MW00824182

ATLAS OF THE BLITZKRIEG 1939–41

ATLAS OF THE
BLITZKRIEG
1939–41

ROBERT KIRCHUBEL

WITH GARY KOMAR

OSPREY
PUBLISHING

OSPREY PUBLISHING
Bloomsbury Publishing Plc
PO Box 883, Oxford, OX1 9PL, UK
1385 Broadway, 5th Floor, New York, NY 10018, USA
E-mail: info@ospreypublishing.com
www.ospreypublishing.com

OSPREY is a trademark of Osprey Publishing Ltd

First published in Great Britain in 2019

© Robert Kirchubel, 2019

Robert Kirchubel has asserted his right under the Copyright, Designs and Patents Act, 1988, to be identified as Author of this work.

All rights reserved. No part of this publication may be reproduced or transmitted in any form or by any means, electronic or mechanical, including photocopying, recording, or any information storage or retrieval system, without prior permission in writing from the publishers.

A catalogue record for this book is available from the British Library.

ISBN: HB 978 1 4728 3499 7; ePDF 978 1 4728 3498 0

19 20 21 22 23   10 9 8 7 6 5 4 3 2 1

Maps by www.Bounford.com
Originated by PDQ Digital Media Solutions, Bungay, UK
Printed in India by Replika Press Pvt. Ltd.

Front cover: TOP German Junkers Ju-87B-2 Stuka dive bombers fly in formation over France in May 1940 (Hulton Archive/Getty Images). BOTTOM German infantry and tanks attacking village defences (ullstein bild via Getty Images)

AUTHOR'S NOTES

This book is written to the glory of God. As usual, first thanks go to my wife Linda, who has had her dining room table covered with maps and map-making impedimenta off and on for the better part of a year. Gary Komar did the basic research from his extensive personal World War II library. For that reason, I'm proud to share the title page with him once again. Joe Wilson assisted with editing, making sure that what I wrote is what I meant. As always, the Purdue University Interlibrary Loan department did a fantastic job getting me all sorts of materials in many languages. Thanks also to Marcus and Russell at Osprey; after painful birthing problems with the first one, these atlases are getting easier with experience!

This *Atlas of the Blitzkrieg 1939–41* is a companion to my earlier *Atlas of the Eastern Front 1941–45* and Steve Zaloga's *Atlas of the European Campaign 1944–45*. More than half the maps here are new and unique to this volume. Of the remaining maps from earlier Osprey titles, some were almost completely redone, while others needed only minor corrections or updates. Pre-existing Osprey maps or bird's-eye view graphics came from the following volumes: *Poland 1939* (Campaign 107), *Crete 1941* (Campaign 147), *River Plate 1939* (Campaign 171), *Denmark and Norway 1940* (Campaign 183), *The Maginot Line 1940* (Campaign 218), *Dunkirk 1940* (Campaign 219), *Fall Gelb 1940, 1 and 2* (Campaigns 264 and 265), plus *German Commerce Raider vs British Cruiser* (Duel 27) and *The Fall of Eben Emael* (Raid 38), as well as hardbound *Case Red* and *We March Against England*.

A word on German organizational names: As with all my earlier books, I use *Panzer-Korps* instead of the cumbersome but technically correct *Armee-Korps (motorisiert)*. I call Germany's *Deutschland*-class vessels 'panzer ship', rather than the usual English 'pocket battleship'. By agreement with the editors and to save the reader from a bewildering stew of military terms in at least 16 languages, only German (Infanterie-Division, etc.) and French (Division Légère Mécanique, etc.) units retain their original names; other nations must make do with English. French translations, e.g. Armée de Terre, provided by the editors.

Osprey Publishing supports the Woodland Trust, the UK's leading woodland conservation charity.

To find out more about our authors and books visit **www.ospreypublishing.com**. Here you will find extracts, author interviews, details of forthcoming events and the option to sign up for our newsletter.

CONTENTS

LEGEND TO MAPS   9

OVERVIEW   10
    Map 1: Strategic Overview

CHAPTER 1: PRE-WAR EUROPE   13
    Map 2: Pre-war Germany
    Map 3: Pre-war Italy
    Map 4: Pre-war France
    Map 5: Pre-war Great Britain
    Map 6: Pre-war Poland
    Map 7: Pre-war Belgium and the Netherlands
    Map 8: Pre-war Balkan Peninsula
    Map 9: Pre-war Soviet Union
    Map 10: Hitler Unopposed

CHAPTER 2: THE POLISH CAMPAIGN   34
    Map 11: Overview
    Map 12: Opposing Plans
    Map 13: The Frontier Battles (I), 1–6 September 1939, Northern Sector
    Map 14: The Frontier Battles (II), 1–6 September 1939, Southern Sector
    Map 15: The Battle of Poland (I), 7–12 September 1939, Northern Sector
    Map 16: The Battle of Poland (II), 7–12 September 1939, Southern Sector
    Map 17: The Bzura Counterattack (I), 9–13 September 1939
    Map 18: The Bzura Counterattack (II), 14–18 September 1939
    Map 19: The Battle for Warsaw, 8–27 September 1939
    Map 20: The end of Poland, 13 September–6 October 1939
    Map 21: Aerial Operations During the Polish Campaign

CHAPTER 3: SOVIET AGGRESSION   58
    Map 22: Overview
    Maps 23 and 24: The Battle of Khalkhin Gol
    Map 25: The Soviet Invasion of Eastern Poland, 17–29 September 1939
    Map 26: The Pre-war Finnish Front
    Map 27: The Karelian Front (I), 30 November–31 December 1939

Map 28: The Karelian Front (II), 11 February–13 March 1940

Map 29: The Lake Ladoga Front (I), 30 November–31 December 1939

Map 30: The Lake Ladoga Front (II), 1–31 January 1940

Map 31: The Central, Salla and Petsamo Fronts, 30 November 1939–15 February 1940

Maps 32 and 33: The Soviet Occupation of the Baltic States and Bessarabia

CHAPTER 4: THE SCANDINAVIAN CAMPAIGN   80

Map 34: Overview

Map 35: Naval Operations and the Norwegian Defences

Map 36: The Invasion of Denmark, 9 April 1940

Map 37: Oslo and Central Norway, 9–30 April 1940

Map 38: South-west Norway, 9–30 April 1940

Map 39: The Central Norwegian Coast, 9 April–2 May 1940

Map 40: The Battle of Narvik (I), 9 April–8 May 1940

Map 41: The Battle of Narvik (II), 9 May–10 June 1940

CHAPTER 5: THE WESTERN CAMPAIGN   98

Map 42: Overview

Map 43: The Evolution of German Plans

Map 44: Opening Moves, 10–12 May 1940

Map 45: Opening Moves: the North, 11–12 May 1940

Map 46: Conquest of the Netherlands, 12–15 May 1940

Map 47: The Approach to Fort Eben Emael, 10 May 1940

Map 48: Capturing Fort Eben Emael, 10 May 1940

Map 49: The German Invasion of Central Belgium, 10–13 May 1940

Map 50: The Battle of Belgium, 14–21 May 1940

Map 51: German Movements Through the Ardennes Forest, 10–12 May 1940

Map 52: The German Meuse River Bridgeheads, 13–15 May 1940

Map 53: The German Breakout, 15–17 May 1940

Map 54: The Drive to the Sea, 18–20 May 1940

Map 55: Closing the Dunkirk–Lille Pocket, 22–24 May 1940

Map 56: Closing in on Dunkirk, 26–28 May 1940

Maps 57 and 58: The German Capture of Dunkirk and the Allied Evacuation, 2–4 June 1940

Map 59: 4 June 1940 – the Eve of *Fall Rot*

Maps 60 and 61: Overcoming the Somme and Oise–Aisne Rivers, 5–7 June 1940

Map 62: The German Encirclement of the 2e Groupe d'Armées, 10–20 June 1940

Map 63: The Fall of Paris, 10–14 May 1940

Map 64: The Conquest of North-west France, 15–30 June 1940

Map 65: The Italian Alpine Front, 20–22 June 1940

Map 66: Aerial Operations During the Western Campaign

CHAPTER 6: THE AIR WAR OVER BRITAIN AND GERMANY — 146

Map 67: Overview

Map 68: RAF Fighter Command Deployment and the Dowding System

Map 69: The Luftwaffe Deployment

Map 70: *Kanalkampf*, 1 July–12 August 1940

Map 71: The Battle of Britain (I), 13–23 August 1940

Map 72: The Battle of Britain (II), 24 August–6 September 1940

Map 73: The Blitz over Britain, 7 September 1940–Spring 1941

Map 74: The Blitz over London, 7 September 1940–Winter 1941

Maps 75 and 76: The Defence of Great Britain, 1940

Map 77: The German Plans for Operation *Seelöwe*

Map 78: The RAF Bombing of Germany (I), 1939–40

Map 79: The RAF Bombing of Germany (II), 1941

CHAPTER 7: THE NAVAL WAR — 172

Map 80: Overview

Map 81: British Convoys and Protective Measures, 1939–41

Map 82: U-boat Operations (I), September 1939–March 1941

Map 83: U-boat Operations (II), April–December 1941

Map 84: German Cruiser Warfare (I)

Map 85: German Cruiser Warfare (II)

Map 86: German Commerce Raiders (I), 1940

Map 87: German Commerce Raiders (II), 1941

CHAPTER 8: THE BALKAN CAMPAIGN — 190

Map 88: Overview

Map 89: Italy Against Greece, 28 October 1940–13 April 1941

Map 90: Operation *25* (I), 6–12 April 1941

Map 91: Operation *25* (II), 13–18 April 1941

Map 92: Operation *Marita*, 6–30 April 1941

Map 93: Air and Sea Action Around Crete, 20 May–2 June 1941

Map 94: Operation *Merkur*, 20 May–2 June 1941

CONCLUSIONS — 206

APPENDIX — 208

Map 95: The Occupation of Poland

Map 96: The Occupation of Scandinavia

Map 97: The Occupation of The Netherlands, Belgium and France

Map 98: The Occupation of Yugoslavia and Greece

BIBLIOGRAPHY — 216

LEGEND TO MAPS

XXXXX	Army group
XXXX	Army
XXX	Corps
XX	Division
X	Brigade
III	Regiment
II	Battalion
I	Company
...	Platoon

	Infantry
	Motorized
	Mountain
	Mountain artillery
	Engineer
	Armoured: German Panzer, French *division cuirassée de reserve*
	Mechanized infantry
	Cavalry
	German Leichte, French *division légère Mécanique*
	Anti-tank defence
	Belgian Chasseurs Ardennes, French *division légère de cavalerie*
	Artillery
BG	Border guard
	Headquarters

	Airborne
	Glider and air transport
	Air unit
	Bomber
	Fighter
	Air defence
	Air landing
	Air base
	Naval
	Naval base
	Fortified city
	Fortification

UNIT BOUNDARIES

—— XXXXX ——	Army group
—— XXXX ——	Army
—— XXX ——	Corps
—— XX ——	Division

UNIT ABBREVIATIONS

General:

Lt	Light

British and Commonwealth:

AIF	Australian Imperial Force
ASH	Argyle and Sutherland Highlanders
BEF	British Expeditionary Force

German:

G.A.K.	*Grenzschutzabschnittkommando* (Border Guard Sector Command)
SS DF	SS Regiment Der Führer
SS GD	SS Grossdeutschland
SSLAH	SS Regiment/Brigade Leibstandarte Adolf Hitler
SS R	SS Division Reich
SS T	SS Totenkopf
SS V	SS Verfügungsdivision

French:

Co	Colonial
NA	North African
AF	French African
FL	Foreign Legion

Soviet:

OCK	*Otdel'nii strelkovii korpus* (Independent Rifle Corps)

Belgian:

ChA	Chasseurs Ardennes

A NOTE ON NATIONAL COLOURS

As so many nations were involved in the many theatres of war covered in this atlas, it is not possible to represent the symbols for each nation in a different colour. Therefore, red symbols have been used throughout to symbolize those who might be considered the agressors (usually the Axis powers), and blue to represent the defenders. Although this means that on occasion the Soviets, for example, appear as red symbols in some maps, and blue symbols on others, the keys to the maps and the main text should offer clarity and it is hoped that this will not hamper the interpretation of the information presented. Where more than one nationality is represented among the units fighting on the same side on a single map, abbreviated national identifiers are used as per the opposite column.

NATIONAL ABBREVIATIONS:

Note that national abbrevations are not used in every case, but only where more than two nationalities of unit appear on the same side on one map. In many maps, where the units on one side are shown within their own borders their national identifiers are not shown. Likewise, if most allied units on a map are of one nationality, with only a few variations, only the nationality of the variants is shown. It is hoped that this aids clarity and prevents overcrowding of information.

Au	Australian	It	Italian
Be	Belgian	Ja	Japanese
Br	British	Mo	Moroccan
Bu	Bulgarian	NA	North African
Ca	Canadian	NL	Netherlands
Du	Dutch	No	Norwegian
Fr	French	NZ	New Zealand
Ge	German	Po	Polish
Gr	Greek	Sv	Slovakian
Hu	Hungarian	Yu	Yugoslavian

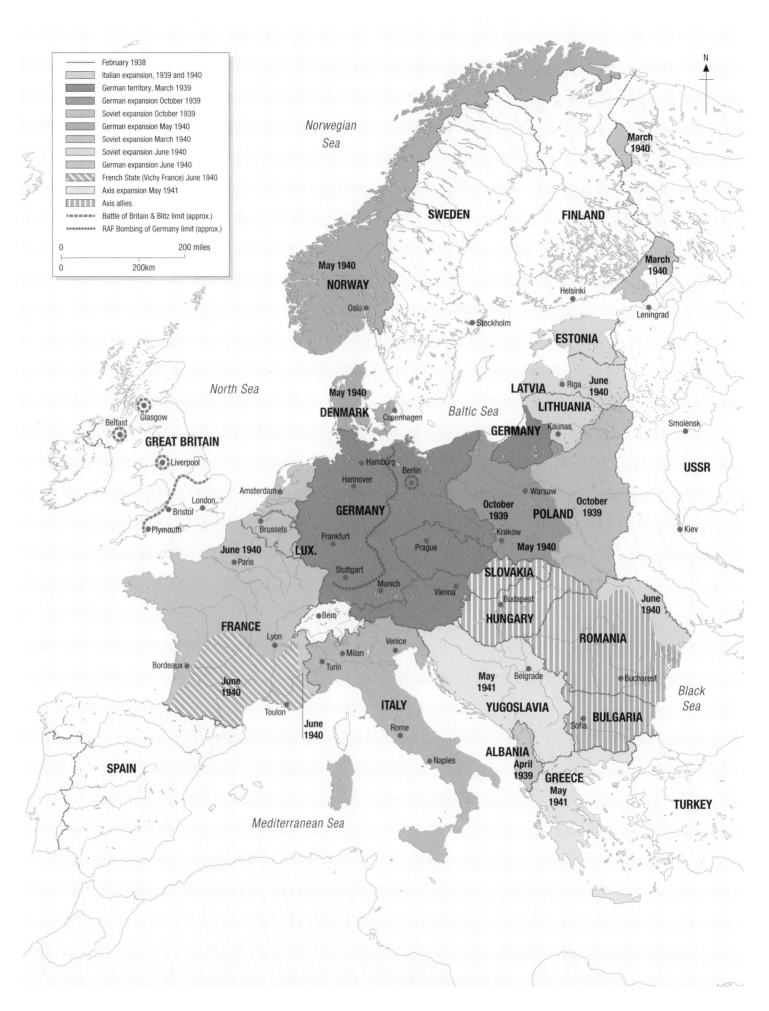

Legend

- February 1938
- Italian expansion, 1939 and 1940
- German territory, March 1939
- German expansion October 1939
- Soviet expansion October 1939
- German expansion May 1940
- Soviet expansion March 1940
- Soviet expansion June 1940
- German expansion June 1940
- French State (Vichy France) June 1940
- Axis expansion May 1941
- Axis allies
- Battle of Britain & Blitz limit (approx.)
- RAF Bombing of Germany limit (approx.)

0   200 miles
0   200km

Norwegian Sea

SWEDEN

FINLAND

March 1940

NORWAY May 1940

Oslo

Helsinki

Stockholm

Leningrad

March 1940

North Sea

Belfast Glasgow

GREAT BRITAIN

Liverpool

London

Bristol

Plymouth

ESTONIA

Baltic Sea

DENMARK May 1940

Copenhagen

LATVIA Riga June 1940

LITHUANIA

GERMANY Kaunas

Smolensk

USSR

Amsterdam

Hamburg Berlin

Hannover

GERMANY

Frankfurt

Warsaw

October 1939 **POLAND** October 1939

Krakow

May 1940

Kiev

Brussels

LUX.

June 1940 Paris

Stuttgart

Prague

Munich

Vienna

SLOVAKIA

Budapest

HUNGARY

June 1940

Bern

FRANCE

Lyon

Milan

Venice

ROMANIA

Bucharest

Bordeaux

Turin

June 1940

Toulon

June 1940

ITALY

Rome

May 1941

Belgrade

YUGOSLAVIA

BULGARIA

Sofia

Black Sea

SPAIN

ALBANIA April 1939

GREECE May 1941

TURKEY

Naples

Mediterranean Sea

OVERVIEW

World War II was the most destructive event in human history ... so far. Its origins can be summarized in two words: Adolf Hitler. Numerous complex factors led Europe to 'sleepwalk' into World War I: antagonistic empires, arms races, revenge and revisionism, nationalism, miscalculation and misunderstanding, wishful thinking and dynastic tensions – among other causes. All these factors contributed to World War I, but none of them caused it. Conversely, World War II began for the simple reason that the Nazi Führer wanted it and no one could stop him from starting it. Neither Germany's defeat in 1918 nor the Versailles Treaty predetermined World War II. Given the continuing unrest around the world during the interwar period, there was every chance of limited or regional wars, but conventional wisdom deemed another global war unlikely. While the widespread effects of the Great Depression dramatically increased domestic and international tensions, fundamentally war came to Europe in 1939 because of Hitler. However, that is not to say he simply woke up on 31 August 1939 and decided to start a war the next day.

After World War I, Britain and France stood alone to rebuild the shattered international system. Of the war's other victors, Italy and Japan were soon shoved aside, while the United States withdrew of its own volition. Russia cannot be considered a victor and did not participate in the peace process. Ignoring the example of the Congress of Vienna in 1815, which created a fairly successful system that prevented a general European war for nearly a century, the Allies did not allow defeated Germany to have any input in the post-World War I peace, or even attend the proceedings. The Versailles Treaty had many flaws, but could have worked. It selectively violated President Woodrow Wilson's principal of self-determination, which could have led to the creation of Greater Germany, i.e., the union of Germany and Austria, Danzig and the Sudetenland. The treaty forced Germany to pay reparations for death and destruction in World War I, which international opinion judged it alone had caused. Germany claimed it could not pay the debt, but it certainly

could have done so, just as France did after 1871. However, many post-World War I Germans considered paying even one ounce of gold too much to ask.

Though Britain and France were victorious in World War I, the war devastated both. Neither had the wherewithal to rebuild Central or Eastern Europe, nor did they have the Tsar to assist in the east. They did not have the strength to act as the global 'power of last resort', the role played by the USA and USSR after World War II. By 1924, the volatile immediate post-war period stabilized somewhat and collective security under the leadership of the armed liberal democracies kept the peace. Britain and France tried, with mixed results, to peacefully divert German commercial and economic energies towards Central and Eastern Europe, but seem to have been a generation too early for this tactic. Disarmament – not the same as pacifism – became a major movement in the 1920s and early 1930s and sapped the resolve of the once and future allies. Further weakened by the Depression, France and Britain drifted apart and towards self-preservation, while the US and USSR remained self-absorbed and largely uninvolved in world affairs. These conditions conspired to give the revisionist states Italy, Japan, and especially Germany, unique opportunities to make mischief. The democracies could not adapt to the likes of Hitler, Benito Mussolini and the Japanese militarists, while Stalin in the Soviet Union actively exacerbated the situation.

Within a year of Hitler coming to power, British national security experts began to anticipate war with Germany in three to five years, a notion France soon adopted. Nevertheless, by the mid-1930s, Britain and France turned their backs on each other. In April 1935, Britain concluded a naval treaty with Germany, doing Hitler's work of dismantling Versailles for him. Six months later, France acquiesced to Mussolini's invasion of Abyssinia, breaking with its partner. Despite his own weak position, Hitler assessed even greater weakness in the two allies. By the winter of 1936, he announced German conscription and remilitarized the Rhineland. France had no response short of mobilization and so did nothing. Belgium, France's first line of defence, also noticed this lack of resolve and declared its neutrality the same year. Joseph Stalin observed these developments and saw weakness, too.

Hitler consolidated suzerainty in the Danube basin and cleverly redirected Mussolini towards the Mediterranean and potential conflict with Britain. Italy soon became embroiled in the Spanish Civil War, with Germany in a supporting role. The two fascist states concluded the 'illusory façade' of the Rome–Berlin Axis and grew closer, with Italy increasingly as the junior partner. Hitler continued dismantling Versailles by annexing Austria in March 1938. He then turned his sights on Czechoslovakia. Not as invested in the Little Entente (Czechoslovakia, Romania and Yugoslavia) as France, Britain could not imagine going to war over the new Central European democracies. By September, Neville Chamberlain, buying into Hitler's definition of national self-determination, threw the Czechs to the wolves to avoid war and to buy time to continue rearmament. France went along with appeasement, even though it lost the support of Czechoslovakia's 35 divisions. In the mind of the French, the cost Britain had to now pay after Munich was to make up for the loss of its Czechoslovak ally. The German people cheered Chamberlain and loved the Munich agreement. Their Führer, however, hated it, since he believed he had been cheated of a perfect *casus belli*.

In six years Hitler had undone Versailles without firing a shot. Two months later, he continued redrawing the map with the First Vienna Award, while France and Britain stood by passively. The last straw came in March 1939, when Hitler occupied the remainder of Bohemia and Moravia, took Memel and set up a fascist puppet state in Slovakia. Within weeks, Britain and France had their first general staff conference, while Britain doubled the size of its Territorial (reserve) Army and guaranteed Polish security. But by then, Hitler had remade Germany into a great power in the old European mold and was now intent on overturning the Continental and global system as well. The Axis dictators were not finished. That spring, the Spanish Civil War ended and a week later Mussolini occupied Albania. In August, Hitler shocked the world by cutting a deal with Stalin. It began with a credit agreement on the 19th, followed four days later by a non-aggression pact. Too late, the British dropped their decades-long anti-communism, but they had nothing to offer Stalin except collective security. He wanted real estate in Central and Eastern Europe, something only Hitler could deliver. The Führer believed that he had completely wrecked the European order and assumed there was no way Britain and France would now go to war over Poland. This time he was really wrong.

***

During the interwar period (incidentally, not the same as a time of peace), each major combatant decided on its solution to the problems of World War I. The French would make miserable dirt trenches into comfortable steel and concrete, the British would fly over the trenches to bomb the enemy heartland, the Germans would punch through the trenches in tanks, while the Soviets would just sit out the slaughter. The reasons for each were entirely logical given the experiences these nations faced in the Great War. Contemporary future-war theorists fell into two main camps: those advocating armour, or bombers. Supporters of the tank option at least could look to successful Allied – mainly French – mobile operations in the summer and autumn of 1918. Air-power enthusiasts, on the other hand, without proof, claimed that 'the bomber would always get through' and predicted that bombing raids would cause destruction and social upheaval worthy of apocalyptic science fiction. The first part of their equation was not unreasonable, given that until the late 1930s, many bombers flew faster than most fighters, anti-aircraft artillery was small and weak, while radar was in its infancy. The second part of their claims would have to wait until August 1945 to be close to coming true.

Hitler's racially charged concept of endless struggle for world domination went way beyond generic German conservative revisionism. Among the German rank and file, sons wanted to accomplish what their fathers had failed to do. Like their fathers in 1914, they believed enemies encircled Germany. In the summer of 1939, most Germans thought they were fighting a defensive war forced on them by the liberal democracies; after all, in 1939 Britain and France declared war first. Policy planning in the German 'Führer state' barely existed – there had been no cabinet meetings debating the subject of war – the notion came out of Hitler's head. His so-called expertise did not come from any government coordination, institutional assessment, intellectual sense of proportion, or experience in the wider world; except for the World War I battlefields of Flanders and two visits to fascist Italy, he had not been outside of Austria and Germany. Hitler mastered opportunism and exploitation of adversaries' mistakes and weaknesses. He operated on wishful thinking, his 'superior' judgement and exaggerated reactions to events like small successes such as the Rhineland militarization or Sudetenland occupation, which he extrapolated into geopolitical truisms.

Having lived through trench warfare, Hitler wanted something bigger and bolder, Hitleresque if you will. His new technique would be the blitzkrieg. Ironically, the word (though German in origin) was used mainly by the Western media and was not a doctrinal term used by the Wehrmacht. Towards the end of World War I, both sides had solved the problem of 'breaking into' enemy lines, but not subsequently 'breaking through'. The blitzkrieg combination of flexible command and control, the internal combustion engine, radios, close air support, infiltration, risk taking and combined arms ruled European combat from 1939 to 1942. By myriad other names, it was arguably the dominant form of land warfare at least for the last 60 years of the 20th century. It operated on all three levels of warfare: strategic – picking on one digestible enemy nation at a time; operational – destroying enemy cohesion at the critical point of a combat theatre; and tactical – locating and exploiting the enemy's weak points with penetrations and breakthroughs. Blitzkrieg also represented the indirect approach, as described by Basil Liddell-Hart and John Boyd. It was not the cavalry raid 'command paralysis' method advocated by some interwar armour theorists. In the spring of 1940, for example, the Wehrmacht aimed for the English Channel and a traditional Prussian–German encirclement battle of annihilation, rather than capturing or disrupting Allied military headquarters or even capital cities. Enemy command paralysis, therefore, came as a byproduct. During the period described in this atlas, no opponent of Germany developed a suitable counter to blitzkrieg, leading Hitler to a string of spectacular victories.

CHAPTER 1:
PRE-WAR EUROPE

War is a learning competition, at the strategic, operational and tactical levels. As mentioned previously, the militaries of the world worked to understand the lessons of World War I and incorporate new interwar ideas and technologies to prepare for the next war. Decisions made in the late 1930s would determine the course of the first years of World War II. This chapter covers how Europe prepared for the coming war and how it dealt with the last years of peace.

German war aims evolved between 1919 and 1939, from overturning Versailles and reclaiming the 'stolen lands' of Alsace-Lorraine and western Poland, to conquering *Lebensraum* (space to live) for the German people in Central and Eastern Europe and finally to taking over the world. Consistent with Hitler's disorganized thinking, Nazi diplomatic, domestic, industrial and rearmament policies all suffered from constant change and poor-to-non-existent coordination. However, Hitler excelled at turning small political successes into larger victories, such as the plebiscite to return the Saarland to Germany on 1 March 1935, which the Führer used as an opening to announce Germany's return to military conscription on the 16th. This law envisioned an army of 36 divisions (up from 21 in the December 1933 plan), to an anticipated 43 divisions 13 months later, then to 72 divisions and finally to 102 divisions when World War II began. By the autumn of 1936, the German Army numbered 520,000 men, an increase of 500 per cent in just three years. It planned for 3.6 million men under arms by 1940–41, a phenomenal 700 per cent jump[1]. Unfortunately for them, German resource and industrial capacity could not keep pace, a problem that dogged the Third Reich throughout World War II. Their Four Year Plan of August 1936, meant to address World War I shortcomings and problems of the Depression, as well as insure German autarchy in the coming war, failed to meet its lofty goals.

Mirroring Hitler's strategic naivety, the German Navy (Kriegsmarine) played a very junior role in German planning. Naval personnel numbers multiplied by a factor of five between 1932 and 1939, but still counted only 79,000 men at the start of World War II. Hitler's Luftwaffe (Air Force) took over the destabilizing role played by the Kaiser's 'Risk Theory' navy a quarter of a century earlier. Its personnel numbers jumped from 17,000 in the spring of 1935 to 370,000 some 30 months later. One third of this total served in the Flak (anti-aircraft artillery) branch, a tremendous combat multiplier that is often

---

1   By comparison, the Kaiser's 1914 army had 87 divisions, 44 militia brigades, totalling 2.1 million men.

underestimated in World War II histories. However, unrealistic proposals, such as the late 1938 plan to build 19,500 aircraft (which would have required 90 per cent of known global aviation gasoline reserves), again demonstrated that Hitler was simply unaware of Germany's true industrial capacity. One German success story would be in keeping the home front motivated throughout most of the war, Hitler's answer to the perceived problems of the Kaiser's war effort.

Italy was largely united in name only prior to World War I. Wartime casualties, social disruption (internal migrations, industrialization) and the growth of socialism added to post-war debt, marginalization at Versailles and domestic political and economic woes, to create chaos in the early 1920s. In a desperate but completely constitutional move, in October 1922 King Victor Emmanuel III named fascist leader Mussolini the Italian premier. Over the next ten years, the Duce consolidated power, so by the early 1930s he believed Italy stood ready to create a new Roman Empire. Previously, in the 1920s, like Germany, Italy took a revisionist but cautious stance. However, in the 1930s, it followed a revisionist but incautious direction. Hitler's growing power, first in Germany and then in Central Europe, forced Mussolini to look towards the south and the Mediterranean, auguring potential conflict with erstwhile allies Britain and France. He soon went to war over Ethiopia (1935–36), Spain, (1936–39) and Albania (1939).

The Italian military reached peak preparedness in the early 1930s, well ahead of the remainder of Europe. For example, the country had one of the first independent air forces. Initially, Britain, France and the League of Nations did not know how to cope with Mussolini's Italy. Overseas adventurism, especially involvement in the Spanish Civil War, took funds away from Italian military modernization. By the late 1930s, its tanks were too small, its aircraft too few and too old, while its ships could not compete against future enemies, especially the British. Despite Italian bombast and aggression against hapless neighbours like Albania, the country had many limitations. Only from a position of relative weakness did Mussolini join with Britain to create a new Concert of Europe at the end of September 1938, to keep the Continent from going to war over Czechoslovakia. This same weakness hamstrung Italy throughout World War II.

For centuries, Great Britain had had global, not just European concerns. 'Never again' dominated British thinking on a national scale following World War I: males of child-rearing and working age had been nearly wiped out in many towns and counties, overseas exports and investments had been drastically hurt and its dominions began to clamour for independence. The British Empire seemed to be coming apart and its ability to 'go it alone' in the world had been exposed. Critically, it now took on the role of status-quo power, challenged just to maintain its empire. By 1934–35, British defence experts assumed the country would be at war with Germany by the end of the decade. Maintaining post-World War I global peace devolved to Britain, France and the League of Nations, but these could not agree on how. Neither Britain nor France trusted the Soviet Union and the former especially put its own anti-communism ahead of self-preservation. Britain wanted no more war, so showed a willingness to work with Germany as members of a European community; this philosophy concurred with

Hitler's (who had inherited the Kaiser's love–hate relationship with the island nation). It gave legitimacy to Versailles revisionism and German rearmament by concluding a bilateral naval agreement and breaking with France over Ethiopia. The only winner in such cases was Hitler.

Also, for centuries, the Royal Navy had been Britain's first line of defence. Although many ships were from the World War I era, it comprised the world's largest and most efficient navy and was getting bigger and more modern all the time. It had learned aircraft carrier operations and equipped its ships with radar and sonar; no Germans other than downed airmen, prisoners of war and turned spies ever made it to the British Isles. Fuelled by 'never again' thinking, during the interwar period, the Royal Air Force had overtaken the army as Britain's second service. Bombers would take the war to the enemy, while fighters would help defend the home islands. By the late 1930s, British aircraft production neared German levels, while a belt of primitive but efficient radar assets faced threats flying in from the Continent. The army came in a distant third, both in terms of budget and quality of manpower. A poorly trained and equipped Territorial Army augmented an undersized, under-motorized colonial Regular Army. It was as unprepared for global war as its 1914 predecessor had been.

World War I devastated France, killed off the better part of a generation of men and ravaged some of its most productive countryside. But in victory and at the peace table it had avenged 1870–71, reacquired Alsace-Lorraine and humbled Germany. Its Plan XVII of 1914 proved to be a failure, so reverting back to a national strategy used since Louis XIV, the country hunkered down behind a line of frontier fortresses. Considering its national character, post-war demographic challenges and resource limitations, the Maginot Line made perfect sense for France in the mid-1920s when it was conceived. Consistent with this thinking, it also eschewed Marshal Ferdinand Foch's 1918 mobile warfare, for the more set-piece 'methodical battle' in line with French capabilities. Internally, in terms of politics, culture and economics, the French nation had difficulty settling its course, a fact obscured by its World War I legacy and large overseas empire.

France would likewise depend on collective security for its defence, including the League of Nations and a ring of small allies surrounding Germany. Having just defeated the Kaiser, the French Army took on the mantle of Europe's – and therefore the world's – best. France reduced its navy's role against Germany in the Atlantic and instead concentrated on the Mediterranean. Its air force did not develop a large heavy bombing arm as seen elsewhere, but would defend the homeland and support the army. All these measures protected French interests until the depths of the Depression struck in the mid-1930s. At that point, external pressures and the breakdown of the domestic consensus over France's role in the world fractured the nation's resolve.

Until the rise of fascism, the two main competing post-World War I global political poles were Wilsonian democracy and Leninist bolshevism. Although the communists prevailed in the Russian Civil War, they basically failed to export their ideology, so settled on a policy of 'socialism in one country': the consolidation of Stalin's authority and power. Components of this policy consisted of establishing the primacy of the Communist Party, destruction of the Russian middle class and other competing power centres, collectivization of agriculture and modernization of industry, largely through successive Five-Year Plans. Although still a disruptive rule breaker in world affairs, Stalin chose to sit out most international conflicts during the late interwar period. However, historical precedent, global opposition to communism and foreign intervention during the civil war, all indicated that enemies surrounded the Soviet Union in a hostile world.

All these factors pointed toward a need to expand and upgrade Soviet preparations for war, in particular their military. By the mid-1930s, they had made the Red Army into the world's largest and led the way in several innovative techniques and technologies: mechanized warfare, airborne forces and heavy bombers. However, the chaotic nature of the Stalinist dictatorship meant that nothing was certain for long. This meant that an admiral today could be a firing-squad victim tomorrow, or what was accepted doctrine today could end up discredited on the trash heap tomorrow. Stalin's purges of top leaders in the late 1930s are perhaps the best examples of this. Combined, these factors led to poor performances by the Soviet military around the end of the decade and the severe (and incorrect) underestimation of the USSR by most of the rest of the world.

Besides describing in further detail these major World War II combatants, this chapter will look at the smaller powers surrounding Germany or living in its vicinity. All eventually succumbed to Hitler, either through coercion or conquest. It will also investigate the Führer's 'fairy tale wars' where, without firing a shot, he expanded the Third Reich in every direction. At the top of his class in the interwar generation of rule-breaking tyrants, he took advantage of other befuddled European leaders who were simply not up to the task of stopping him. This then brings us to the brink of World War II.

MAP 2: PRE-WAR GERMANY

Germany on the eve of World War II can be considered an armed camp. Every branch of its military expanded faster than training facilities, raw materials, armaments enterprises and construction industry could keep up. The entire German economy teetered on the brink of disaster as it produced weapons of war that contributed nothing of commercial value. As Hitler had once said, however, 'Armies for the maintenance of peace do not exist, they exist for the successful exertion in war.' He soon set out to make good on this implied threat.

With his limited experiential and intellectual foundations, Hitler thought in terms of pre-1914 European strategy, where a relatively small, practically isolated and almost land-locked country like the Third Reich could successfully compete against global empires such as Britain's or the continental-sized, proto-superpowers of the USSR and USA. He also mainly thought in purely military terms, discounting factors such as coalitions, economics and geography. His only ally was Italy, which he knew was weak by most measures and for which he had thinly disguised contempt. Likewise, he had boundless contempt for potential adversaries and enemies. In his calculations this more than compensated for Germany's poor material wealth and weak diplomatic support network. In no way could the country's resource base be considered adequate for a major war. The fortitude and steadfastness of the German people, trusting and enamoured of the Führer but ambivalent concerning Nazism, represented the main strength of the Third Reich.

As it had for generations, in Hitler's coming war, the German Army would do the heavy lifting. The nation had long been divided into corps-sized military districts (*Wehrkreis*) and the army remained principally recruited along geographic lines. Losses in World War I, lack of modernity and, most critically, Hitler and the Nazi Party, had ruined any previous cohesion among its officer corps. Reflection on the reasons for losing World War I concentrated on personalities, i.e. Kaiser Wilhelm, so systematic failures remained uninvestigated and many would be repeated in World War II. Germany possessed no real strategists worthy of the name, whether in or out of uniform.

Despite new panzer forces, which soon grabbed most headlines in the battles described in this atlas, the army stood on a foundation of marching infantry. The average infantry division consisted of about 16,000 men organized into three regiments, plus supporting arms and services. Like much of the army's logistical tail, infantry relied heavily on horses, which required 50 tons of fodder per day per division, along with considerable veterinary and other support. The quality of army formations in many instances hinged on when and where the division was established and how it was equipped, which varied widely depending on its mobilization 'wave'.

In 1939, Germany had six panzer divisions, each with around 14,000 men, 320 tanks in two panzer regiments, plus mechanized artillery, infantry and support carried by nearly 3,000 motor vehicles. It had no remarkable tank designs; most mounted only a machine gun or 20mm cannon. The army had just begun to think in terms of panzer corps (named 'motorized') and using panzers as operational weapons. It had four 'light' divisions, each with two regiments of motorized infantry and a panzer battalion plus mechanized supporting arms and services. After the Polish campaign, the army converted these to panzer divisions. The German order of battle also initially included four motorized infantry divisions, where infantry rode half-tracks or trucks into battle but fought dismounted. Mechanized forces also included the motorized Infanterie-Regiment 'Grossdeutschland', SS-Verfügungstruppe division and the Leibstandarte SS Adolf Hitler regiment. Together, these forces represented the spearhead of the blitzkrieg. In general, German mechanization was haphazard, limited and rudimentary, although superior to that of its neighbours. They used 100 truck, 50 car and 150 motorcycle types – a logistical (i.e. maintenance and repair parts) nightmare. Upon mobilization, approximately 16,000 civilian vehicles were pressed into service, hurting the economy.

The Luftwaffe was also administratively divided into *Luftgaue* (air districts). Like the rest of the German military, operationally and logistically, it had limited range and could only seriously threaten close neighbours. The main operational formation was the *Geschwader* (group in Britain, wing in the US). The main aircraft types – Ju 52, He 111, Ju 87, Bf 109, etc. – had been in use since the Spanish Civil War and had already peaked in terms of performance. During the 1930s, the Luftwaffe had investigated heavy ('strategic') bombing, but had no enthusiasm for the concept. As a land power, there was no doubt that supporting the army would be a top Luftwaffe mission. Having only one truly high-performance aircraft engine, the DB601, hamstrung the German aviation industry. The Luftwaffe's threatening reputation sprung mainly from unsubstantiated pre-war propaganda. Only when compared to its non-RAF competition can it be considered cutting-edge and war-changing.

Naval expansion and modernization were just getting started in 1939 and the sea service was a second-class citizen compared to the army and air force's prestige and resources. *Deutschland*-class panzer ships represented its main strength when Hitler came to power. Two super-*Deutschland* battlecruisers plus numerous heavy cruisers and destroyers soon followed. The Third Reich developed grandiose naval plans, but only the two *Bismarck*-class battleships ever materialized from them. After surreptitiously experimenting with Dutch, Finnish and Turkish submarines following World War I, the first domestic *U-1* launched in June 1935. Within a year of the Anglo-German Naval Treaty, the Kriegsmarine counted 24 U-boats (21 short of the total allowed). Thereafter, submarines – the 770-ton Type VIIC and 1,120-ton IXC – represented Germany's main seagoing threat. However, of the 300 U-boats which navy plans required for an effective commerce campaign, Germany began the war with only 57.

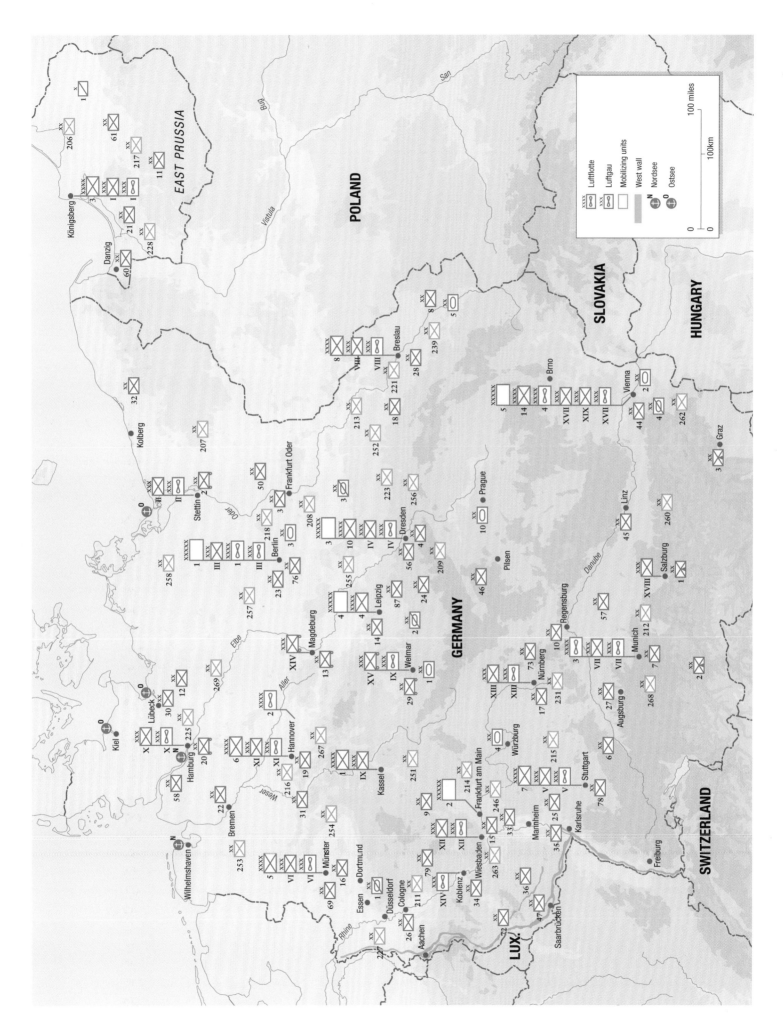

EAST PRUSSIA

POLAND

SLOVAKIA

HUNGARY

GERMANY

SWITZERLAND

LUX.

Königsberg

Danzig

Stettin

Kolberg

Berlin

Frankfurt Oder

Breslau

Dresden

Leipzig

Magdeburg

Weimar

Hannover

Lübeck

Kiel

Hamburg

Bremen

Münster

Dortmund

Essen

Düsseldorf

Cologne

Aachen

Koblenz

Wiesbaden

Frankfurt am Main

Kassel

Würzburg

Mannheim

Karlsruhe

Freiburg

Saarbrücken

Stuttgart

Nürnberg

Regensburg

Munich

Augsburg

Salzburg

Linz

Vienna

Brno

Prague

Plisen

Graz

Bug

San

Vistula

Oder

Elbe

Aller

Weser

Rhine

Danube

100 miles

100km

Luftflotte

Luftgau

Mobilizing units

West wall

Nordsee

Ostsee

17

MAP 3: PRE-WAR ITALY

Although Germany and Italy both became nations around the same time, roughly 1860–70, the latter had more difficulty moving beyond mere geographical conception. Despite the growth of nationalism during World War I, the old divisions along the lines of north–south, urban–agrarian and wealthy–poor continued to hinder Italy. It would be up to Mussolini and his fascists, along with some serendipity such as championship soccer teams in 1934 and 1938, to finally unify the country.

Italian foreign policy and fascist theory came together in the glorification of war. Mussolini's vision had been the domination of southern Europe, but the more dynamic and powerful Third Reich pushed him away from the Alpine and Danubian regions. Echoing pre-World War I Italian modernism, in 1931 he wrote, 'War alone brings all human energies to their highest state of tension and stamps with the zeal of nobility the nations which dare face it.' In an effort to distract his dissatisfied countrymen from internal problems and weaknesses in the fascist state, he pivoted to overseas adventurism. He sent Italian armies abroad in 1935 (Ethiopia), 1936 (Spain) and 1939 (Albania). Reluctantly, the nation followed its Duce.

The Abyssinian operation started as a frontier dispute over Italian Somaliland. It began slowly for Mussolini, as his troops were ill prepared. They ground out a victory of sorts in 1936, although real success took three more years. Envious of King Victor Emmanuel's title of military commander-in-chief, upon creation of the Italian Empire in 1936, Mussolini invented the position First Marshal of the Empire for them both, creating an imaginary equality between the two men. To the north, Hitler approved of Mussolini's southwards push, since that would reduce Italian interference in Europe and put Italy on a collision course with Britain and France, Germany's expected future opponents. By October 1936, Mussolini began to speak in terms of a Rome–Berlin Axis.

Italy's interwar adventures had several negative consequences. The commitment of 300,000 men to garrison the Horn of Africa was far beyond what Italy could support. The war also raised the country's financial deficit from 2.5 to 16 billion lire. Involvement in the Spanish Civil War then required 50,000 men, cost 700 aircraft and 9 million rounds of ammunition, at a time when Italy could not afford such expenditure. The defeat by Republican forces at Guadalajara rates as an unmitigated disaster. Worst of all, Mussolini's wars drove Italy away from Great Britain and further into Hitler's arms. By 1939, Italy had a war economy despite the fact that most Italians did not share Mussolini's warmongering. Just days before the start of the Polish campaign, the Duce warned the Führer that he could intervene in a general European war only if Germany propped up its economy with 17 million tons of oil, coal, steel and rubber, plus numerous weapons systems 'at once'. Hitler politely left his confederate out of the upcoming conflict.

In August 1939, the Italian military was in desperate straits. Mussolini's 1930s wars had consumed resources that the country did not have. The adjacent map shows nearly 70 divisions, of which only 19 were at full strength and combat ready. Of the remainder, 34 were rated 'efficient' but lacked about 25 per cent of assigned personnel and equipment. The remaining 20 divisions were completely unprepared for war. Italy's two-regiment infantry divisions would have been called brigades in most other armies. Their hoped-for increased mobility, the trade-off for their small size, did not materialize. Italy's best World War II artillery had been captured from the Central Powers in the Great War, while its tanks fell short of the competition by every measure. Italy's best units were its mountain divisions, although these suffered from many limitations. Its *Celere* ('fast') divisions were partially mechanized and included an elite Bersaglieri regiment. Armoured divisions consisted of an armoured regiment with three to five tank battalions of 55 tanks each, plus a Bersaglieri regiment and supporting arms and services. Italians called their primary tank design, the M11, 'medium', when in reality other armies would consider it light.

Mussolini's overseas aggression had been very costly to the air force. In 1938, Italy began a programme to replace obsolete biplanes, the majority of its models, with modern monoplanes. While Italian industry proved capable of producing aircraft that set many interwar speed records, it could not mass produce competitive fighters in numbers required for a world war. Its bombers were small, slow and had limited range. Therefore, of more than 3,000 aircraft on the books, only 600 were operational in August 1939 and, of these, only 166 were modern.

The navy represented Mussolini's favourite branch of service, despite a royalist, anti-fascist officer corps. Government policy and an excellent shipbuilding industry allowed Italy to compete for naval dominance in the Mediterranean during the 1920s. Speed and gun range took precedence over armour and weight of broadside in Italian designs. In theory, this meant that the Italians could break contact with better-crewed Royal Navy ships at will. In reality, it lagged in terms of technology such as radar and sonar and likewise took a beating supporting Mussolini's wars in Ethiopia and Spain. In August 1939, it possessed two modern battleships, 22 cruisers, 126 destroyers and torpedo boats and 105 submarines.

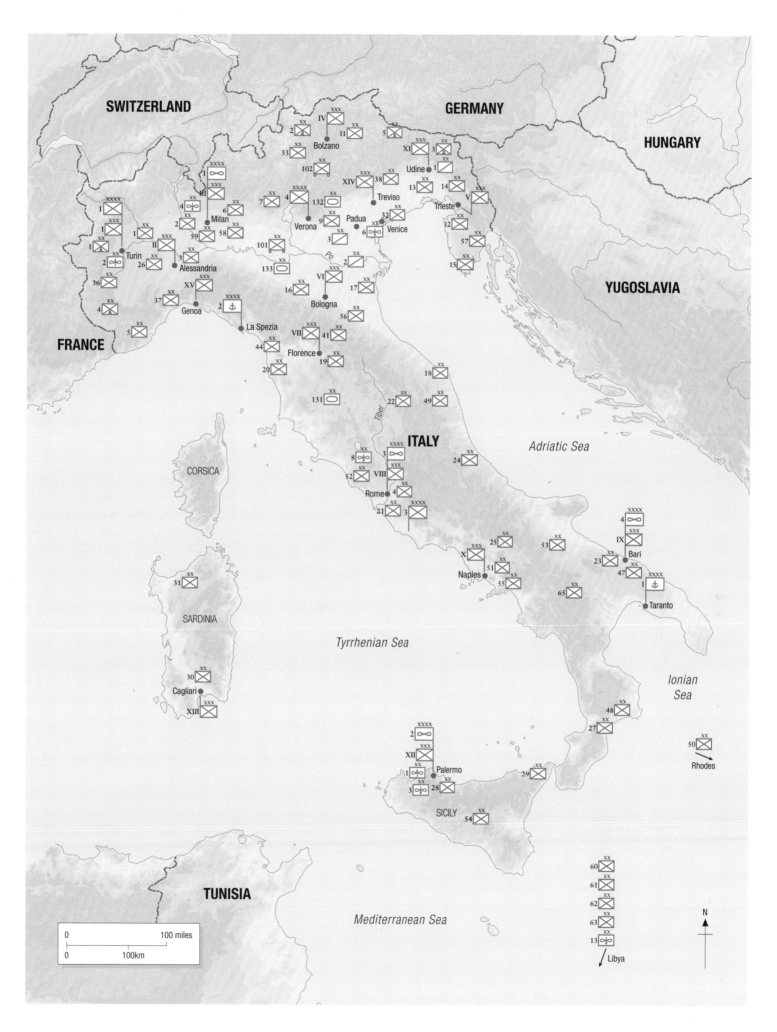

SWITZERLAND

GERMANY

HUNGARY

FRANCE

YUGOSLAVIA

ITALY

Adriatic Sea

CORSICA

Tyrrhenian Sea

SARDINIA

Ionian Sea

SICILY

TUNISIA

Mediterranean Sea

Bolzano

Milan

Verona

Padua

Treviso

Venice

Udine

Trieste

Turin

Alessandria

Genoa

La Spezia

Bologna

Florence

Rome

Naples

Bari

Taranto

Cagliari

Palermo

Rhodes

Libya

N

0   100 miles

0   100km

19

MAP 4: PRE-WAR FRANCE

At the Versailles negotiations, Prime Minister Georges Clemenceau's France frustrated and somewhat surprised the British and Americans. Revenge dominated French thinking. With no serious rivals on the Continent, some even feared a return of French hegemony reminiscent of Louis XIV or Napoleon. However, the country had been greatly weakened by World War I – demographically, diplomatically, financially and colonially. The disappearance of Russia and differences of opinion and mistrust with its allies left pre-World War II France largely on its own.

Despite this, French strategy rested on collective security. Relations with Britain remained the keystone, augmented by the League of Nations and the patchwork of agreements in Central Europe: Poland (1921 and 1925), Czechoslovakia (1925), Romania (1926) and Yugoslavia (1927). The Locarno Treaty (1925) supposedly guaranteed Europe's new borders; however, it contained more spirit than hard realities. The tenuous situation worked so long as Germany stayed contrite (it joined the League in 1926) and Europe's economic and employment numbers looked healthy. The Great Depression, however, destroyed the post-World War I European consensus. As first Mussolini, then Hitler, gained power, the fragility of the new and flawed Concert of Europe became clear. This clarity was especially true within France itself; the country retreated into a shell of conservatism, divided society, antiquated and weak economy and a crumbling empire.

The Maginot Line is the enduring symbol of interwar France's defensive mentality and strategy. The term conjures images of resignation and even self-deception. But the line was perfectly logical given the nation's history, World War I experiences and post-war realities. France simply no longer had the manpower, industrial base, or allies east of Germany to think offensively. Not all Frenchmen would agree; the fortifications spawned a long national debate and Marshal Philippe Pétain, for one, decried the fortress mentality. In sum, the Maginot Line was modern, defensive, relied on firepower rather than manpower and was methodical, all advantages to France. Initially, the fortifications ran from Switzerland to the Ardennes Forest. It is important to point out here that French planners considered the Ardennes easily defended, *not* impassible.

The Maginot Line followed the Franco-German frontier, but planners assumed it would eventually tie into Belgian fortifications all the way to Antwerp. As relations with Mussolini deteriorated, the French extended the line opposite the Italian frontier. Marshy lowlands with high water tables approaching the English Channel were rightly considered poor ground for massive underground structures. Engineering and financial problems meant France did not complete the line until 1938. Smaller, lighter positions screened the immediate border areas, giving way to larger, heavier forts to the rear. Between 500 and 1,000 soldiers manned the latter, built to withstand 420mm artillery. The Maginot Line only represents half of the French strategy, however, a frequently forgotten fact. The other half was a large mobile force that in case of war would swing clockwise into Belgium to augment that nation's defences.

On the eve of World War II, France had the world's largest army in terms of numbers of divisions, artillery pieces and tanks. It had 110 divisions, 65 of which were active and 25 that could be mobilized very quickly; of these, nearly 70 stood against Germany. The French Armée de Terre counted some 2.75 million men and the Armée de l'Intérieur another 2.25 million. An army, however, needs leadership and its generals were lacklustre and line officers and sergeants lacked experience. In addition, many troops suffered from poor training, while reservists were undisciplined. These problems were not caused by financial constraints; in the late 1930s, the military left huge percentages of its budget unspent. Curiously, France exported many of its tanks and guns, even as late as the spring of 1940. Military reforms in the last years of peace held out some promise. French infantry possessed many good weapons and its artillery outclassed the Germans in many categories. French tanks bested German panzers in quantity and, in some cases, quality. Even the best models were hamstrung, however, by small two-man turrets and a paucity of radios. The small anti-aircraft artillery arsenal would have drastic repercussions in 1940.

The Armée de l'Air (air force) had been a political football for much of the 1930s. It suffered from constantly changing missions and priorities and cannot be considered ready for war in 1939. Somewhat like the Luftwaffe, the Armée de l'Air eschewed heavy bombers and concentrated on lighter aircraft and supporting ground operations. Its command and control was very ineffective, from its convoluted organization to the low number of good radios. It had radar as good as the RAF's, but critically without the corresponding ground controller system. The French aviation industry struggled to produce aircraft in sufficient numbers, although by 1940, new models were roughly equivalent to their British and German peers. France relied heavily on aircraft purchased abroad, especially from America.

The Marine Nationale (navy) made many improvements over its World War I predecessor. Civilian and uniformed leaders were good, crews were well trained and ships (except for cruisers) were of high quality. On the eve of war, it had three modern and two old battleships, 19 cruisers of all types, 32 large destroyers, 38 regular destroyers and 77 submarines.

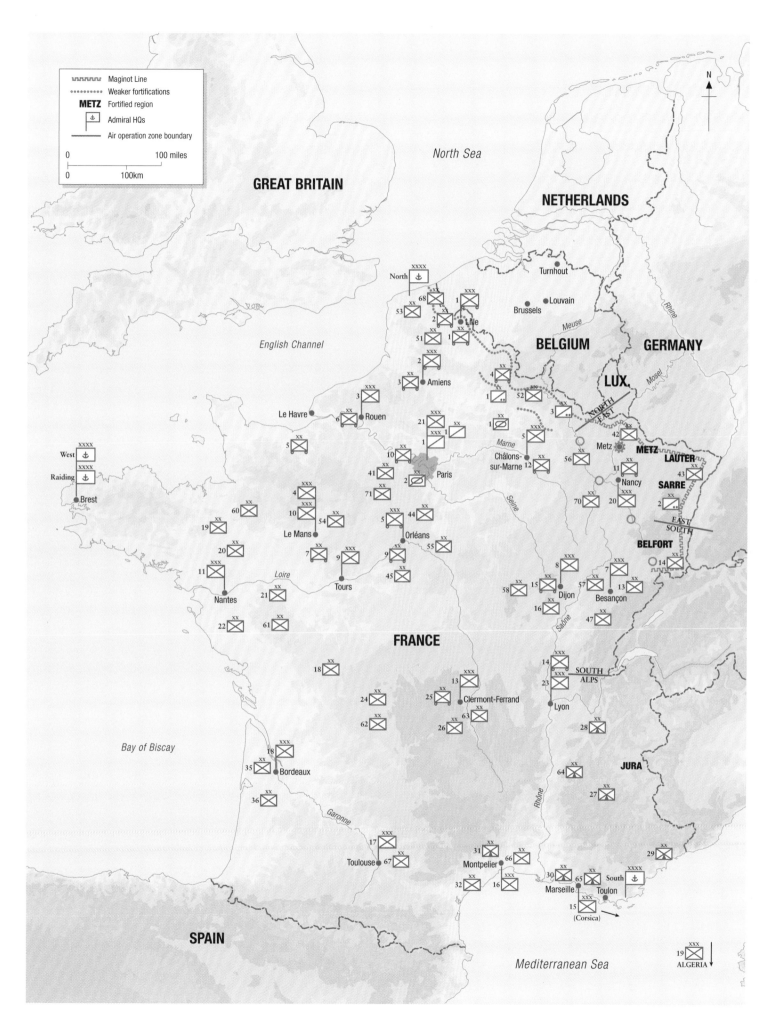

MAP 5: PRE-WAR GREAT BRITAIN

The British Empire escaped World War I in good shape. By any estimation, it received the better parts of the German and Ottoman empires as League of Nations mandates. Its overseas possessions accounted for over half its trade and provided numerous locations to which British citizens could relocate. Accordingly, the empire sent a constant stream of food and raw materials back to the metropole. At home, however, the war had seriously damaged the British economy. It reduced overseas investments by two-thirds and threatened financial instability through inflation and war debts. Attempts to recover the country's economic position and balance budgets by both Conservative and Liberal governments took a heavy toll on military and security spending. According to the cabinet's 'ten-year rule' adopted in 1919 (and reiterated by Churchill in 1928), Great Britain would always have at least a decade in which to catch up with any external threat; further, Churchill told the Royal Navy it could expect 20 years.

The Great Depression exacerbated the Great Britain's problems, as it did the rest of the world. In times of shrinking budgets, it was difficult to keep intact the far-flung empire. Post-World War I independence movements in the dominions (mainly white-dominated lands such as Canada, South Africa, Australia and New Zealand) plus nationality problems in India, Egypt, Palestine and elsewhere, added layers of complexity. In the face of threats to the world order, by Japan in Manchuria in 1931 and those by Hitler and Mussolini already mentioned, Britain abdicated its international leadership role and retreated into its shell, saying 'Let the League handle it'.

After years of idling, by 1936 the British economy showed signs of recovery. New prime ministers, first Stanley Baldwin (1935) and then Neville Chamberlain (1937), devoted more attention to the military, Britain's security and the Continent. Chamberlain initiated negotiations with Europe's two most prominent fascist dictators in an attempt to calm the worsening situation. Unfortunately for the prospects of European peace, in 1938 Hitler took Austria and the Sudetenland and then in 1939, Bohemia, Moravia and Memel. These German moves galvanized British resolve and, in the spring of 1939, it offered security guarantees to Poland, Romania and Greece. Military cooperation with France increased and Britain even swallowed decades of anti-communism and made fruitless overtures to the USSR.

The three British services reflected the emphasis during the interwar years on frugality, home defence and securing the empire at the expense of Continental involvement. By mid-1939, hoped-for peace and disarmament had been dashed by harsh reality, so that most segments of British society, plus its overseas dominions, now recognized the extreme danger posed by Hitler. The liberal world order, which had been Great Britain's work-in-progress for generations, would be put to the test again in the struggle between democracy and fascism.

The Royal Navy held pride of place in British strategy since at least the days of the Spanish Armada. Its main strength lay in its 10,000 officers and 110,000 men (supplemented in wartime by 73,000 reservists), all skilled, professional and trained. Like many navies around the world, the Royal Navy placed battleships at the forefront when considering the next war. However, due to a weak economy, only two of a planned 15 had been built since 1918. It had only one purpose-built aircraft carrier, HMS *Ark Royal,* although six others were in various stages of construction. Cruisers and destroyers were good enough, mostly of recent construction and augmented by dominion vessels, although there were too few of the latter. It had 69 recent-vintage submarines. After 1936, British government budgets paid more attention to adding new ships, monoplane aircraft and technology to the fleet.

The interwar Royal Air Force benefited from the fascination with new technologies and doctrine, not to mention appealing to tight-fisted parliamentarians and taxpayers (even at a time when warplanes did not cost hundreds of millions of pounds apiece). Prime Minister Baldwin gave Britain its first modern security strategy, including Scheme F covering the RAF. This plan called for a Home Defence Air Force of 124 squadrons by March 1939. The RAF and British aviation industry largely met this objective, just in time for the two Czechoslovak crises, after which it concentrated on heavy bombers and fighters. They had begun to solve the problem of bomber range with the Hamden, Wellington and Whitley models and then mastered the issue with later Stirlings, Halifaxes and Lancasters. By mid-1939, of 35 fighter squadrons, 29 flew Hurricanes and Spitfires. An evolving command and control system with rudimentary radar (but good enough, begun in 1935) backed up the fliers. All in all, the RAF had put the year between Munich and Poland to better use than the Luftwaffe.

Neville Chamberlain, target of much scorn, and his Secretary of State for War, Leslie Hore-Belisha, began turning around the British Army in 1937. While not as good as its 1914 antecedent, it had prepared reasonably well and ranks high among Allied armies facing the Wehrmacht. No post-war government would consider conscription, so Britain had an all-volunteer army of 227,000 men (not counting those in India). Part of the Hore-Belisha reforms included increased pay, better living conditions and more respect and responsibility for the Territorial Army (428,000 men). Infantry divisions counted around 13,600 men in nine infantry plus three machine-gun battalions. The 25-pdr was the standard divisional artillery piece. Despite the recent creation of the 1st Armoured Division, British tanks were handicapped by being mainly conceived and used for infantry support. The British plan for the first half of 1939 would initially send four regular and four Territorial Army Divisions to France in the event of war; four more divisions eventually followed, for a total of 12 deployed.

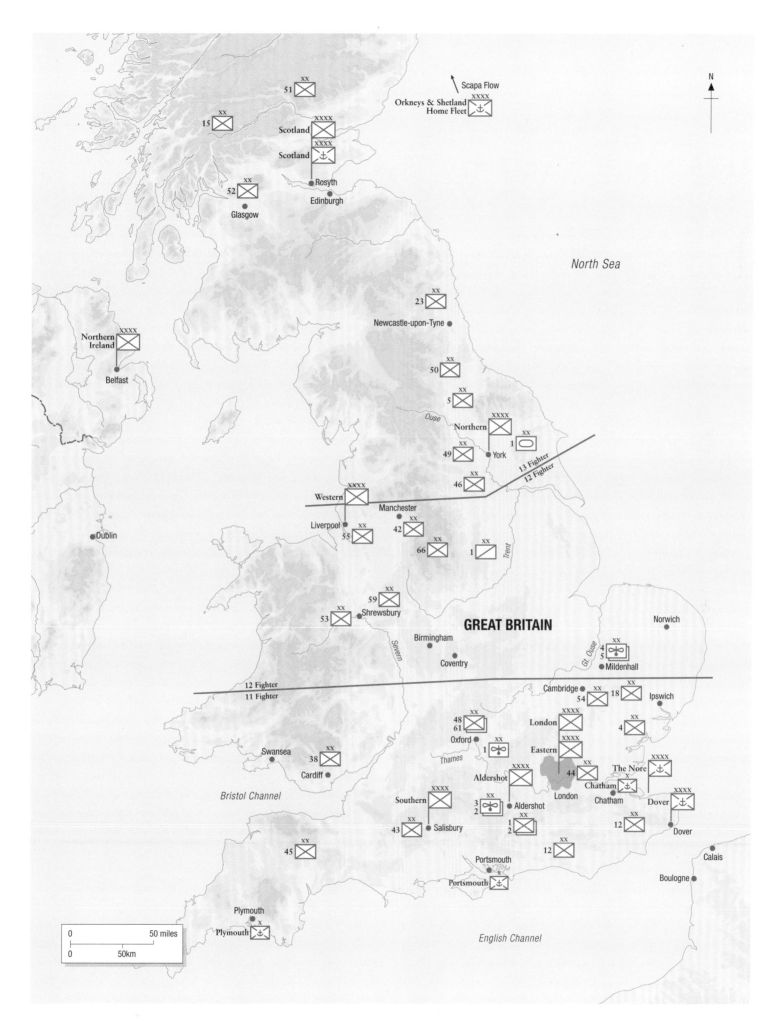

North Sea

Scapa Flow

Orkneys & Shetland
Home Fleet

51

15

XXXX
Scotland

XXXX
Scotland

52
Glasgow

Rosyth

Edinburgh

Northern
Ireland

Belfast

Dublin

23

Newcastle-upon-Tyne

Ouse

50

5

Northern

49

York

1

13 Fighter
12 Fighter

46

Western

Manchester

Liverpool

55

42

66

1

Trent

59
Shrewsbury

53

GREAT BRITAIN

Norwich

Severn

Birmingham

Coventry

Gt. Ouse

4
5

Mildenhall

12 Fighter
11 Fighter

Cambridge

54

18

Ipswich

48
61

Oxford

1

London

XXXX

Eastern

4

Thames

Swansea

38

Cardiff

Southern

Bristol Channel

Aldershot

3
2

Aldershot

London

44

London

Chatham

Chatham

The Nore

Chatham

Dover

Dover

Dover

43

Salisbury

1
2

12

45

Portsmouth

Portsmouth

12

Calais

Boulogne

Plymouth

Plymouth

English Channel

0   50 miles

0   50km

N

MAP 6: PRE-WAR POLAND

In 1918, Poland reappeared in Central Europe, more than 100 years after the dissolution of Napoleon's Duchy of Warsaw. The young country immediately went to war against communist Russia. By June 1920, Polish armies (with temporary Ukrainian help) had taken Kiev and Minsk, but three months later were pushed back to the very gates of Torun, Warsaw and L'wow (L'viv). The Peace of Riga in March 1921 ended the war, although formal establishment of Poland's borders had to wait two more years. An unwieldly constitution, revisionist neighbours and nagging nationality problems (despite Woodrow Wilson's self-determination pledges) hamstrung the new Second Republic. Economic woes finally brought an end to the brief democratic experiment as Marshal Josef Pilsudski's coup d'état toppled the government in May 1926. Civilian politicians went through the motions of leading Poland, while Pilsudski held real power as a non-fascist authoritarian until his death in 1935. The Depression hurt Poland as everywhere else and, with Nazi Germany to the west and the USSR to the east, security issues dominated Polish foreign policy. A new general, Edward Rydz-Śmigły, filled the dead marshal's military role, but not his political one. In the late 1930s, the government tried to reinvigorate the economy, especially the largely unmotorized agricultural sector.

Through the mid-1930s, Poland occupied a unique place in the security planning of most European nations: Military prowess demonstrated over centuries had earned universal respect; It played a lynchpin role in British and French strategy for its anti-communist/Soviet and anti-German attitudes. Its anti-communist/Soviet credentials also attracted the attention of Germany, which at one point even considered war with Poland against the USSR. Stalin, ever the opportunist, looked for any good reason to undo the Treaty of Riga. For Poland, however, the Western Allies' weak response to Hitler's remilitarization of the Rhineland (see Map 10) caused it to doubt the entire collective security arrangement. For the next two years, Poland seemed eager to cooperate with Germany. In October 1938, it received payment of sorts at the First Vienna Award, when Hitler gave the Czechoslovak coal region around Tschen (Cieszyn) to Poland. But soon thereafter, Polish–German relations deteriorated over agricultural policies and disagreements about Danzig and the Polish Corridor. Hitler did not push the issue, since he did not want to drive Poland back into the arms of Britain and France, and he hoped to use Poland's 30 divisions in a potential war against the Soviet Union. Any good will between the two evaporated after March 1939, when Hitler took over the rump of Czechoslovakia and created a puppet state in Slovakia,

thereby increasing mortal danger to Poland. Within days of the German occupation of Prague, Poland asked for and received security guarantees from Britain. This amounted to a Polish rejection of Hitler, who on 3 April 1939 ordered the Wehrmacht to draw up plans to conquer his neighbour.

By March 1939, Poland was surrounded on all sides. With a frontier approaching 2,000 miles, it had to defend well forward along this entire length. No responsible government could simply abandon large segments of the country and its population to the enemy. Principal population and resource areas around Warsaw and Krakow were within easy striking distance from German units in East Prussia and Silesia, respectively. It possessed a small industrial base, also mostly west of the Vistula River and close to Luftwaffe bases, and its mobilization infrastructure was very vulnerable. The Nazi–Soviet Non-Aggression Pact of August 1939 had one principal target: Poland. The little country could not defend itself without substantial and immediate British and French assistance, and knew it.

Poland therefore had a defensive strategy. Its military consisted of a combination of past and present. Its mixture of modern plus old Austro-Hungarian and tsarist fortifications dotted the country in an uneven fashion. The army consisted of approximately 300,000 active duty soldiers plus almost 1.5 million reservists in various stages of preparedness and training. Plans called for 30 to 60 days to mobilize for war, but the Germans gave Poland only between one week (preliminary) and two days (full mobilization), so hundreds of thousands of reservists were in transit when the war began. The Polish order of battle counted 30 infantry divisions, a dozen cavalry brigades, plus numerous smaller units. In each division, one brigade was active and the other two inactive, waiting on reservists. Field armies were made up of four to five divisions, essentially glorified corps in other contemporary militaries. Mechanization was in the early stages of implementation. Poland had 250 modern and 90 obsolete tanks of British and French origin, plus an assorted mix of small or obsolescent tankettes, reconnaissance vehicles and armoured cars. Artillery was modern but small in terms of calibre and numbers. Command and control suffered from absence of the corps echelon and an over-reliance on inflexible and easily interdicted landline communications.

The Polish Air Force, while of a good size, suffered from small obsolete models. Modern fighters were almost non-existent, while modern bombers (e.g., the P.37B) were too few in number. The navy consisted of four destroyers and five submarines, some of which sailed for Great Britain when the war began, plus numerous smaller craft.

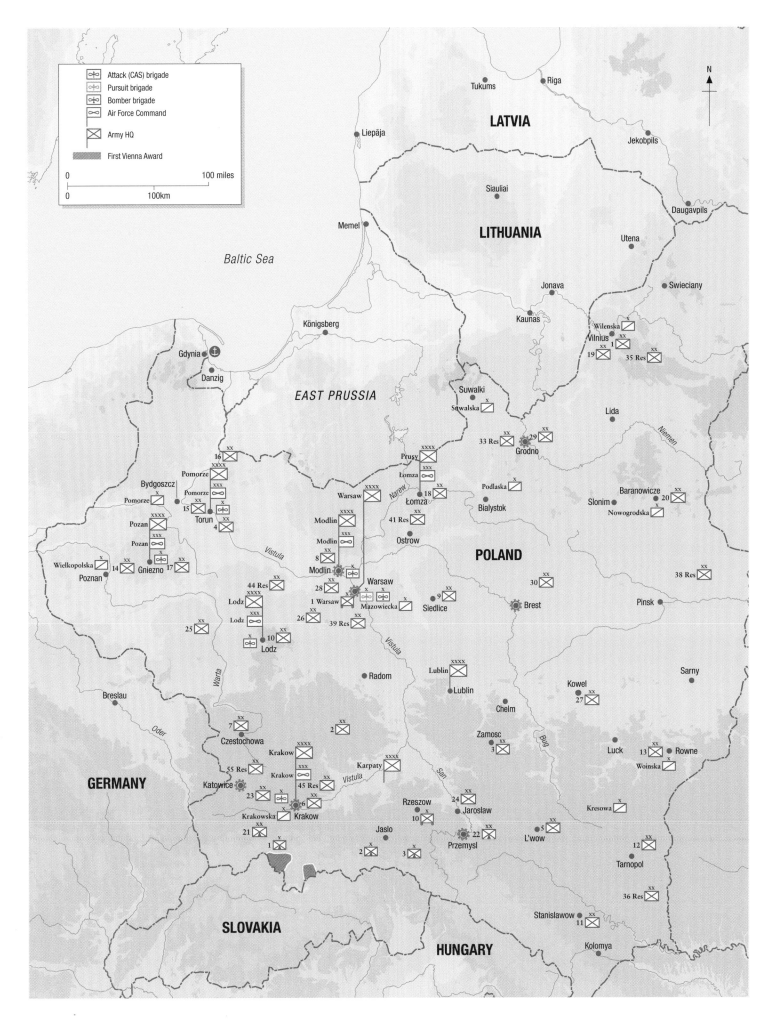

Legend:
- Attack (CAS) brigade
- Pursuit brigade
- Bomber brigade
- Air Force Command
- Army HQ
- First Vienna Award

0 — 100 miles
0 — 100km

Baltic Sea

LATVIA

Tukums
Riga
Liepāja
Jekobpils

LITHUANIA

Siauliai
Memel
Daugavpils

Königsberg

Utena
Swieciany

Jonava
Kaunas

Wilenska
Vilnius   1
19   35 Res

Gdynia
Danzig

EAST PRUSSIA

Suwalki
Suwalska

Lida

33 Res   29
Grodno

16
Pomorze
Bydgoszcz
Pomorze
Pomorze   Prusy
15   Torun   Łomza   18
4   Warsaw   Narew   Podlaska   Baranowicze   20

Pozan   Modlin   Bialystok   Slonim
Pozan   Modlin   41 Res   Nowogrodska
Wielkopolska   14   Gniezno   17   Modlin   Ostrow   POLAND
Poznan   8   Modlin   38 Res

44 Res   28   Warsaw
Lodz   1 Warsaw   Warsaw   30
Lodz   26   Mazowiecka   9   Brest   Pinsk
25   39 Res   Siedlice

10   Lodz   Vistula

Radom   Lublin   Sarny
Breslau   Lublin   Kowel
Chelm   27

Oder   Zamosc
7   3   Luck   13   Rowne
Czestochowa   Woinska

2
Krakow   Karpaty
55 Res   Krakow   24   Kresowa
Katowice   45 Res   Vistula   Rzeszow   Jaroslaw
23   6   10   5
Krakowska   Krakow   San   22   L'wow   12
21   Jaslo   Rzeszow   Przemysl   Tarnopol
1   2   3

GERMANY

SLOVAKIA   36 Res

Stanislawow   11

HUNGARY   Kolomya

25

MAP 7: PRE-WAR BELGIUM AND THE NETHERLANDS

Both Belgium and the Netherlands had been neutral leading up the Great War. Belgium became Germany's first victim on 4 August 1914 and was sucked into the war, while the Netherlands managed to remain neutral as 'Germany's windpipe' to the rest of the world (along with Sweden). Both declared their neutrality at various times during the interwar period, although they suspected that a future war might not exclude them.

The historiography of the two world wars has been unkind to Belgium; the country is scapegoated for Allied failures in both cases. During World War I, human and property losses due to combat in Belgium had been great, but not as great as from the German occupation. Reparations levied by the Versailles process were assumed to make good on the destruction, but this was not the case. Not helped by the Franco–Belgian occupation of the Ruhr, the Belgian economy struggled until 1926. Its interwar politics remained generally civil until 1936, when radical parties on both left and right grew in influence and power. Tensions between isolationist Flemings and pro-French Walloons remained very divisive (and spilled over into the national security debate). Regarding foreign and security policies, Belgium is roughly analogous to Poland in that it too was a small nation caught between two large and antagonistic foes. Between 1920 and 1936, it had a military accord (not a treaty) with France; both countries strained under its terms. Neutrality, declared in 1936, neither prevented Belgium from surreptitiously making military plans with the Western Allies, nor saved it from becoming a future battleground for the French, who would rather not fight in their own country again (and would enter Belgium by force, if necessary). To the Belgians, the (too short) Maginot Line and French reliance on 'methodical battle' provided cold comfort.

Hitler's 1936 remilitarization of the Rhineland and the Belgian elections that followed soon after led the country to declare its neutrality and go it alone. It therefore developed a defence-in-depth strategy tied to fortresses around Antwerp and Namur to the west plus Liège and Maastricht jutting towards Germany in the east – all tied into natural and man-made obstacles. In this way, Belgium's policy looked curiously like France's: appear so strong that Hitler would attempt to invade somewhere else. Belgium had a peacetime army of six infantry and two cavalry divisions. It added a frontier screening force, the Chasseurs

Ardennais, in 1934. Wartime reserves raised the army to 22 divisions numbering around 650,000 men, including fortress troops. Cavalry forces underwent considerable mechanization in the late 1930s. In early September 1939, with the official beginning of World War II, Belgium called up the first two classes of reserves, while controversial King Leopold III took command of the army on the 4th of that month. During the autumn of 1939 and the winter of 1940, the country dealt with numerous false war scares. Compared to the army, the Belgian Air Force seemed obsolete and unprepared.

The Netherlands sat out as a neutral and continued this policy until 1940. As Hitler began to take threatening actions during the late 1930s, the Dutch increased their military preparedness (they also had to plan on the Japanese menacing their East Indies colonies). After many years of financial and policy neglect, these changes proved to be too little, too late. The Dutch defensive strategy relied on traditional geographic advantages consisting of many large rivers and easily flooded lowlands and areas of reclaimed polders. Their plans assumed that the Germans would quickly overrun most of the eastern Netherlands, from which the Dutch would grudgingly withdraw. Thereafter, parallel defences roughly along the Peel, Grebbe and New Water lines and demolished bridges would slow the German advance. Of these positions, the Grebbe Line was the key, consisting of many modern fortifications. The Dutch would then make a final stand in Fortress Holland, the heavily populated space around Amsterdam and Rotterdam.

The army consisted of nine small (10,000-man) divisions – eight infantry and one light (bicycle-mounted), plus many battalions of frontier defence forces. It fielded approximately 114,000 men when mobilized in August 1939. An ad hoc unit, the Peel Division, guarded the marshy south-east of the country. Although it eventually included 23 battalions defending five 'boxes' (Schajik, Erp, Bakel, Asten and Weert – not mutually supporting), it cannot be considered a cohesive formation. Dutch artillery and armour branches were small and ill-equipped with old, small weapons. Anti-tank forces had modern guns, just too few of them. The air force was also small and outdated.

Luxembourg represented the third neutral in question (Hitler had guaranteed its neutrality a year before he violated it). It had no army, merely a 500-man paramilitary gendarmerie, in wartime the main duty of which consisted of manning roadblocks.

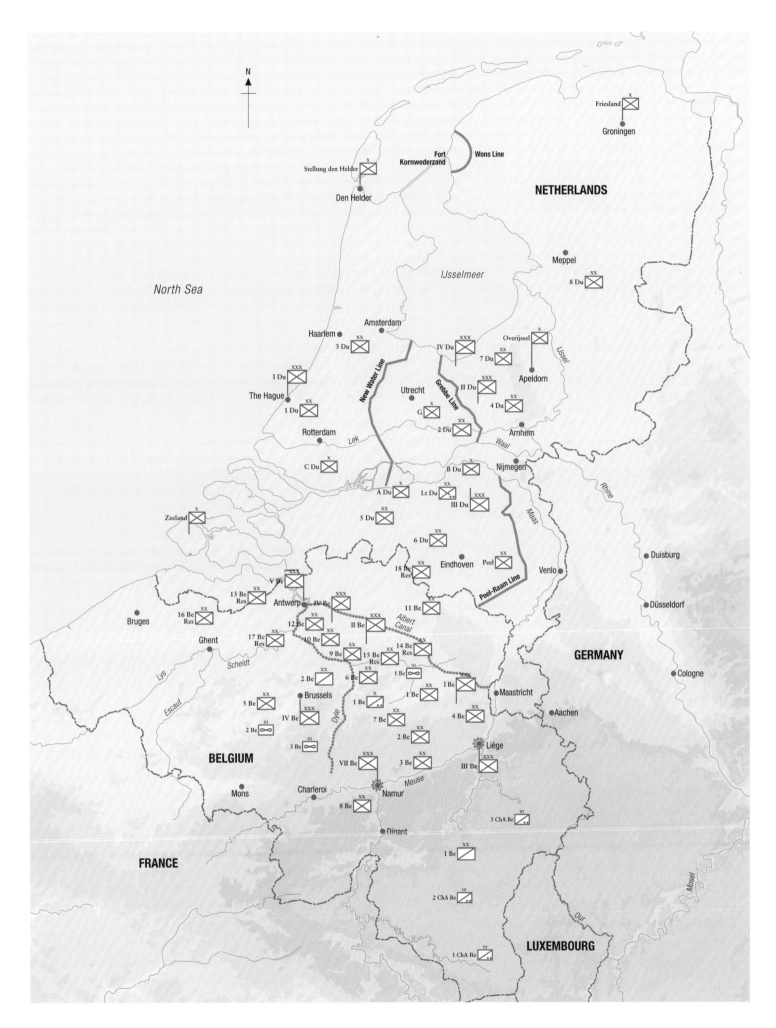

MAP 8: PRE-WAR BALKAN PENINSULA

For generations, the Balkan Peninsula represented a fracture zone disputed by the three Eastern European empires, while Germany considered the region its hinterland. Apart from Greece, nations covered here came into being in the 42 years preceding the Versailles Treaty. They benefited especially from the demise of the empires and, very unevenly, from Wilson's self-determination policy. Greece, Romania and Serbia were rewarded for their part in the winning coalition, while defeated Central Powers states Hungary and Bulgaria became revisionist. These alignments basically continued through the interwar period. All were economically disadvantaged monarchies and, by the late 1930s, often leaning towards authoritarianism or fascism.

Though on the losing side of World War I, Bulgaria survived the Treaty of Neuilly (1919) basically intact and ethnically unified, though the ceded lands cost it over 1 million countrymen. Primarily an agrarian nation with many small enterprises but little industry, the Depression hit Bulgaria less severely than some nations. After 1935, King Boris III ran a virtual dictatorship (with democratic trappings) advised by a clique of loyal army officers. Despite official neutrality, the Bulgarian military had been aligned with Germany due to numerous Wehrmacht advisors. The army consisted of four corps (called field armies, directly subordinated to the war ministry), ten infantry and two 'rapid' (cavalry) divisions plus some brigade- and regiment-sized units. The air force mainly flew plundered Czechoslovak and French machines.

Greece earned its nationhood in 1830 and grew considerably thanks to the treaties of Neuilly and Sèvres (1920). However, war with the new Turkish Republic (1920–23) ended disastrously, both in terms of military defeat and civilian atrocities. Chaos and turmoil dominated interwar Greece, which alternated between civil and military governments or monarchy and republic. After early problems absorbing a flood of war refugees following 1923, the economy adjusted as successfully as it could, given Greece's agrarian and small business emphasis. A military dictatorship ruled the country from a 1936 coup d'état until defeat in 1941. In 1940, Greece had two field armies, named the Western and Eastern Macedonian Armies, five corps, plus 20 infantry and one cavalry division. Equipment and weapons came principally from Czechoslovakia, France and Germany, with obvious negative connotations for ammunition and repair parts after 1940. The air force possessed 90 fighters and bombers.

Within one year of the World War I armistice, Hungary went from a republic, to communist dictatorship, to counterrevolutionary monarchy. The Treaty of Trianon (1920) awarded 'Hungarian' lands to Romania and the new nations of Czechoslovakia and Yugoslavia, causing flags in Budapest to be flown at half-mast until the 1938 First Vienna Award. Ruled by a conservative regent, former Habsburg admiral Miklós Horthy, propped up by a dominant Magyar nobility, governed by a pliant parliament, and with only a trace of democracy, Hungary slipped towards fascism. The Depression and the rise of Hitler drove the country towards greater radicalism and revisionism. By 1939, Hungary had withdrawn from the League of Nations and signed the Anti-Comintern Pact. Prior to the war, the army consisted of three field armies, nine corps and 20 divisions. In peacetime, each division had two active regiments, joined by the third regiment upon mobilization.

Romania began World War II in the Allied camp, but ended it as possibly Hitler's most steadfast ally. Its participation in World War I began disastrously, but the country also nearly doubled in size due to the treaties of Nueilly and Trianon. New territories contained considerable natural resources, while German capital pushed the growing oil industry. However, non-Romanians made up almost 30 per cent of the population. National politics ran a course typical of the region: monarchs coming and going, alternating experiments with democracy and dictatorship, etc. Defending newly acquired lands became the military's main purpose. Military policy relied on collective security with regional neighbours (aimed against both Hungary and the USSR). In 1940, Stalin's absorption of Bessarabia (Map 33) and the fall of its French patron led to great loss of territory, the end the country's Francophile leanings, a new alliance with Germany and a royally sanctioned military dictatorship (in an uneasy alliance with fascists). The country was divided into two army and seven corps districts, numbering 20 infantry, three cavalry, two mountain and one armoured division. Romania had an advanced aviation industry for a country its size.

As a brand-new nation with Treaty of Versailles origins, Yugoslavia was surrounded by revisionist neighbours and torn by ethnic strife. A strong Croat minority challenged the Serbian majority to the point of assassinating the Serbian king (and virtual dictator) Alexander in 1934. Up to that point, the country favoured the French and modelled its military on France. The new regent Prince Paul and the realities of Hitler's rising power in Europe signalled a shift in Yugoslav foreign policy. This culminated after Munich in 1938, with its abandonment of France and wholesale alliance with Germany (with which it now shared a common border). The Serbian military had earned great respect for its performance in World War I. It dominated the new Yugoslav Army, including 161 of 165 generals. During the late 1930s, defence consumed 30 per cent of the national budget and the fully mobilized army numbered 1.5 million men armed with relatively modern Czechoslovak weapons.

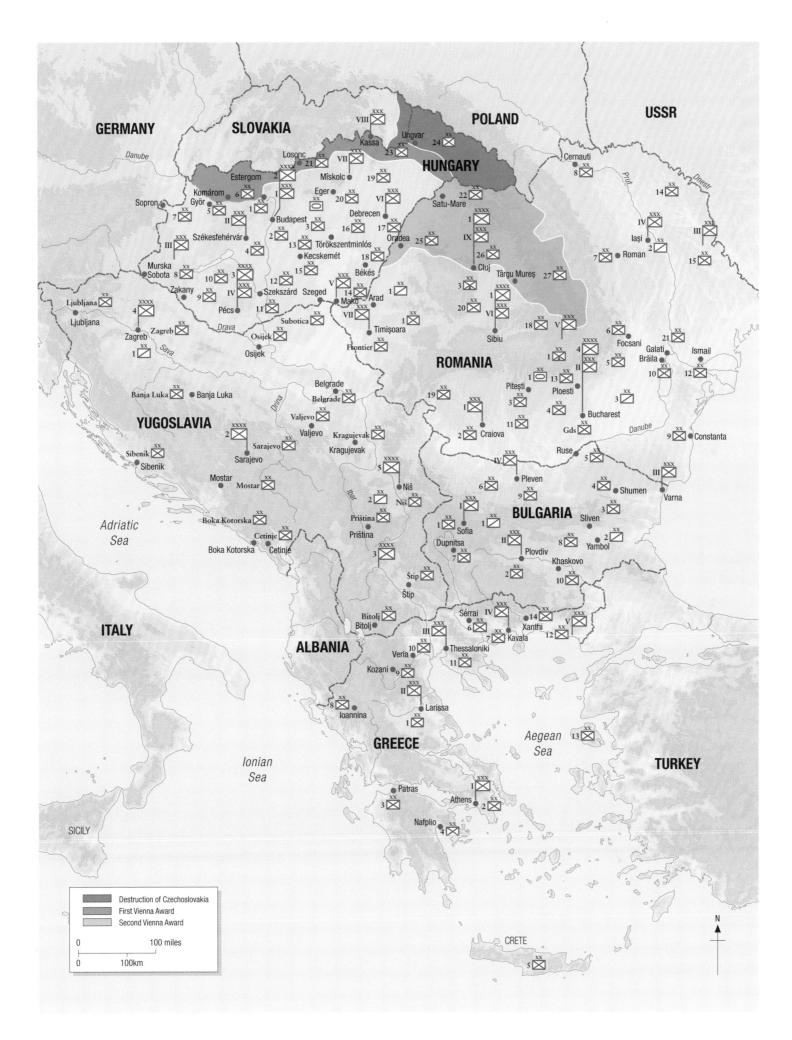

GERMANY

SLOVAKIA

POLAND

USSR

Danube

VIII XXX

Kassa

Ungvar 24 XXX

23 XXX

Cernauti
8 XXX

Prut

Dnestr

Losonc
21 XXX

VII XXX

HUNGARY

14 XXX

Estergom 2 XXXX

Miskolc 19 XXX

22 XXX

Komárom 6 xx

1 XXX

Eger
20 XXX

VI XXX

Satu-Mare

IV XXX

III XXX

Györ 5 xx

1 XXX

Debrecen 17 XXX

1 XXXX

Iași 2 XXX

Roman

Sopron 7 XX

II XXX

Budapest 3 XXX

16 XXX

Oradea

IX XXX

7 XXX

15 XXX

Székesfehérvár III XXX

2 XXX

13 XXX

Törökszentmiklós

25 XXX

26 XXX

Murska
Sobota 8 XX

4 XXX

18 XXX

Békés

Cluj

Târgu Mureș 27 XXX

Ljubljana XX

10 XX

3 XXXX

Szeged

XX
14

Makó

3 XXX

20 XXX

1 XXX

Zakany 9 XX

IV XXXX

Szekszárd

Arad

VI XXX

Ljubljana

Pécs

11 XXX

VII XXX

Timișoara

Sibiu

18 XXX

V XXX

ROMANIA

6 XXX

Focsani

21 XXX

4 XXXX

Zagreb 4 XXXX

Subotica

Frontier

1 XXX

II XXX

Galati
Brăila
10 XXX

Ismail
12 XX

Zagreb 1 XX

Sava

Osijek

5 XXX

Drava

Osijek

Belgrade

19 XXX

Pitești

13 XXX

Ploesti

3 XXX

Banja Luka XX Banja Luka

Belgrade XX

I XXX

3 XXX

4 XXX

9 XXX Constanta

YUGOSLAVIA

Valjevo XX

2 XXX Craiova

11 XXX

Gds XX

Danube

2 XXXX

Valjevo

Kragujevak XX

Bucharest

Ruse XX

Sarajevo XX

Kragujevak

IV XXX

5 XX Shumen

Varna

Sibenik XX

Sarajevo

5 XXXX

6 XXX

Pleven

III XXX

Sibenik

Mostar XX

Niš

9 XXX

Mostar

2 XXX

Niš XX

I XXX

BULGARIA

Sliven XX

Boka Kotorska XX

Priština XX

1 XXX

Sofia

1 XXX

8 XXX

2 XXX Yambol

Cetinje XX

Priština

II XXX

Boka Kotorska

Cetinje

3 XXXX

Dupnitsa

7 XXX

Plovdiv

Khaskovo

Štip XX

2 XXX

10 XXX

Štip

Bitolj XX

Sérrai
6 XXX

IV XXX

14 XXX

V XXX

Bitolj

III XXX

Xanthi

12 XXX

ALBANIA

10 XXX

7 XXX Kavala

Veria

Thessaloniki

Kozani 9 XXX

11 XXX

8 XX

II XXX

Ioannina

Larissa

1 XXX

GREECE

*Aegean
Sea*

TURKEY

*Ionian
Sea*

Patras

I XXX

3 XXX

Athens

2 XXX

Nafplio 4 XXX

13 XXX

SICILY

*Adriatic
Sea*

ITALY

CRETE

5 XX

	Destruction of Czechoslovakia
	First Vienna Award
	Second Vienna Award

0   100 miles

0   100km

N

MAP 9: PRE-WAR SOVIET UNION

After World War I, Russia (and the post-1922 USSR) was a dreaded and hated pariah state. Nations around the globe held anti-communist beliefs and strategies, crusader-like in intensity, which in many cases turned into fascism. During the Russian Civil War, the Allies deployed fleets and expeditionary forces and gave other support to White forces. By 1920, Poland had dashed Lenin's hopes that the Red Army would bring bolshevism into the heart of Europe. Tsarist Russia had shown countless failings and weaknesses during its final years, so Stalin set about consolidating 'socialism in one country' and preparing the Soviet Union for a showdown with capitalism that both Lenin and he knew would come.

The fearful Soviet world view justifiably saw danger and threats everywhere. In 1928, ten years after the revolution, Soviet industry had only reached 1913 levels. To preserve Lenin's dream, Stalin initiated successive Five-Year Plans to boost capital expenditures, build heavy industry, train skilled workers and extract raw materials – all with the goal of strengthening the Soviet state and military. According to Soviet figures, by 1932 industrial output had doubled. Soviet rearmament dwarfed that of any other power, including the Third Reich. Starting in 1930, its tank inventory jumped from 170 to 5,000 in six years, while numbers of aircraft went from 1,000 to 10,000 by 1940. With the Depression and advent of widespread fascism, Stalin believed that the USSR could only survive if it made common cause with the capitalist West. This attitude did not last long, however: Allied support of Republican Spain was anaemic, the League of Nations was toothless in the face of Japanese, Italian, German and other rule-breaker regimes, and then Britain and France adopted a policy of appeasement. To make British and French pusillanimity worse, Stalin did not get invited to Munich.

Slightly earlier, beginning in 1936, Stalin turned on his own people, with his purges and show trials that targeted top party and military leaders, but also lowly lieutenants and aircraft designers. The USSR seemed to have lost its earlier lead in key defence and security areas: doctrine (Mikhail Tukhachevsky's deep battle and shock armies), techniques (airborne operations) and weapons systems (modern tanks). This beheading of the Red Army happened just as it underwent a massive expansion and needed all the qualified leaders it could get. After Hitler occupied Bohemia and Moravia in March 1939, Britain gave assurances to Poland and Romania – exactly what Stalin opposed. Then, at the end of May, Hitler's government told its ambassador in Moscow to begin negotiating with the Soviets. Only Hitler could offer Stalin what he really wanted: freedom of action and territory in Central and Eastern Europe. In addition, the Germans showed much more earnestness than Britain and France did in their simultaneous negotiations. The final result of course was the 23 August Nazi-Soviet Non-Aggression (a.k.a. Molotov–Ribbentrop) Pact, which shocked the world and gave both dictatorships what they needed and wanted.

Stalin had long taken a keen interest in all military questions, especially the development of new weapons. After the purges, all senior military leaders owed their position to Stalin. This brought marginally incompetent personal acquaintances into most top jobs (the so-called 'Cavalry Army clique' from the Civil War) and also put new and untrained men into lower jobs as well. Command and control also suffered greatly as a result – the Soviet military struggled to adopt to the post-Tukhachevsky world and digest the lessons from the Spanish Civil War and early blitzkrieg campaigns. Fortunately for the USSR, General G.K. Zhukov did not fall victim to the purges.

Prior to the invasion of Poland, the Red Army had 1.7 million men in 120 divisions. That autumn it called up two additional year groups, swelling the ranks to 4.7 million. Despite impressive moves towards motorization, it still depended heavily on horses, both for its 30 cavalry divisions (the largest such force in the world) and to pull artillery and logistics. Old tsarist models made up most small arms and artillery, although excellent new models of the latter were coming online. The Red Army had the planet's largest tank park and although the trendsetting T-34 still lay in the future, most other Soviet armour was as good as any found in Germany, Britain, or France. Soviet obsession with easily quantifiable data, like gun calibre or tank weight, however, meant that more intangible measures, such as quality of optics or radios, lagged behind.

The Red Army Air Force was huge, but its quality was poor, although some new models were approaching operational deployment. Again, Stalin made all the important decisions in this area as well. The air force (not an independent branch of service) had as its primary mission support of the army. Stalin's purges had likewise taken a severe toll on naval officers and ship designers. The dictator had wanted an independent and offensive blue-water navy, while most of his purge victims advocated a defensive force, dependent on submarines. For the Soviet Navy, World War II began too early to see this goal realized.

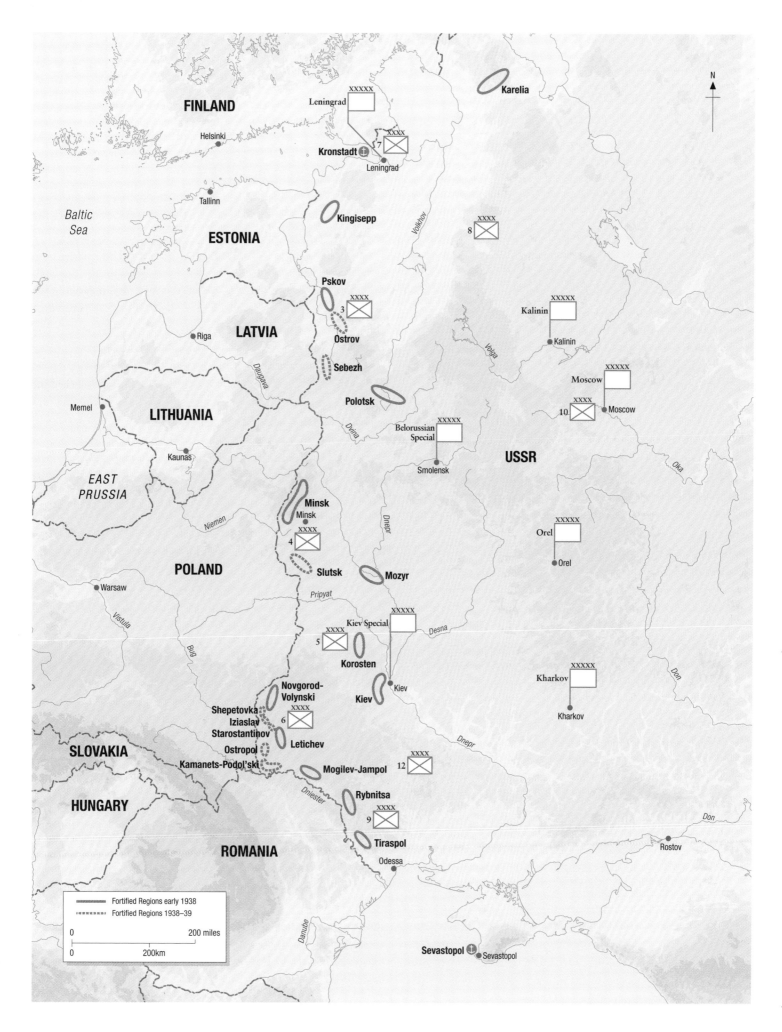

N

FINLAND

Helsinki

Baltic
Sea

Tallinn

ESTONIA

LATVIA

Riga

LITHUANIA

Memel

Kaunas

EAST
PRUSSIA

POLAND

Warsaw

SLOVAKIA

HUNGARY

ROMANIA

USSR

Karelia

Leningrad XXXXX

Kronstadt ⚓ 7 XXXX
Leningrad

Kingisepp

8 XXXX

Pskov
3 XXXX

Ostrov

Sebezh

Polotsk

Belorussian
Special XXXXX

Smolensk

Minsk
Minsk
4 XXXX

Slutsk

Mozyr

Kiev Special XXXXX

5 XXXX

Korosten

Novgorod-
Volynski

Shepetovka
Iziaslav
Starostantinov

6 XXXX

Letichev

Ostropol

Kamanets-Podol'ski

Mogilev-Jampol

12 XXXX

Rybnitsa

9 XXXX

Tiraspol

Odessa

Kiev

Kalinin XXXXX

Kalinin

Moscow XXXXX

10 XXXX
Moscow

Orel XXXXX

Orel

Kharkov XXXXX

Kharkov

Rostov

Sevastopol ⚓ Sevastopol

Volkhov

Volga

Oka

Dvina

Dnepr

Desna

Daugava

Niemen

Vistula

Bug

Pripyat

Dniester

Danube

Dnepr

Don

Don

Fortified Regions early 1938
Fortified Regions 1938–39

0   200 miles
0   200km

31

MAP 10: HITLER UNOPPOSED

From the beginning of his political career, Hitler had wanted to 'restore German greatness', as he described it: undo Versailles, return Germany to the first rank of European nations and expand its borders. He was not alone, however: as early as 1926, the Weimar Republic's Reichswehr began planning to retake or conquer all the territory shown on this map. A self-styled bohemian artist who operated by inspiration and instinct, the Führer did not have fixed plans or timetables and seldom wrote anything down. Therefore, when an international situation and his foreign policy goals aligned, he moved quickly. While this appears to be mere opportunism, it was more than that. Often it was a case of either exploiting some small success to restore sagging popularity, or an attempt to distract popular opinion from unfavourable domestic news onto an external issue. In any event, for more than three years prior to starting World War II, Hitler went from one bloodless success or conquest to the next (*Blumenkriege*, or Flower Wars), increasing his standing both at home and abroad each time.

OPERATION SCHULUNG (TRAINING)

The Versailles Treaty had 'permanently' demilitarized the Rhineland (the part of Germany between the Rhine and its western neighbours, plus three bridgeheads on the right bank), initially occupied immediately after World War I. Hitler wanted it back. He often used some provocation to justify his actions, in this case, the Franco–Soviet Mutual Assistance Treaty signed in early March 1936. Therefore, on 7 March, he sent three battalions towards the three cities shown here, covered by 54 Luftwaffe fighters. Orders told them to quickly retreat (not 'flee') if the Allies offered any resistance. The remainder of the Wehrmacht stood by in case of joint French–Czech action. With few options short of mobilization, France mainly sent reservists to the Maginot Line. Otherwise, the Western democracies did little. Hitler had correctly judged their lack of resolve.

OPERATION OTTO

After a quiet year, when among other things, Hitler wanted to put on a good show hosting the Olympic Games, he looked to his next move. With the Allies distracted by the Italians in Ethiopia and simmering problems in Spain, in June 1937 he ordered the German Army to plan to invade Austria. The process began slowly, with Austrian Nazi agitators stirring up trouble. Then, on 12 February 1938, the Führer demanded that Austria both coordinate their foreign and economic policies with the Reich government and allow Nazis to participate in government. The Austrian chancellor rejected the ultimatum and ordered a national plebiscite on these questions for 13 March. Hitler would not wait for the vote. His army finalized plans on the 10th, Hermann Göring strong-armed the Austrians into 'inviting' in the Wehrmacht on the 11th and the two nations were defacto joined starting the next day. Wehrkreis VII and XIII under the 8. Armee conducted the operation. The Germans' first mechanized campaign suffered many teething problems, but otherwise *Otto* went smoothly with only 25 deaths (mostly to vehicle wrecks on icy roads). Despite post-war claims of being

'Hitler's first victim', on 10 April Austrians voted by a margin of 99 per cent for *Anschluss* (Joining) with Germany.

OPERATION GRÜN (GREEN)

The feeble Allied response to Austria emboldened Hitler to set his sights on Czechoslovakia next. Tensions escalated throughout the spring until 30 May, when he ordered the Wehrmacht to be ready by 1 October to invade Czechoslovakia from north and south. Nazis agitated trouble among the German minority in the Sudeten Mountains in far-western Czechoslovakia and the summer crisis seemed to be heading towards certain war. Stalin's purges almost guaranteed no response from the Soviets. During the second half of September, Prime Minister Neville Chamberlain, painfully aware of British unpreparedness, engaged in shuttle diplomacy in the name of peace. At Mussolini's invitation, on the 29th and 30th leaders of Germany, Italy, Britain and France met in Munich and agreed to all of Hitler's demands. German troops occupied the Sudetenland on 1 October; it was the beginning of the end for Czechoslovakia. *Grün* (not shown on map) also marks the early first example of Hitler injecting himself into the Wehrmacht's planning process with the OKW (Oberkommando der Wehrmacht, Military High Command)

On 17 December 1938, Hitler ordered the Wehrmacht to prepare to occupy the rest of Czechoslovakia. In the upcoming scenario, the Slovak minority (one-quarter of the 10 million population) would take over the role played earlier by earlier Austrian Nazis and Sudeten Germans. Again, tensions rose as a prelude to military action. On 10 March 1939, Czech President Emil Hacha dismissed Slovak Premier Jozef Tisa and two days later sent troops into Slovakia. The next day, Tisa reported to Hitler and announced the new Slovak state. On the 14th, Slovakia and Ruthenia declared their independence, sounding the death knell of Czechoslovakia, no longer a viable nation (and therefore voiding British security guarantees). Under the command of Gruppenkommando 3 in Dresden, on 15 March the Wehrmacht entered what was left of the country, which became a German protectorate.

OPERATION STETTIN

Hitler's final bloodless victory came just days later at the Lithuanian port of Klaipeda (German: Memel) and right bank of the Neman River (not shown on map). As usual, the takeover began with ethnic and political agitation by the German minority, so Hitler could come to the rescue of 'his Germans'. On 22 March, the Lithuanian foreign minister reported to Berlin to receive the German ultimatum regarding the city. Seasick Hitler, aboard the panzer ship *Deutschland,* prepared for his triumphal arrival. In Berlin, the Lithuanians played hard to get and only agreed to the German terms at 1330 hours on the 23rd. Hitler disembarked later that day to a hero's welcome by the 'liberated' Germans in the region.

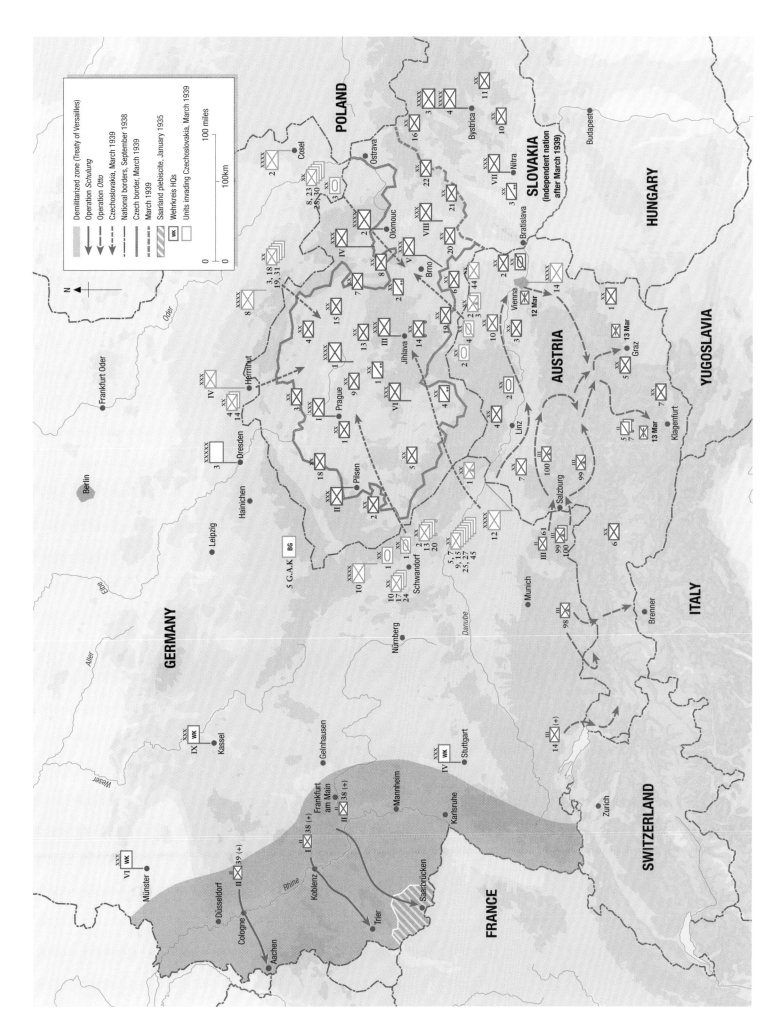

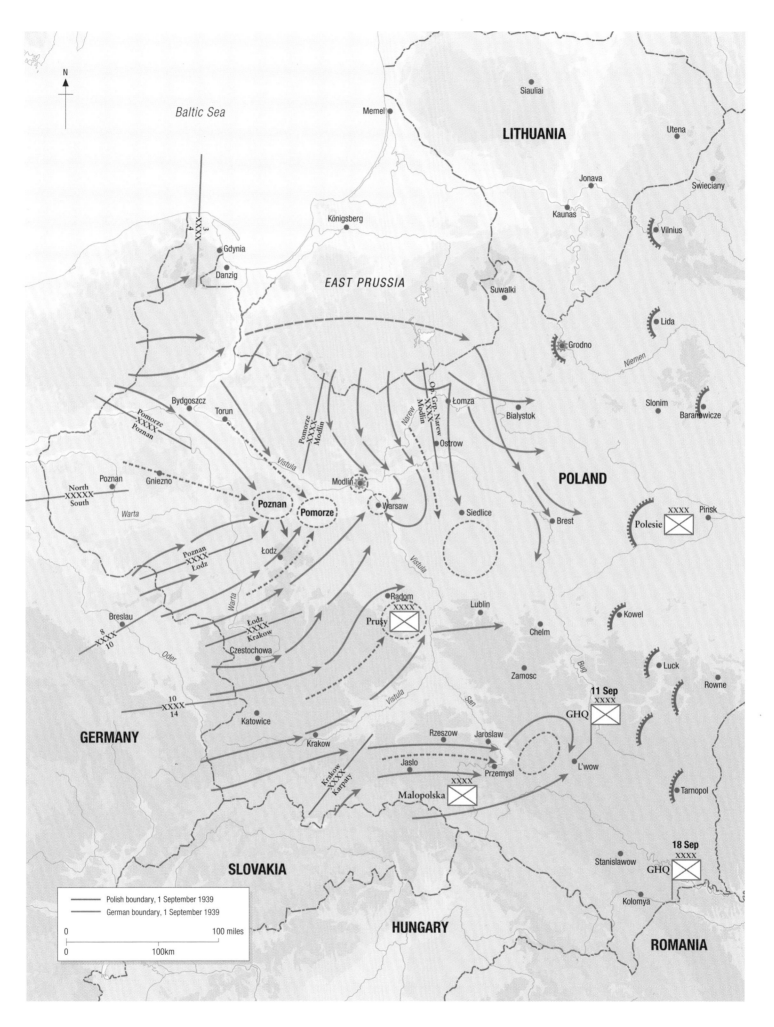

Baltic Sea

LITHUANIA

Memel

Siauliai

Utena

Swieciany

Königsberg

Jonava

Kaunas

Vilnius

EAST PRUSSIA

Gdynia

Danzig

Suwalki

Lida

Grodno

Niemen

Bydgoszcz

Torun

Łomza

Slonim

Baranowicze

Pomorze
XXXX
Poznan

Vistula

Pomorze
XXXX
Modlin

Narew

Op. Grp. Narew
XXXX
Modlin

Ostrow

Bialystok

POLAND

Modlin

Poznan

Gniezno

Warta

Warsaw

Siedlice

Brest

Pinsk

North
XXXXX
South

Poznan
XXXX
Łodz

Łodz

Polesie
XXXX

Warta

Kowel

Vistula

Radom
XXXX

Lublin

Breslau

Łodz
XXXX
Krakow

Prusy

Chelm

Luck

8
XXXX
10

Czestochowa

Zamosc

Rowne

Oder

Bug

San

10
XXXX
14

Katowice

Vistula

Rzeszow

Jaroslaw

11 Sep
XXXX

GHQ

L'wow

Tarnopol

GERMANY

Krakow

Jaslo

Przemysl

Krakow
XXXX
Karpaty

Malopolska
XXXX

18 Sep
XXXX

SLOVAKIA

Stanislawow

GHQ

Kolomya

Polish boundary, 1 September 1939
German boundary, 1 September 1939

0   100 miles

0   100km

HUNGARY

ROMANIA

CHAPTER 2:
THE POLISH CAMPAIGN

I would have to be an idiot to skid into a war over Poland, like those incompetents did in 1914.[2]

Adolf Hitler

On 1 September 1939, Hitler began 'the German War' by invading Poland. Only the night before he had gone on the radio to tell the German people about his 16-point peace plan, but he was not genuine. At Munich a year earlier, he believed that he had been talked out of the war he desired and vowed to not allow that to happen again. Most Germans did not share the Führer's enthusiasm for war, but in the year or two leading up to the conflict, had grown resigned to the prospect of another major struggle.

A week before hostilities broke out, Hitler and Stalin shocked their own countrymen and the rest of the globe by signing a non-aggression pact. In the spring of 1939, the Soviets had opened the door to a relationship with the Third Reich, but at that point Hitler did not want to be nailed down. Mid-way through another tense summer, on 18 August, the Führer decided perhaps the two dictatorships could come to an accommodation in Central and Eastern Europe. Two days later, he sent a personal telegram to Stalin, asking him to receive the German foreign minister. On the 23rd, Joachim von Ribbentrop flew to Moscow for final negotiations and he and Vyacheslav Molotov signed the treaty, with secret protocols, in the early hours of the 24th. For his part, Stalin had the added advantage of knowing that the Red Army had just defeated Imperial Japanese forces in Manchuria (see Maps 23 and 24), so probably would not have to worry about future threats to his Far East flank. In the meantime, both dictatorships would enjoy relative freedom of action in the unfortunate fracture zone separating their two regimes. On 24 August, the propaganda organs of both went into overdrive justifying a pact with a state that only days earlier had been a mortal enemy. The rest of the world did not know what to make of the 180-degree policy change; Hitler had to write to a perplexed and anxious Mussolini to assure him that the move was only a temporary expedient; he also alerted the Duce to the coming war.

---

2 Rolf-Dieter Müller, *Enemy in the East: Hitler's Secret Plans to Invade the Soviet Union*, I. B. Tauris: London, 2015, quoting Ian Kershaw, *Hitler: Nemesis*, p. 1,141, footnote 50.

The final week of peace saw a flurry of activity in Berlin, London, Paris, Rome, Warsaw and elsewhere, a miniature version of the crisis of July 1914, complete with meetings of heads of state, foreign ministers and ambassadors, plus additional treaties (the Anglo-Polish Mutual Assistance Pact, 25 August). Hitler's cynical insincerity represented the main difference between events 25 years earlier; recalling Munich, he said he was 'afraid that a *Schweinehund* will make a proposal for mediation.[3] To provide a suitable provocation, Heinrich Himmler's deputy Reinhard Heydrich had the SS stage a phoney attack by Poland against a radio station in Gleiwitz, Silesia, 3 miles inside Germany. Corpses dressed in Polish uniforms at the site fooled no one. Hours later, early on 1 September, German units swept into Poland. The next day, a secret delegation of five Red Army officers arrived in Berlin to coordinate respective activities in the two parts of Poland. On 3 September, the British and French declared war on Germany, prompting Hitler to ask Ribbentrop, 'What now?' He had hoped to localize the war between Germany and Poland only. With these twin declarations, however, he had already lost control of events in the war's first hours. That same day, Ribbentrop asked his counterpart in Moscow if the USSR was going to attack Poland as agreed in the secret protocols. Not yet, Molotov replied: he did not want the Western Allies to also declare war on the Soviet Union!

The Germans attacked with two army groups (Nord and Süd, under Generaloberst Fedor von Bock and recently reactivated Gerd von Rundstedt respectively), consisting of five armies (3., 4., 8., 10. and 14.), with 17 corps and 52 front-line divisions and three brigades. Their operational objective was the destruction of the Polish military by two pincers west of the Vistula River. Poland defended with six armies forward, (Karpaty, Krakow, Łodz, Modlin, Pomorze and Poznan) plus various reserve groups, made up of 30 front-line divisions and 14 (mostly cavalry) brigades. Their goal was to hold out until relieved by the British and French, according to treaty. Hitler could attack with fully mobilized forces while, in forlorn hopes of peace, the Western Allies pressured the Poles not to call up all their military assets. In the north, the German 4. and 3. Armeen launched simultaneous attacks east across the Polish Corridor and south from East Prussia into the modern Mława defences. Here, the first attack went better than the second. The German *Schwerpunkt* (main effort) came in the south, where the 8. and 10. Armeen smashed into the Łodz and Krakow Armies. In this case, the second assault achieved more than the first. With four panzer and four light divisions, 10. Armee represented the Wehrmacht's mechanized fist. The 1. and 4. Panzer-Divisionen promptly split the seam between the Łodz and Krakow Armies and made straight for Warsaw. Reserve forces belonging to Army Prusy, placed exactly to guard against such a move, proved inadequate. By 5 September, the Polish high command ordered all three armies back to the Vistula. Similar instructions went to the relatively unengaged Army Poznan.

After the first week, the campaign's outlines could be seen clearly. Warsaw appeared threatened, so Marshal Edward Rydz-Śmigły

displaced his headquarters to Brest; moving more than 100 miles during this critical juncture of a fluid battle hamstrung Polish command and control. Meanwhile, German commanders on the ground saw that the Poles were attempting to escape across the Vistula without offering serious resistance in the west. This would deny them the sought-after *Kessel* (pocket). From the German viewpoint, however, two positive developments occurred: Firstly, the Western Allies were doing very little, thereby virtually guaranteeing Polish defeat; and secondly, panzer forces were advancing faster than the Poles could withdraw. After delays caused when the Oberkommando des Heeres (OKH, Army High Command) doubted its own success, it finally allowed Bock to attack down the right (east) bank of the Vistula. This move would negate the Pole's Vistula defence gambit, now further in doubt due to the speed differential already mentioned.

Disaster stared Poland in the face, strategically thanks to the feckless British and French, operationally due to the worsening situation on the ground. The Germans had largely bypassed Army Poznan, the commander of which argued that he be allowed to attack the left flank of Heeresgruppe Süd. Aided by surprise when German intelligence committed the first of very many mistakes to mar its staff work in World War II, on the evening of 9 September, the Poles attacked along the Bzura River with three infantry divisions and two cavalry brigades. Within 24 hours, they had the two German divisions screening the flank on the run. But with the Polish high command in transit, however, the attack lacked any overall coordination. Rundstedt saw opportunity in chaos and began redirecting mechanized counterattack forces towards the rupture. By the 12th/13th, the Germans outnumbered the encircled Poles 19:9⅔ divisions. Harried remnants of the Pomorze and Poznan Armies now attempted to breakout eastwards. Surrounded on all sides and pounded by the Luftwaffe from above, three days later the defender's situation looked grim. Cohesive resistance inside the pocket ended on 18 September and over the next couple of days, the Germans rounded up 120,000 POWs. The Bzura River counterattack represented a temporary German tactical reversal very early in World War II. It delayed the final assault on Warsaw for a week, but did not alter the campaign's ultimate outcome.

Having mastered this situation, the Germans returned to the developing siege of the Polish capital. Earlier, when the 4. Panzer-Division attacked the city's Ochota suburb on 8–9 September, they learned that there were limits to what this kind of formation could accomplish, especially unsupported in a large urban area. A more significant threat to Warsaw came a week later from the north, along both banks of the Vistula. With the Bzura battles still raging to the west, reinforcements (often scattered remnants of Army Poznan) trickled in from that direction. However, by the 21st, the Germans had 13 divisions closing in on the city. The first direct assault two days later accomplished little against the stout defences. On 25 September, Luftwaffe bombers and heavy artillery pounded Warsaw (but also caused many casualties among attacking friendly infantry). The following evening, the commander of the new Army Warsaw, defending the capital, asked his opponent at 8. Armee for surrender terms. The encircled garrison capitulated on the 27th, with the Germans taking 140,000 more

---

3   Louis Snyder, *The War: A Concise History, 1939–1945*, Dell: New York, 1964, p. 83.

POWs. The civil population lost over 40,000 killed, while 50 per cent of the city's structures were damaged or destroyed. Two days after that, the nearby Modlin garrison surrendered, with the 24,000 defenders taken prisoner.

Meanwhile, the Poles' situation deteriorated along the Vistula. Beginning in the north on 9 September, a panzer corps headed from East Prussia towards Brest. In the south, German mountain divisions, with the help of Slovakian units, crossed the Carpathian Mountains to engage the Karpaty Army. The 10. and 14. Armeen neared L'wow by the 12th. Rydz-Śmigły ordered all available forces to the so-called Romanian Bridgehead to hold out at this non-hostile frontier. However, the Soviets, somewhat surprised and unnerved by the speed of the blitzkrieg, quickly ordered a general mobilization on the 11th. The Bzura River attacks could not halt the rampaging panzer units, while Polish countermeasures proved ineffective. The defenders had reason to lose all hope on 17 September, when two fronts of the Red Army invaded eastern Poland to claim their portion of the country (see Map 25). Initial assumptions that the Soviets had intervened on behalf of their Slavic brethren were dashed at the first combat, as lightly armed border defence forces (Korpus Ochrony Poganicza, KOP) – gave way. The Red Army invasion also surprised the Germans, who had exceeded the agreed-upon demarcation lines in numerous places. The OKW began pulling back its units and Hitler took the extraordinary step of personally prohibiting his troops from tangling with the Soviets.

The drift of Polish formations towards the Romanian Bridgehead intensified. A three-way contest developed around L'wow, which surrendered on 22 September. Throughout the shrinking strip of Polish-held territory between German and Soviet invaders, small, isolated, ad hoc Polish formations continued to resist as best they could in a command and control vacuum. In these areas of eastern Poland, Ukrainian and White Russian majorities rose up against the Polish minority, especially taking a toll on the civil and military leadership. Both German and Soviet occupiers stood by and allowed these events to take their bloody course. The last significant group of organized Polish troops to surrender gave up near Kock on 6 October. Thereafter, the terrible five-year occupation of Poland began (see Map 95). During the campaign, Poland lost 66,300 dead and 133,700 wounded, Germany 16,000 dead and 32,000 wounded, the USSR 996 dead and 2,383 wounded. Nearly 100,000 Poles escaped through Romania, Hungary and Lithuania to go on fighting Germany in France (1940 and 1944), fly for the RAF and serve elsewhere for the Allied cause. The Wehrmacht learned valuable lessons and gained irreplaceable combat experience that gave it a significant advantage for the next few years of World War II. The campaign against the brave and skilled Poles prepared the Germans well for bigger battles ahead.

MAP 12: OPPOSING PLANS

Emboldened by his recent success in the dismembering of Czechoslovakia plus British and French passivity, Hitler turned against Poland. He assumed war in the west would degenerate into another stalemate in the trenches, as he had experienced as a young corporal, while his neighbour to the east had outlived its usefulness as a possible ally against the USSR. On 3 April 1939, he ordered the OKW to develop a plan, to be executed anytime after 1 September. The army commander presented his plan for *Fall Weiss* (*Case White*) on 15 June. Consistent with generations of German military thought, the plan envisioned a massive pincer battle. In this, geography greatly assisted them in several ways. Firstly, thanks to East Prussia, Upper Silesia and Slovakia, they had Poland three-quarters encircled from the very start; secondly, most of Poland consisted of plains or gently rolling terrain ideal for mechanized warfare and, due to the late summer heat, most rivers did not present much of an obstacle to modern armies. The Germans wanted to trap the bulk of Poland's military west of the Vistula. Here the infrastructure was more highly developed than in the more primitive east, while being much closer to air and logistics bases in the Reich. The army chief of staff's map exercise in May highlighted problems with the German concept of operations, solutions to which were applied during the summer.

Surprise also represented a key German advantage. Because of their *Welle* ('wave') process of building divisions, they did not have to go through a long mobilization with its formal announcements. They used several subterfuges to conceal their deployments from preparing for the usual summer manoeuvres to celebrating the 25th anniversary of the Battle of Tannenberg. A main goal of the surprise attack was to disrupt the Polish mobilization as much as possible by cutting communications lines, capturing railheads and interdicting rail lines. The Wehrmacht accepted significant risk, especially by allowing a 185-mile gap between the two army groups around Poznan.

The Germans actually planned on a pair of double encirclements, inner and outer. The 3. Armee, starting in central East Prussia and the 8. Armee in lower Silesia, conducted the close-in operation and covered the flanks of the outer pincer. They had the additional mission of keeping an eye on the Poznan Army. In the north, 4. Armee would quickly overrun the Polish Corridor, leapfrog over the 3. Armee, then attack east of Warsaw. The 10. Armee represented the main effort in the south, aiming for Warsaw and the Vistula bend. The 14. Armee would cover its right flank and attack into Galicia. Planners allocated 886,000 men to Rundstedt and 630,000 to Bock.

Finally, Hitler absolutely counted on the Western Allies doing nothing. Facing France's 99 divisions stood Heeresgruppe C, with three armies of 44 divisions, only a dozen of which were first rate. Generaloberst Wilhelm von Leeb had 750,000 men, 160,000 Organization Todt (Labour Service) workers and a small Luftwaffe contingent. The main value of the German Siegfried Line (West Wall) was not military but as a propaganda tool; in this it functioned perfectly by discouraging serious Allied action.

Polish plans underwent substantial changes in the late 1930s as Hitler impacted all of Europe. Their Plan Z (*Zachod*, West) accordingly considered the addition of Slovakia as an enemy and correctly placed the German main effort in the south. Plans of the Western Allies, especially France, played a key role in Polish calculations. French leadership expected the Poles to resist for three to four months. With French urging, the Poles first considered falling back to old fortifications along the Biebrza, Narew, Vistula and San Rivers. Subsequent plans, as adapted, moved defences westwards to both prevent a Sudetenland-type German land grab and shield mobilization efforts in the heavily populated west. Poland was just too small to fall back too far. They would then conduct an active defence until the French launched their supporting offensive. The Molotov–Ribbentrop Pact further complicated Polish planning, although they knew nothing of the secret protocols.

As did many other European nations, Poland misjudged the nature of the coming blitzkrieg and anticipated the wrong war. It was guilty of planning for 'the last war', in this case the Polish–Soviet War and Spanish Civil War. It also had systemic problems: Marshal Rydz-Śmigły held too tightly to power and did not delegate, a fatal flaw when confronting the fluid blitzkrieg. The Poles also lacked the mobility required to adequately counter the Germans. Without being overly deterministic, it would take a miracle for Poland to survive *Case White*, even if the Allies had launched respectable attacks in the west.

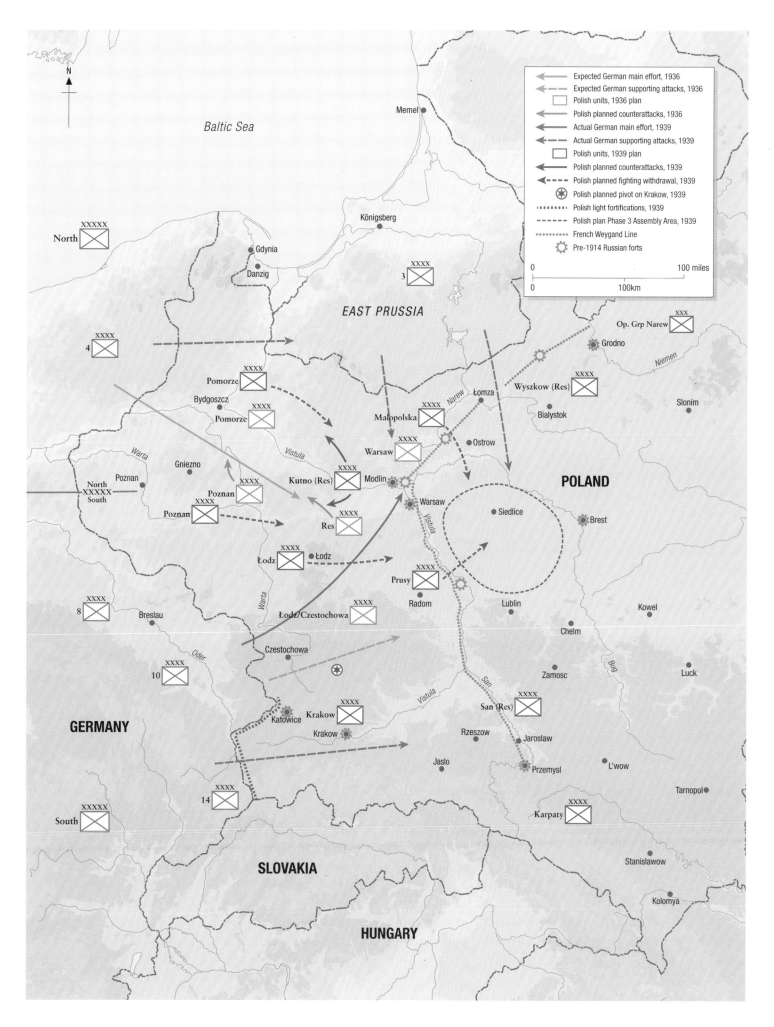

Memel

Königsberg

North XXXXX

Gdynia

Danzig

EAST PRUSSIA

3 XXXX

Op. Grp Narew XXX

4 XXXX

Grodno

Niemen

Pomorze XXXXX

Bydgoszcz

Łomza

Wyszkow (Res) XXXXX

Slonim

Pomorze XXXX

Narew

Bialystok

Małopolska XXXXX

Warsaw XXXX

Ostrow

Vistula

North XXXXX South

Poznan

Gniezno

Kutno (Res) XXXX

Modlin

POLAND

Res XXXX

Warsaw

Poznan XXXX

Poznan XXXX

Siedlice

Brest

Łodz XXXX

Łodz

Vistula

Prusy XXXX

Kowel

8 XXXX

Breslau

Łodz/Czestochowa XXXX

Radom

Lublin

Chelm

Czestochowa

Zamosc

Luck

10 XXXX

Oder

Bug

Krakow XXXX

San (Res) XXXX

Katowice

Rzeszow

Jaroslaw

L'wow

Krakow

GERMANY

Jaslo

Przemysl

Tarnopol

14 XXXX

Karpaty XXXX

South XXXXX

SLOVAKIA

Stanislawow

Kolomya

HUNGARY

→	Expected German main effort, 1936
⇢	Expected German supporting attacks, 1936
☐	Polish units, 1936 plan
→	Polish planned counterattacks, 1936
→	Actual German main effort, 1939
⇢	Actual German supporting attacks, 1939
☐	Polish units, 1939 plan
→	Polish planned counterattacks, 1939
⇠	Polish planned fighting withdrawal, 1939
✳	Polish planned pivot on Krakow, 1939
⋯	Polish light fortifications, 1939
---	Polish plan Phase 3 Assembly Area, 1939
⋯	French Weygand Line
⚙	Pre-1914 Russian forts

0 ——————— 100 miles

0 ——————— 100km

MAP 13: THE FRONTIER BATTLES (I), 1–6 SEPTEMBER 1939, NORTHERN SECTOR

The Kriegsmarine, the smallest branch within the Wehrmacht, fired the opening shots of World War II. The World War I battleship *Schleswig-Holstein*, now a cadet training ship, happened to be in Danzig for a good will visit. Around 0445 hours on 1 September, it began firing on lightly emplaced Polish positions at the Westerplatte base. Soon, other German ships and Luftwaffe aircraft joined in the barrage and for the next week infantry made repeated assaults. The Poles held out against improbable odds until the afternoon of the 7th. In the city itself paramilitaries fought with particular brutality. The SS Heimwehr (Home Guard), joined by irregular troops of Brigade Eberhard (reservists, SA and SS men, discharged veterans, policemen) from East Prussia and Kriegsmarine ships in the harbour, finally prevailed after one week.

On the main front, the Luftwaffe usually led the way by attacking Polish airfields at dawn, troop concentrations and mobilization sites. In the north, General der Flieger Albert Kesselring's 1. Luftflotte (Air Fleet) supported Bock. Army Pomorze defended the corridor with five infantry divisions, one cavalry brigade and four naval battalions. The 4. Armee was also five infantry divisions strong, but also with a mechanized corps of one each of panzer, light and motorized infantry divisions. The Polish 9th Division and much of the Pomorska Cavalry Regiment became separated from the rest of the army and began to drift north towards the Baltic, where it became encircled. It managed to hold out for many days. It was here that, on the first day of the war, one of the lingering episodes of the Polish campaign occurred. While covering the retreat of a friendly unit, two squadrons of the 18th Lancer Regiment of the Pomorska Brigade charged a German column belonging to the 20. Infanterie-Division (mot.) near Krojanty. They slashed their way through the formation until German armoured cars arrived and drove off the cavalrymen. Inaccurate myths of Polish cavalry making fatal, futile charges against panzers sprung from this event.

On the right flank of 4. Armee, the Polish 15th Infantry Division put up stiff resistance in Bydgoszcz against the III Armee-Korps. The German minority in the city initiated an uprising in support of the invaders, but the Polish majority soon put it down. Three days into the war, the Germans were approaching the lower Vistula. Polish forces attempted to make a stand along the river, their 'main defensive line', but the Pomorze Army had reached its limit of endurance. Engineer troops dropped a couple spans of the large bridge at Tczew in an effort to slow the Germans. By the next day, however, the Germans had overrun most of the Corridor except for small pockets of defenders slow to surrender. The III. Armee-Korps continued upriver on the right bank of the Vistula to assist the 3. Armee by hitting the Modlin Army in its western flank. The rest of 4. Armee now raced across East Prussia, some units falling in behind their comrades in 3. Armee; others, like Generalleutnant Heinz Guderian's XIX Panzer-Korps, prepared to attack far into eastern Prussia.

Meanwhile, the 3. Armee attacked towards Warsaw, barely 70 miles to the south. Here, 320,000 Germans in five infantry divisions, the 1. Kavallerie-Brigade and the provisional Panzer-Division Kempf faced Army Modlin's two infantry divisions and two cavalry brigades. Tough and relatively modern fortifications at Mława on the western shoulder held out for three days. To the east, however, elements of Panzer-Division Kempf worked their way around more weakly held defences (at this point, the panzer division operated in infantry-support task forces). Near the Ulatkowka River, the 1. Kavallerie-Brigade and Mazowiecka Cavalry Brigade clashed in one of the only horse vs horse battles of the war. Further east, the Narew Group's Podlaska Cavalry Brigade briefly attacked into Germany, overwhelming the Landwehr territorial reserve force. By the 3rd, Panzer-Division Kempf threatened to break out towards Warsaw, now only 50 miles away. Once levered from its strong initial positions after four days of fighting, Army Modlin would have a hard time finding suitable terrain on which to anchor its defences until it reached the Vistula. Once here, it would centre its defence on its namesake, the fortified city of Modlin.

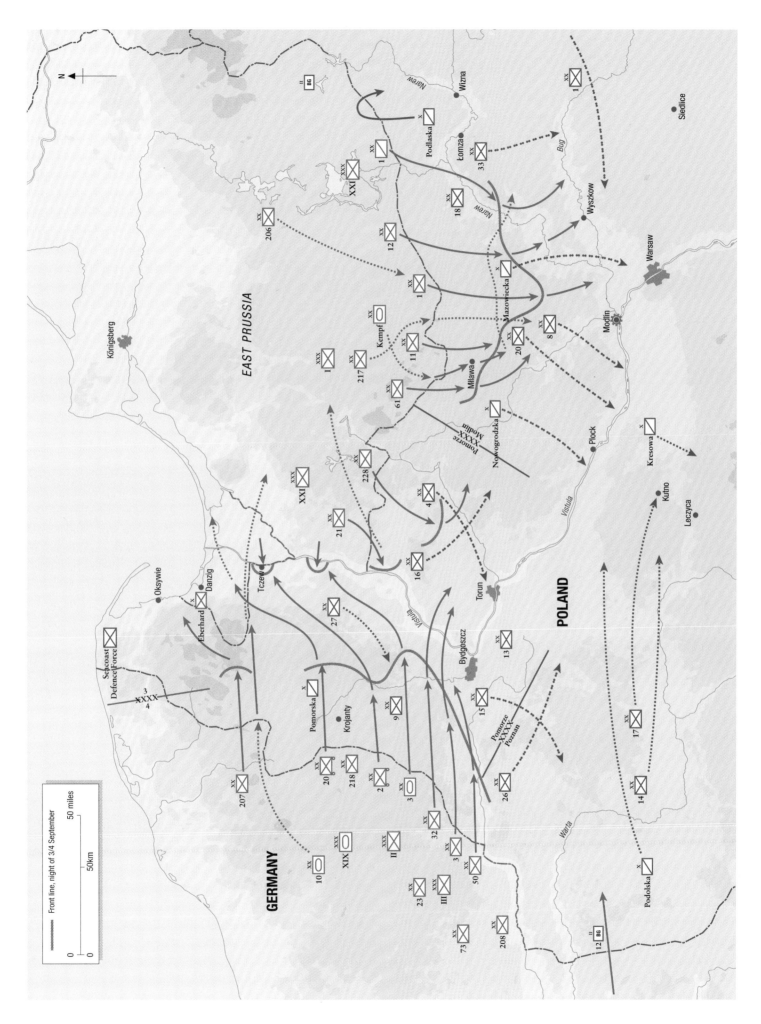

MAP 14: THE FRONTIER BATTLES (II), 1–6 SEPTEMBER 1939, SOUTHERN SECTOR

Rundstedt's army group consisted of three armies: from north to south, 8. Armee (180,000 men in four infantry divisions), 10. Armee (300,000 men in six infantry, three light and two each motorized and panzer divisions) and 14. Armee (five infantry, three mountain, two panzer and one light division). The 8. Armee would help isolate Army Poznan and shield the army group's left, the 10. Armee would smash Army Łodz and make for Warsaw, while the 14. Armee would aim for Krakow, defeat the army named after the city, then turn and pin Army Karpaty against Slovakia and Hungary. Austrian Generalleutnant Alexander Löhr commanded the 4. Luftflotte. Defending, also from north to south, was Army Łodz (four infantry divisions and two cavalry brigades), Army Krakow (four infantry and one mountain division and one each cavalry, mechanized and mountain brigades), Army Karpaty (one each infantry and mountain divisions and two mountain brigades) with Army Prusy in reserve to the rear (six infantry divisions and one cavalry brigade, but not fully massed due to German interference in its mobilization). Clearly, the south represented the main effort for both attacker and defender.

Mechanized forces of both the 10. and 14. Armeen created immediate problems for the defenders. So did paramilitary forces belonging to the sizeable and subversive German minority active in the area, in this case assisted by Abwehr's (Wehrmacht counterintelligence) Brandenburger forces. Neither defenders, mountains, nor rivers seemed to slow them down. However, at Mokra, the Wolynska Cavalry Brigade with the *Smiały* armoured train, and the 10th Mechanized Brigade guarding the road to Krakow both put up determined fights.

The XVI Panzer-Korps quickly found the seam dividing Armies Łodz and Krakow and began to exploit it – never a good thing in combat. The 10. Armee penetrated nearly 50 miles during the first two days, reaching the Warta River. The Poles had hoped to make a stand on the river, but by the 3rd, the Germans had thrown numerous bridgeheads over it and soon headed for the Pilica River. Elsewhere, at Częstochowa, the 7th Infantry Division put up a good defence, but even this ultimately had a downside: it took heavy casualties, lost half

its artillery and now had faster-moving panzers to its rear, as the retreating defenders moved only at the pace of man and horse. After negotiating the Carpathian range, two German mountain divisions supported by Slovak mountain brigades began harassing Army Karpaty.

The Germans' continued success on the critical Warsaw axis spelled real trouble for the Poles. The XVI Panzer-Korps continued to work the inter-army boundary while the Częstochowa defences crumbled. One of the Poles' largest aerial attacks, meant to blunt the panzer thrust, fell victim to excellent German Army Flak. The 10. Armee reinforced its panzers' exploits with an additional light division, adding to Rydz-Śmigły's woes. The defenders enjoyed more success in the less important Krakow sector, where uneven terrain aided their withdrawal and slowed the German follow-through. Overall, however, the Polish high command did not know how to handle the blitzkrieg's speed and violence. Though they had correctly anticipated the German main effort, they could not react to developments fast enough.

By 5 September, Army Prusy could not alter the situation along the seam separating Armies Łodz and Krakow, nor could any other Polish countermeasures. That evening, Rydz-Śmigły ordered all three armies facing Rundstedt back to the Vistula before they were encircled and defeated. He also ordered Army Poznan, generally unengaged and drifting in the gap between the two Wehrmacht army groups, back along with the others. Despite pleas by Poznan's commander that he be allowed to attack into Heeresgruppe Sud's exposed flank (mainly guarded by the stretched-out 30. Infanterie-Division), higher headquarters denied him. Farther south, terrain in front of 14. Armee finally opened up as it approached Krakow. Around 6 September, senior leaders on both sides had crises of confidence created by the radical new form of warfare. On the German side, commanders in the field could see the time was ripe for encircling Polish formations that were obviously trying to escape eastwards with what strength they still had; the OKW did not agree. On the Polish side, army commanders wanted to do something positive, but Rydz-Śmigły, whom history will judge as a micromanager, could only think of escaping over the Vistula.

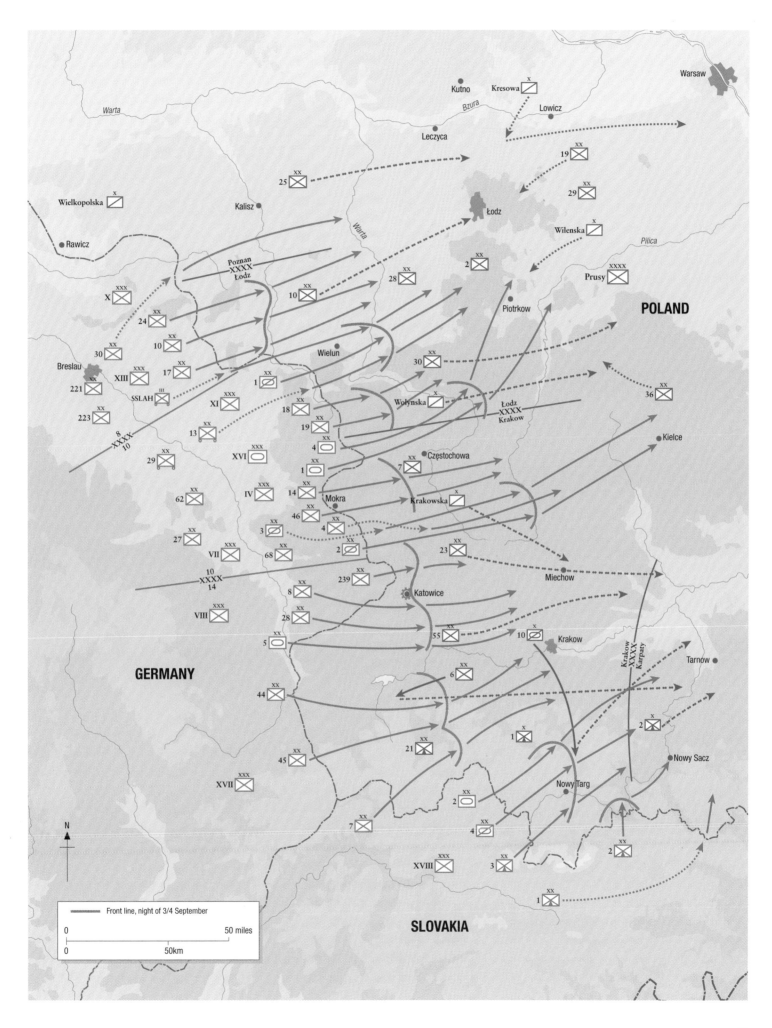

Warta

Kutno

Kresowa [x]

Bzura

Lowicz

Warsaw

Leczyca

25 [XX]

19 [XX]

Wielkopolska [x]

Kalisz

Warta

Łodz

29 [XX]

Rawicz

Poznan
XXXX
Łodz

10 [XX]

28 [XX]

2 [XX]

Wilenska [x]

Pilica

Prusy [XXXX]

POLAND

X [XXX]

24 [XX]

Piotrkow

30 [XX]

10 [XX]

Wielun

30 [XX]

36 [XX]

Breslau
221 [XX]

XIII [XXX]

17 [XX]

1 [XX]

Wolynska [x]

Łodz
XXXX
Krakow

SSLAH [III]

XI [XXX]

223 [XX]

18 [XX]

13 [XX]

19 [XX]

Kielce

8
XXXX
10

29 [XX]

XVI [XXX]

4 [XX]

Częstochowa

7 [XX]

62 [XX]

IV [XXX]

1 [XX]

14 [XX]

Mokra

Krakowska [x]

27 [XX]

46 [XX]

VII [XXX]

68 [XX]

3 [XX]

4 [XX]

23 [XX]

10
XXXX
14

2 [XX]

239 [XX]

Miechow

8 [XX]

Katowice

VIII [XXX]

28 [XX]

55 [XX]

10 [XX]

Krakow

Krakow
XXXX
Karpaty

5 [XX]

Tarnow

GERMANY

6 [XX]

44 [XX]

2 [x]

21 [XX]

1 [XX]

45 [XX]

Nowy Sacz

XVII [XXX]

2 [XX]

Nowy Targ

N

7 [XX]

4 [XX]

XVIII [XXX]

3 [XX]

2 [XX]

1 [XX]

Front line, night of 3/4 September

0   50 miles
0   50km

SLOVAKIA

43

MAP 15: THE BATTLE OF POLAND (I), 7–12 SEPTEMBER 1939, NORTHERN SECTOR

By the beginning of the second week of the war, the Germans could feel success while the Poles sensed trouble. Strategically, British and French inactivity in the west reinforced both assessments. Operationally and tactically, there could be little doubt over the course of the campaign so far. The Germans threatened Warsaw with the bulk of the 3. Armee from the north and mechanized elements of the 10. Armee from the south-west. Although the Polish Army had avoided decisive battle, it had done little to slow the Germans; nor was it entirely clear whether it would be able to withdraw over the Vistula in the cohesive fashion necessary to continue viable defensive operations in the east.

On 8 September, the Polish high command issued new defensive instructions to its field armies, including creating two new commands: The Northern Front (Modlin Army and Group Narew) and Southern Front (Armies Krakow and Małopolska). Orders went out to the Northern Front, telling it to hold the Narew and Bug Rivers, covering the approaches to Siedlice. Across the front, 3. Armee continued to drive on Warsaw over a broad front, clearly working its way around either flank of the defence. With temporary assistance from the 10. Panzer-Division, XXI Armee-Korps attempted to turn the Poles' eastern flank and cross the Narew. When the armoured unit rejoined Guderian, the infantry attack bogged down. Nevertheless, by the night of 9/10 September, Army Modlin, now relying on reserve divisions and the Narew Group, began to pull back using a diversionary attack against elements of Panzer-Division Kempf at the fork of the Bug and Narew Rivers to cover their retreat. With the Polish 18th Infantry Division, weakened after an earlier unsuccessful counterattack, pushed out of Łomza on the 12th, the Germans had overcome the Narew line and could now threaten Warsaw from the forests to the north-east. Having taken heavy losses over a dozen days of fighting, Army Modlin retreated with little hope of seriously halting the 3. Armee. Besides, in many places the faster German units were closer to Warsaw that the would-be defenders.

Meanwhile the 4. Armee had split into several parts. Infantry elements were reducing the Polish Seacoast Defence Forces on the Baltic (nearly 20,000 men from KOP battalions, naval infantry, workers' militias and coastal artillery), marching across East Prussia and pursuing the northern shoulder of Army Poznan, now in a bad position, down the lower Vistula. In the forested and marshy region deep within East Prussia, Guderian's XIX Panzer-Korps prepared to break into the massive and largely undefended portions of Poland east of Warsaw and the Vistula.

After transiting East Prussia, Guderian, soon augmented by the 2. Infanterie-Division (mot.) from higher reserves, massed around Johannisburg. Starting on 10 September, XIX Panzer-Korps moved out in the direction of Bialystok and the Bug River, bypassing units of the Narew Group and Podlaska Cavalry Brigade. Despite their failure to anticipate Guderian's move and numerous losses, the Poles managed to hinder German progress in a number of places, causing Guderian to frequently shift his resources to overcome local pockets of resistance. In the Poles' defence, the German high command, also new to the idea of blitzkrieg, had only recently settled on this course of action. By the 12th, the panzer corps advanced detachments had reached Bielsk, halfway between Bialystok and Brest. Few Polish units besides KOP border ones stood in their way. These developments put the entire Polish defensive scheme in jeopardy.

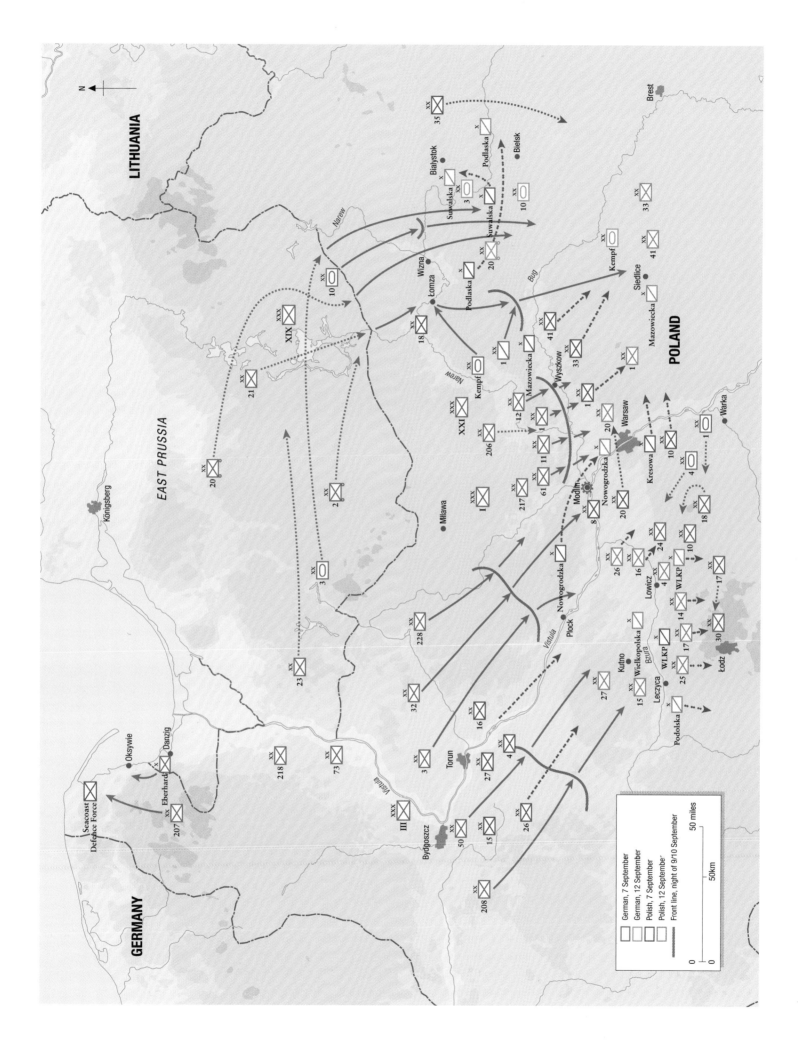

LITHUANIA

GERMANY

EAST PRUSSIA

POLAND

Königsberg

Danzig

Oksywie

Eberhard

Seacoast
Defence Force

Bydgoszcz

Toruń

Brda

Vistula

Vistula

Narew

Narew

Bug

Mława

Płock

Nowogródzka

Modlin

Warsaw

Warka

Łęczyca

Kutno

Wielkopolska

Łowicz

Kresowa

Łódź

Siedlice

Mazowiecka

Wyszków

Łomża

Wizna

Suwalska

Podlaska

Białystok

Bielsk

Brest

N

50 miles

50km

German, 7 September
German, 12 September
Polish, 7 September
Polish, 12 September
Front line, night of 9/10 September

MAP 16: THE BATTLE OF POLAND (II), 7–12 SEPTEMBER 1939, SOUTHERN SECTOR

Although Heeresgruppe Nord seriously threatened Warsaw just a fortnight into the war, Heeresgruppe Süd took the lead in hammering the bulk of the Polish Army. Together, they would accomplish OKH orders of 9 September to encircle and destroy the defenders around the Vistula River. Rundstedt's men shoved the Poles back in many places and penetrated their defences in others.

On the northern end of the front, the Łodz Army drifted north-east towards the fortress city of Modlin with the 8. Armee on its heels. At that moment, it looked like coordinated action with the 3. Armee from Heeresgruppe Nord could quickly lead to the near encirclement of Warsaw. But unfortunately for the Germans, Army Poznan lurked in the gap between Bock and Rundstedt, largely intact.

To the south, attacked by the 14. Armee, the new unified Southern Front command of Lieutenant-General Kazimierz Sosnkowski, gave up the city of Krakow and fell back to the San River. The beginning of the end for Krakow came when the 2. Panzer and 3. Gebirgs Divisionen levered the 22nd Infantry Division off the Dunajec River. The 5. Panzer-Division's breakthrough at the Holy Cross Mountains to their north finished the job. Near the Slovak border, the new Army Małopolska withdrew on its own accord, further harming the defence of Krakow. Deprived of its critical anchor, the defences gave way to the 2. Panzer and 4. Leichte-Divisionen, which burst east through Rzeszów and over the middle San River.

The most significant action, however, came in the centre, where the 10. Armee's mechanized forces penetrated in numerous places the combined remnants of Armies Łodz, Krakow and Prusy. At this point of the war, Polish defences in the very centre of the southern front were virtually non-existent. The 4. Panzer-Division broke through the seam dividing Armies Łodz and Krakow all the way to the south-western suburbs of the Polish capital. Combat and mechanical losses had reduced the 4. Panzer-Division's strength, so the city's defences rejected its attempted *coup de main* with relative ease by 9 September. The 1. Panzer-Division pulled up along to its south, but could not swing the battle in the Germans' favour. In the centre, 1. Leichte-Division and 13. Infanterie-Division (mot.) attacked past Radom to the bend of the Vistula at Deblin. Finally, the 2. and 3. Leichte-Divisionen and 29. Infanterie-Division (mot.) drove through Kielce to the Vistula to the east. These manoeuvres equated to a triple penetration and encirclement, trapping numerous Polish units in the process. The Polish high command, which spent much of this time moving from Warsaw to Brest (and preparing to jump again to L'wow), cast about for viable units to put in the Germans' way.

However, there just were not enough Polish forces remaining to staunch the bleeding. Already on 11 September, Rydz-Śmigły ordered his troops to begin moving to the country's south-east corner, the Romanian Bridgehead. That plan immediately was put into doubt; on the following day, the 14. Armee's 1. Gebirgs-Division reached the environs of L'wow. Across the front, we can see that during the second week of the month the Wehrmacht began to understand the nascent blitzkrieg, employing panzer, light and motorized divisions together in groups of two or three against deep objectives. The XIV, XVI and XIX Armee-Korps were giving armies around the world lessons in operational mechanized warfare. The Germans' rush eastwards would soon reveal the weak side of their 'don't look back, the flanks will take care of themselves' thinking. The Poles still had one trick up their sleeve.

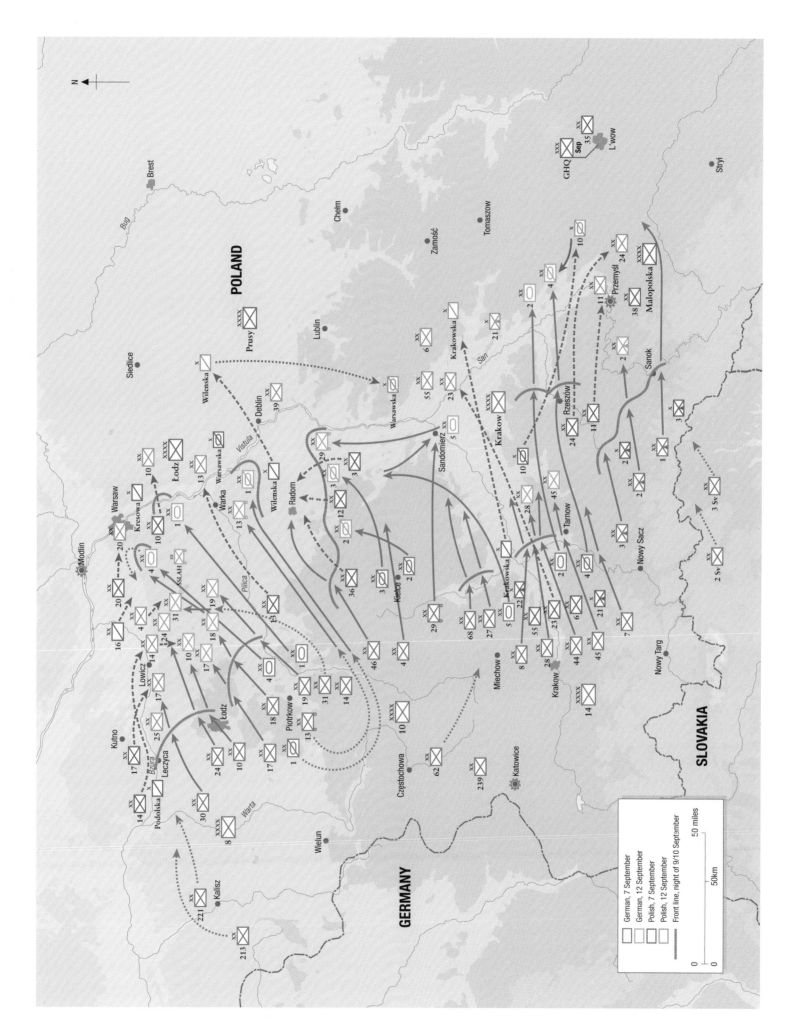

POLAND

GERMANY

SLOVAKIA

Brest

Bug

Chełm

Zamość

Tomaszów

Stryi

L'WOW

GHQ
XXX
Sep
35 XX

Siedlice

Lublin

Prusy
XXXX

Warsaw
Modlin
Kresowa
Łódź

Deblin
39

Wilenska

Warka
Warsawska
Wilenska

Radom

Sandomierz
5
Krakowska

San

Warsawska
55 23

Krakowska
x
21

6 XX

Przemyśl
24
Małopolska
38 XXXX

Sanok

Rzeszów
24 11

Kraków
XXXX

Tarnow
45

Nowy Sacz

Krakowska

Kielce

Kutno
Łowicz
Łódz
Łęczyca
Piotrkow

Podolska

Warta

Kalisz

Wielun

Częstochowa
62

Miechow
Kraków
XXXX
14

Katowice
239

Nowy Targ

3 Sv

2 Sv

Key:
☐ German, 7 September
☐ German, 12 September
☐ Polish, 7 September
☐ Polish, 12 September
━━ Front line, night of 9/10 September

0 ____ 50 miles
0 ____ 50km

MAP 17: THE BZURA COUNTERATTACK (I), 9–13 SEPTEMBER 1939

With some minor exceptions, the Polish campaign was going just as the Germans wished. There had been casualties and the mechanical reliability of their armoured fighting vehicles (AFVs) caused concerns, but on the positive side, the Western Allies had done next to nothing and Poland showed serious signs of disintegration. On top of these factors, the Soviets had not even weighed in yet, so remained a question mark for both sides. From the beginning, however, German staffs had worries over what to do about Army Poznan. In particular, Rundstedt considered his left flank vulnerable and had detailed 8. Armee with the mission of covering it. The decision by the Polish high command to withdraw without offering lengthy resistance – in other words, to avoid becoming fixed in costly battles – exaggerated the problem. In its zeal to keep up the pursuit of fleeing Polish formations, 8. Armee's own left flank had become overextended. It tasked X Armee-Korps (the 30. and 24. Infanterie Divisionen) with the mission of securing Heeresgruppe Süd's spread out northern boundary.

As early as 3 September, the commander of Army Poznan Lieutenant-General Tadeusz Kutrzeba saw an opportunity to strike the already exposed flank guards of X. Armee-Korps and 8. Armee. He had been involved in pre-war operational planning that had anticipated exactly this situation, so argued for an immediate counterattack. At this early stage of the war, however, Rydz-Śmigły still wanted to avoid a decisive engagement, so refused. While the overall situation developed in the Germans' favour, during the next few days in this sector at least, the relative positions of the two enemies seemed to favour the Poles. Running out of options, the Polish high command gave its blessing to Kutrzeba's idea; it had to take pressure off Army Łodz in any way possible.

The Bzura battles played out in two phases: Kutrzeba's initial counterattack and Rundstedt's reaction. For more than a week, Army Poznan had basically been drifting eastwards without attracting much attention from either German army group. A little to the north-west, two divisions of Army Pomorze that had escaped the earlier Polish corridor battles were doing the same, albeit pursued by the right wing of Bock's army group. Kutrzeba attacked on the evening of 9 September just south of the Bzura with three divisions abreast and cavalry brigades screening each flank. The stretched-out 30. Infanterie-Division took the brunt of the assault and made a brave stand at Piątek, but eventually gave up the town, losing 1,500 POWs in the process. Nevertheless, by 10 September, 8. Armee realized it could not both continue its drive on Warsaw and blunt this new threat, so asked Heeresgruppe Süd for a panzer division as reinforcement.

Another German intelligence failure, incorrectly believing that Army Poznan was making for Warsaw, contributed to the surprise. Their two divisions fell back nearly 7 miles. Kutrzeba initially wanted to break out to the south-east and possibly escape to the Romanian Bridgehead, but soon settled on the more realistic objective of joining the defence of Warsaw. A couple of days into the attack, three more divisions from Army Pomorze arrived and entered the fray against the 24. Infanterie-Division. Partially due to poor Polish command and control caused by its moving headquarters, the attack was not as coordinated and effective as it could have been. Meanwhile, the 221. Infanterie-Division from Heeresgruppe Süd reserves arrived on the western edge of the battlefield. Three days into the counterattack, the Germans were regaining their numerical superiority.

Polish troops had advanced up to a dozen miles in places, but to the south, Army Łodz was falling back, ruling out any coordinated action from that quarter, either. On 12 September, Kutrzeba ordered his forces to fight their way to Warsaw. By this time, the Germans had recovered from the initial shock and managed to limit the damage to 10–12 inconsequential miles lost. What had seemed like a good plan a few days earlier had merely produced a temporary tactical reverse. The Poles did not know it then, but at the same time, Heeresgruppe Süd prepared to pivot 90 degrees (in some cases, almost 180 degrees) to address the immediate problem and even go beyond that to inflict a crushing defeat.

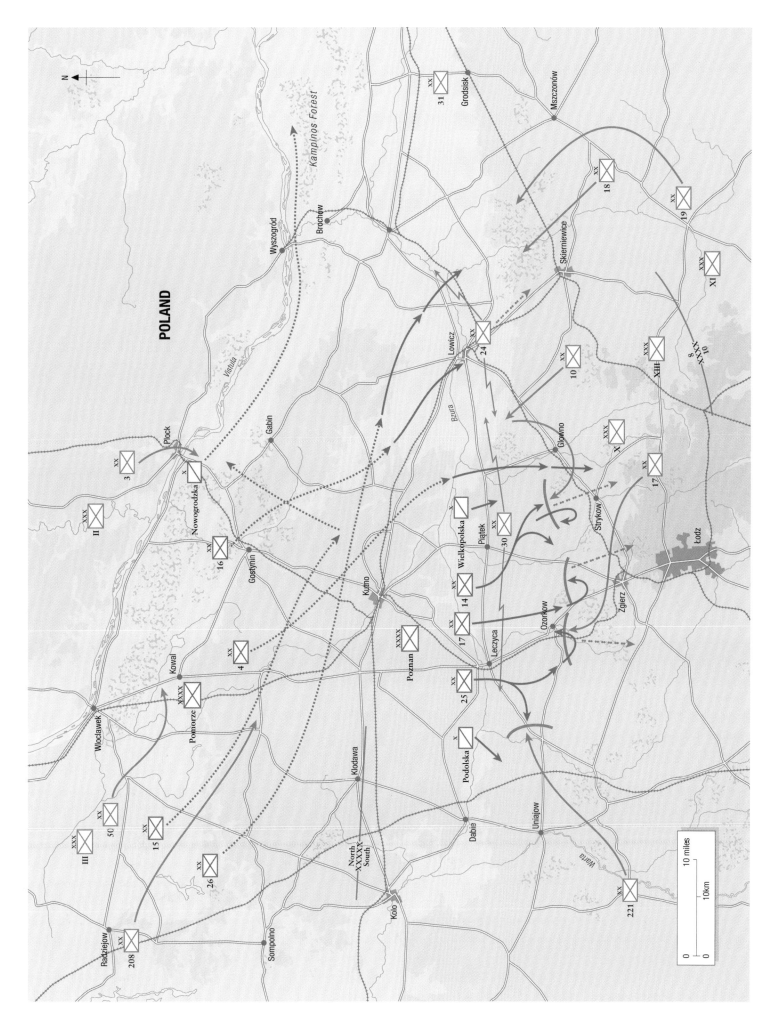

POLAND

Kampinos Forest

Vistula

Bzura

Warta

Radziejow

Włocławek

Kowal

Sompolno

Kłodawa

Dąbie

Koło

Uniejow

North
XXXXX
South

Gostynin

Gąbin

Płock

Wyszogród

Brochów

Nowogrodzka

Kutno

Łęczyca

Ozorkow

Zgierz

Łódź

Strykow

Głowno

Piątek

Łowicz

Skierniewice

Grodsisk

Mszczonow

Podolska

Poznan

Wielkopolska

0   10 miles

0   10km

49

MAP 18: THE BZURA COUNTERATTACK (II), 14–18 SEPTEMBER 1939

The Germans had anticipated just such a Polish counterattack during pre-war wargames, so only its exact location and time really came as a surprise. As mentioned earlier, the Polish high command did not do well coordinating the manoeuvres of three of its armies involved, either. During the attack's early going, 8. Armee had asked for a panzer division to help stabilize its lines. The OKW plus Rundstedt and his chief of staff, Generalleutnant Erich von Manstein, had a bigger operation in mind, however. This eventually involved half the army group (and even some of Bock's) plus most of its mechanized units. In so doing, they turned a tactical Polish counterattack into a German operational victory.

As decided on 13 September, Heeresgruppe Süd would leave two divisions (4. and 14. Infanterie) to screen the Vistula bend between Deblin and Sandomierz while the bulk of the 8. and 10. Armeen, plus part of the 4., focused on the Bzura River area. For this operation, Rundstedt had overall command and control. The reinforced 8. Armee, now almost exclusively oriented on the Polish attack, would stop withdrawing and begin pushing back from the west and south. The 10. Armee would come in the east with a phalanx of mechanized units, including the 4. Panzer-Division, fresh from its failed Warsaw attack and its sister 1. Panzer-Division. Finally, III Armee-Korps, on loan from Bock, pursuing fleeing elements of ArmyPomorze, would come in from the north-west.

By 14 September, the Germans had completed this reorganization while in contact with the enemy and stood ready to launch their own counterattacks. Rundstedt brought substantial forces to bear, causing Kutrzeba to change his direction of escape from south-east to due east. On the 16th, 820 Luftwaffe sorties dropped nearly 350 tons of bombs on the encircled Poles. This broke new ground in the annals of airpower, using close air support as an operational weapon. Polish antiaircraft batteries had long since run out of ammunition for their 40mm Bofors guns. Massive, accurate and well-coordinated German artillery joined

in the pounding as Rundstedt's divisions constricted the defenders' perimeter. That same day, with his offensive over and any organized withdrawal out of the question, Kutrzeba issued what amounted to a *sauve qui peut* order to his men to break out any way they could. The only real escape route lay to the east, north of the 4. Panzer-Division's positions and through the Kampinos Forest.

Army Pomorze's forces, intended to shield Kutrzeba's attacks from the north-east, merely became encircled themselves. Elements of its 15th and 25th Infantry Divisions plus remnants of the Podolska and Wielkopolska Cavalry brigades made it out of the trap, only to stumble into another one developing around Warsaw. By the 18th, organized resistance in the *Kessel* came to an end, although it took the Germans another three days to digest their haul of between 120,000 and 150,000 POWs, found mainly hiding in the Kampinos Forest. Kutrzeba managed to avoid capture, but the commander of Army Pomorze was not so fortunate. Of the nine divisions encircled, one-third had their commanding generals killed in action.

The Poles' Bzura counterattacks were a logical and valid reaction to the situation which the exposed 8. Armee flank presented. Throughout World War II, numerous armies – especially the Germans and Soviets on the Eastern Front – resorted to exactly this type of quick, local counterattack as an attempt to blunt an enemy drive and regain the initiative. Even a relatively small force, employed at the right time and place, could distract the attacker enough to regain control of a battle. Unfortunately for the Poles, the Bzura counterattacks received no outside help, such as a coordinated manoeuvre against the weak German screen on the Vistula. This meant that Rundstedt could defeat the Bzura threat almost at his leisure, with the main downside being a delay in completing the siege of Warsaw. With the Germans concentrating on – I would argue overreacting to – the Bzura battle, the Poles had some breathing space to partially recover from the initial shock of the first two weeks of the blitzkrieg and for the coming battles around their capital.

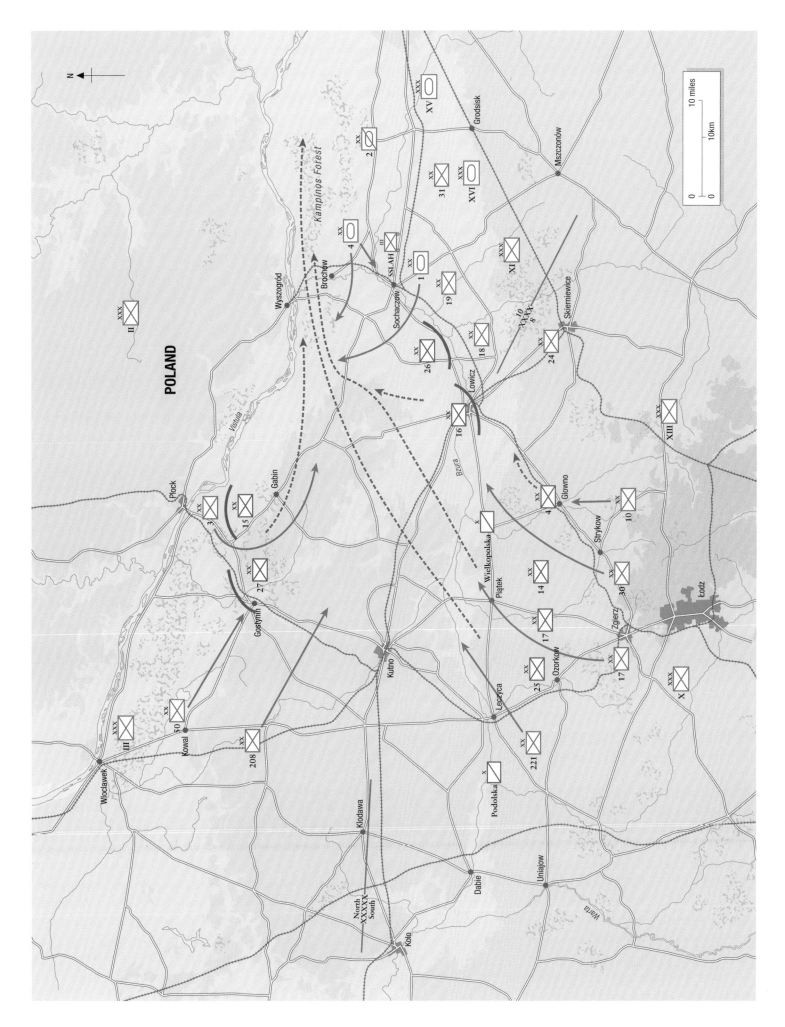

POLAND

Kampinos Forest

Vistula

Bzura

Warta

XV 0

Grodsisk

Mszczonów

XX 2 0

XX 31

XVI 0

XX 4 0

III SSLAH

SSLAH 1 0

XX 11

XX 19

XX 18

Sochaczew

Brochów

Wyszogród

XXX II

XX 26

XX 24

Skierniewice

10 8

Łowicz

XX 16

XXX XIII

Płock

XX 3

XX 15

Gabin

XX 27

Gostynin

XX 14

Piątek

Wielkopolska

Głowno

XX 4

XX 10

Stryków

XX 30

Zgierz

Łódz

Kowal

XX 50

Kutno

Leczyca

XX 25

Ozorków

XX 17

XX 17

XXX X

XXX III

Włocławek

XX 208

XX 221

Podolska

Kłodawa

Dabie

Uniajów

North XXXXX South

Koło

51

MAP 19: THE BATTLE FOR WARSAW, 8–27 SEPTEMBER 1939

When the 4. Panzer-Division reached the south-western outskirts of Warsaw on the afternoon of 8 September, the high command could hardly believe their good fortune. German radio played patriotic music and the community of military attachés in Berlin went into shock. On the same day, the Luftwaffe started bombing the city (and interdicting transport into it), while a short time later, the 1. Panzer-Division created a small bridgehead over the Vistula to the south at Gora Kalwaria. German success was short-lived, however, as Major-General Walerian Czuma's defenders, augmented by civilian auxiliaries led by the popular mayor Stefan Starzyński ('Stefan the Stubborn'), turned back the 4. Panzer-Division, which lost more than half of its panzers, damaged or destroyed. About this time, Kutrzeba began his Bzura counterattack, which redirected German attention and forces. In the meantime, eschewing any more costly, hasty, frontal assaults on Warsaw, the Wehrmacht relied on aerial bombardment to reduce casualties while it tightened the noose from nearly every direction.

An ad hoc defence would have to hold the city of half a million souls, at this point mostly women plus the young and old. One- to two-person fighting pits dotted the city and trenches zig-zagged across open spaces such as streets and parks, all backed up by camouflaged 37mm anti-tank guns and artillery. Remnants of Armies Łodz and Modlin stumbled into Warsaw, later joined by units from Armies Poznan and Pomorze that had escaped the Bzura debacle. In numerous cases, Polish divisions shown on the adjacent map consisted of perhaps the headquarters and one regiment, plus whatever other random troops it could bring under its control; these were usually not cohesive formations. Wehrmacht units closed in right behind them, from the north, east and south – probing attacks began on 15 September – and finally from the west. Polish units that could not reach the capital soon initiated guerrilla operations behind enemy lines, further slowing the Germans.

The Luftwaffe, planning its first major bombing of a large city to begin on the 16th, dropped millions of leaflets telling civilians they had 12 hours to evacuate the city and encouraging Polish soldiers to surrender. Largely uninvolved in the Bzura battles, Bock's 3. Armee attacked first in the east, initially against the Praga suburb on the east bank of the Vistula and then in the north. As if things could not get worse for the Polish Republic, on 17 September the Soviet Union launched its massive offensive all along the extensive eastern border (see Map 25). The following day President Ignacy Mościcki and Marshal Rydz-Śmigły left the capital and headed south-east in the direction of the Romanian Bridgehead. By the 18th and 19th, Polish units that had fled the Bzura and Kutno traps began to appear.

Rundstedt's men arrived soon thereafter and eventually 13 divisions ringed Warsaw (although only 11 are shown here – not counting the 4. Panzer-Division). On 20 September, 1,000 heavy guns joined the Luftwaffe to herald the final phase of the siege. Buildings collapsed into the streets, crushing people underneath. Fire raged throughout Warsaw, with dust and smoke turning day into night. The Germans stepped up ground and air attacks on the 23rd. Fighting on the 25th was so bad, the day became known as 'Black Monday'. German 8. Armee troops finally joined the battle 24 hours later. Rundstedt reorganized his army group: The 8. Armee took control of the Warsaw battle, freeing up the 10. Armee to continue driving into southern Poland. The same day, forts Mokotow, Dabrowski and Czerniakow fell, and that evening, Army Warsaw commander General Juliusz Rómmel requested surrender terms. The Germans initially refused and increased their assaults on the 27th.

With food and water in short supply, unburied corpses everywhere, fires uncontrolled and hospitals overflowing, hostilities ended at 1400 hours on 27 September. Rómmel surrendered with 140,000 soldiers, one-tenth of them wounded. Many Polish troops did not give up, but took off their uniforms and melted into the civilian population; they would fight another day. Nearly 10,000 civilians perished and approximately 50 per cent of Warsaw's structures had been damaged. For the next five years, repairing them would be very low on the Germans' list of priorities. Two days later, the Modlin fortress north-west of the city surrendered its 24,000-man garrison. One-sixth of its soldiers were wounded and the outpost had run out of food and water. Together, these forces represented the last sizeable resistance to the German conquest of Poland.

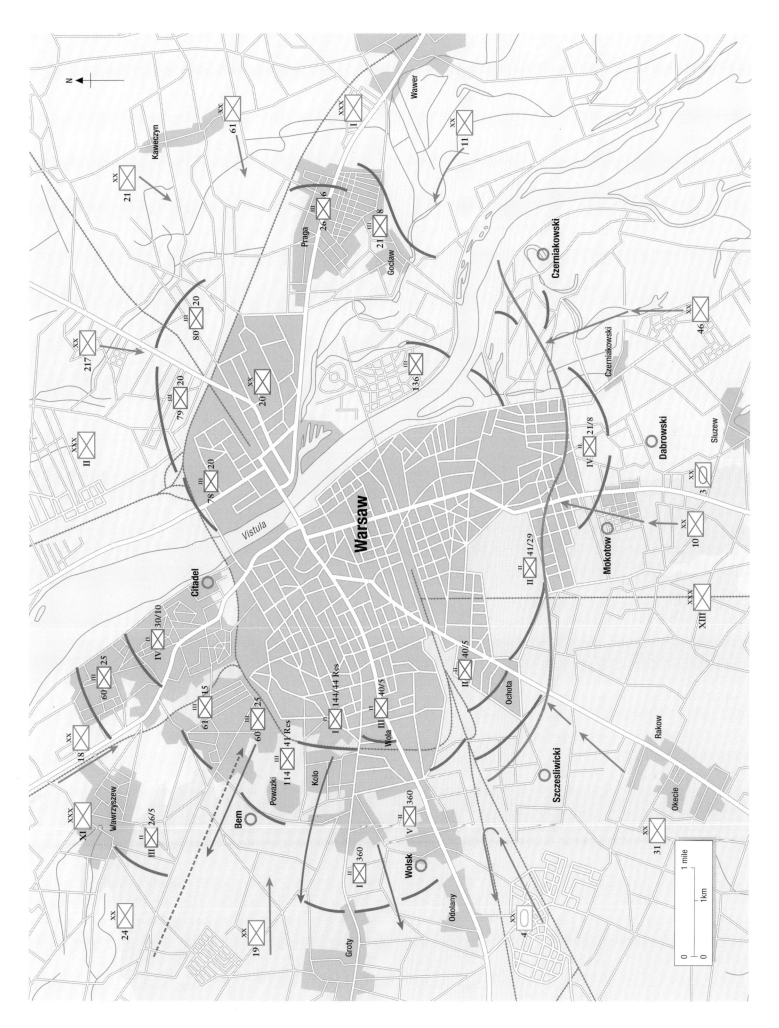

MAP 20: THE END OF POLAND, 13 SEPTEMBER–6 OCTOBER 1939

While battles in the centre of Poland around the Bzura River and Warsaw dominate the history of the campaign, they were certainly not the only fighting. Significant operations took place between the Vistula River and the German–Soviet demarcation line. So far, Army Krakow had managed to maintain some cohesion, at this stage of the war the only Polish field army so to do, but this too was about to change.

Bock's 3. Armee continued its drive south, culminating at Warsaw, as described previously. The 4. Armee crossed East Prussia. Its Korps Brand and XXI Armee-Korps had the mission of attacking towards Grodno (off this map, to the north) and Bialystok, respectively. Unaware of Stalin's exact intentions, the OKH issued Guderian's XIX Panzer-Korps a change of mission order. It would attack towards Brest and link up with Rundstedt's forces somewhere on the middle Bug, preventing the eastwards escape of as much of the Polish Army as possible. Heavily reinforced, XIX Panzer-Korps took about three days to defeat the Narew Group. Little in the way of cohesive, organized Polish defence barred the Germans' route, as scattered remnants attempted to offer some resistance. Guderian reached Brest on 14 September and took all of the town, except for the heavily defended citadel. Thereafter, his forces launched inconsequential probes to the south and east, technically into the Red Army's zone of occupation.

While the bulk of Rundstedt's 10. Armee turned 180 degrees to respond to the Bzura situation, a few divisions remained to guard the army's rear along the Vistula bend. Later, these pushed across the river towards Lublin and the much smaller Wieprz River, with Chełm as their ultimate objective. Even against this weak force, clearly a tertiary German thrust, Polish units could only throw up occasional and improvised defences.

At Sandomierz and points south, the 14. Armee had its own mechanized formations and made good use of them. These soon had the new Southern Front (remnants of Armies Krakow, Karpaty and Małopolska) further broken into small bits, which they easily encircled in wide open spaces between the San and Bug Rivers. Army Krakow's plan to fall back on Zamość came to nothing. Unable to fight in a coordinated fashion because the panzer thrust created isolated pockets, the Southern Front's defence foundered. On 14 September, Guderian's tankers linked up with 14. Armee soldiers at Włodawa, completing the deep encirclement. Rydz-Śmigły and his staff, now constantly on the run, had virtually no command and control over the fighting. Creating a new Lublin Army and Central Front did little to change the situation on the ground. Nor could subsequent Polish experiments with combining and recombining its scattered forces ever really amount to more than form over substance.

On 15 September, the OKW ordered Rundstedt to drive south-east, as before, to cut off any Polish escape in that direction. German mountain divisions, now clear of the Carpathian range, made for the Galician capital of L'wow. They lacked the strength to capture the city, so began manoeuvring to encircle it. The Polish government and high command had just arrived there and now had to contemplate evacuating yet again. Even before the Soviets' intervention, the forlorn notion of a Romanian Bridgehead was in danger of being overcome by events.

On the 17th, the republic's president and the rest of the government headed for Romania in hope of ultimately setting up a government in exile in France. Initially, the Romanians sounded sympathetic to the plan, but when the Poles arrived, they were quickly interned. It seems that the Germans had applied considerable diplomatic pressure on Romania. The Red Army's invasion that same day represented the last straw. The limited and local counterattacks the Poles could mount, such as the one at Tomaszów Lubelski during 18–20 September, did not appreciably slow the Germans. Except for defenders holding out in Warsaw, Modlin and on the Hel Peninsula, fighting devolved into a series of attempted Polish escapes and German pursuits; on 23 September, the OKW declared combat elsewhere ended. Isolated pockets held out at Nisko until 2 October and Kock until the 6th.

None of this discounts the Poles' skill against Europe's two largest armies. Their abilities shone brightly even while defending the somewhat featureless countryside of eastern Poland or cities like Warsaw, Modlin, Brest, L'wow and Tomaszów. Heeresgruppe Süd, for example, suffered more casualties during the second half of September than it did during the first half. Despite their numerous strategic, geographic and command and control disadvantages, the Poles killed 16,000 Germans and wounded twice again that number. Of 674 panzer losses, nearly one-third were completely written off. For their part, the Germans learned valuable lessons fighting against Poland that they would apply in later wars. Perhaps most important of these was the need for more aggressive leadership at all levels and enhanced combined-arms training.

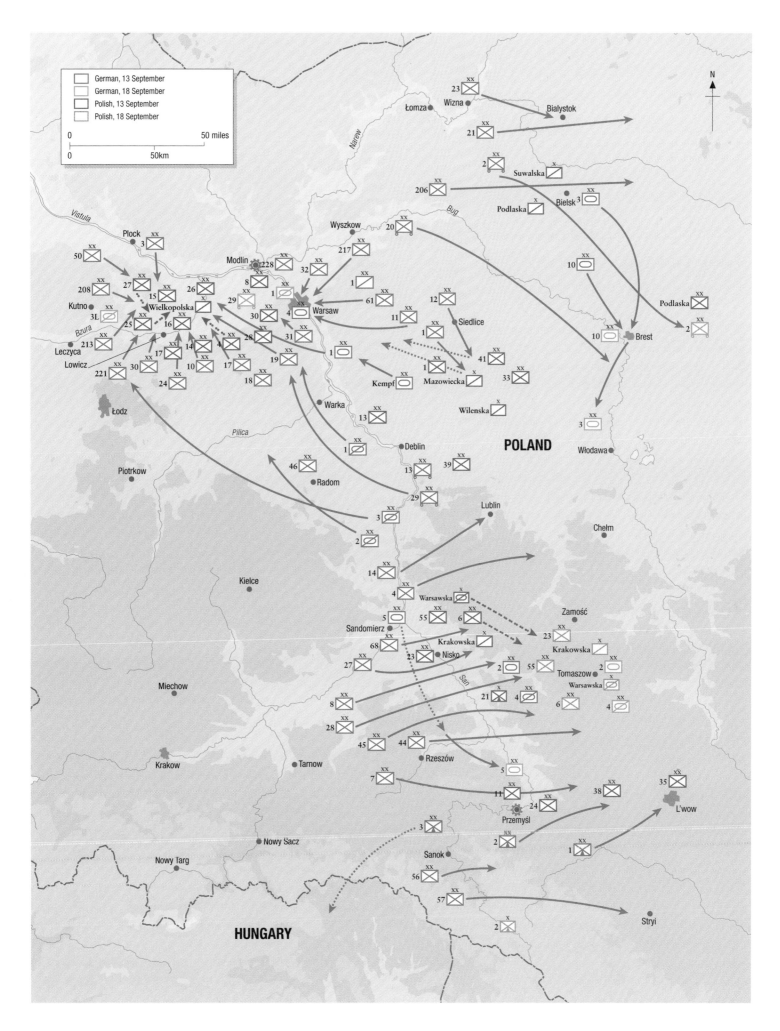

MAP 21: AERIAL OPERATIONS DURING THE POLISH CAMPAIGN

Fall Weiss set the standard for beginning an attack used by nearly every conventional operation since: An aerial assault against the enemy's air force, ground troops and national infrastructure. Contrary to popular myth and German propaganda, the Luftwaffe did not obliterate the Polish Air Force in the campaign's first couple of days, although German numbers and quality eventually did turn the tide in the attackers' favour.

Approximately one-third of the Luftwaffe's aircraft – 1,939 of an available 2,775 – took part in the east. At this early stage of World War II, the air force had not been completely subordinated to the army, so had its own independent plan against Poland. Some Luftwaffe leaders, aircrew and ground staff had tasted combat in Spain, but most had no practical experience. The Poles had about 1,929 machines, almost half of which carried bombs, mostly for tactical missions. Around half of its inventory comprised first line aircraft, though even many of these were obsolete. Most of the Polish Air Force flew in support of the army.

During the initial period, the Luftwaffe largely gained air superiority while also interdicting Poland's infrastructure, especially portions involved with mobilization, reservist assembly points and rail nodes. Sixty He 111 bombers hit Krakow on the first day while others bombed Łodz, L'wow and Lublin; thick fog prevented the Warsaw attack. Stukas (Ju 87s) and Do 17s attacked airfields at Deblin, Goclaw, Krosno, Ktowitz, Moderowski, Mokotow, Toruń, Wadowice and Warsaw-Okęcie. They mainly destroyed older models, since as a precaution on the last day of peace, the Poles had withdrawn their best planes to scattered secondary bases. Polish mobilization stations and troop trains came under heavy bombardment, as did Polish bases and ships in the Baltic. The Luftwaffe provided close air support for the advancing army from day one. Of particular note was Generalmajor Wolfram Freiherr von Richthofen's Fliegerführer zbV, made up of five *Gruppen* of 140 Stukas and one each of Bf 110s and Hs 123 biplanes. This outfit went on to become Flieger-Korps (Air Corps) VIII, which along with its commander, achieved near-legendary status throughout World War II. Thanks to its concentrated mass, it could apply close air support operationally.

Poland's Pursuit Brigade rose up, notably over Warsaw, and scored some early victories over German Stukas and Hs 123s. The Bomber Brigade and other close air support aircraft flew to assist the army. Losses from defending Polish cities and attacking German spearheads roughly halved the Polish Air Force in the war's first five days.

During the second phase of the war, the Luftwaffe could basically operate with impunity as the Polish Air Force retreated eastwards. Most missions were in support of the army, in particular the blitzing panzers. When the 4. Panzer-Division reached south-west Warsaw on 8 September, the Luftwaffe arrived in force, first to assist the division's attacks and then to cover its defence and withdrawal. Around the 11th, however, both air forces concentrated their efforts in the region of the Bzura counterattack. After initial German surprise, the Luftwaffe arrived in force in support of the 8. and 10. Armeen. Medium bombers called off their attacks against industrial and infrastructure targets in order to contribute to the ground combat. With this crisis mastered, German planes once again helped the advancing army negotiate the Vistula River crossings.

The concentrated bombing of Warsaw marked the next phase of aerial operations. Beginning on 13 September, Luftwaffe bombers started hitting the city in earnest. After dropping millions of leaflets warning the civilian population to evacuate the city, the assault began on the 16th in concert with army heavy artillery. Large raids followed on the 18th, 19th, 22nd and 24th, as the two sides negotiated the capital's surrender. By that point, the German high command had grown tired of Polish stalling, so ordered a massive bombardment for the 25th. More than 400 bombers flying three to four sorties dropped over 500 tons of high-explosive and 72 tons of incendiary bombs on government buildings, water, gas and electric utilities, and military targets. Surrender negotiations began the next day and were signed on 27 September.

At a cost of 743 aircrew and 285 machines (including 109 bombers), the Luftwaffe learned some valuable lessons for the future. Air–ground cooperation was good but needed improvement. A harder to fix problem was its equipment, since from now on the Germans would have to fight with what they had on hand: Aircraft that were too small, too slow, under-armed and with short ranges. As for Poland, many of its aviators escaped to fight another day, under more even odds.

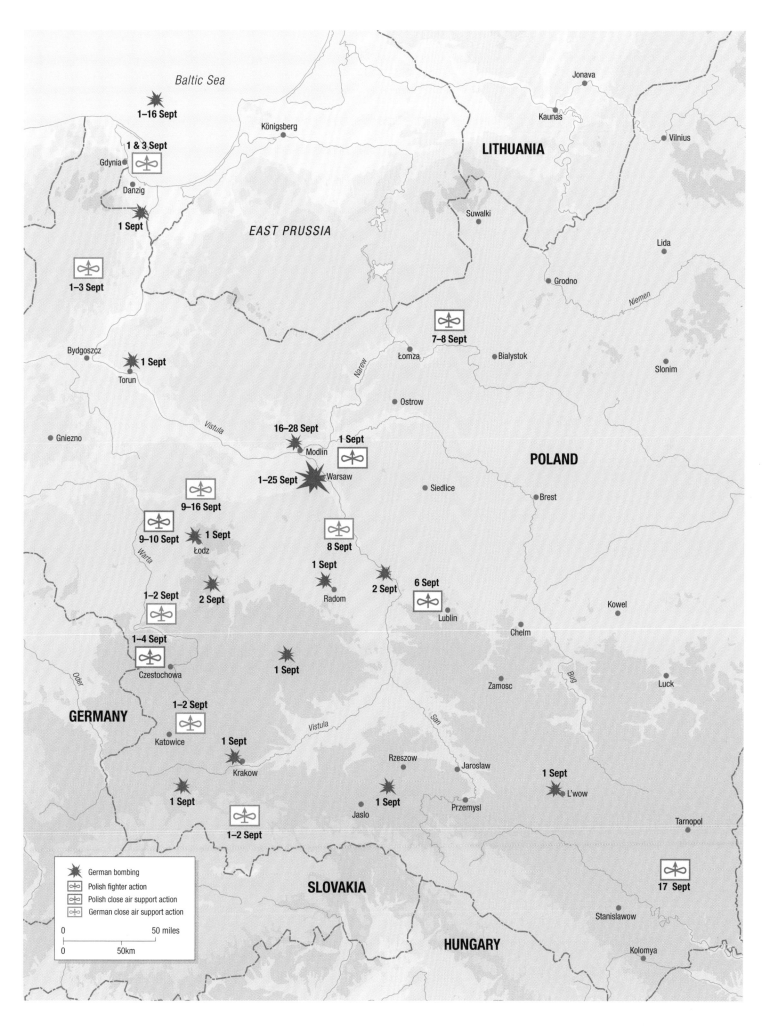

Baltic Sea

1–16 Sept

1 & 3 Sept

Königsberg

Gdynia

Danzig

1 Sept

EAST PRUSSIA

1–3 Sept

Bydgoszcz

1 Sept

Torun

Vistula

Gniezno

16–28 Sept

Modlin

1 Sept

1–25 Sept Warsaw

9–16 Sept

9–10 Sept **1 Sept**

Łodz

Warta

8 Sept

1 Sept

Radom

1–2 Sept **2 Sept**

2 Sept

6 Sept

Lublin

1–4 Sept

Czestochowa

Oder

GERMANY

1–2 Sept

Katowice

1 Sept

Vistula

1 Sept

Krakow

1 Sept

Jaslo

1–2 Sept

Rzeszow

Jaroslaw

1 Sept

Przemysl

San

1 Sept L'wow

LITHUANIA

Jonava

Kaunas

Vilnius

Suwalki

Lida

Grodno

Niemen

Łomza

Bialystok

Slonim

Ostrow

POLAND

7–8 Sept

Siedlice

Brest

Kowel

Chelm

Zamosc

Bug

Luck

Tarnopol

17 Sept

Stanislawow

HUNGARY

Kolomya

SLOVAKIA

German bombing
Polish fighter action
Polish close air support action
German close air support action

0   50 miles

0   50km

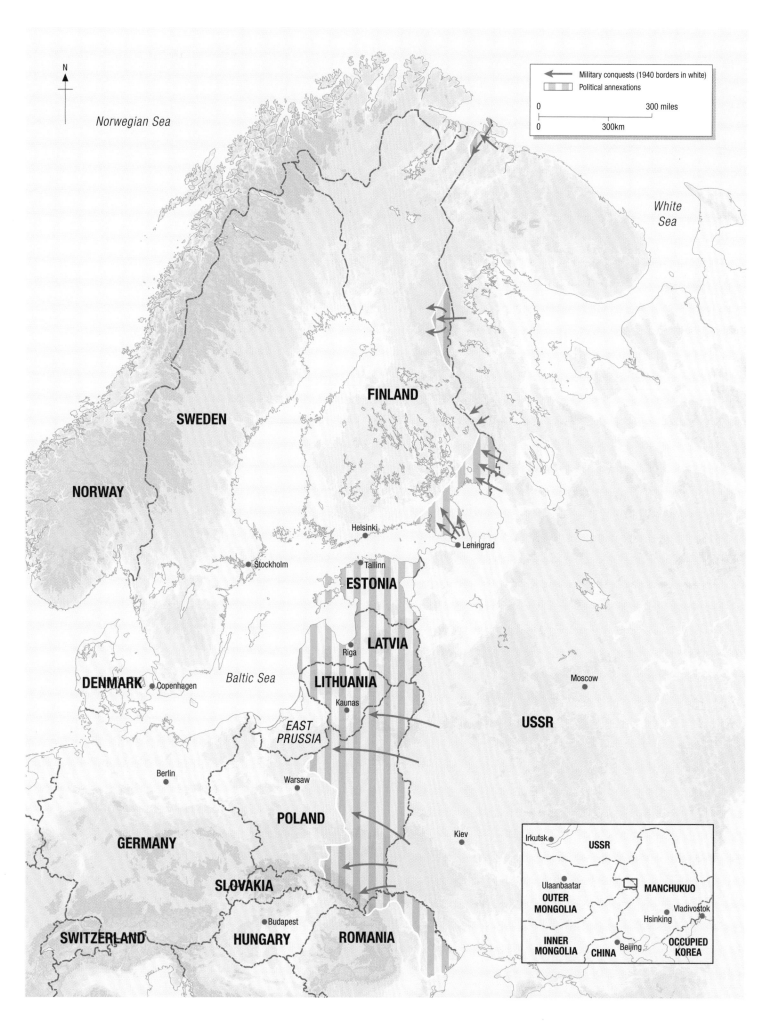

CHAPTER 3:
SOVIET AGGRESSION

Global chaos in the immediate post-World War I years seemed like the perfect place to marry centuries-long Russian expansionism to Bolshevik world revolution. However, national exhaustion, counter-revolutionary Whites, interventionist Allies and military overextension at the gates of Warsaw, to name but a few causes, threw cold water on such ideas. In addition, the difficulties in creating a new society and state meant that Lenin had to scale back his foreign policy plans and concentrate on establishing and stabilizing 'socialism in one country'. A generation later, Stalin felt strong enough to take abroad the combination of Russian tradition and Soviet revolution. With capitalist, imperialist and militarist renegades – like those in Germany, Italy and Japan – leading the way in undermining the existing structures in the mid-1930s, he likewise believed the international situation was ripe for exploitation.

For generations leading up to the Great War, Russia had sided with Prussia/Germany against French liberalism, Napoleon and British imperial designs in southern Asia. For many reasons, this orientation turned 180 degrees in the quarter century preceding the Russian Revolution. An updated 1930s version of the World War I arrangement might have even boxed in Hitler and deterred World War II. However, the critical year between Munich and Poland convinced Stalin he could not count on Britain, France and the West in general. Therefore, in the summer of 1939, he returned to the historical schemes favoured by Alexander I and Friedrich Wilhelm III, and Alexander II and Otto von Bismarck; in August, he entered into a treaty with Hitler. Far from trusting Hitler, he would be able to quietly work his plans while the Germans grabbed the world's attention. Over the next year, Stalin greatly expanded the borders of the USSR while avoiding the general European war.

Perhaps the most important battle of World War II, which many people are not aware of, had almost ended before the ink dried on the Molotov–Ribbentrop Pact. Japan had been a sworn enemy of Russia so far during the 20th century; the two nations had already come to blows in 1904–05 and 1918–22. While the Imperial Japanese Navy prepared for future war against the British Empire and the United States, the Japanese Army anticipated fighting Russia/the USSR. During the 1930s, the rogue Kwantung (Guandong) Army, on occupation duty in the Japanese puppet state of Manchukuo, had grown used to acting in a completely unaccountable fashion, murdering civilian ministers and its own generals, and unilaterally launching provocative military operations. Sensing the same Soviet and Red Army weaknesses the rest of the world did around the time of

Stalin's purges, the Kwantung Army planned to grab disputed frontier areas in Manchuria. Border incidents in 1935 escalated into full-blown combat in August 1939 with the battle of Khalkhin Gol (Nomonhan in Japanese). Overwhelming Soviet counterattacks quickly reversed initial Japanese gains at the exact time the Nazis and Soviets were meeting in Moscow. Hitler had no idea what was going on a world away; the Japanese were in no hurry to admit their humiliation to the globe, while Stalin had every reason to remain silent. Having learned their lesson in the summer of 1939 at the hands of General G.K. Zhukov, who was destined to become the outstanding operational field commander of World War II, the Japanese had no stomach for further conflict with the Soviets. This would be of decisive importance two years later. When Hitler launched Operation *Barbarossa*, he did it without Japanese assistance.

Hitler invaded Poland during the closing stages of Khalkhin Gol. The larger war in the heart of Europe and the secrecy of the two regimes fighting in faraway Asia, meant the world heard little from Manchuria. When, on 3 September, Britain and France declared war on Germany, Stalin the chess player knew he had Hitler the gambler right where he wanted him. According to the Molotov–Ribbentrop Pact, the USSR had the eastern half of Poland for the taking. The Nazis and Soviets promised to keep in close contact during any upcoming hostilities. However, the speed and violence of the blitzkrieg surprised the Soviets, since they had developed a healthy respect for the Polish military during their 1919–21 war. Soon it became clear to them that they would have to act quickly if they wanted to secure their share of this most recent partition of Poland. The day the 4. Panzer-Division reached Warsaw, Ribbentrop asked about 'the military intentions of the Soviet government'. The next day, Molotov replied that it would move 'within the next few days'[4]. The Germans wanted the Soviets to act faster and to change their justification for entering Poland lest the two dictatorships look like enemies. Molotov would not budge and stuck to his story that the Red Army was moving to save 'fraternal' Belorussian and Ukrainian nationalities from the Germans.

The Soviets quickly mobilized their two military districts adjacent to Poland and moved out on 17 September with seven armies consisting of 25 rifle and 16 cavalry divisions and two cavalry–mechanized groups. The defenders, already battered by the Germans, could not hold them back. In addition, Red Army claims that it had come to help its Slavic brethren against the Nazis thoroughly confused the Poles. It took the invaders just days to reach Vilnius, Brest and L'wow. Their haphazard advances, especially in the south, allowed many Poles to escape to Romania and Hungary. Thereafter, the Soviets entered into an informal competition with the Nazis for 'most brutal occupier' honours.

Next on Stalin's list was Finland, a Russian grand duchy from 1809 until 1917. With the assistance of Germans and Whites, the Finns kicked out the Bolsheviks and secured Petsamo (Russian Pechenga) in the far north and captured part of Karelia, only 18–20 miles from Petrograd (St Petersburg, soon renamed Leningrad). In 1939, Stalin wanted to create a defensive hinterland around the city by pushing back the new Finnish border. If possible, he wanted to set up a puppet communist government as well. On 5 October, the same day Hitler staged his victory parade in Warsaw, the Soviets invited the Finns to send a negotiator to Moscow to discuss 'certain questions of a concrete political nature'[5]. A week later, Stalin demanded an exchange of territory and guarantees of Finland's 'friendly relations'. Negotiations dragged on for a month, but the Finns would not agree to all the Soviet terms.

On 30 November, the Red Army invaded Finland with four armies of 750,000 men, versus about 160,000 Finns (mostly reservists). The main Karelian front saw 26 Soviet divisions face off against nine Finnish ones. The Soviets underestimated the fighting qualities of the Finns and the challenges of fighting a war in the far north during winter. They had a weak plan, poor leadership and unmotivated, untrained masses of conscripted soldiers, so made small progress in limited sectors. The Finns' advance guards skillfully gave way until they reached the main defences along the Mannerheim Line (actually a series of semi-parallel lines of differing quality). Here, their commander, Marshal Carl Mannerheim, member of the old Swedish nobility and war of independence hero, adeptly shifted reserves from one threatened locale to another, frustrating the Soviets. The Finns overcame their fear of Soviet artillery and tanks and perfected their own 'Motti' (encirclement) tactics (trapping isolated and attacking over-extended Red Army formations up to division size). By the end of 1939, the Finns had stabilized their front and began launching counterattacks.

On 7 January, Stalin named General S.K. Timoshenko as new overall commander, who immediately began retraining leaders and soldiers. On 1 February 1940, Timoshenko launched a new series of assaults. In the largest artillery bombardment since Verdun, in 24 hours he poured 300,000 shells into the Finnish defences. After a dozen days, the Finns could take it no more and the government approached Stalin for terms. By 19 February, the Soviets neared the fortress of Viipuri (Vyborg in Swedish), which anchored the southern end of the Mannerheim Line and it surrendered two days later. Finally, in late February, Britain and France seemed ready to do more than ship weapons to Finland, so readied expeditionary forces for deployment. In hope of outside relief, the Finns continued to defend into early March. Wanting to pre-empt the Western Allies, Stalin urged on his troops. The Finnish government soon realized no rescue effort would arrive, so surrendered on 13 March. Not wanting to push his luck, Stalin's new demands looked much like his original ones. At a cost of unnumbered casualties (estimates run as high as 200,000 dead and twice that wounded), he picked up 16,000 square miles of Karelia. Finland lost 25,000 dead and 200,000 civilians evacuated from the occupied territories.

According to the secret protocols of the Molotov–Ribbentrop Pact, the three Baltic States and Bessarabia fell into the Soviet sphere – basically a return to pre-World War I frontiers. Before the Germans had even concluded their war with Poland, Ribbentrop returned to Moscow (27 September) to finalize the common Nazi–Soviet frontier. Immediately, Stalin started to bully his three tiny neighbours on the

---

4   William Shirer, *The Rise and Fall of the Third Reich*, Simon and Schuster: New York, 1960, p. 627.

5   Snyder 1964, p. 99.

Baltic (Estonia on 29 September, Latvia on 5 October, Lithuania on 10 October). He forced them to declare their friendship and give the Soviets military basing rights. In the spring of 1940, while Hitler was focused on his war against France, Stalin upped the ante. In mid-June, the Soviets began to issue ultimatums, staging border incidents and sending trusted lieutenants to each of the Baltic capitals. The message to all three countries was clear and, on 21 July, the USSR annexed them as constituent republics. Between 1 and 6 August, the Red Army invaded and occupied the three Baltic States.

A similar fate befell Romania over its provinces of Bessarabia and Bukovina (the latter had never belonged to Russia, instead being part of the Austro-Hungarian Empire prior to World War I). Again, with the war in the West as a backdrop, in May 1940, the Soviets massed troops on the Dniestr River and made threatening diplomatic noises. Governed by the secret protocols, Germany could do little, so pressured Romania to give in without a fight. Red Army troops moved in on 28 June. Stalin had completed his takeover of key areas of Eastern and Central Europe without firing a shot.

MAPS 23 AND 24: THE BATTLE OF KHALKHIN GOL

This obscure tactical battle in eastern Asia had strategic implications completely disproportionate to its small size. It humbled the arrogant Kwantung Army and ensured that in World War II Japan would confine itself to fighting in China, south-east Asia and the Pacific.

The Kwantung Army began making trouble in Manchuria and northern China in the late 1920s. It represented the muscle behind Japan's puppet state of Manchukuo. It mainly fought local bandits until 1934, when it transformed from a counter-insurgency force to an operational field army. As Imperial Japan moved closer to the Third Reich in the mid-1930s, relations worsened with the USSR. Border skirmishes between small patrols in 1935 grew to regimental raids four years later. This became too much for Emperor Hirohito, who wanted raids kept local and small. Even this imperial scolding could not restrain the impudent Kwantung Army, which planned even bigger operations against the Soviets. It would attack into the disputed frontier area between the settlement of Nomonhan and the Khalkhin Gol River. But the Japanese did not plan on Zhukov, who arrived on 5 June.

MAP 23: JAPANESE ATTACKS

The Kwantung Army attacked on 3 July with the inexperienced 23rd Division and a brigade from the veteran 7th Division, two tank regiments and 180 aircraft. Task Force Kobayashi, a mixed force of four regiments from both divisions, crossed the Khalkhin Gol River. The Soviets offered little resistance and the Japanese defeated their limited counterattacks. Higher headquarters did not know what to do with Kobayashi's success and the attack stalled. The Soviets fought back and without a clear mission, Kobayashi quickly withdrew to the Japanese bank.

Meanwhile, near the village of Nomonhan, the Japanese 3rd and 4th Tank regiments attacked (only battalion-sized by European standards). This Task Force Yasuoka forfeited any semblance of combined arms when the 64th Infantry Regiment provided only weak support. Stranded and alone, the 3rd Tank Regiment quickly retreated, while the 4th got lost, driving around in a 180-degree semicircle. They tried similar attacks over the next couple days with similarly dismal results. Many senior Japanese officers considered *hara-kiri* (ritual suicide).

With the Kobayashi relocated, the two task forces attempted unified attacks between 5 and 9 July. The 4th Tank Regiment continued its weak performance, but the infantry regiments made progress, especially through the 9th. Their attacks included nighttime bayonet charges (mainly to avoid enemy artillery during the day), forcing the Soviets to conduct a fighting withdrawal to the river. Red Army reinforcements soon arrived. The Japanese discovered that their scorn for the Soviet military was unfounded and that fighting them was nothing like scrapping with the ragtag Chinese masses.

The 23rd Division began its 'General Offensive' on 23 July. Showing that they had learned something during the past weeks, they started with counter-battery fire. However, the Japanese 64th and 72nd Infantry Regiments gained little advantage from this. Combined-arms tactics and any significant cooperation between the left and right were still lacking. Japanese generalship was highly suspect. Japanese losses now totalled nearly 5,000 men killed; the General Offensive petered out after a couple days with the Japanese no closer to the Khalkhin Gol.

MAP 24: SOVIET COUNTERATTACKS

Zhukov sensed the momentum swinging his way. While he prepared for his own attack, he also continued the artillery duel, a contest that the Japanese could not win. Zhukov would attack in the north and centre with the 36th Motorized Rifle Division and south with the 82nd Rifle Division. Both aimed at Nomonhan and the piecemeal encirclement of isolated and spread-out Japanese formations. Their artillery and close air support attacks on 20 August surprised the Japanese. That afternoon, the Japanese committed their reserves, while Zhukov added numerous fresh units until they outnumbered the enemy nearly 2:1. His forces made good progress with their main effort in the south, but the defenders held in the centre. The next day, the Japanese Sixth Army assumed command and control of the battle from the struggling 23rd Division.

This belated move could not change the course of the fighting, however. On 23 August, the Soviet 9th Mechanized Brigade, curling around from the north, took Nomonhan, cutting off many Japanese units. A day later, the 8th Mechanized Brigade fought its way through stiff Japanese defences to link up with the 9th Mechanized, creating a bigger pocket. On the 24th, the Japanese launched a hasty counterattack by the 72nd Infantry Regiment, but this did little.

Those Japanese units that escaped encirclement began a general withdrawal on 25 July, with Zhukov's spent troops taking up a cautious pursuit. Inside the various pockets, defenders burned their unit colours while senior officers committed suicide. The Soviets entered Manchukuo in numerous places. A ceasefire took effect on the 16th. What months earlier seemed like a good idea to the Kwantung Army had turned into a full-blown debacle. It lost 17,000 men over four months of fighting, including 8,440 dead. Soviet casualties of all types amounted to 9,284. This was a cheap price for Stalin to pay for never again having to worry about his far eastern flank during World War II.

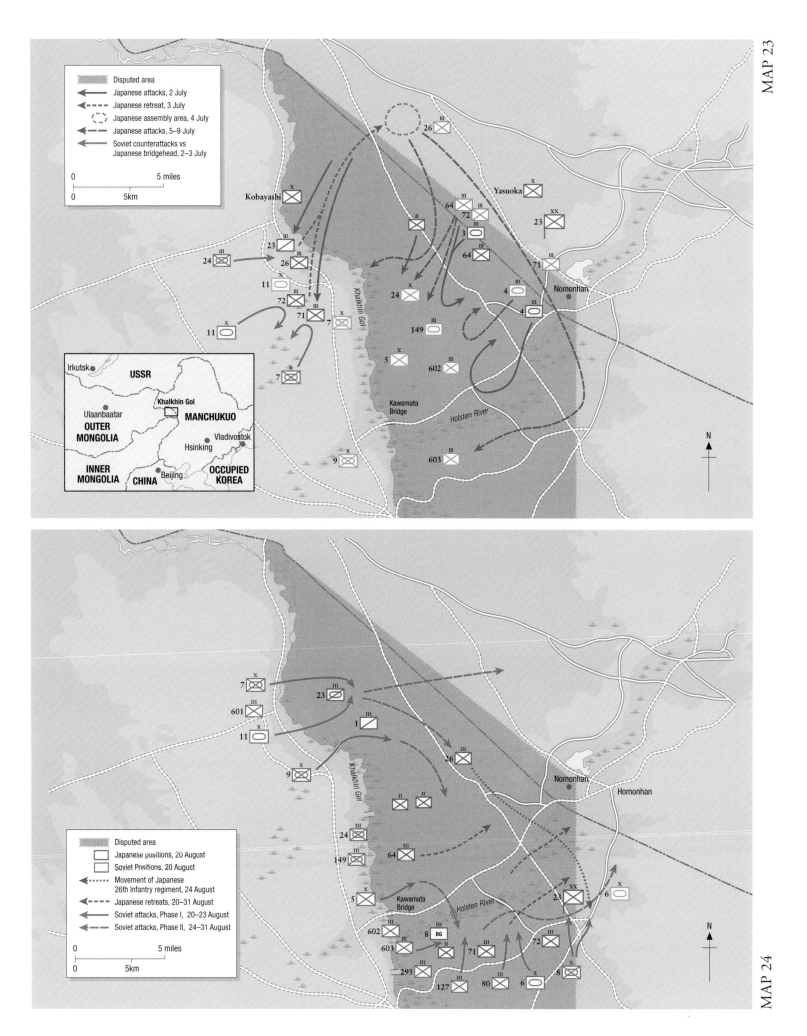

MAP 23

MAP 23 (top map)

Legend:
- Disputed area
- Japanese attacks, 2 July
- Japanese retreat, 3 July
- Japanese assembly area, 4 July
- Japanese attacks, 5–9 July
- Soviet counterattacks vs Japanese bridgehead, 2–3 July

0 — 5 miles
0 — 5km

Kobayashi
Yasuoka
26
64
72
3
64
71
23
Nomonhan
24
26
23
11
72
24
4
4
71
7
149
11
7
5
602
USSR
Irkutsk
Ulaanbaatar
OUTER MONGOLIA
Khalkhin Gol
MANCHUKUO
Hsinking
Vladivostok
INNER MONGOLIA
CHINA
Beijing
OCCUPIED KOREA
Kawamata Bridge
Holsten River
9
603
N

MAP 24 (bottom map)

Legend:
- Disputed area
- Japanese positions, 20 August
- Soviet Positions, 20 August
- Movement of Japanese 26th Infantry regiment, 24 August
- Japanese retreats, 20–31 August
- Soviet attacks, Phase I, 20–23 August
- Soviet attacks, Phase II, 24–31 August

0 — 5 miles
0 — 5km

7
23
601
1
11
26
9
Nomonhan
Homonhan
Khalkhin Gol
24
149
64
5
23
6
Kawamata Bridge
Holsten River
602
8 BG
72
603
71
293
8
127
80
6
N

MAP 24

MAP 25: THE SOVIET INVASION OF EASTERN POLAND, 17–29 SEPTEMBER 1939

The USSR had been lusting for the return of its Polish lands since Russia lost them at the Treaty of Brest-Litovsk in March 1918. Hitler was just the man to give most of them back: 12 million souls and 78,000 square miles of territory. The Soviets would have to be careful with their justification and timing of an invasion. They could not attack too early, in case Britain and France smelled a rat and declared war on them, too. Yet, if the Germans simply rolled up to the demarcation line and stopped, i.e. no longer threatened the Belorussian and Ukrainian peoples there, then the Red Army would have no excuse to intervene. By mid-September 1939, the Poles naively waited for news of the long-delayed Allied offensive against western Germany, but instead the 17th greeted them with news of advancing Red Army troops. The Third Reich and Soviet Union wanted to issue a joint communiqué on the intervention, but Stalin considered Hitler's version too frank and honest, so wrote his own, a masterpiece of obfuscation. The Führer, now in a general war and beholden to the chairman more than ever, had to accept it.

The Soviets invaded with the Belorussian Front under Army Commander II M.P. Kovalev, consisting of three armies (3rd, 10th and 4th) and the army-sized Dzherzhinsk Cavalry–Mechanized Group, all totalling 16 divisions and five brigades and the Ukrainian Front under Army Commander II Timoshenko, consisting of three armies (5th, 6th and 12th) and the Vinnitsa Cavalry–Mechanized Group, 21 divisions and seven brigades in all. The 12th Army and Group Vinnitsa had the sensitive mission of dashing across Galicia and Volhynia to prevent Polish units from reaching Hungary and Romania. Facing them stood up to 20 KOP frontier-guard battalions (totalling 11,000 men at their peak strength just before the war) and perhaps (at most) remnants of a couple of divisions and as many cavalry brigades as had managed to evade destruction at the hands of the Wehrmacht.

Red Army forces swarmed across the entire 800-mile Polish–Soviet border on 17 September. Polish units did not know what to do because of confusing orders from above, ambiguous (to them) reasons for the Soviets' arrival and even white flags of truce on Soviet vehicles. With little to hinder their movement, some Soviet formations covered 60 miles per day on the first couple of days, often actively avoiding combat with the Poles. To them, scattered Polish Army units, generally heading for Lithuania and Romania, represented little more than bands of guerrillas and were treated accordingly. Problems with command and control and vehicle maintenance hamstrung the Soviet advances and eventually 80,000–100,000 Poles made it to friendly neighbouring countries and thence to France and Britain.

By 19 September, Molotov had lodged a complaint with the German ambassador to Moscow, Friedrich-Werner von der Schulenburg, that numerous Wehrmacht units had overshot the agreed-upon military demarcation line. Potential German–Soviet hostilities loomed in these areas, principally around Bialystok, L'wow and Brest. On the 22nd, the Germans dutifully pulled back from the demarcation line and Guderian handed Brest over to his Red Army counterpart. A week later, the two countries formalized the Molotov–Ribbentrop line, generally following the Bug and San Rivers, as their new mutual border and signed a friendship treaty. The USSR received 78,000 square miles of Poland to Germany's 73,000. A terrible occupation began for all Poles, regardless of whether they had German or Soviet overseers. Stalin achieved all of this at a cost of 737 men killed. Lithuania received a sliver of land around Vilnius, given to Poland in 1919, but only after Red Army soldiers had pillaged the city.

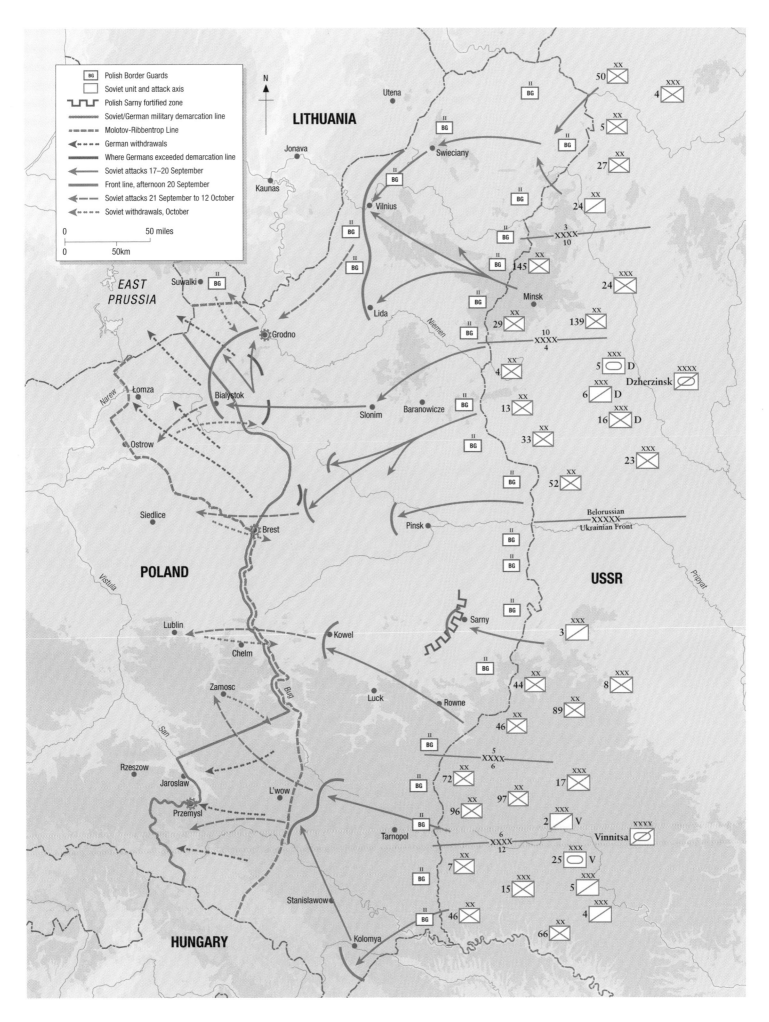

MAP 26: THE PRE-WAR FINNISH FRONT

According to the Molotov–Ribbentrop Pact, the Germans and Soviets considered Finland a 'Baltic State' and therefore within the latter's sphere of influence. Stalin worried that, with their existing border, the Finns could threaten Leningrad and the Murmansk railway, hinder shipping to and from the Kronstadt naval base (also within artillery range of Finnish Karelia), plus he wanted to control his neighbour's access to the rest of the world via the Arctic Ocean port of Petsamo. Finland had also come into being and fought off the Russian Revolution with Germany's help; if that relationship continued, it would be another concern for Stalin. Therefore, Soviet designs on Finland were not purely expansionist, but included a healthy dose of defensive thinking, a point lost on the West both at the time and since. That is not to say that Stalin's intentions did not include the hope that he could create another socialist republic on the Baltic if he could.

As for the Finns, they remained non-aligned. Prior to independence, they had led a fairly autonomous existence under both Swedish and Russian rule. Finland was a republic, but had flirted with quasi-fascism between 1929 and 1932 and had outlawed the Communist Party in 1931. Its small army depended heavily on regionally recruited reserves (i.e. frequently defending their actual homes), often made up of hearty rural settlers very familiar with fieldcraft, terrain and climate, and belonging to units with almost a family atmosphere – officers were often considered 'one of the guys'. The World War I Prussian 27th Jäger Battalion was the unofficial training ground for many senior officers. Finland bought equipment and weapons from all over Europe and America, so had an almost unmanageable mix – a maintenance and supply nightmare. Finland had the manpower for 14 divisions, but only equipment for ten (with much of it obsolete). Their commander-in-chief was Carl Mannerheim, a former Russian Guards cavalry officer who had fought in the Russo-Japanese War, commanded the 25th Cavalry Division during World War I and served on the staff of General A. A. Brusilov, perhaps Russia's most talented Great War general. Among other awards, he received an Iron Cross from Kaiser Wilhelm II during the fighting against Russia in the summer of 1918. During the interwar period, he had a loose relationship with the fascist Lapuan Movement (outlawed in 1932).

The blitzkrieg against Poland had convinced Stalin that Hitler was not only unpredictable but dangerous. On 5 October 1939, before the last Poles had surrendered, he invited a Finnish delegation to Moscow to discuss the situation between the two countries. When the Finns arrived a week later, Stalin presented a list of demands, including a land swap and assurances of Finland's peaceful intentions. Among other things, he would push the border 25 miles farther away from Leningrad, give the USSR islands around Kronstadt, a 30-year lease of the port and naval base at Hango in the Gulf of Finland and territory in the far north. Both sides made counter- and counter-counterproposals over the next month. Perhaps counter-intuitively, Mannerheim favoured coming to terms, but Finnish public opinion, and the government, did not. This surprised Stalin, who thereafter had to be talked into war by Kremlin hardliners. Negotiations ended on 14 November and Stalin ordered war preparations immediately. The press and propaganda attacks then began, as did the de rigueur claims of Finnish border skirmishes and violations.

The Leningrad Military District began planning and preparing, with no intelligence on the enemy and obsolete maps; Stalin gave it fewer than two weeks. General K. A. Meretskov had four armies: The main effort 7th Army (13 rifle divisions, a mechanized corps and three tank brigades comprising 1,000 tanks) attacking across lower Karelia towards Viipuri and ultimately Helsinki; the 8th Army (six rifle divisions and two tank brigades) attacking counterclockwise around Lake Ladoga in support of the 7th Army; the 9th Army (five rifle divisions) attacking across central Finland to split the country in two; and the 14th Army (three rifle divisions) attacking in the far north against Petsamo to cut off Finland from any outside help.

Finland's strategy looked much like Poland's: Hold out until some larger power came to save it. Operationally, its Army of Karelia had II and III Corps (three and two divisions respectively), while north of Lake Ladoga stood IV Corps (two divisions) and the North Finland Group – an assortment of army units, reservists and border guards. Soviet strength lay in its masses, unfortunately road-bound without mobility and lacking winter clothing. Finland depended on the morale of its troops and knowledge of the daunting forests, marshes and poor infrastructure in the east.

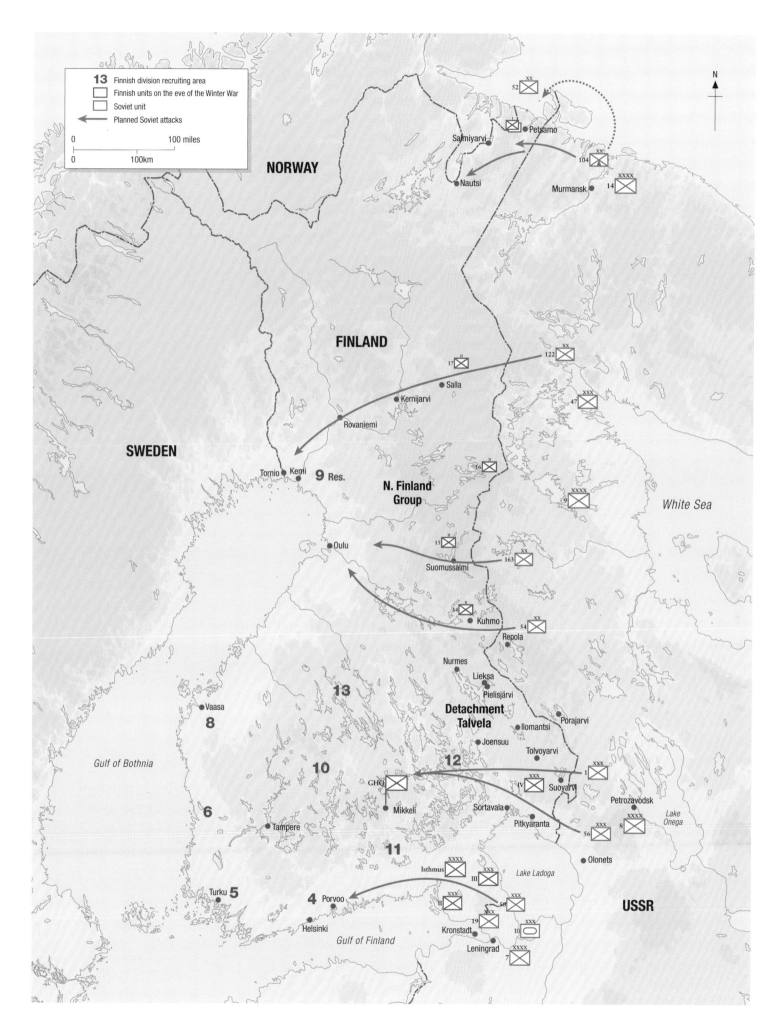

Legend

13 Finnish division recruiting area
Finnish units on the eve of the Winter War
Soviet unit
Planned Soviet attacks

0   100 miles

0   100km

NORWAY

FINLAND

SWEDEN

52

Salmiyarvi   Petsamo

Nautsi

104

Murmansk   14

17   122

Salla

Kernijarvi   47

Rovaniemi

9

Tornio   Kemi   **9** Res.

16

N. Finland Group   White Sea

15   Oulu

Suomussalmi   163

14   Kuhmo

54   Repola

Nurmes

Lieksa

Pielisjärvi

13   **Detachment Talvela**   Porajarvi

Vaasa

8   Ilomantsi

Joensuu   Tolvoyarvi

Gulf of Bothnia

10   **12**   GHQ   1

IV   Suoyarvi

Mikkeli   Sortavala   Petrozavodsk

6   Lake Onega

Tampere   Pitkyaranta   56   8

11   Olonets

Isthmus   III   Lake Ladoga

Turku **5**

4 Porvoo   II   50

Helsinki   19   Kronstadt   10   **USSR**

Gulf of Finland   Leningrad   7

MAP 27: THE KARELIAN FRONT (I), 30 NOVEMBER–31 DECEMBER 1939

Soviet planning against Finland mirrored the turmoil at the top levels of the USSR seen since Stalin's purges. Two plans were advanced, one by the army high command and one by the Leningrad Military District; each had its political patrons. In the end, the Leningrad plan prevailed. It put inordinate trust in Finnish workers, expected to rise up against their own government and support Leninist world revolution. It underestimated the Finns' skill and will to resist and difficulties posed by climate and weather. The Leningrad Military District commander estimated his men would need three months. Their main effort would aim past Viipuri for Helsinki, the population and economic heart of the country. The Finns' defensive main effort lay in the same area for similar reasons.

Red Army and Army Air Force units attacked on 30 November 1939. Between 500,000 and 600,000 men in 26 divisions supported by 900–1,000 mainly vintage aircraft were pitted against 150,000 Finns in nine divisions (the tenth division was being formed), covered overhead by 145 planes manufactured by every major nation in Europe plus the US. Each Soviet division had more tanks supporting it than in the entire Finnish Army. On the main southern Karelian front, 120,000 Soviet troops, 1,000 tanks and 600 guns attacked across the Finnish buffer zone, 12–30 miles wide and leading to the Mannerheim Line. In the initial assaults into the buffer zone, often a single Finnish covering force battalion faced down one Soviet division. Snowstorms and traffic jams slowed the invaders. The weather was terrible – often too cloudy for the Soviets to assert their air superiority, and cold, but not cold long enough to provide the frozen ground needed to support Red Army armour.

Many Finns had never seen a tank, not even in training, so frequently fled on account of mere rumours. By 4 December, the defenders had settled down, even learning to attack Soviet tanks one-on-one. They launched local counterattacks against isolated enemy columns. Covering force engagements were largely over by the 6th; the main takeaway was that the Finns now realized the Soviets could be beaten. Within a few days, fighting centred on the Mannerheim Line. The Red Army liked to exaggerate its features and strength, equating it to the Maginot Line. In reality, it was a series of trenches with occasional log-covered dugouts. The 80-mile-long line had only about 100 reinforced concrete bunkers. It also shared the same deficiencies as the rest of the army: Too few anti-tank guns and too little artillery. Its main strength came from how Finnish engineers knitted together natural and man-made features.

In mid-December, Meretskov brought his artillery forward and prepared to take on the Mannerheim Line. Clearing weather aided him by making possible numerous close air support sorties. His main effort came on the left, on the most direct route to Viipuri, but he also made significant attacks on the indirect route on the right. Soviet attacks followed the standard World War I model: A heavy artillery barrage followed by infantry, sometimes supported by tanks (which, limited to roads, usually became stuck in snowdrifts). They had all arms on the battlefield, but these did not always cooperate in true combined-arms operations. Nevertheless, they pressured the defenders, in particular the 5th Division holding the vulnerable elbow in the line at Summa. The Finns honed their defensive abilities, especially in the area of pinpoint artillery fire. Their ski patrols, dressed in white, moved around enemy units at will. Mannerheim wanted to launch a double-envelopment counter against exposed Red Army attackers, but subordinates and staff officers talked him out of the idea. His army was too new and inexperienced for such a manoeuvre and it had no training in the coordinating artillery in the attack, too few radios (Finnish defenders mainly relied on landlines) and no tanks.

In the end, Mannerheim decided on numerous less ambitious counterattacks all along the line bearing his name. However, even these limited manoeuvres during the last week of December proved too much for the Finns. Attacks begun at 0630 hours often foundered by 1000 hours. Luckily, further Red Army attacks launched against the Mannerheim Line accomplished little. On the critical Karelian front, the Finns held and the Soviets failed. By the end of 1939 the mortal danger to Finland seemed over, at least for now. On 2 December, Finland had appealed to the League of Nations, which first promised to intervene, and then expelled the USSR 12 days later.

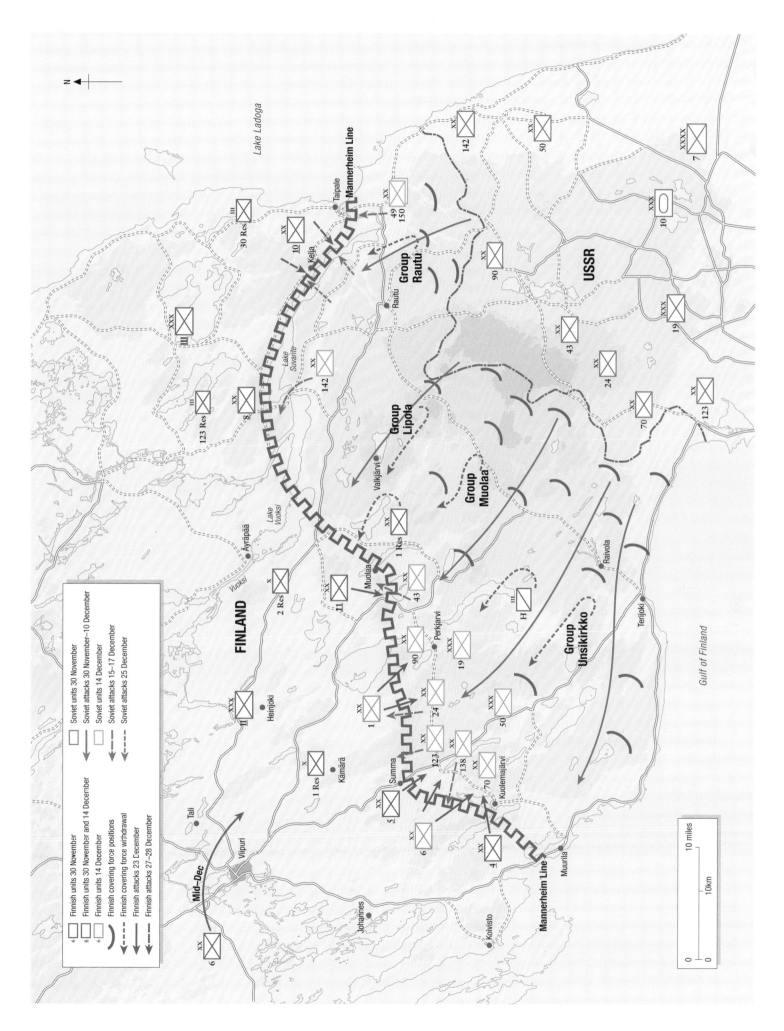

MAP 28: THE KARELIAN FRONT (II), 11 FEBRUARY–13 MARCH 1940

During December 1939, the Soviet invasion fell short of its ambitious objectives along the entire front. The Finns sustained serious casualties and lost some territory, but believed they had survived the worst and had most global opinion on their side.

Meretskov had clearly failed and Stalin had enough of the 'Leningrad clique' and the David versus Goliath nature of the war so far. The dictator sacked the general and on 7 January 1940, replaced him with the Red Army's senior soldier, Timoshenko, at the head of the newly renamed North-Western Front (with Zhukov as his chief of staff). Fresh from leading the southern wing of the Polish invasion, he immediately set to work attempting to correct the great number of problems that had bedevilled the whole campaign so far. He instituted new training for leaders and soldiers, concentrating on combined-arms tactics. Timoshenko increased patrolling along the front line so his commanders could have current and reliable intelligence. He brought in additional winter clothing and equipment and beefed up the already massive artillery park. The first months revealed many problems with the air force: A lack of initiative on the part of leaders, indifferent bombing and gunnery skills, poor communications, lack of coordination with ground forces and avoiding flying in bad weather or at night. Timoshenko also reorganized the forces facing the Mannerheim Line, dividing them into two armies by adding the new 13th Army.

Marshal Mannerheim and his troops did not remain idle during the first half of January either. They formed (but could only partially equip) two new divisions and began digging new defensive lines behind the main Mannerheim Line, especially on the western half, where they expected to see the Soviets' main attacks. In mid-January, Timoshenko began a massive weeks-long bombardment of the Finnish defences, concentrating on the Summa sector in the south and Taipale, the anchor of the north. With a few days of good flying weather, the Red Army Air Force added to the destruction. Together, these caused significant damage to Finnish fieldworks and gave the defenders no rest. Mannerheim's men had to ration their scarce artillery ammunition, but somehow managed to hold on to the same battlefields as December.

By 11 February, Timoshenko had moved up 18 rifle divisions and five tank brigades and began his new offensive, concentrating on a 12-mile portion of the line. Large concrete bunkers with heavy guns fell on the first day. Mannerheim ordered his 5th Division to counterattack, blunting the Soviet assault and causing 12,000 casualties (Finnish losses were 10 per cent of this figure). Nevertheless, by the 14th, the depleted II Corps fell back approximately 10 miles to the Interim Line, a weak shadow of the defences they abandoned. To the north, the III Corps beat back numerous attacks. In late February, the 7th Army stepped-up its assaults on the Interim Line, which bent but did not break. On the last day of the month, Mannerheim ordered II Corps back to the Rear Line. When Timoshenko's men moved out again, they hit abandoned, empty positions. However, improved Soviet morale and combined-arms tactics impressed the marshal.

Meanwhile, the international situation intensified. Britain and France were finally moved to intervene, but Norway and Sweden (pressured by the Germans) would not allow them passage. Hitler caught wind of these plans and began to prepare his own Scandinavian operations (see Chapter 4). Both combatants had grown tired of the fighting and on 25 February, the Soviets demanded the old frontier of Peter the Great, to which, days later, the Finns agreed 'in principal'. The Western Allies tried to bribe Finland into fighting on with promises of support that both parties knew they could not keep.

As if the Finns needed much more convincing, on 4 March, Timoshenko began his final offensive against the Rear Line with 30 divisions backed up by 2,000 aircraft and 1,200 AFVs. Within three days, he had a bridgehead across the bay south of Viipuri, where his artillery could interdict the road to Helsinki. The same day a Finnish delegation arrived in Moscow to discuss terms. House-to-house fighting took place in Finland's second city over the 9th and 10th and the two parties agreed on a ceasefire on 13 March. Just minutes before the shooting was scheduled to stop, the Soviets began a murderous 15-minute barrage on Finnish positions before they withdrew to the new (or rather, 1721) border.

Finland began the 105-day war with 150,000 men; half had become casualties. While there are no solid figures, estimates of Soviet losses include a quarter of a million dead and as many wounded. It seems that Timoshenko's battlefield reforms had worked, yet another indication that many had overrated the effects of Stalin's purges. The Soviet terms have been seen as fairly moderate, a tribute to plucky Finland's strong defence against improbable odds.

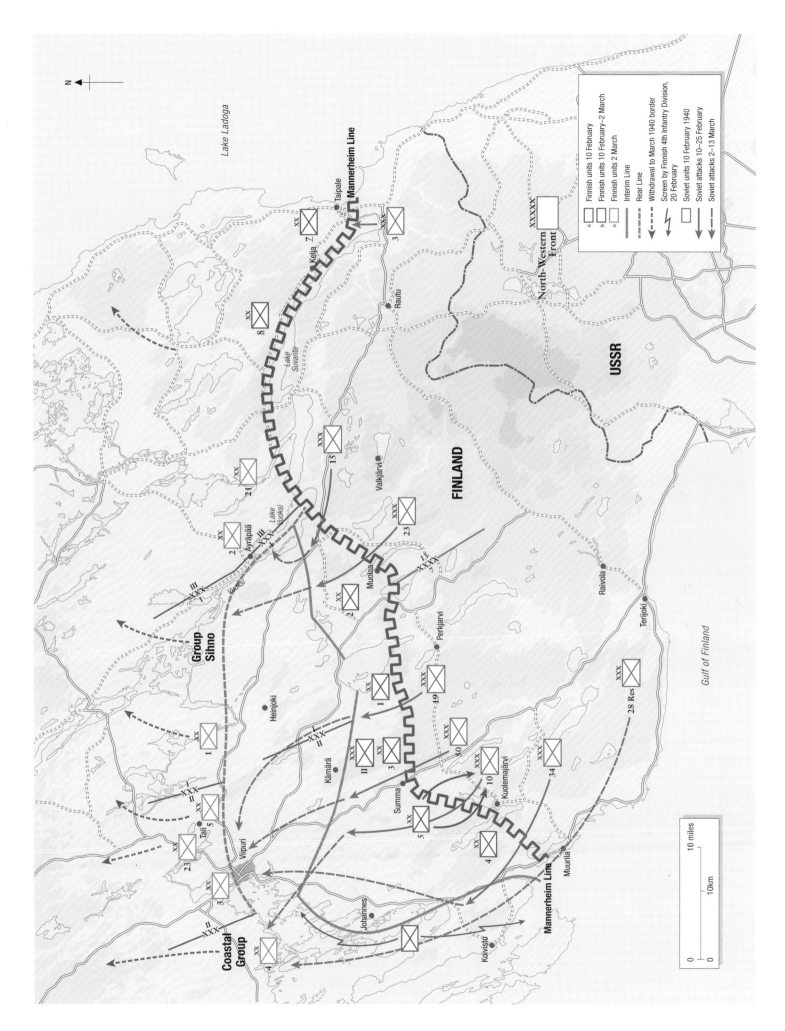

Lake Ladoga

Mannerheim Line

Taipale

Kelja

Lake Suvanto

Rautu

Lake Vuoksi

Valkjärvi

Äyräpää

Vuoksi

Muolaa

Raivola

Perkjärvi

Group Sihno

Terijoki

Heinjoki

Kämärä

Summa

Kuolemajärvi

28 Res

Tali

Viipuri

Johannes

Koivisto

Muurila

Mannerheim Line

Coastal Group

USSR

FINLAND

North-Western Front

Gulf of Finland

0   10 miles
0   10km

Finnish units 10 February

Finnish units 10 February–2 March

Finnish units 2 March

Interim Line

Rear Line

Withdrawal to March 1940 border

Screen by Finnish 4th Infantry Division, 20 February

Soviet units 10 February 1940

Soviet attacks 10–25 February

Soviet attacks 2–13 March

71

MAP 29: THE LAKE LADOGA FRONT (I), 30 NOVEMBER–31 DECEMBER 1939

Meretskov's plan included a supporting attack north of Lake Ladoga. The 8th Army was supposed to breakthrough and push aside the Finns, make a great counterclockwise arc around the north of the lake and finally come in behind the Mannerheim Line position. This enveloping manoeuvre would make the principal Finnish position untenable and open the way into the heart of Finland. As before in southern Karelia south of the lake, the defenders' main mission here was also to prevent this from happening. The Soviets enjoyed a sizeable advantage: Six divisions and two tank brigades against two divisions near Ladoga, plus some screening forces and border guards to the north.

The Red Army attacked here on 30 November, with the 56th Corps in the north aiming for Kitilä, backdoor to the Mannerheim Line and 1st Corps to its north. The 1st Corps surprised Marshal Mannerheim with the weight of its attack in the far north, opposite the lightly screened Suojärvi. Not yet being aware of Soviet mobility limitations, he believed it could easily turn south, first behind his own IV Corps and thence behind the main defences.

As depicted earlier on Map 27, after about a week of fighting on the main Karelian front, the Finns knew they had escaped destruction. This was not the case in the IV Corps sector, where things went badly, especially on the Tolvoyarvi road. Here, two rifle divisions roughly handled the small Group Räsänen and by 7 December, stood half way to the railway junction of Värtsilä, the logistical hub for IV Corps and gateway to southern Karelia. Even farther north, the 155th Rifle Division worked its way through the one Finnish battalion guarding the area and began to threaten the important regional town of Ilomantsi. Using the advantages of interior lines and the superior Finnish rail system, Mannerheim shuffled three regiments as reinforcements to the

threatened area to serve as the nucleus of a new defensive arrangement. Before the first week of December was out, he also fired IV Corps commander General Juho Heiskanen and replaced him with General Woldemar Hägglund, a fellow 27th Jäger Battalion alumnus. At the same time, Mannerheim also reorganized his forces there, creating a new Group Talvela to take control of the fighting north of IV Corps.

In addition to having only half the number of men in this area as the Soviets did, the Finns had no tanks or close air support and only limited indirect-fire weapons. The 1st Corps was having its way in the north, fighting to within 5 or ten miles of Ilomantsi, while the well-led 139th Rifle Division reached the outskirts of Tolvoyarvi. During the third week of December, the Finns launched numerous hasty counterattacks in these areas, often using only a few companies or a couple of battalions at the most. The semi-fresh 75th Rifle Division came forward to replace the heavily attrited 139th, but the Finns kept coming. The lines stabilized on about 23 December and thereafter the Group Talvela portion of the front quietened down for the remainder of the war.

Not so on the 56th Corps axis of attack. The Soviets easily pushed aside screening regiments and then quickly overcame the Finns' main defensive line. Without retreating too far, the 12th Division managed to make a stand on the Kollaa River (actually a stream). To the south, the 13th Division was not so fortunate, being outnumbered 3:1. With the 168th Rifle Division leading the attack in the south, within a week Red Army forces levered the Finns off their main defensive line there. They pushed on to a point just short of Kitilä, where the defences finally halted them. It appeared that the tide had finally turned, but Soviet commanders and troops were about to learn some hard lessons about being too successful.

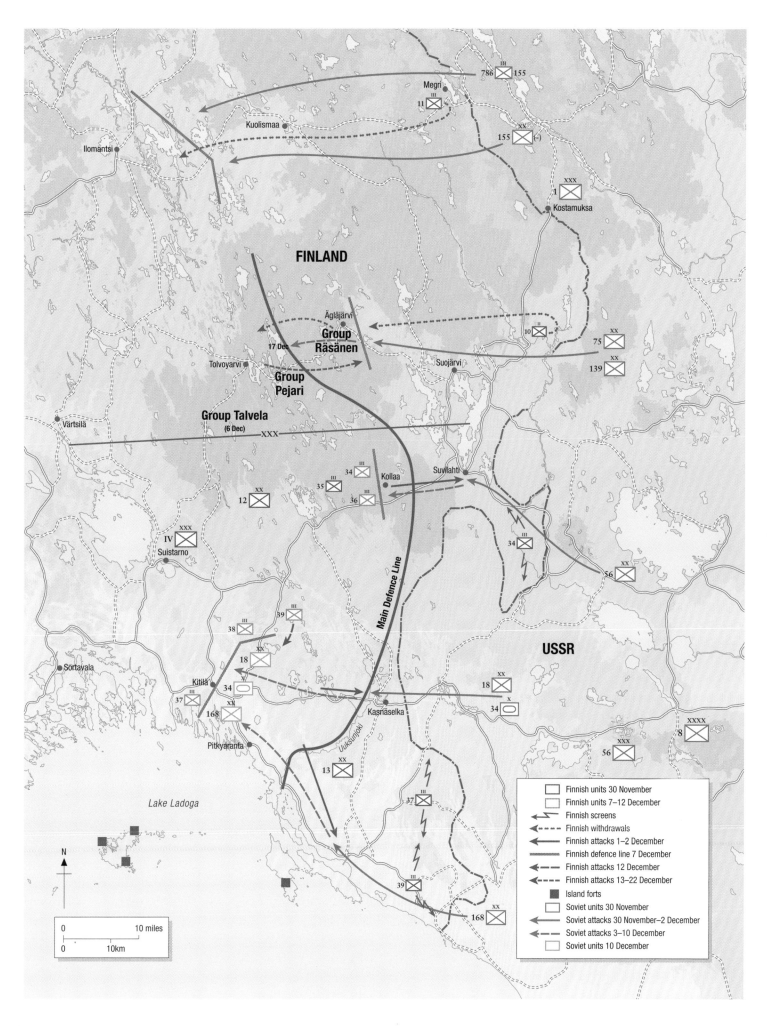

FINLAND

Megri

155
786

11

Kuolismaa

155
(-)

Ilomántsi

1

Kostamuksa

Group Räsänen

Ägläjärvi

17 Dec

Group Pejari

10

75

Tolvoyarvi

139

Suojärvi

Group Talvela
(6 Dec)

Vártsilá

34

35

Kollaa

Suvilahti

12

36

34

56

IV

Suistarno

39

38

18

USSR

Sortavala

34

18

Kitilä

34

37

Kasnäselka

168

56

8

Pitkyáranta

13

37

N

Lake Ladoga

39

168

	Finnish units 30 November
	Finnish units 7–12 December
	Finnish screens
	Finnish withdrawals
	Finnish attacks 1–2 December
	Finnish defence line 7 December
	Finnish attacks 12 December
	Finnish attacks 13–22 December
	Island forts
	Soviet units 30 November
	Soviet attacks 30 November–2 December
	Soviet attacks 3–10 December
	Soviet units 10 December

0   10 miles

0   10km

MAP 30: THE LAKE LADOGA FRONT (II), 1–31 JANUARY 1940

Two Soviet rifle divisions and a tank brigade barrelled towards Kitilä in mid-December. The 13th Division, three regiments abreast, stopped them short of the town. The new IV Corps commander Hägglund ordered counterattacks on 12, 17 and 26 December, but these failed to destroy or even turn back the Red Army forces. What these manoeuvres did do, however, was split the attackers into 11 small pockets, usually strung out along a road and lacking mutual support. This is the genesis of the Motti tactics, now part of World War II lore.

As with the word blitzkrieg, Motti tactics were not official Finnish military doctrine, but instead an ad hoc creation. The technique involved a three-step process: Conduct reconnaissance to fix enemy locations; launch local attacks to isolate and trap enemy groups; and then destroy the pockets in detail. The Finns could usually accomplish the first two steps (often on skis), but in a few cases could not complete the job with the third. First, they simply lacked the manpower to overwhelm and destroy the encirclements, especially the larger ones. Next, they also did not have the necessary artillery, tanks, close air support, or perhaps most importantly, time to reduce the Soviet groupings. Finally, Motti tactics actually favoured the Red Army's key strength, its defensive fighting. Each pocket essentially became an all-round 'hedgehog' perimeter, often resupplied by air or, for pockets near the Lake Ladoga shore, water. For example, the three largest Mottis held out until the end of the war. Often, the Finns' best bet to destroy a Motti was to wait for the Soviets to attempt to break out and kill them in the open. Other than digging in and trying to wait out the Finns, the Soviets had no counter to the Mottis due to their weak command and control, poor winter training and lack of skis or other proper equipment.

If nothing else, Hägglund's Mottis brought the 56th Corps attacks to a halt. The Soviets only helped create more encirclements when they sent in fresh divisions to save the trapped one – which they frequently did. In this way, by late December, the 18th and 168th Rifle Divisions with the 34th Tank Brigade, fought their way close to Kitilä, where the reinforced 13th Division blocked their way. When Hägglund ordered the counterattacks, at first they seemed to fail, but the Finns soon saw them as presenting new opportunities. They learned that the pockets created as byproducts of their attacks could not advance, retreat, nor even be saved from the outside. While some Mottis were too big or strong to be taken, others were the right size to be destroyed or at least to be left to waste away in isolation. Relief attempts from the direction of Salmi likewise failed. This temporarily ended the threat to Kitilä, although the so-called Great Motti at the gate of the town still had much combat potential within its 20-mile perimeter. As often before, Stalin ordered courts martial and executions following this debacle.

As part of his mid-January reorganization, Timoshenko divided his forces north of Lake Ladoga into two armies. The new 15th Army now had responsibility for operations around Kitilä. Its relief force of six divisions attacked in late January, but did not advance much beyond the frozen Uuksunjoki River. At the north end of the IV Corps sector, another six Soviet divisions lined up against the 12th Division, but never made it past Kollaa. This sector saw much fighting but very little movement for the rest of the war: its outcome was being decided farther south on the main front.

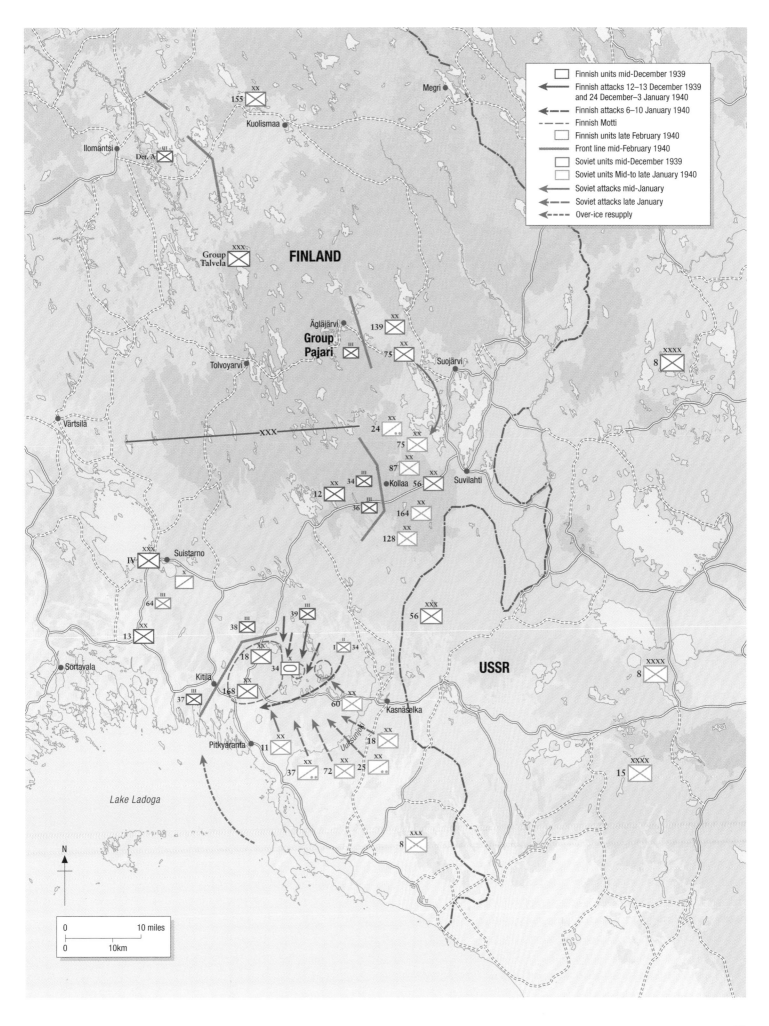

	Finnish units mid-December 1939
←	Finnish attacks 12–13 December 1939 and 24 December–3 January 1940
◄– – –	Finnish attacks 6–10 January 1940
– – –	Finnish Motti
	Finnish units late February 1940
▬▬	Front line mid-February 1940
	Soviet units mid-December 1939
	Soviet units Mid-to late January 1940
←	Soviet attacks mid-January
◄– – –	Soviet attacks late January
◄·····	Over-ice resupply

155

Megri

Kuolismaa

Ilomantsi

Det. A

Group
Talvela

FINLAND

Ägläjärvi

139

Group
Pajari

75

Suojärvi

8

Tolvoyarvi

Värtsilä

XXX

24

75

87

Kollaa 56

Suvilahti

34

12

36

164

128

XXX

IV

Suistarno

64

56

13

38

39

Sortavala

18

I 34

USSR

34

Kitilä

168

60

Kasnäselka

8

37

Pitkäranta 11

Uutsunjoki

18

37 72 25

15

Lake Ladoga

N

8

0   10 miles

0   10km

75

MAP 31: THE CENTRAL, SALLA AND PETSAMO FRONTS, 30 NOVEMBER 1939–15 FEBRUARY 1940

The Soviets attached much importance to the Petsamo and Salla operations shown here, but not so much on the central front (at the bottom of the adjoining map). Finnish strategy mirrored these priorities, as losing Petsamo and contact with the outside world (except through the German-controlled Baltic) and being split in two from Salla to Kerni would clearly be disastrous for the country.

In the far north, the Soviet 14th Army, basically on its own above the Arctic Circle, launched its attack against Petsamo in December and also sent some elements farther northwards towards the Rybachi Peninsula. In a clever manoeuvre, the White Sea Fleet carried the 52nd Rifle Division directly to the Petsamo area. Considering the port's strategic importance, the Finns left it barely defended, with only a couple of companies supported by artillery dating back to the 1880s on station. The two Soviet divisions easily shoved these aside and occupied Petsamo on 15 December. They then set down the deceptively named Arctic Highway (actually little more than a dirt track cleared through the tundra parallel to the Norwegian border) towards the town of Nautsi. As insignificant as the Arctic Highway may sound, it represented the only avenue the Finns could ever use to retake Petsamo. Group Pennanen conducted a fighting withdrawal down the road, strongly pursued by the 52nd Rifle Division. The numbers of troops involved clearly favoured the attackers. They reached the Nautsi area in mid-February and took the town a week prior to the ceasefire. Finland simply lacked the luxury of sufficient troops to make much of an effort in this theatre.

Meretskov's plan also had high hopes for the 9th Army's thrusts, nothing less than reaching the Gulf of Bothnia. In a pair of attacks, the 122nd Rifle Division took the lead against Salla and the 163rd Rifle Division headed for Suomussalmi. In lopsided combat, they quickly overwhelmed the battalion-sized screens that tried to bar their way. Both towns fell within two weeks, although the Soviets soon realized movement in this region would be very slow. Meanwhile, the Finns railed reinforcements to counter the threats, now under the command and control of the 9th Division. Within days of taking Salla, the 122nd Rifle Division, seeking to cut the Arctic Highway at Kemijärvi and reach the port of Kemi, had advanced 20 miles and launched a right-hook flanking attack. The Finns halted both thrusts,

counterattacked and managed to throw the Soviets halfway back to Salla. By the end of January, stalemate set in on this axis.

In the Suomussalmi area, Red Army forces, with the port of Oulu as their objective, never advanced much past the town. Not only did the narrow roads constrict their movement, but lakes crisscrossed the entire region, further isolating them. In very deep snow and with temperatures of -40°F, Finnish patrols dressed in white and on skis harassed them the whole way. The 9th Division used all this to its advantage when, without its slow-arriving artillery, it counterattacked against the 163rd Rifle Division on 12 December. It soon had the Soviets split into isolated parts. A week later, the 44th Rifle Division entered the fray in an attempt to reach and reinforce the 163rd. Finnish roadblocks easily prevented any sort of union, in the process creating numerous Motti pockets, similar to those shown on Map 30. Brutal fighting continued through the first week of January 1940. The two Soviet divisions suffered 27,500 killed and frozen to death, 300 tanks lost and much booty captured (including all the Soviet artillery and 50 tanks). Finnish casualties amounted to 900 dead and twice that wounded – heavy casualties for little Finland. But fighting here also came to a halt until the end of the war.

Soviet plans set up the lone 54th Mountain Division for failure in the Kuhmo, Lieksa and Ilomantsi sector. Its widely separated and non-mutually supporting attacks had little chance of success. By mid-December, it had failed to get close to either town. The Finnish 9th Division, itself very spread-out, dispatched a regiment to help the scattered battalions hold back the attackers. Near Kuhmo, these forces created several Mottis around two regiments of the 54th Mountain Division. Timoshenko sent the 23rd Rifle Division in support, but to no avail. This marked the Red Army's first use of ski troops –2,000 of them – but the Finns managed to kill or capture most. As with the failed assaults around Salla and Suomussalmi, this marked the end of the 9th Army's mediocre contributions to the Winter War[6].

---

6 Somehow, the 9th Army's fiascos did not negatively affect the career of its commander, General Vasily Chuikov, who went on to save Stalingrad and take the surrender of Berlin.

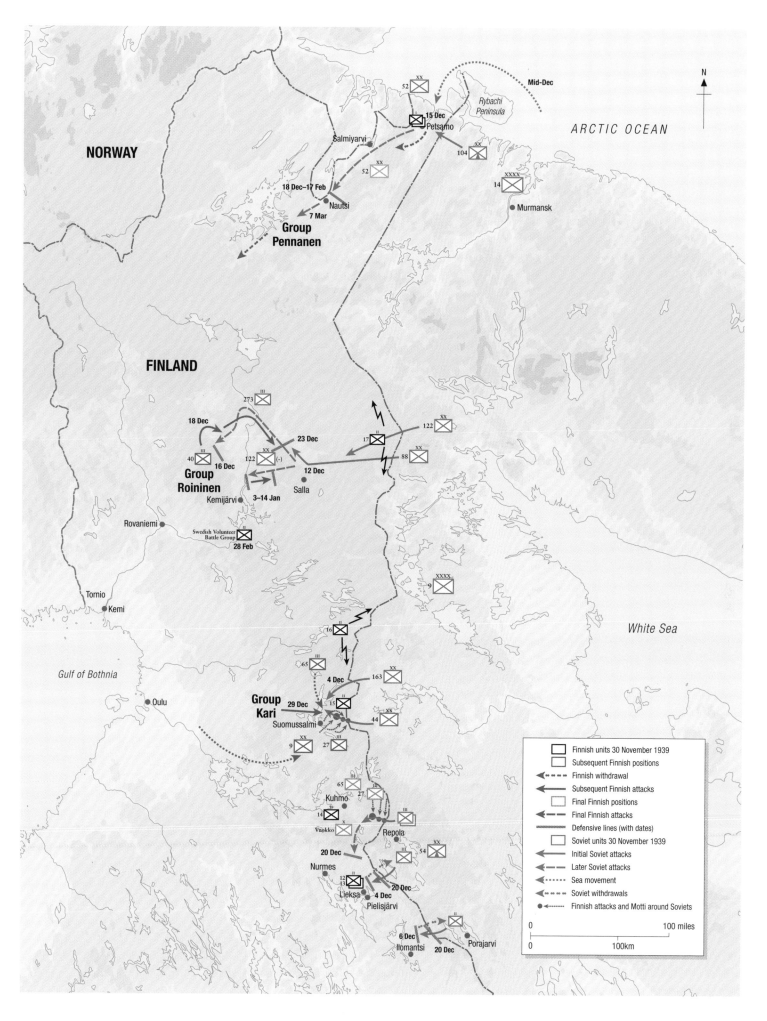

NORWAY

FINLAND

Rybachi
Peninsula

ARCTIC OCEAN

Mid-Dec

52 XX

15 Dec
Petsamo

Salmiyarvi

104 XX

52 XX

14 XXXX

18 Dec–17 Feb

Nautsi

7 Mar

Murmansk

Group
Pennanen

273 III

18 Dec

23 Dec

122 XX

17 II

88 XX

40 III

16 Dec

122 XX (-)

12 Dec

Group
Roininen

Kemijärvi

Salla

3–14 Jan

Rovaniemi

Swedish Volunteer
Battle Group

28 Feb

9 XXXX

Tornio

Kemi

White Sea

Gulf of Bothnia

16 II

65 III

4 Dec

163 XX

Oulu

Group
Kari

29 Dec

15 II

44 XX

Suomussalmi

9 XX

27 III

65 XX

27 II

Kuhmo

14 II

III

Vuokko

X

Repola

20 Dec

III

54 XX

Nurmes

12 13 II

Lieksa

4 Dec

20 Dec

Pielisjärvi

6 Dec

Ilomantsi

20 Dec

Porajarvi

☐	Finnish units 30 November 1939
☐	Subsequent Finnish positions
◀---	Finnish withdrawal
◀━━	Subsequent Finnish attacks
☐	Final Finnish positions
◀━	Final Finnish attacks
━━	Defensive lines (with dates)
☐	Soviet units 30 November 1939
◀━	Initial Soviet attacks
◀ – –	Later Soviet attacks
◀······	Sea movement
◀- - -	Soviet withdrawals
●·······	Finnish attacks and Motti around Soviets

0   100 miles

0   100km

MAPS 32 AND 33: THE SOVIET OCCUPATION OF THE BALTIC STATES AND BESSARABIA

Stalin's last landgrab came in the spring and summer of 1940, while war with France and Britain distracted Hitler. His final efforts to recreate the national boundaries of the tsars came in the north-west and south-west of the USSR. Along the way, in its mostly bloodless wars (except for Finland) between 1939 and 1940, the Soviet military learned some valuable lessons in command and control and airborne and mechanized operations and showcased at least one general from the new generation that would win World War II: Zhukov.

MAP 32: SOVIET OCCUPATION OF BALTIC STATES

In September and October 1939, the USSR forced lengthy treaties of mutual assistance on the Baltic States. This gave it some army and air force basing rights, access to raw materials and began the process of undermining the new republics, struggling to find their way in the harsh region between Hitler and Stalin. It is hard to see that the three little nations accrued any 'assistance' from these arrangements. When Molotov met the Estonian foreign minister to discuss the treaty, he said the USSR would station 35,000 troops in the country. The Estonian pointed out this meant the Red Army would outnumber his own army, so Molotov reduced the number to 25,000. Himself a master of creeping aggrandisement, Hitler knew immediately what Stalin intended to do, so days later ordered nearly 90,000 *Volksdeutsche* (ethnic Germans) living in the Baltic region 'home' to the Reich.

In May 1940, Molotov turned up the pressure on the three republics, accusing them of 'provocative acts' against Soviet citizens and solders within their borders. The USSR then initiated a hostile propaganda campaign and started massing troops in the north-east. In early June, it began staged border incidents and commenced blatant interference in the domestic politics of all three states. Lithuania, large and thickly populated (including significant Belorussian, Jewish and Polish minorities), had been a political football. Hitler and Stalin kicked it back and forth in August and September 1939 as they negotiated spheres of influence. Stalin ultimately won the game and would make the country his first Baltic target.

An ultimatum to Lithuania followed on 14 September, which demanded that the Red Army be allowed in. The small republic had no real options other than to agree to the terms. On the next day, the 3rd and 11th Armies entered the country unopposed, aided by Soviet troops already stationed there as part of the September 1939 deal that returned the historical capital of Vilnius. On the 16th, Stalin repeated the process with Latvia and Estonia. Days later, the 8th Army took over both countries.

The Soviets immediately stationed large garrisons in all three countries, which as of 3 August were referred to as Soviet Socialist Republics. New elections chose only 'working class' candidates and almost all private businesses were nationalized. The Soviets murdered or deported to the interior of the USSR thousands of native Balts.

MAP 33: SOVIET OCCUPATION OF BESSARABIA

Stalin also coveted Bessarabia, part of Russia since 1812 but awarded to Romania by the 1920 Treaty of Paris (not signed by Moscow). The Molotov–Ribbentrop Pact confirmed that the region lay within the Soviet sphere of influence. Even before Hitler invaded Western Europe, the Soviets began making moves towards Bessarabia. This included ordering the Odessa Military District to begin planning for offensive operations. Command and control soon passed to the new Southern Front under Zhukov, consisting of the 5th, 9th and 12th Armies, numbering about 40 divisions, 15 brigades and numerous smaller units. Zhukov planned for opposed and unopposed attacks.

Molotov intensified Soviet bullying on 26 June 1940, with an ultimatum demanding Romania evacuate Bessarabia. The Romanian government initially wanted to resist, so began diplomatic activity to support this decision. But four days earlier, its main interwar patron, France, had surrendered to Germany and was treaty-bound to not care about Romania. The next day, Molotov upped the ante and threatened prompt military action if the Romanians continued to dawdle. On the advice of Hitler and Mussolini, they agreed on the 28th. That same day, the Romanians began withdrawing their civil and military authorities, including abandoning numerous defensive fortifications.

Zhukov moved out immediately with his three armies abreast and the Romanians offered no resistance. His troops entered the cities of Chisinau and Chernauti the same day the Romanians left. By the 30th, they had reached the Prut River, completing the occupation. They also took northern Bukovina – as Molotov put it, 'the last missing remnant from a United Ukraine'[7]. Stalin had increased the USSR by 20 million people and 286,000 square miles.

7 Alan Bullock, *Hitler and Stalin: Parallel Lives*, Knopf: New York, 1992, p. 678.

MAP 33 (top map)

USSR

POLAND · ROMANIA

Tarnopol · Vinnitsa · Uman

Bug · Dnestr · Prut · Prut · Danube

Kamanets Podolsk · Chernauti · Balti · Chisinau · Iasi · Tiraspol · Odessa · Galati · Focsani · Ploesti · Bucharest · Constanta

Soviet Occupied Poland · Kolomya

Black Sea

XXXX 12/5 · XXX 15 · XXX 17 · XXX 13 · XXX 8 · XXX 49 · XXX 36 · XXXX 5/9 · XXX 35 · XXX 37 · XXX 5 · XXX 7 · III 55 · III 201 · III 204

MAP 33

0 — 50km · 0 — 50 miles

N

MAP 32 (bottom map)

Occupied Polish territory

0 — 100km · 0 — 100 miles

Gulf of Finland

Kingisepp · Pskov · Ostrov · Tartu · Rezekne · Tallinn · Haapsalu · Parnu · Valga

ESTONIA

HIIUMAA · MUHU · SAAREMAA

Gulf of Riga

Riga · Tukums · Ventspils · Liepaja · Memel

LATVIA

Jekabpils · Daugavpils · Utena · Sventiany · Vilnius · Jonava · Kaunas · Siauliai · Alytus · Lida · Grodno

LITHUANIA

Königsberg

EAST PRUSSIA

POLAND · Suwalki · Minsk · Niemen

USSR

XX 11 · XXX 1 · XXX 19 · XXX OCK · III 201 · XX 16 · III 214 · XX 67 · XXXX 8/3 · XXX 4 · XXX 3 · XXX 24 · XXXX 3/11 · XXX 10 · XXX 11 · XXX 6

N

MAP 32

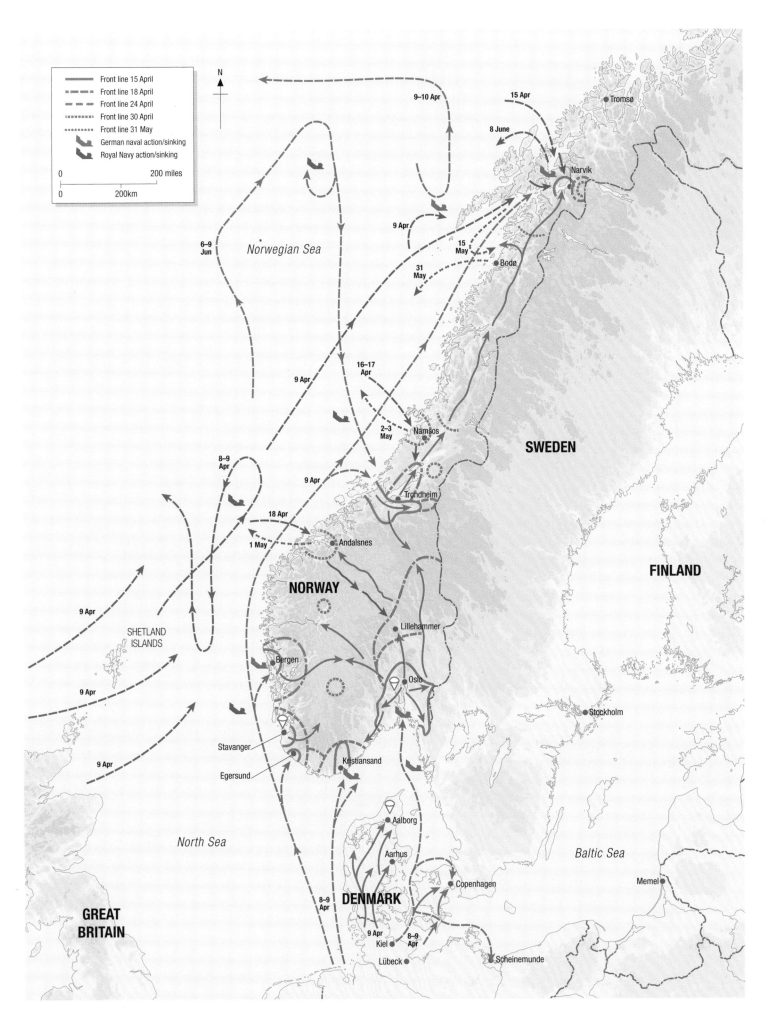

Front line 15 April
Front line 18 April
Front line 24 April
Front line 30 April
Front line 31 May
German naval action/sinking
Royal Navy action/sinking

0   200 miles
0   200km

N

Norwegian Sea

9–10 Apr

15 Apr

8 June

Narvik

Tromsø

9 Apr

15 May

31 May

Bodø

6–9 Jun

16–17 Apr

2–3 May

Namsos

SWEDEN

9 Apr

8–9 Apr

9 Apr

Trondheim

18 Apr

1 May

Andalsnes

NORWAY

FINLAND

Lillehammer

9 Apr

SHETLAND ISLANDS

9 Apr

Bergen

Oslo

Stockholm

9 Apr

Stavanger

Egersund

Kristiansand

North Sea

Aalborg

Aarhus

Baltic Sea

Copenhagen

Memel

8–9 Apr

DENMARK

GREAT BRITAIN

9 Apr

Kiel

8–9 Apr

Lübeck

Scheinemunde

CHAPTER 4:
THE SCANDINAVIAN CAMPAIGN

German geography did not favour its navy. During the Great War, except for sailings by individual ships and a few notable episodes involving large groups, the Royal Navy limited the fleet to the German Bight. During the interwar period, German naval commanders and staffs wrestled with potential problems of geography in a future war.

Commander-in-chief of the Kriegsmarine, Admiral Erich Raeder, had toyed with the idea of naval bases in Norway, particularly in Trondheim and Narvik. He believed this would give his ships many more options to get to the open ocean and conduct operations against Allied navies. In addition, he thought possessing Norway would allow Germany to indirectly control commodities exported from Sweden, which came through Narvik, most notably in winter when much of the greater Baltic froze over. He raised these points with Hitler during the first half of October 1939, but at the time the Führer could only think of the pending Western campaign. Additionally, keeping Norway neutral for the moment represented the best course for Germany, which imported Swedish iron ore (20 per cent of all its imports) through Narvik and the ports along the Norwegian coast.[8]

Weeks later everything changed when Stalin invaded Finland. Immediately, the League of Nations began to talk of giving assistance to Finland, most likely British and French troops. When the Finns lost their port at Petsamo (see Map 31), attention shifted to Narvik as the best possible entrepôt. History does not treat kindly British and French promises to help Finland and besides, Norway and Sweden showed no enthusiasm for getting involved in the Winter War, or jeopardizing their neutrality. Demonstrating excellent political skills, Raeder encouraged a series of meetings in mid-December between Hitler and Vidkun Quisling, leader of Norway's fascist Nasjonal Samling (National Unity Party, which had around 15,000 members in a country of 3.5 million). During these meetings, Hitler determined on the eventual invasion of Norway. At the same time, winter weather caused repeated postponements of the Western campaign, freeing Hitler's hands (see Maps 42 and 43). He therefore created an OKW planning staff on 27 January 1940, but did not inform the OKH. Preparations received an impetus in mid-February, when the Royal Navy destroyer *Cossack* violated Norwegian neutrality

8   By 1939, Germany imported approximately 10 million tons of ore from Sweden, with between one-quarter and one-third coming through Narvik, in particular between December and April.

by pursing the German merchantman *Altmark* into Jossing Fjord[9]. Days later, Hitler demanded the Wehrmacht expedite its preparations of the Scandinavian operation, now named *Weserübung* (Training Exercise Weser).

On 20 February, after a brief meeting, Hitler chose Generalleutnant Nikolaus von Falkenhorst and his XXI Armee-Korps to conduct the invasion (again, he left the OKH out of the decision). The corps staff included capturing Denmark in the operation and on 1 March, Hitler approved the plans. The staff finally brought the three services into the planning process when it started demanding troops, ships and planes. Thanks only to middle- and lower-echelon commanders and staffs, preparations proceeded professionally. Four days later, Hitler had a conference with his very angry service chiefs to smooth their ruffled feathers. The plan included paratroopers from the 7. Flieger-Division and 'Trojan Horse' merchant ships in Norwegian harbours, full of troops ready to jump ashore when ordered. Assaults against Trondheim and Narvik represented the touchiest part of the operation; German ships would be at sea for a long time, far from Luftwaffe air cover and vulnerable to the vastly superior Royal Navy. Capturing Oslo would be a joint air–sea operation, while the Luftwaffe had sole responsibility against Stavanger and its airfield at Sola; however, ship-borne army troops would attack most Norwegian locales. Most of the Kriegsmarine, including 28 U-boats (recalled from their anti-commerce shipping duties), would be involved. Flieger-Korps X had command and control responsibility for the Luftwaffe contribution, including 500 Ju 52 transports, 220 bombers and more than 100 fighters. One of its most critical tasks would be to capture the Sola airfield and to quickly establish a Luftwaffe base there to cover both ground and sea operations in central and southern Norway.

Two infantry divisions augmented by one motorized brigade would conduct the invasion of Denmark, *Weserübung Süd*. Airborne troops would seize the two Aalborg airfields in north Jutland, while the World War I battleship *Schleswig-Holstein* was pressed into first-line duty again, landing troops in central Denmark.

Hitler's directive for the twin invasions called for 'a peaceful occupation' due to begin on 15 March. That date got pushed back for a number of reasons, including effects of the same extreme winter that had hindered the Soviets in Finland. Foreign intelligence services and military attachés began hearing rumours of the operation in late March. Spies and their own sighting of the massive German flotilla heading for Norway could not convince the Danes of the impending danger. On 2 April, Hitler set the invasion date as the 9th. The next day, the Trojan Horse freighters set sail, followed on the 6th and 7th by the warships. Around the same time, British and French militaries finally awoke to the danger. There would be many chance encounters between German and British ships and planes on 7 and 8 April, but on the morning of the 9th, most invading Germans arrived at the appointed time and place.

History's first airborne combat operation took place early on 9 April, as the Luftwaffe took the Aalborg airfields and bridges leading to southern Zeeland (Copenhagen). Civilian ferries, warships and cargo ships (including Trojan Horses) carried the 198. Infanterie-Division to the various islands making up eastern Denmark. Copenhagen's docks were close to the Amalienborg Palace and most government buildings in the city centre, making for a short march for the Landsers. Luftwaffe bombers buzzed the capital and dropped leaflets, while King Christian X personally ordered his royal guardsmen to stop fighting back. Meanwhile, the reinforced 170. Infanterie-Division advanced up the Jutland Peninsula. By noon, limited and uncoordinated Danish resistance ended. Worst from a Wehrmacht perspective, 12 British submarines could now operate in the previously neutral Kattegat and Skagerrak, eventually scoring numerous hits on the many German ships heading to and from Norway. Luftwaffe planes flying out of the Aalborg airfields somewhat cancelled this advantage.

A little late, on 7 April, the Royal Navy Home Fleet left Scapa Flow in search of the Germans, assumed to be breaking out into the Atlantic. The next day, Royal Navy ships laid several minefields at various places in Norwegian waters (as they had done in World War I). Norway had not been at war since 1814 and the attitude of the current Labour government bordered on pacifism, although it leaned towards the Allies. Except for mobilizing single battalions at four key port cities, it did little against the German threat that was growing by the hour. Early on the morning of 9 April, flotillas of Kriegsmarine warships and merchantmen sailed up the various fjords leading to the Norwegian ports they intended to occupy: Narvik, Trondheim, Bergen, Kristiansand and Oslo, while paratroopers took Stavanger. The Germans expected to encounter little to no resistance, but the Norwegians had other plans.

The cities taken by the Germans on day one of *Weserübung* did not merely represent the small nation's largest conurbations and gateways to the wider world, they also housed the mobilization stations for five of its six divisions. Therefore, as the Germans had done in Poland, they seriously disrupted Norway's mobilization; this would affect the entire campaign. Capturing the Sola airfield, and the Luftwaffe's ability to quickly make it into a forward operating base, turned out to be the major coup of the war. The mere threat of Stukas and other bombers flying out of Sola kept the Royal Navy at arm's length. It also caused the Allies to implicitly abandon southern Norway to its fate. Most landings went off without serious incident, except for at Oslo, where turn-of-the-century defences sank a German heavy cruiser. Elsewhere along the coast, the Germans came ashore with few losses. Norwegian Army units therefore had to mobilize in the rough terrain of the sparsely populated countryside, mostly without access to their heavy equipment and weapons depots, which the Germans controlled.

After one week, the Germans had 24,700 troops in Norway and 40,000 after two weeks. Greatly aided by near-total Luftwaffe air superiority, German troops spread out from each of the port cities. However, with no prospect of outside assistance, the Norwegians fought a losing battle in the south. Hoping to take advantage of Norway's great length, the Allies planned relief operations in the far north, supposedly out of range of most German aircraft. Fighting devolved to a collection

---

9   *Altmark* was indeed unarmed, as Norwegian authorities told the captain of *Cossack*, but below decks she had c.300 British POW sailors from ships captured by *Admiral Graf Spee* (see Map 81).

of separated, non-mutually supporting actions for both sides. Initial landings in mid-April at Namsos and Åndalsnes (against Trondheim) plus Narvik went sufficiently well, but unfortunately for the Allies, several factors condemned the two missions. First, judging command and control facilities in Norway to be inadequate, the British commander of the landings tried to direct them from faraway London. Assuming that the Germans had only landed light detachments, the Allies brought little artillery and no tanks and suffered from inefficient loading of their transport ships. Finally, they had no air support of any type, a major handicap in any World War II battle. The Namsos operation seemed aimless and foundered against the even-odds situation around Trondheim. Nor could the Allies capitalize on their superior weight at Narvik.

Despite Allied naval superiority, in two months the Germans made 249 successful sailings to Norway, delivering 108,000 troops and more than 100,000 tons of supplies at a cost of 21 ships sunk. By the end of April, Hitler felt confident enough about the course of *Weserübung* to approve the invasion of France and the Low Countries for early the next month. This offensive, and in particular the clear indications of overwhelming success within its first ten days, put the final nail into the coffin of Allied efforts in Norway. On the last day of May, the British cabinet approved the evacuation of Narvik. A week later, the Allies had abandoned Norway and the country sued for peace.

Combat deaths for both sides amounted to nearly 3,600, although men lost at sea made up 60 per cent of the German total. Naval losses were approximately equal, but extremely lopsided as a proportion of the two fleets. Kriegsmarine losses crippled German naval strategy for the remainder of the war; after Norway, only U-boats represented any sort of strategic naval threat. *Weserübung* seemed like another audacious triumph for Hitler and another inept humiliation for the Allies. The debacle brought down prime ministers Neville Chamberlain and Édouard Daladier. However, Norway turned into a hollow victory and a strategic dead end for Germany: It never became the haven for the Kriegsmarine that Raeder had hoped, and, throughout the war, Hitler insisted on a ridiculously large garrison that deprived the Wehrmacht of valuable troops needed elsewhere.

MAP 35: NAVAL OPERATIONS AND THE NORWEGIAN DEFENCES

While not a single battle like Jutland in 1916, the various naval engagements during the Norwegian campaign represented the largest connected combat between the Royal Navy and Kriegsmarine in World War II. As is often the case in war, a few hours can mean the difference between life and death, or success and failure. So it was here, as the Germans got the jump on the British by the slightest of margins. Taking place right in the massive Royal Navy's backyard as it were, the heavily outnumbered Kriegsmarine's audacious plan and execution is remarkable. Although the Luftwaffe's materiel effect on the naval battles was more limited than, for example, off the coast of Greece and Crete, its psychological effect was great.

Raeder's naval staff contributed significantly to planning *Weserübung*, in particular Kapitän zur See Theodore Krancke, whose recommendations were adopted almost entirely. The small Kriegsmarine would have to employ just about every surface unit in the invasion of Norway. Its role was not limited to fighting the Royal Navy or escorting transports, but included delivering many soldiers to target port cities. U-boats acted as lookouts while searching for targets of opportunity. The navy had only a small role to play in the invasion of Denmark. The many missions of the Royal Navy, despite its size, stretched the fleet very thin. Numerous small groups of its small ships mined Norwegian waters. Winter weather also limited British air reconnaissance, much to the Germans' advantage.

The German groups were as follows. Group 1: Battlecruisers *Scharnhorst* and *Gneisenau* plus ten destroyers carrying 2,000 mountain troops had the farthest to go, Narvik, so left Germany on the night of 6 April. Group 2: Heavy cruiser *Admiral Hipper* and four destroyers combined to ferry 1,700 troops to Trondheim. Groups 3 and 4: Army–navy groups in light cruisers made for Bergen and Kristiansand. Group 5: Panzer ship *Lützow* and heavy cruiser *Blücher* plus light cruisers and smaller craft headed for Oslo.

Meanwhile, the British could not decide if they wanted to make their own landings in Norway, simply frustrate the Germans, or maybe try a third option. On 8 and 9 April, heavy seas made things dangerous for sailors and ships on both sides. There were many near misses, but an engagement between *Admiral Hipper* and the destroyer HMS *Glowworm* on the 8th ended with *Glowworm* sunk and *Admiral Hipper* limping into Trondheim a day later with a 4-degree list to starboard.

All the German naval groups generally arrived at their appointed invasion sites on the designated morning. All had managed to avoid the British aircraft and ships with minimal interference. Perhaps most remarkable, Group 1 made it to faraway Narvik. As it neared Westfjord, the two battlecruisers peeled west to draw away the Royal Navy while the ten destroyers arrived at Narvik with their load of (doubtless seasick) soldiers. In a ten-minute duel, three 15in. hits from HMS *Renown* caused some damage to *Gneisenau* before the German ship escaped (*Renown* suffered only minor damage from 11in. hits). Light cruisers *Köln* and *Königsberg* made it to Bergen, while despite heavy fog, light cruiser *Karlsruhe* landed successfully at Kristiansand. However, that same day, Skua dive-bombers sank *Königsberg*, while a British submarine sank *Karlsruhe*. Worst from the German perspective was the Oslo operation: the turn-of-the-century Oscarborg fortress guarding Oslofjord sank *Blücher* (just short of the city, with the loss of hundreds of crewmen and soldiers,) while another British submarine damaged *Lützow*, which returned to Germany

The Royal Navy scored a major victory at Narvik. Ten German destroyers lay in the nearby fjords after torpedoing two Norwegian coastal defence ships on 9 April. Five British destroyers came at them on the 10th, sinking two German destroyers and six merchantmen at a cost of two of their own. Three days later, the battleship HMS *Warspite* and nine destroyers entered the fjord and sank the remaining German ships, leaving the soldiers completely isolated and unsupported. *Warspite* and her escorts returned to bombard German ground troops two weeks later.

Naval combat tapered off markedly after that, as the Kriegsmarine licked its wounds and the Royal Navy avoided the Luftwaffe. British submarines sank the occasional German transport. In mid-April, the Allies landed three groups of troops along the central coast without incident. However, when the Allies evacuated their Trondheim expedition in early May, the Luftwaffe sank one British destroyer and one French destroyer.

The Royal Navy's worst loss came following the Narvik evacuation. On 8 June, aircraft carrier HMS *Glorious* and two escorting destroyers encountered the two German battlecruisers, repaired and returned to battle. With planes unable to fly due to weather and heavy seas, it was an unfair fight. All three British ships went down, losing 1,515 of 1,561 sailors, while both battlecruisers sustained damage, one from the engagement, the other from mines on the way home. Though the Kriegsmarine definitely contributed to the operational success of *Weserübung,* the Royal Navy never lost its dominant position.

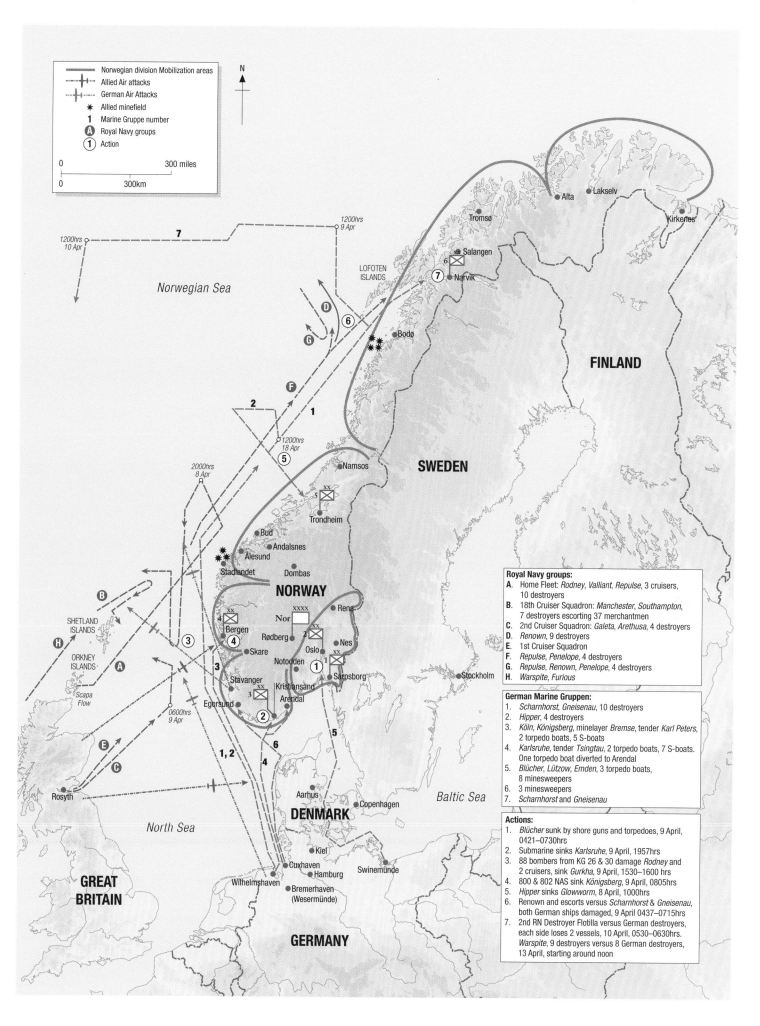

Norwegian division Mobilization areas
Allied Air attacks
German Air Attacks
⁕ Allied minefield
1 Marine Gruppe number
Ⓐ Royal Navy groups
① Action

0 ———— 300 miles
0 ———— 300km

N

Norwegian Sea

LOFOTEN
ISLANDS

FINLAND

Alta • • Lakselv
Tromsø •
⁎ Salangen
⑦ Narvik

1200hrs
10 Apr

7

1200hrs
9 Apr

Ⓓ
⑥
Ⓖ
• Bodø
⁕⁕

Ⓕ

2
1

1200hrs
18 Apr
⑤

• Namsos

SWEDEN

2000hrs
8 Apr

xx
5 ⊠
Trondheim

• Bud
Andalsnes
⁕⁕
Alesund •
Stadlandet
Dombas

NORWAY

Rena •

4 xx
⊠
Bergen
④
Rødberg
xxxx
Nor ☐ 2 xx
⊠
• Nes
Skare
Oslo
Notodden ①
Stavanger
xx
3 ⊠
Kristiansand
Arendal
Egersund
②
③
④
5
6
1, 2
4

Sarpsborg

• Stockholm

Baltic Sea

SHETLAND
ISLANDS
Ⓗ

ORKNEY
ISLANDS
Ⓐ
③
Ⓑ
Scapa
Flow

0600hrs
9 Apr
Ⓔ
Ⓒ

Rosyth

Aarhus •
• Copenhagen

DENMARK

North Sea

Kiel •

**GREAT
BRITAIN**

Cuxhaven •
• Hamburg
Wilhelmshaven •
• Bremerhaven
(Wesermünde)

Swinemünde •

GERMANY

Royal Navy groups:
A. Home Fleet: *Rodney, Valliant, Repulse*, 3 cruisers,
   10 destroyers
B. 18th Cruiser Squadron: *Manchester, Southampton*,
   7 destroyers escorting 37 merchantmen
C. 2nd Cruiser Squadron: *Galeta, Arethusa*, 4 destroyers
D. *Renown*, 9 destroyers
E. 1st Cruiser Squadron
F. *Repulse, Penelope*, 4 destroyers
G. *Repulse, Renown, Penelope*, 4 destroyers
H. *Warspite, Furious*

German Marine Gruppen:
1. *Scharnhorst, Gneisenau*, 10 destroyers
2. *Hipper*, 4 destroyers
3. *Köln, Königsberg*, minelayer *Bremse*, tender *Karl Peters*,
   2 torpedo boats, 5 S-boats
4. *Karlsruhe*, tender *Tsingtau*, 2 torpedo boats, 7 S-boats.
   One torpedo boat diverted to Arendal
5. *Blücher, Lützow, Emden*, 3 torpedo boats,
   8 minesweepers
6. 3 minesweepers
7. *Scharnhorst* and *Gneisenau*

Actions:
1. *Blücher* sunk by shore guns and torpedoes, 9 April,
   0421–0730hrs
2. Submarine sinks *Karlsruhe*, 9 April, 1957hrs
3. 88 bombers from KG 26 & 30 damage *Rodney* and
   2 cruisers, sink *Gurkha*, 9 April, 1530–1600 hrs
4. 800 & 802 NAS sink *Königsberg*, 9 April, 0805hrs
5. *Hipper* sinks *Glowworm*, 8 April, 1000hrs
6. Renown and escorts versus *Scharnhorst* & *Gneisenau*,
   both German ships damaged, 9 April 0437–0715hrs
7. 2nd RN Destroyer Flotilla versus German destroyers,
   each side loses 2 vessels, 10 April, 0530–0630hrs.
   Warspite, 9 destroyers versus 8 German destroyers,
   13 April, starting around noon

MAP 36: THE INVASION OF DENMARK, 9 APRIL 1940

Germany (Prussia) had last invaded Denmark in 1864. As part of the 1935 Anglo-German Naval Treaty, the Royal Navy agreed to vacate the Baltic; Britain would allow Germany and the Soviet Union to struggle over that body of water. After that, Denmark fell increasingly under the influence of the Third Reich. In his February 1940 plan, General von Falkenhorst added the capture all of this small nation, not just the airfields in Jutland, as a change to Operation *Weserübung*.

The Germans had a number of reasons for taking their small neighbour to the north. Of immediate importance was the fact that Denmark stood astride both sea and air lines of communication for its forces attacking Norway. Of more long-term importance, German air defences extended no farther north than Schleswig, so RAF bombers could easily fly over Denmark to avoid the flak. Planning and preparation took longer than the actual 2–3-hour attack. As for the Danes, 'preserving Danish society' and avoiding unnecessary destruction topped their list of national objectives. However, they did strengthen their defences during the eight months of the Phoney War.

The invasion began with two parachute attacks early in the morning of 9 April. A platoon from 4. Kompanie of Fallschirmjäger-Regiment 1 jumped into the two airfields in Aalborg and captured them without a shot. The rest of the company landed near the bridge joining the islands of Falster and Zeeland and took them and the adjoining Fort Vordingborg easily. The III. Bataillon of the 305. Infanterie-Regiment arrived by ferry to join them shortly thereafter. History's first airborne attack ended in success. Within an hour, Ju 52s delivered III./

Infanterie-Regiment 159 to Aalborg, cementing the victory. The Luftwaffe then used these airfields to support operations in Norway.

In Copenhagen 1,000 men from II./Infanterie-Regiment 308 (198. Infanterie-Division) aboard a Trojan Horse merchant ship tied up at the port for two days, disembarked and marched towards the royal palace. At a cost of six dead and a dozen wounded guardsmen (half of all Danish casualties that morning), the bodyguard of King Christian X put up a brief fight until the 70-year-old monarch ordered them to stop. The sight of German soldiers marching through their capital amazed Danes, riding their bicycles to work that morning. A flight of He 111 bombers and Bf 110 fighters buzzed the capital to reinforce the message of the all-conquering Wehrmacht. The 198. Infanterie-Division subdued the other Danish islands with little trouble.

On the Jutland Peninsula, the forewarned Danes barely screened their border with Germany for fear of providing a provocation, not that any was needed. The 170. Infanterie-Division, reinforced by 11. Schützen-Brigade (a motorized infantry brigade of two regiments of two battalions each) and a battalion of panzers raced north on roughly parallel courses. The Jutland Division's widely separated regiments did not put up much of a fight. The Germans reached the north of Jutland as fast as their vehicles could carry them.

Hitler hoped to make Denmark a model of German–Nordic cooperative occupation. However, by 1943, the Danish resistance was so active and strong that the Germans unleashed a reprisal campaign. Eventually, like Norway, a disproportionately large occupation force was required to keep this small country at heel.

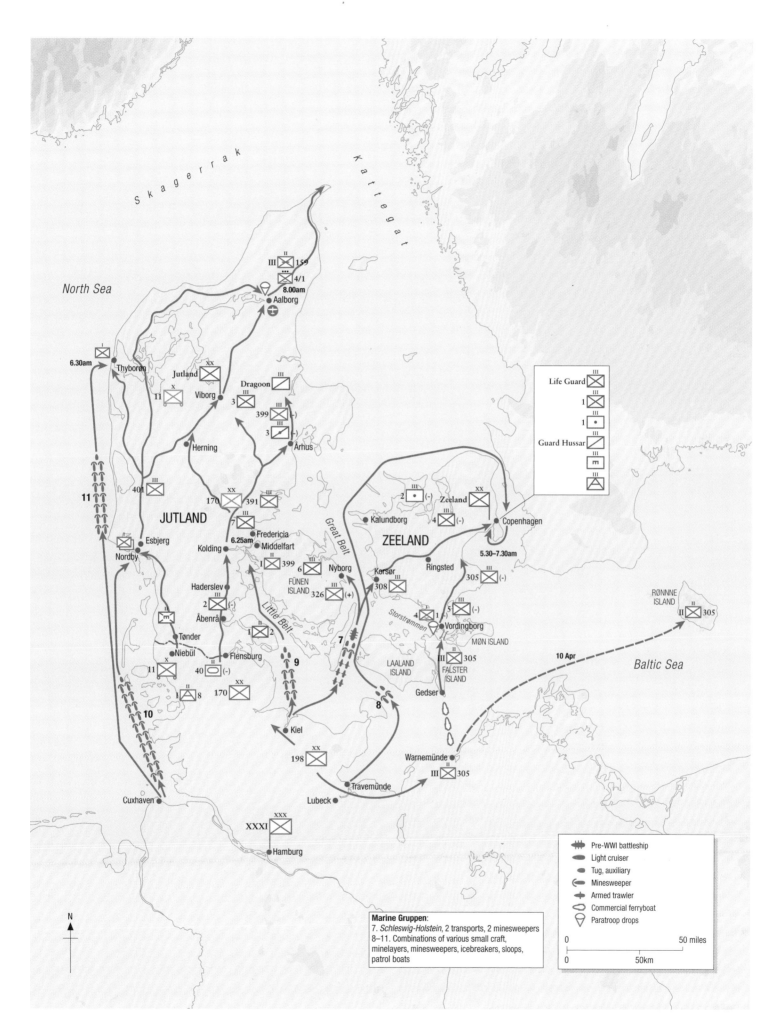

Skagerrak

Kattegat

North Sea

III II 159

*** 4/1
8.00am

Aalborg

6.30am

Thyborøn

Jutland   XX

11   X

Viborg

Dragoon   III

3   III

399   III (-)

3   (-)   Århus

Herning

401   III

170   XX   391   III

JUTLAND

7   III

Fredericia

Kolding   6.25am   Middelfart

I   II   399

6   III   Nyborg

FÜNEN
ISLAND

326   III (+)

Haderslev

2   III (-)

Åbenrå

1   II   2

Little Belt

Esbjerg

Nordby

Tønder

Niebül

11   X

40   (-)   Flensburg

1   II   8   170   XX

9

Kiel

10

198   XX

Cuxhaven

XXXI   XXX

Hamburg

Great Belt

ZEELAND

2   III (-)   Zeeland   XX

4   III (-)

Kalundborg

Copenhagen

5.30–7.30am

Korsør   Ringsted   305   III (-)

308   III

Storstrømmen

4   III   1   5   III (-)

Vordingborg   MØN ISLAND

LAALAND
ISLAND

III   305

FALSTER
ISLAND

Gedser

7

8

Warnemünde

III   305

Travemünde

Lubeck

10 Apr   Baltic Sea

RØNNNE
ISLAND

II   305

Life Guard   III   XX

1   III   XX

1   III

Guard Hussar   III

III   m

III

N

Marine Gruppen:
7. *Schleswig-Holstein*, 2 transports, 2 minesweepers
8–11. Combinations of various small craft,
minelayers, minesweepers, icebreakers, sloops,
patrol boats

Pre-WWI battleship
Light cruiser
Tug, auxiliary
Minesweeper
Armed trawler
Commercial ferryboat
Paratroop drops

0   50 miles
0   50km

MAP 37: OSLO AND CENTRAL NORWAY, 9–30 APRIL 1940

Despite being isolated geographically, close to Germany and under the Luftwaffe umbrella, fighting here nevertheless lasted until the end of April. Bounded by Sweden to the east and high mountains with steep valleys to the north and west, the region had large flat areas around Oslo and was home to nearly half of Norway's population.

German staffs had inadequate maps of Norway, so to begin planning *Weserübung*, Falkenhausen had to buy his own Baedeker travel maps. They planned a straightforward attack on the capital, followed by ground forces fanning out in all directions. The assault on Oslo began disastrously. Between 0300 and 0400 hours, Marinegruppe 5 sailed up Oslofjord and managed to capture three forts guarding its entrance, but in so doing lost the element of surprise. The flotilla continued up the narrow channel when, at 0521 hours, the forewarned Oscarsborg fort opened fire, hitting the large, brand new *Blücher* with 11in. guns and torpedoes from both sides. She sank two hours later, taking 320 German sailors and soldiers down with her, including many from the 163. Infanterie-Division staff.

The rest of the ships retreated and dropped off their army passengers at Son and Moss, over 20 miles from Oslo. Meanwhile, the bulk of I./Fallschirmjäger-Regiment 1 encountered bad weather and then alerted defenders at the Oslo airfield at Fornebu. Parachutists coming in around 0720 hours turned back on account of fog. The second wave, II./Infanterie-Regiment 324, coming in 20 minutes later aboard 52 Ju 52s supported by eight Bf 110s, expected to land at an already secured airstrip. Instead, they encountered deadly anti-aircraft fire. The *Zerstörer* (Bf 110) fighters suppressed as many of the Norwegian gunners as they could, until all aircraft fuel tanks had mere drops remaining. Higher headquarters ordered them to abort, but there was little point in doing that at this stage, so the commander on the scene disobeyed. Within a couple hours, a stream of transports landed at Fornebu, the Landsers captured it and began marching for Oslo, where their comrades emerging from Trojan Horse ships already had the upper hand. Thanks to the *Blücher* fiasco, the capture of Oslo remained in doubt until that night.

With the German timetables hours behind due to these problems, King Haakon VII, his cabinet, the Storting (parliament) and much of Norway's gold reserves escaped north-west towards Elverum, covered

by a battalion from the 5th Regiment. Nine German companies had sufficed to capture Oslo. Transport sinkings meant that the two infantry divisions involved –163. and 198. Infanterie Divisionen – arrived piecemeal and created improvised battle groups. They pushed around partially mobilized elements of the 1st and 2nd Divisions; these two could barely put together a brigade of troops between them. Within a couple days of arriving, the Germans had commandeered motor transport and began pushing defenders towards internment in Sweden or other German units coming from the direction of the North Sea. Colonel Otto Ruge, recently promoted to overall command of the Norwegian defences, attempted to pen in the Germans. On 14 April, a company of *Fallschirmjäger* dropped into Dombas to block any aid coming to Ruge. They held out for five days without any outside reinforcements or resupply, before being forced to surrender.

The defenders conducted a fighting withdrawal towards Trondheim, where Ruge expected Allied relief expeditions to arrive at any time. The British 148th Infantry Brigade indeed landed at Åndalsnes on the 18th (Sickleforce), minus much of its transport (see Map 39). This weak force helped capture the paratroopers at Dombas, but arrived too late to really augment the defence. Instead, they covered the Norwegian withdrawal from the Lillehammer area northwards. On a parallel route to the east, the Germans pushed through Rena on the 23rd and Tynset, 100 miles north, a day later. The Norwegians defended the valley floors, so the Germans had improvise, often attacking at night. Allied fortunes did not improve on the Lillehammer–Åndalsnes road, despite the arrival of another British brigade. By the end of the month, the Allies had evacuated the entire Åndalsnes venture. To the west of Oslo, elements of the 163. Infanterie-Division drove in the direction of Bergen against remnants of the 2nd Division.

Remnants of three Norwegian divisions tried to contain two German ones in the general area of Oslo and its environs. Luftwaffe support was particularly decisive. On 24 April, obsolete Gloster Gladiator biplane fighters from the RAF's No. 263 Squadron flew off HMS *Glorious* to lend some air support. Lacking a proper airfield, they landed on the frozen Lake Lesjaskog in the Romsdal Valley, where 24 hours later, the Luftwaffe had destroyed all but one machine on the ground. However, with the failure of the Åndalsnes operation, the Norwegians could not defend Oslo and eastern Norway alone.

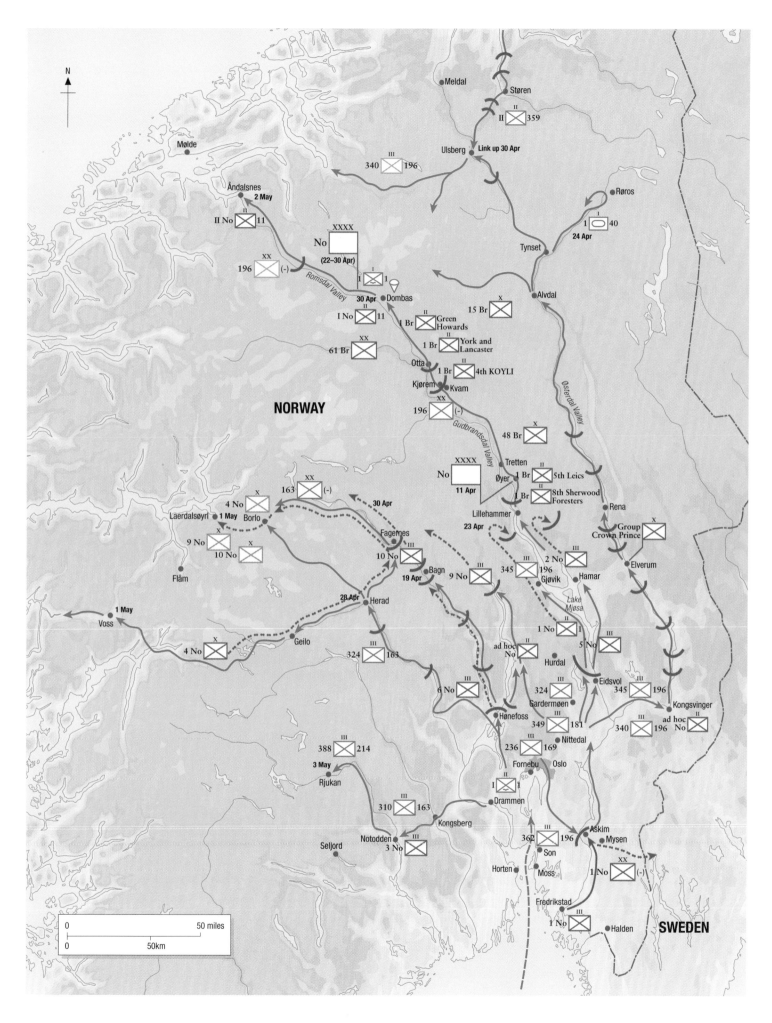

N

Meldal

Støren

II II 359

Ulsberg   **Link up 30 Apr**

Mølde

340 III 196

Røros

1 I 40
24 Apr

Åndalsnes
2 May

II No II 11

Tynset

XXXX
No
(22–30 Apr)

196 XX (-)

Romsdal Valley

I I 1
30 Apr Dombas

Alvdal

15 Br X

I No II 11

II Green
1 Br Howards

1 Br II York and
Lancaster

61 Br XX

Otta

1 Br II 4th KOYLI

Kjørem Kvam

NORWAY

196 XX (-)

Østerdal Valley

Gudbrandsdal Valley

48 Br X

XXXX
No
11 Apr

Tretten
Øyer 1 Br II 5th Leics

1 Br II 8th Sherwood
Foresters

Rena

163 XX (-)

4 No X

Lillehammer
23 Apr

Group X
Crown Prince

Laerdalsøyrl **1 May** Borlo

30 Apr

Fagernes

9 No X

10 No X

III
10 No

Bagn
19 Apr

9 No III

345 III

2 No III

196 III
Gjøvik

Hamar

Elverum

Flåm

28 Apr Herad

Lake
Mjøsa

1 No III I

5 No III

1 May
Voss

Geilo

324 III 163

6 No III

ad hoc No II

Hurdal

324 III

Eidsvol

345 III 196

Kongsvinger

4 No X

Gardermøen

349 III 181

340 III 196 ad hoc No II

Hønefoss

388 III 214

236 III 169 Nittedal

Fornebu Oslo

3 May
Rjukan

310 III 163

Kongsberg

I II 1

Drammen

Seljord

Notodden

3 No III

362 III 196

Askim Mysen

Son

1 No XX (-)

Horten Moss

Fredrikstad

1 No III

Halden

SWEDEN

0 _____ 50 miles
0 _____ 50km

MAP 38: SOUTH-WEST NORWAY, 9–30 APRIL 1940

The three operations depicted on this map represent German efforts to secure three ports along the Norwegian western and southern coasts. From north to south they are Bergen, Stavanger and Kristiansand; the Germans also attacked a couple of smaller locales nearby.

Marinegruppe 3, consisting of two light cruisers and several smaller ships, sailed into Bergen in the morning of 9 April. Norwegian shore batteries fired off a few shots before German soldiers overtook these from the land with the help of flight of He 111s. Approximately 1,900 troops from the 69. Infanterie-Division, under Generalmajor Hermann Tittel, then came ashore and quickly captured the city, Norway's second largest. The 4th Command District, premobilization headquarters of the 4th Division, evacuated to Voss. Indecision by the Royal Navy failed both to support the Norwegians and to intercept and sink the greatly outnumbered Germans. However, Fleet Air Arm Blackburn Skua dive-bombers, at extreme range from their base at Scapa Flow, did score two fatal hits on *Königsberg* (already suffering from significant damage from the shore guns) tied up in the harbour. Tittel dispatched his men on roads and by boat to secure the Bergen area. They defeated Norwegian resistance by the end of the month.

Fighting at Stavanger and nearby Sola airfield provoked much more excitement. At about 0930 hours, a dozen Ju 52s carrying 3./Fallschirmjäger-Regiment 1 made it through the thick clouds over the Skagerrak to Sola, accompanied by two Bf 110s (of an original eight). With 3/ZG 76 *Zerstörer* strafing the airport defenders, the parachutists jumped out at 400ft and floated down. The fight ended after half an hour. More Ju 52s soon arrived, with forward air controller teams and other ground crew to establish a completely capable Luftwaffe air base.

Within a couple of hours, a stream of transports began landing with the bulk of the 193. Infanterie-Regiment, which soon captured Stavanger. Other reinforcements eventually arrived by air and, as above, these forces spread out and chased the Norwegian defenders into the mountains to the east. The large and modern Sola airbase arguably made the difference in *Weserübung*. On 17 April, the cruiser HMS *Suffolk* attempted to bombard it, but Luftwaffe bombers flying from there chased her off with heavy damage. This made sure the Royal Navy never came near again, with dire consequences for Allied hopes in Norway.

The third major assault from the sea took place at Kristiansand, where Marinegruppe 4 arrived to land 1,100 men from 163. Infanterie-Division. First, they had to get by Norwegian shore batteries, which kept the German ships at a safe distance until repeated Luftwaffe bombing raids silenced the guns. Troops from 310. Infanterie-Regiment landed, quickly took over the town and then marched off into the hinterland. That evening the submarine HMS *Truant* put three torpedoes into *Karlsruhe* as she sailed back to Germany. This damaged the light cruiser so badly that her crew had to scuttle and abandon her.

Two smaller operations also took place on 9 April. A group of four minesweepers landed a company of scouts from the reconnaissance battalion of the 69. Infanterie-Division at Egersund, south of Stavanger. They easily took the fishing village and cut cable communications to the rest of the world. A little east of Kristiansand, the torpedo boat *Greif* landed 100 bicycle troops (also from the 69. Infanterie-Division's reconnaissance battalion) at Arendal, also capturing an undersea cable station unopposed. At a cost of two light cruisers sunk, the Germans had captured the parts of Norway closest to Great Britain.

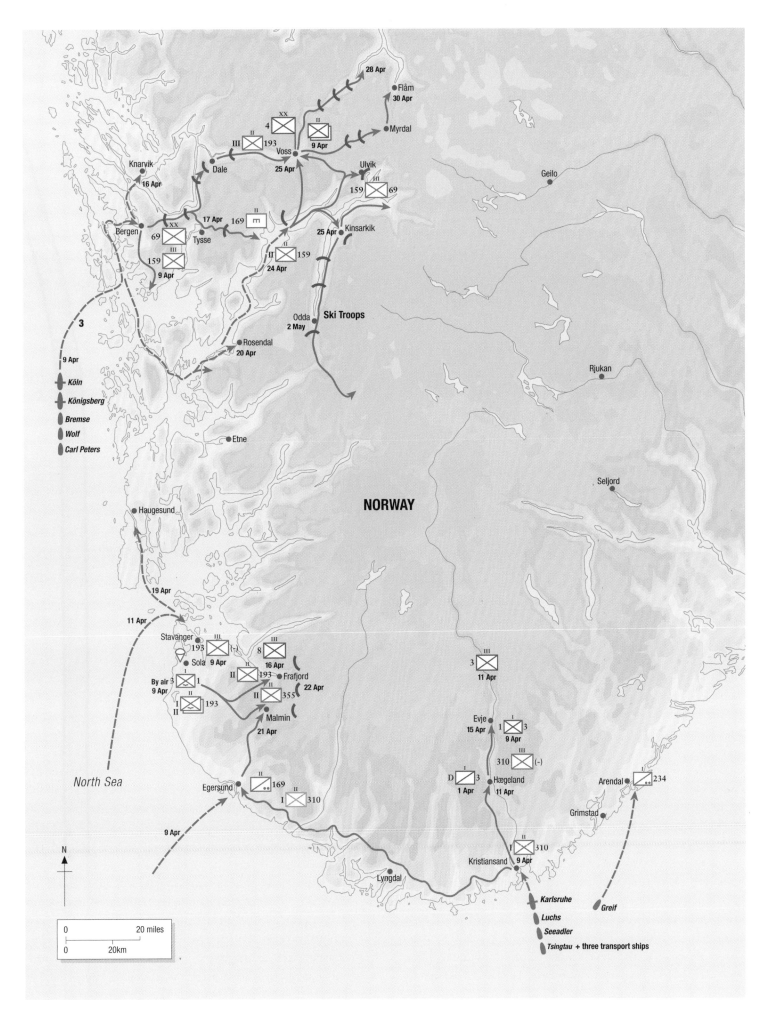

28 Apr
Flåm
30 Apr

XX
4
II
III 193 9 Apr
Voss
25 Apr
Myrdal

Knarvik
16 Apr
Dale

Ulvik
III
159 69

II
III 169

Bergen
69 XX
159 III
9 Apr

Tysse
17 Apr

II
159 24 Apr

Kinsarkik
25 Apr

Geilo

Odda
2 May
Ski Troops

Rosendal
20 Apr

3
9 Apr

Köln
Königsberg
Bremse
Wolf
Carl Peters

Etne

Rjukan

NORWAY

Seljord

Haugesund

19 Apr

11 Apr

Stavanger
III
193
(+)
III
8
16 Apr
Frafjord
22 Apr

Sola
9 Apr

By air 3
9 Apr
I
1
II 193
II
193
II
355
Malmin
21 Apr

III
3
11 Apr

Evje
15 Apr
I
1 3
9 Apr

III
310 (-)

D I
3
1 Apr
Hægeland
11 Apr

Arendal
234

Grimstad

North Sea

Egersund
II
169
II
I 310

9 Apr

Kristiansand
I
II
310 9 Apr

Lyngdal

Karlsruhe
Luchs
Seeadler
Tsingtau + three transport ships

Greif

N

0   20 miles
0   20km

91

MAP 39: THE CENTRAL NORWEGIAN COAST, 9 APRIL–2 MAY 1940

An interesting variety of activity took place around Trondheim, a key port on Norway's central coast. Following the German landings, the Allies made concerted efforts to swing the course of the battle their way.

Fresh from its encounter with *Glowworm*, Marinegruppe 2, ferrying 1,700 men from the Gebirgsjäger-Regiment 138 (3. Gebirgs-Division) sailed through the multi-arm Trondheimsfjorden leading to the port, representing themselves as British. After landing at the town's wharves largely without incident thanks to this deception, the troops took coastal guns from the land and manned them against anticipated Allied counterattacks. They also quickly marched 25 miles east to the airfield near Stjørdal. The Norwegians abandoned it without a fight, depriving the Allies of significant air cover for the remainder of the fighting there. As had happened elsewhere, the speed and surprise of *Weserübung* greatly hindered mobilization efforts of the local defenders. The 5th Command District withdrew towards Steinkjer to assemble, but had to do so without its artillery, left in the Trondheim depots. A volunteer force of artillerists withdrew to the old fort of Hegra, where they blocked a major road and held out until early May. Two days after the initial invasion, Swordfish torpedo bombers from HMS *Furious* arrived to attack *Admiral Hipper*, but the German cruiser had already left for Germany.

For weeks, the Allies had been toying with the idea of ignoring Norwegian neutrality and landing troops there anyway. They therefore had assault forces ready to go soon after *Weserübung* began. As a preliminary to the main Allied attack against Trondheim, the Allies landed troops north and south of the town. The British landing at Åndalsnes has already been mentioned (see Map 37). Between 15 and 19 April, they made a joint landing with the French at Namsos, north of Trondheim and relatively close to the Norwegian 5th Division. The British 146th Infantry

Brigade (Operation *Henry*) and French 5e Demi-Brigade de Chasseurs Alpins came ashore and soon linked up with the 5th Division. Unfortunately, the Allies had arrived to a mix of deep snow and slushy thaw, often with incomplete equipment (skis missing straps, etc.), no mules, little artillery and transport, plus no air cover, anti-aircraft guns or armour. The main assault on Trondheim never happened, chiefly due to the Royal Navy's healthy respect for the Luftwaffe.

Meanwhile, despite Royal Navy superiority, the Germans had reinforced their forces at Trondheim with the 159. Infanterie-Regiment (69. Infanterie-Division) and 359. Infanterie-Regiment (181. Infanterie-Division). These Landsers joined the Gebirgsjäger in spreading out to the north, east and south. Between 19 and 21 April, Kriegsmarine destroyers and torpedo boats braved the ice pack and narrow waters to deliver troops behind the main Allied defences at Verdalsøra. All the while, Luftwaffe bombers plastered the Namsos harbour and town, making Allied reinforcement and resupply very difficult, even if their admirals wanted to risk the ships.

Luftwaffe attacks soon also made Steinkjer uninhabitable and imprudent to defend. Within a few days, nearly half the British contingent of 1,500 men (many of them Territorials with one year of training) had become casualties. Conflicting orders from the War Office in London told them to fight, evacuate and withdraw farther north. Steinkjer generally marked the planned German limit of advance, so they did not pursue very energetically. The disparity in air power had become acute, so simultaneously the Allies decided to abandon the Trondheim expedition. Under heavy Luftwaffe attack, they abandoned the central Norwegian coast and 5th Division to its fate. The Allied relief effort had been poorly planned, resourced and executed from the start. They had landed basically a division of troops north and south of Trondheim, yet accomplished almost nothing.

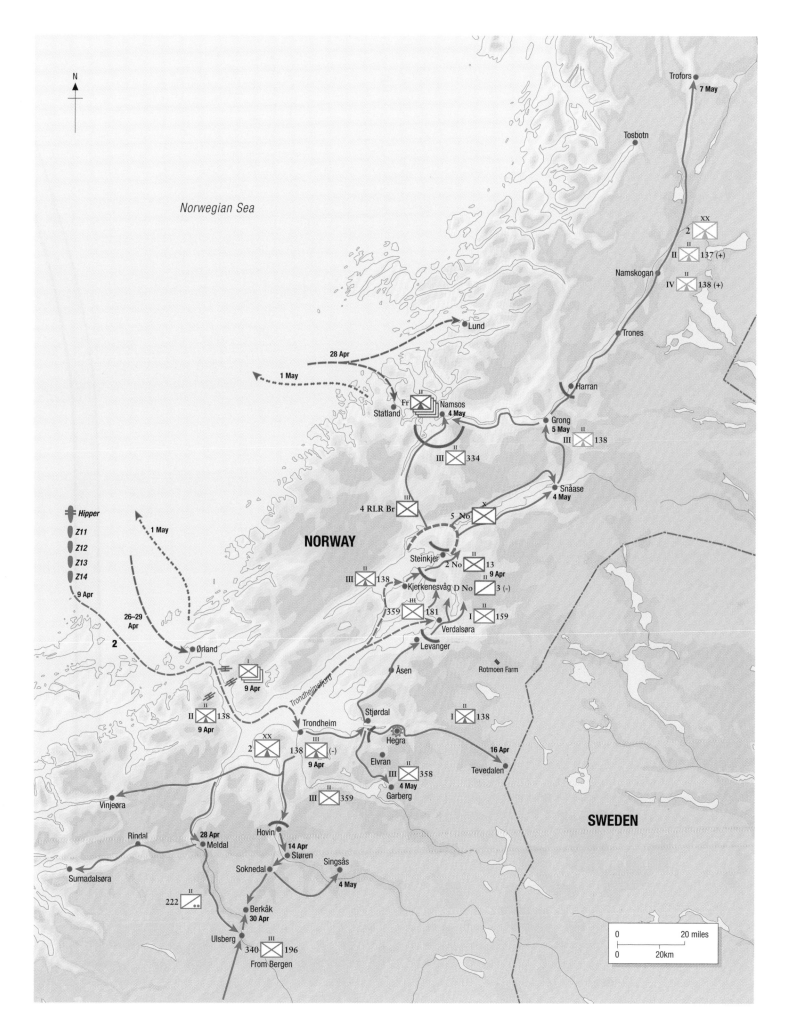

N

Norwegian Sea

Trofors
7 May

Tosbotn

XX
2

II 137 (+)

Namskogan

IV 138 (+)

Trones

Lund

28 Apr

1 May

Harran

Fr Namsos
Statland 4 May

Grong
5 May

III 138

III 334

Snåase
4 May

4 RLR Br

5 No

Hipper

Z11

Z12

Z13

Z14

1 May

9 Apr

26–29 Apr

2

Ørland

NORWAY

Steinkjer

2 No 13

9 Apr

III 138

Kjerkenesvåg D No 3 (-)

359 181

I 159

Verdalsøra

Levanger

Åsen

Rotmoen Farm

9 Apr

II 138
9 Apr

Trondheimsfjord

Stjørdal

Hegra

I 138

2

XX

138 (-)
9 Apr

Elvran

III 358

16 Apr

Tevedalen

III 359

Garberg
4 May

Vinjeøra

SWEDEN

Rindal

28 Apr

Hovin

Meldal

14 Apr

Støren

Soknedal

Singsås

4 May

222

Berkåk
30 Apr

Ulsberg

340 196

From Bergen

Surnadalsøra

0   20 miles

0   20km

93

MAP 40: THE BATTLE OF NARVIK (I), 9 APRIL–8 MAY 1940

The fighting around Narvik is one of the best-known episodes from the Scandinavian campaign. It also represents the battle for Norway in microcosm: An audacious and barebones *Weserübung* versus a much larger Allied response. It is a David and Goliath story where skill and willpower defeated bigger numbers. The ultimate German victory at this faraway outpost fits the Nazi narrative perfectly.

Ten destroyers of Marinegruppe 1 peeled off from the capital ships with 2,000 men from the command and staff of 3. Gebirgs-Division and its Gebirgsjäger-Regiment 139 and headed up Ofotfjord. Two turn-of-the-century coastal defence ships tried to intercept the Germans, but torpedoes from the destroyers soon sank both. The division headquarters, Generalmajor Eduard Dietl and II. Bataillon landed in Narvik, while the I. and III. Bataillone continued up the fjord to Bjerkvik. Dietl bluffed the Narvik garrison commander and a battalion of the Norwegian 13th Regiment to surrender. The Germans then braced themselves for the expected Allied counterattack. To the north, the 6th Division, the only Norwegian formation to mobilize somewhat successfully that day, prepared to resist.

The German destroyers each carried 200 of Dietl's men, but none of his heavy equipment, including artillery. Transports that failed to arrive carried this, so the destroyers provided his only heavy gunfire support. However, they had orders to return to Germany as soon as they refuelled, an extra-slow process since only one of two oilers had arrived. Early on the 10th, five Royal Navy destroyers sailed up the fjord and sank two German destroyers and damaged two others and six merchant ships, at a cost of two of their number. Dietl lost valuable supplies, including much of his ammunition. This represented a serious setback for the Gebirgsjäger and the remaining warships. Three days later, the battleship HMS *Warspite* and nine more destroyers entered Ofotfjord and finished off the remaining Kriegsmarine vessels. Occasionally, a Ju 52 arrived with equipment, supplies and weapons, but essentially Dietl's troops were on their own now, although eventually nearly 400 Ju 52 sorties brought some outside assistance. The general also had approximately 2,600 surviving sailors from the sunken destroyers

(armed with captured Norwegian weapons) – an ad hoc unit given the exaggerated title of a naval brigade.

Between 14 and 15 April, the British 24th Guards Brigade arrived at Harstad and set up command and control for the coming Allied reaction. Within a couple of days, its battalions had moved to the north side of Ofotfjord. But the British Army commander, Major-General Pierse Mackesy, would not budge until reinforced. It would take nearly a month to replace him. On the 24th, *Warspite* returned with four escorts to shoot up Narvik. During this diversion, four Norwegian battalions attacked the northern bulge in the German lines at Gratangsbotn and Lapphaug. Mackesy passively looked on as the Germans defeated the attackers in detail. In the meantime, elements of the 27e Demi-Brigade de Chasseurs Alpins arrived at the end of April to further strengthen the Allied effort. Together, they had Dietl greatly outnumbered.

Thereafter, a stalemate set in as the Germans barely held on, the Norwegians licked their wounds and the British did very little. Dietl received real and promised future reinforcements from the sister 2. Gebirgs-Division. First, hastily trained Gebirgsjäger volunteers parachuted into Narvik, while others first sailed to Trondheim and then began the 400-mile (as the crow flies) march to Narvik. The Allies finally had an energetic commander worthy of his men: The French commander of the 27e, Général de Brigade Antoine Béthouart. Supported by recently landed tanks, commencing 1 May, he began attacking north of Bjerkvik. Béthouart pushed his men like Mackesy should have, but the I./Gebirgsjäger-Regiment 139 held on for ten days. The German defence received much needed close air support beginning on the 4th, as Luftwaffe bombers operating out of Trondheim could now reach Narvik.

Exploiting their control of the seas, between 6 and 9 May the Allies landed the 13e Demi-Brigade de Légion Étrangère and two battalions of the Polish Brigade (known as the Chasseurs du Nord, mountain troops) on the south banks of Ofotfjord, 30 miles west of Narvik. Nine days into May, it looked like Dietl's days might be numbered.

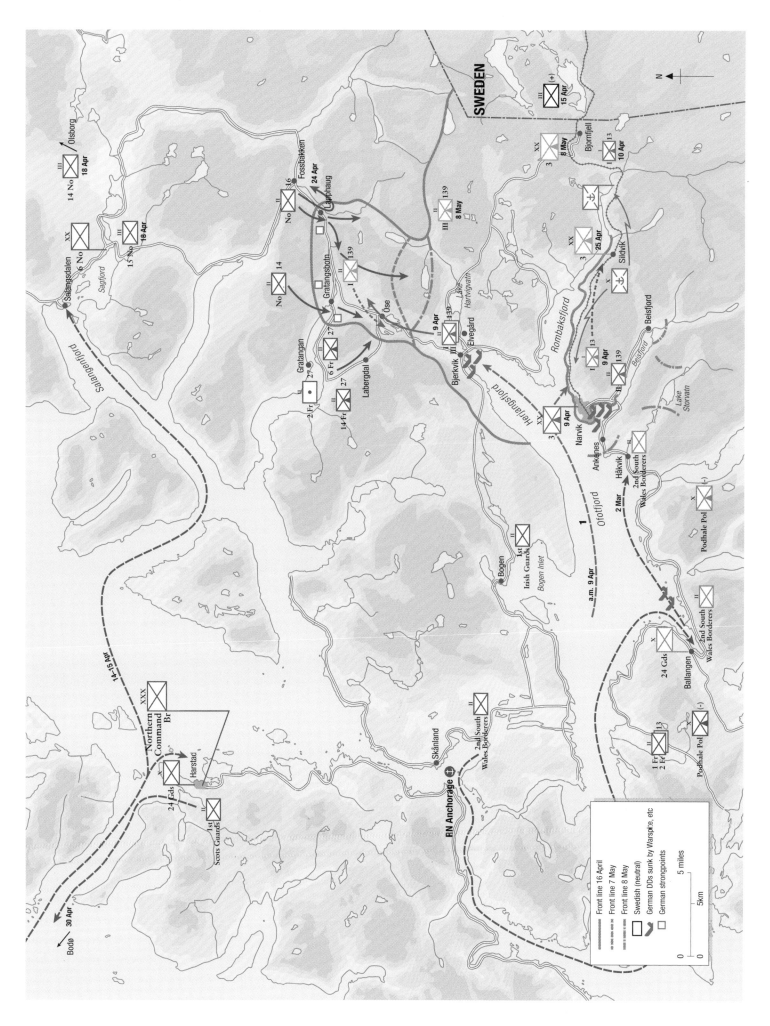

SWEDEN

N

III
15 Apr (++)

XX
3
8 May
13
10 Apr
Bjørnfjell

III
14 No
18 Apr
Olsborg

III
1.5 No
18 Apr

XX
6 No
18 Apr
Salangsdalen
Salangen

III
No 16
24 Apr
Fossbakken
Lapphaug

1.5
25 Apr
Sildvik

X
13
9 Apr
139
9 Apr
Beisfjord

Sagfjord

II
No 14
Gratangsbotn

1
139
Øse

II
139
8 May

III
139
9 Apr
Elvegård
Lake Hartvigvatn

Rombaksfjord

X
3
9 Apr
Narvik

XX
3
9 Apr
Bjerkvik
Helljangsfjord

II
27
Gratangan

II
27
6 Fr
II
27
14 Fr
Labergdal

Lake Storvatn

II
2 Fr
Gratangen

Ankenes
Håkvik
2nd South Wales Borderers

2 Mar

X
Podhale Pol (-)

Ototfjord
1
a.m. 9 Apr

II
1st Irish Guards
Bogen
Bogen Inlet

14–15 Apr

XXX
Northern Command Br

X
Harstad

24 Gds

II
1st Scots Guards

Salangenfjord

30 Apr
Bodø

X
24 Gds
Ballangen
2nd South Wales Borderers

II
2nd South Wales Borderers
Skånland
RN Anchorage

II
1 Fr
2 Fr
Podhale Pol (-)

13

Front line 16 April
Front line 7 May
Front line 8 May
Swedish (neutral)
German DDs sunk by Warspite, etc
German strongpoints

5 miles
5km
0
0

95

MAP 41: THE BATTLE OF NARVIK (II), 9 MAY–10 JUNE 1940

Just when it looked darkest for Dietl, like he might have to withdraw to Sweden and internment, everything changed. On 10 May, Hitler invaded France and the Low Countries (see Chapter Five). The worst news came about ten days later when it became clear to the world that Hitler would win. Suddenly, Norway and Narvik mattered much less.

Général Béthouart's attacks north of Bjerkvik finally bore fruit on 9 and 10 May. Dietl had no reserves left and slowly evacuated the bulge that he had held for almost a month, as the French moved ahead supported by tanks. Inland, Norwegian forces advanced beside them. On the 11th and 12th, the battleship HMS *Resolution* with cruisers and destroyers initiated the next attack both north and south of the Ofotfjord. Béthouart and his French and Polish mountain troops plus Norwegians assaulted on a wide front. They easily infiltrated the German lines, sparsely manned by machine-gun nests and observation posts every few hundred yards. More hopeful news met the Allies when a new overall Allied commander arrived to replace the timid Mackesy: Major-General Claude Auchinleck took over on 13 May.

The newcomer Auchinleck had to delegate the Narvik attacks to the French general because the 2. Gebirgs-Division had made steady progress from Trondheim and now was closing in from the south. This developing threat demanded his attention, since a new group of enemy soldiers coming from an unexpected direction would upset Allied plans. Norwegian defenders demolished bridges, but this barely slowed the Germans. On the 14th, the Irish Guards battalion shipped south to Bodø to help block the way; Luftwaffe attacks made sure many did not make it. In any event, they abandoned Bodø on the 31st.

Béthouart kept shoving the Germans back along the Rombaksfjord. Dietl's headquarters and supply base lay practically at the Swedish border and would soon be within range of the approaching Allied artillery[10]. By the 21st, the German lodgement north of Narvik shrank to a fraction of its size a month earlier. On that day, another French regiment landed on the Rombaksfjord; Allied naval power and amphibious capability could not be denied. Even the Luftwaffe had

little influence over events. At least Dietl received some much-needed reinforcements in the form of airborne troops and Gebirgsjägers trained to parachute, who landed on some of the last flat, sparsely foliated areas within the German's shrinking perimeter.

A week later, on 28 May, French, Polish and Norwegian troops began a series of overland and amphibious assaults, again preceded by Royal Navy bombardment. They took the town of Narvik and advanced in the face of weak German counterattacks. It looked like Dietl's men were about to be crushed in a pincer. The Allies even finally had some aircover provided by 18 Gladiators and as many Hurricanes thanks to expedient airstrips they had constructed in the area. At the height of their success, on the last day of May, the British cabinet ordered their troops out of Norway: The situation in France and at home was too problematic. With Dietl backed up practically to Sweden, the Allies cancelled their planned final assault. Allied ships evacuated Narvik on 7 June and Harstad on the 8th. A week later, the first of the German volunteer relief force from Trondheim linked up with Dietl's group. Damage caused mainly by Royal Navy bombardment put Narvik's port facilities out of use for seven months.

Norway sued for peace on 3 June and its military surrendered four days later. King Haakon, government officials and the country's gold reserves departed aboard HMS *Devonshire* from Tromsø on the 7th. The massive Norwegian merchant fleet, equivalent to 16 months of average U-boat sinkings, transferred to the Allies. A spirited resistance to the Nazi occupation sprang up immediately. Germany used Norway for air and naval bases, somewhat limited by available German resources and undeveloped Norwegian infrastructure. These bases became especially active after Operation *Barbarossa*, when the Arctic Ocean became a prime avenue to get supplies to the USSR. Over 400,000 German troops in Norway surrendered in May 1945, basically lost to the life-and-death war effort on the main fronts in Europe. Ultimately however, when we ask whether *Weserübung* was worth it for Germany, we must ask what would have happened if Hitler had not taken Scandinavia in the spring of 1940? How would Allied bases in Norway have changed World War II? This would probably have been to Germany's disadvantage.

---

10   Under German diplomatic pressure, Sweden did allow some illicit logistical help to reach Dietl.

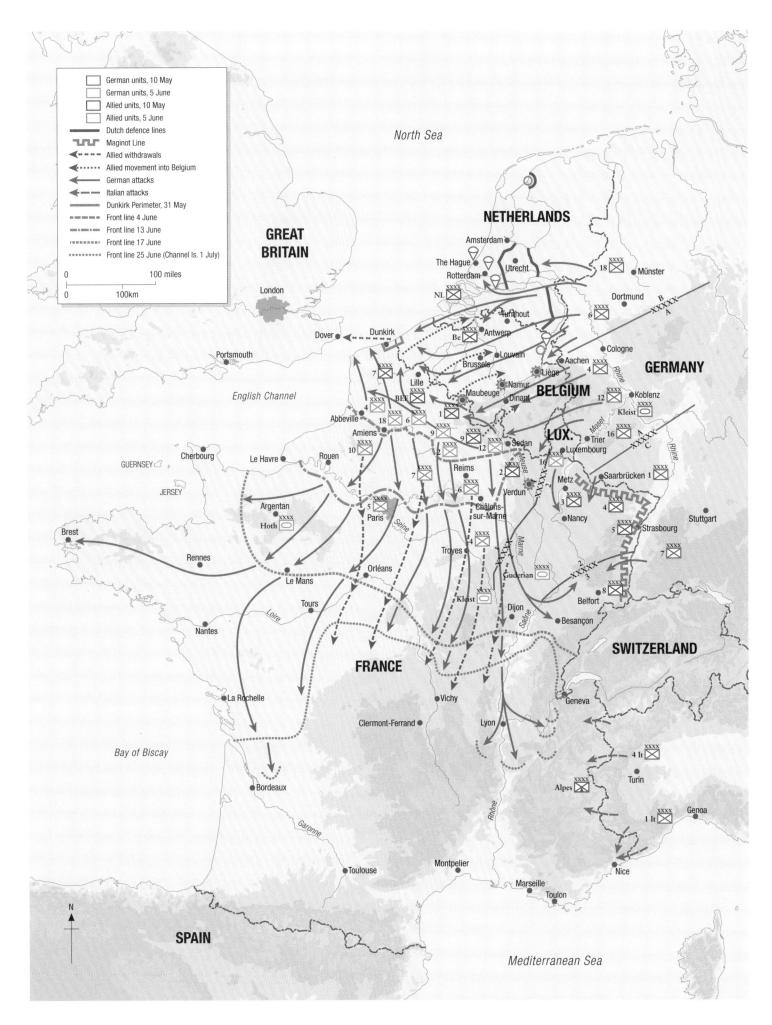

North Sea

NETHERLANDS

Amsterdam

The Hague

Rotterdam

Utrecht

18 XXXX Münster

NL XXXX

6 XXXX Dortmund B XXXX A

GREAT BRITAIN

London

Dover

Portsmouth

English Channel

Turnhout

Be XXXX Antwerp

Louvain

Brussels

Namur

Liège

Maubeuge

Dinant

Cologne

Aachen 4 XXXX

GERMANY

BELGIUM

12 XXXX Koblenz

Kleist ▭

7 XXXX

Lille XXXX

BEF XXXX

1 XXXX

16 XXXX A C XXXX

Rhine

Moselle

Abbeville 18 XXXX 6 XXXX

Amiens

9 XXXX

2 XXXX

9 XXXX

12 XXXX Sedan

LUX:

Luxembourg

Trier Saarbrücken 1 XXXX

Cherbourg

Le Havre

Rouen

10 XXXX

7 XXXX Reims

2 XXXX

16 XXXX

Metz

3 XXXX

4 XXXX

GUERNSEY

JERSEY

Argentan

Hoth ▭

5 XXXX

Paris

Seine

6 XXXX

Verdun

Marne

2 XXXX

Meuse

Nancy

5 XXXX Strasbourg

Stuttgart

Brest

Rennes

Le Mans

Loire

Orléans

Châlons-sur-Marne

Troyes

4 XXXX

Kleist ▭

Saône

Dijon

Guderian ▭

2 XXXXX 3

8 XXXX

Belfort

7 XXXX

Nantes

Tours

Besançon

SWITZERLAND

La Rochelle

FRANCE

Vichy

Geneva

Clermont-Ferrand

Lyon

Rhône

4 It XXXX

Turin

Bay of Biscay

Bordeaux

Alpes XXXX

1 It XXXX Genoa

Toulouse

Montpelier

Marseille

Toulon

Nice

N

SPAIN

Mediterranean Sea

Legend:
- German units, 10 May
- German units, 5 June
- Allied units, 10 May
- Allied units, 5 June
- Dutch defence lines
- Maginot Line
- Allied withdrawals
- Allied movement into Belgium
- German attacks
- Italian attacks
- Dunkirk Perimeter, 31 May
- Front line 4 June
- Front line 13 June
- Front line 17 June
- Front line 25 June (Channel Is. 1 July)

0   100 miles

0   100km

CHAPTER 5:
THE WESTERN CAMPAIGN

France, the French Army and the Maginot Line stood guard as the first line of defence of the non-fascist world in the winter of 1940. Great Britain, the USA and even the USSR (not to mention numerous smaller nations) put their hopes for stopping Hitler on France. For most of the world, Hitler's invasion of the West, *Fall Gelb* (*Case Yellow*), did not come as a surprise. Few expected the Phoney War or 'Sitzkrieg' or 'drole de guerre' to go on indefinitely and most could see the Wehrmacht's build up for a Western campaign.

The completeness, decisiveness and speed of Hitler's victory did shock the globe just ten days after the invasion began. By that point, diplomats, military and security experts and statesmen alike could see that France was beaten, both materially and, more importantly, psychologically. The surviving major powers had to immediately rethink their plans for a future without France. Britain had to consider war in Europe alone. American President Franklin D. Roosevelt had to earnestly work for eventual involvement in another general European war. Stalin had to come up with a new idea for exporting communist revolution; his hoped-for prerequisite, 'the self-laceration of capitalism and its fascist afterbirth', now looked decidedly unlikely. All had to look forward to the unhappy prospect of Hitler immeasurably bolder and stronger after his relatively bloodless victory over France.

Although clearly a defeat, apart from the lingering British blockade, World War I ended on terms generally favourable to Germany: Its army marched home intact, only a small corner of the country was occupied, Berlin did not have to endure enemy victory parades and its post-war government and other structures were of its own choosing. Likewise, radical anti-Versailles revisionism aside, the peace treaty did not make another war inevitable. That honour goes to the Great Depression. World War II began just weeks short of the tenth anniversary of Black Thursday on the New York Stock Exchange. Yet France was not really ready for what came next.

The French invasion of Germany on 7–8 September 1939 in support of Poland was a joke. With the Wehrmacht outnumbered in divisions 85:34, the French 4e and 5e Armées crept into Germany in battalion strength along a 15-mile front. German units, overwhelmingly reservist and lacking artillery, armour and aerial support, gave way. They pulled back a dozen miles or so to the Siegfried Line, Germany's weak answer to the Maginot Line. The dozen or so attacking divisions of the Saar Offensive easily occupied some deserted villages and sent out small reconnaissance patrols. Two weeks after they began, the French withdrew back behind the Maginot Line; the threat to Germany had passed.

Soon after Hitler invaded Poland, on 10 September, the British Expeditionary Force (BEF) began arriving in France. Within a month, 158,000 men in four divisions made it across the Channel, too late to help Poland even if they tried. By December, Indian troops had joined them. The following month, Belgium and the Netherlands began mobilizing. Both, however, stubbornly maintained their neutrality, Belgium going so far as to say it would regard any invading French soldiers as enemies and stood ready to 'repulse by force any foreign unit of whatever nationality which violated Belgian territory'.[11] They would grant no transit privileges to Britain and France. Seeming to understand, that same month Prime Minister Chamberlain nevertheless promised British aid if Germany attacked Belgium. Belgium reiterated its position three months later, two days after Hitler invaded Scandinavia, when they could clearly see how the Führer treated small neutrals. A week later, the Netherlands followed suit. While declaring a state of siege, it also refused any assistance, 'whether offered or actually forced on us'.[12] A month later, on 7 May, the Dutch completed their defence mobilization plan, just days before Hitler struck.

During the final six months of the Phoney War, things in France went from bad to worse. Its political right and left disagreed on everything except not wanting to go to war against Germany, although they had diametrically opposed reasons: The right because it admired the Third Reich, the left because of its pacificism. Hitler's vacuous peace offer of 19 September 1939 divided the French cabinet; Foreign Minister Georges Bonnet believed it 'merited some attention'. The Soviet invasion of Finland further divided France. Allied pusillanimity brought down the Daladier government a week after the Finnish capitulation. This time France would have no Leon Gambetta or Georges Clemenceau. The new Prime Minister Paul Reynaud, governing with a majority of one vote in the Chamber of Deputies, put on a brave face, somewhat in contrast to his predecessor, who was tainted by Munich. Three weeks later, Operation *Weserübung* gave the French another thing to disagree about and again they did very little. Reynaud wanted to replace Army Commander Général Maurice Gamelin with Général Maxime Weygand, but encountered political resistance from many quarters, including President Albert Lebrun. Meanwhile, by early May, indications of a pending German invasion from military intelligence sources all over Europe, including from within Germany, were pouring in.

***

Hitler had his own problems with his cautious generals and baulky ally Mussolini. Only on 18 March, when the two dictators met at the Brenner Pass, did Italy agree to join the upcoming war. Getting agreement from the Wehrmacht brass took more effort. Before Warsaw had even fallen, Hitler told his generals he wanted to invade the West that autumn. Except for the pathetic Saar Offensive, combat between the two sides had been limited to the air (see Chapter 6) and sea (see Chapter 7). The army especially did not believe it was ready for another war in Belgium and France. In one way, the generals were more correct than they knew: The weak invasion plans of that autumn and winter were little more than unimaginative rehashed copies of 1914. Also, as mentioned earlier regarding the Winter War and Operation *Weserübung*, the winter of 1939/40 was one of the most severe in recent memory. Between the unenthusiastic generals and pessimistic meteorologists, Hitler postponed the invasion of the West repeatedly until May. The story behind the evolving Wehrmacht plans is one of the most interesting in World War II. Even more risky than the Norway attack on account of the stronger enemy, the Allies' countermoves played into the Germans' hands perfectly.

The campaign that would shock the world began with little surprise on 10 May. In a classic 'feint right, go left' manoeuvre, Heeresgruppe B got off to a noisy start through the Netherlands and northern Belgium. The inadvertent bombing of Rotterdam and high visibility aerial assault on Fort Eben Emael confirmed the ruse. According to plan, the Allies rushed into Belgium as per their Dyle River defence: Plan D. With the world's attention fixed on this sleight of hand, Panzergruppe Kleist took two days to work its way through the Ardennes Forest. When the four panzer corps of Heeresgruppe A broke through the rough woods, the Allies did not know how to react. By the 13th, the panzers had crossed the Meuse River between Dinant and Sedan, near the northern terminus of the Maginot Line and, more critically, at the vulnerable joint where French and Belgian forces met. With their best formations engaged and tied down in central Belgium, the Allies had little with which to counter Kleist.

Around 14–15 May, the Allies figured out what had happened, but by then it was too late. On the 18th, Reynaud finally relieved Gamelin. Breaking contact and withdrawing while engaged is one of the most difficult military manoeuvres. Besides, the panzers were closer to the English Channel and moving westwards faster than the Allies' marching infantry. The Germans drove on relentlessly, fuelled by the amphetamine 'Pervitin'. Forward elements of Guderian's XIX Panzer-Korps reached the coast on 20 May, with the three others not far behind. The very best of the French Army and BEF, along with the entire Belgian Army, had been cut off and trapped. A couple of French and British counterattacks against the flanks and spearheads of the panzer group caused only a few hours' delay and minimal casualties. The Germans operated entirely within the Allies' decision loop, manoeuvring way too fast for the defenders. As it turned out, the panzers' speed also made their own commanders (including Hitler) uneasy to the point where they halted the tankers more than once, so that marching infantry could catch up and close any gaps.

The British government decided to evacuate the BEF from the developing pocket; nonessential personnel began leaving on 18 May. Pinched between Heeresgruppen A and B, the BEF would have to depend on the sacrifices of the Belgians and French to hold the Germans at bay long enough for an evacuation fleet to carry them to Britain and safety. The Allies' greatest succour, however, came from Hitler and the Wehrmacht. They halted the army and put their hopes on the Luftwaffe.

---

11 William Shirer, *The Collapse of the Third Republic*, Simon and Schuster of Canada: Ontario, 1971, p. 573.

12 Robert Goralski, *World War II Almanac, 1939–1945*, Perigee Books: New York, 1981, p. 111.

Their work apparently done, the panzers withdrew for the Somme River, France's new defensive line. The Luftwaffe turned out to be unequal to the task and between 27 May and 4 June, the plucky armada of British ships and boats withdrew the BEF and over 120,000 Allied troops from other nations. Instead of a crushing, history-changing win, the Germans had to settle for a massive but 'ordinary' victory.

On 5 June, the day after the last Tommy left Dunkirk, the Germans began phase two of the conquest of France, *Fall Rot* (*Case Red*). Except for a small British contingent, France was on its own, greatly handicapped by the fact that it had lost its best men and units during that terrible May in Belgium. The so-called Weygand Line along the Somme, Oise and Aisne Rivers could not derail the energized Wehrmacht. They penetrated the defences at numerous bridgeheads and within a week closed in on the River Seine and Paris. The capital surrendered on the 14th without a fight. Thereafter, important French cities quickly fell day after day. Further east, Wehrmacht troops had already turned the exposed flank of the Maginot Line and even frontally assaulted its forts in places. By mid-month, the Germans had crossed the Rhine and the French in the east began a general withdrawal. Guderian, now commanding his own panzer group, played an important role here as well, assisting in encircling the 2e Groupe d'Armées, generally along the Vosges Mountains.

All through central and southern France, penetration and breakthrough turned into pursuit. Forces from both sides competed for road space with masses of refugees fleeing the combat. Twenty days after *Fall Rot* began, the Germans reached the eventual demarcation line, although some units continued down the Atlantic coast. To near-universal derision, on 21 June, Mussolini launched his army into the south-western Alps, but their success against the already defeated French was extremely limited. The next day, Hitler accepted the surrender of the French nation. German dead and missing totalled approximately 40,000 (71 per cent of which occurred during *Rot*); French numbers were greater than 100,000; Britain lost fewer than 10,000; and Belgium 6,500. Wounded and prisoners for all combatants amounted to more than 2 million men (three-quarters of those were French POWs). Germany's great victory came at a relatively cheap price: Fewer killed during the entire campaign than in a few days of battle during the Great War. The day after the surrender ceremony at Compiègne, Hitler made a whirlwind tour of central Paris; he stood at the pinnacle of his success.

MAP 43: THE EVOLUTION OF GERMAN PLANS

Like any good general staff anticipating contingencies, the Wehrmacht had a plan for attacking the West before September 1939 and, on 9 October, Hitler issued his first directive on the invasion. Quite inexplicably, however, by the end of the month, the generals could come up with nothing better than the 'Son of the Schlieffen Plan'. They replicated the counterclockwise sweep through the Low Countries, with one striking difference: Unlike the overly ambitious 1914 plan, in 1939 the German Army did not even hope to land a knockout blow. It fully intended to advance into Belgium and northern France, but then halt in the face of the Allies' expected defence. It was not a war-winning plan.

In the far north, General von Bock's Heeresgruppe B wielded the *Schwerpunkt*, three armies, 43 divisions and eight of ten panzer divisions. Rundstedt's Heeresgruppe A in the centre, with 22 infantry divisions, merely covered Bock's left flank. Leeb's Heeresgruppe C remained on guard duty opposite the Maginot Line.

Even the dilettante Hitler could see that the generals' plan would accomplish little more than recreate the stalemate he had lived through as a young soldier a quarter of a century earlier. On 20 November, he called on his staffs to revisit the matter and to be open to better solutions. Fortunately for the Germans, they never implemented this plan; problems caused by logistical delays in shifting the army from Poland, bad weather and even hesitation and resistance from the generals repeatedly pushed back the invasion timetable. Eventually, autumn turned to winter and the constant rescheduling allowed time for a new, radical, war-winning plan to come forward.

The adjacent map shows the evolving Wehrmacht plan. In response to repeated requests from the frustrated Führer for a war-winning operation, the army shifted its main effort, the mass of panzers, slightly south. But this adjustment represented a minor tweak to the existing flawed plan, not a decisive new concept. Two points jump out: the Wehrmacht leadership seemed complacent about neither avoiding a stalemate nor winning the war and it evidently had learned little from the Polish campaign about the potential of massed panzers employed for operational objectives. The lack of creativity on the part of senior German leaders is striking.

More than institutional envy motivated Rundstedt and his chief of staff – still Manstein – to make Heeresgruppe A the offensive's *Schwerpunkt* and develop a radically new solution to the operational problem of the campaign. They wanted a clear-cut victory. Ironically, since mid-November

Hitler had been advocating a very similar idea. Rundstedt's attempts to pass an alternate plan up the chain of command met professional opposition from the army commander, Generaloberst Walter von Brauchitsch and his chief of staff General Franz Halder. They even reassigned Manstein ('promoting' him to command an infantry corps) to mute his innovative ideas. Simply put, Heeresgruppe A wanted to take the mass of mechanized units through the Ardennes in a clockwise thrust to the Channel, behind the Allies and trapping them in Belgium. Coincidentally, during a chance meeting at a luncheon with Hitler on 17 February 1940, Manstein presented his plan to the Führer.

On the 18th, a day after speaking to Manstein, Hitler met Brauchitsch and Halder to fashion a new concept of the operation. Not very long prior to this, Halder had been a guest at wargames put on by Rundstedt, so he was already in a flexible state of mind. Six days later, on the 24th, the OKH issued the new deployment order. This put the *Schwerpunkt* and most of the mechanized formations under Heeresgruppe A. Accordingly, in Phase I Bock would attack first through the Netherlands and Belgium to draw the Allies there. Meanwhile, Heeresgruppe A, in particular Panzergruppe Kleist, would work its way through the Ardennes. The plan's outstanding feature would follow, the panzers' race from the Meuse to the Channel. This would accomplish the classic Prussian/German *Kesselschlacht* ('cauldron battle'), annihilating the main Allied armies. Phase II would be the anticlimactic coup de grâce: The speedy occupation of an already defeated France.

The Allied plan, fundamentally defensive, assumed the Germans would repeat 1914. Despite Belgian neutrality, British and French forces would rush into the small nation on day one of hostilities. Gamelin came up with the plan and, although it took some convincing, the British had signed on by September 1939. Their concept also had two phases: Advance to the Scheldt River (Escaut in French, therefore Plan E) and then to the Dyle River (and adjoining canals and rivers, Plan D). In November, Gamelin even considered advancing into the Netherlands and up to the Albert Canal in Belgium, on the German border. He refused to give up this idea, which also meant losing his last reserve army. As for the Dutch, they had, without informing the Allies, eschewed any sort of forward defence, and planned, after brief resistance in their east, to withdraw to *Vesting Holland* (Fortress Holland) – basically Amsterdam, Rotterdam and the Hague.

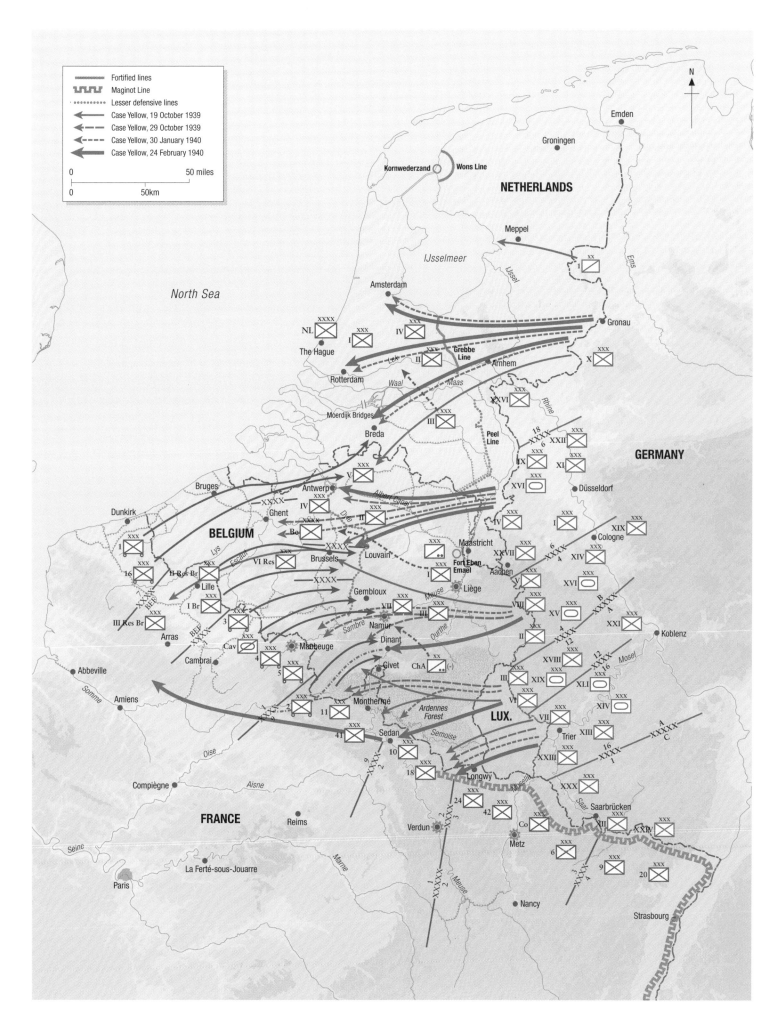

Fortified lines
Maginot Line
Lesser defensive lines
Case Yellow, 19 October 1939
Case Yellow, 29 October 1939
Case Yellow, 30 January 1940
Case Yellow, 24 February 1940

0 — 50 miles
0 — 50km

NORTH SEA

NETHERLANDS

Kornwederzand — Wons Line

IJsselmeer

Groningen

Emden

Meppel

Amsterdam

The Hague

Rotterdam

Moerdijk Bridges

Breda

Grebbe Line

Arnhem

Gronau

Peel Line

GERMANY

Düsseldorf

Bruges

Antwerp

Albert Canal

Dunkirk

Ghent

BELGIUM

Brussels

Louvain

Fort Eben Emael

Maastricht

Aachen

Cologne

Lille

Gembloux

Liège

Arras

Namur

Dinant

Givet

Koblenz

Cambrai

Maubeuge

Abbeville

Amiens

Montherme

Ardennes Forest

Sedan

LUX.

Trier

Saarbrücken

Compiègne

FRANCE

Reims

Verdun

Longwy

Metz

Nancy

La Ferté-sous-Jouarre

Paris

Strasbourg

MAP 44: OPENING MOVES, 10–12 MAY 1940

In the winter and early spring of 1940, intelligence reports flooded into French, British, Belgian and Dutch headquarters, correctly putting the German centre of gravity in the centre (i.e. near the Ardennes), accurately locating seven of ten panzer divisions and fairly closely identifying the offensive's start date. Not to be confused by these new facts, Gamelin and the Allies stuck to their existing plans. This lack of agility would be the first of many during the six-week war.

Several distinctions between 1914 and 1940 are immediately apparent: The Germans only had to fight on one front in 1940; the earlier French aggressive attitude had been replaced by defensive thinking; the Wehrmacht had gained some familiarity with the blitzkrieg in Poland, whereas the Allies had very limited combat experience; and German ground and air forces cooperated to a very high degree. In addition, German command and control only had to concern itself with German forces, while the Allies fought coalition warfare, and the quality differential between first-line, regular German divisions was not as marked as with the French. All these factors had a major impact on the upcoming battle.

At 2100 hours on 9 May, the codeword 'Danzig' went out, alerting the entire Wehrmacht that *Fall Gelb* would launch the following morning. Like almost every military operation from then on, it began with an aerial onslaught against myriad targets. Just after midnight on the 10th, the Luftwaffe began laying mines along both coasts of the Channel. Before the sun came up, about 500 bombers attacked enemy airfields, barracks, anti-aircraft batteries and bridges. Two more waves of approximately 500 bombers each lifted off later in the morning. Stukas appeared at daylight, taking out their victims with unique accuracy. At numerous important locales, transports either dropped parachutists or delivered troops directly to their objectives. Fighters and Flak sought to keep enemy aircraft away from their army comrades, especially Panzergruppe Kleist. In numerous places, Allied planes rose to intercept or fly close air support missions of their own. Allied aircraft losses alarmed senior leaders, who quickly decided to limit their attacks to absolutely critical targets. Thereafter, Luftwaffe planes filled the skies of north-west Europe (see Map 66).

The Germans also deployed a few special operations forces. The Netherlands was particularly hard hit in this regard. Brandenburgers, dressed in Dutch uniforms and escorting a group of German 'POWs', worked with local Nazi sympathizers to capture a bridge at Gennep from the surprised guards. This opened the road west for the 9. Panzer-Division[13].

Luftwaffe paratroopers captured Dutch airfields near The Hague and Rotterdam and bridges at Dordrecht and Moerdijk. Another group of soldiers rode old He 59 floatplanes to capture the Mass River bridges in Rotterdam[14].

In the far north, the Dutch gave way as planned. The 1. Kavallerie-Division broke through the border screen, crossed Friesland and made for the fortified Wons Position. The SS also had important roles to play capturing bridges here during the war's first days, in the form of regiments Der Führer (largely Austrian and leading the way for the SS-Verfügungstruppe Division, strung out far to the east along crowded roads) and Leibstandarte SS Adolf Hitler. Advancing 50–60 miles on the first day, they were only partially successful against Dutch demolitions, but then used improvised rafts instead. The Germans easily negotiated the appendix in the south-east of the country and were soon at Fort Eben Emael in Belgium (see maps 43 and 44).

The Allies reacted as planned; all eyes were on central Belgium and the expected German offensive. As soon as word of the invasion arrived, 1re Groupe d'Armées moved into Belgium with its cavalry corps screening the advance. Initially, the advance had a number of problems. The French had kept commanders below divisional level in the dark about the 'secret' Dyle Plan, so they did not always know what their units were supposed to do. The first day did not go well for the BEF, either. Its commander, Field Marshal Lord John Gort, anxious to get into battle, left his headquarters and set up an advanced command post near Lille[15]. This created a command and control nightmare, as commander and headquarters staff could not communicate for many critical hours. Also as planned, the Belgians pulled back from their eastern border towards the Dyle River defences. As of the first day of the war, there was still no communication or cooperation between the three southern Allies and the neutral Dutch.

In the centre, the left of the French 9e Armée swung clockwise into the Ardennes, using Sedan as its pivot. This did not go well, with deleterious effects on the Allied plan. Although few knew it at the time, the quiet German advance represented the key manoeuvre of the entire campaign. As yet undiscovered by the Allies, the French sat comfortably behind the Maginot Line with their false sense of security.

---

13 Bock's panzer units had a high proportion of Pz Is and IIs, considered good enough against Dutch and Belgian anti-tank guns.

14 The army's 22. Infanterie-Division, trained in 'air landing' – flying into battle aboard Ju 52s – would fly in as reinforcements soon after the paratroopers dropped.

15 For Gort control and command was problematic: militarily he was subordinated to a French general, yet his political guidance came from London.

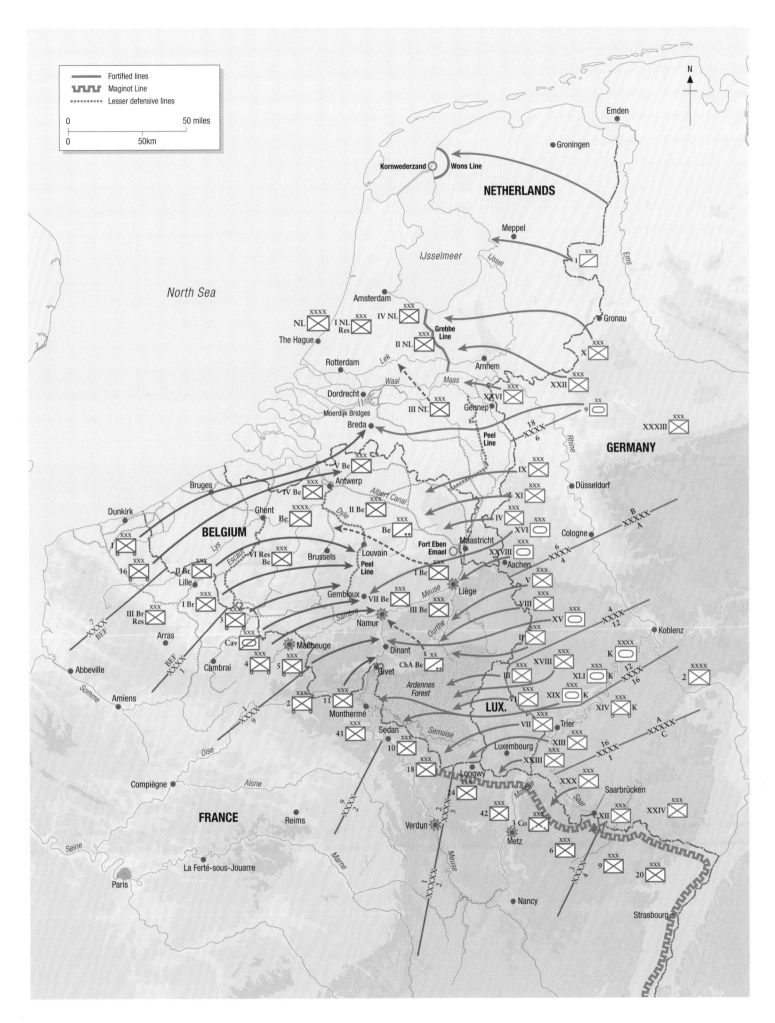

MAP 45: OPENING MOVES: THE NORTH, 11–12 MAY 1940

All went according to plan for the Allies again on 11 May; they had no inkling of the German manoeuvre through Luxembourg. On the North Sea coast, 1. Kavallerie-Division reached the Wons Position, manned by the I./33rd Infantry Regiment, guarding the eastern end of the Great Dyke. The Germans fought their way to Fort Kornwerderzand on 12 May, but even after a good pounding by Stukas, the fort held out as long as the Netherlands did. A little to the south, the 18. Armee easily crossed the Ijssel River on its way to the Grebbe Line at the tip of the Ijsselmeer, the strongest of the various Dutch lines. The XXVI Panzer-Korps and northern elements of the 6. Armee likewise made short work of the Peel Line (Grave to Weert). Counterattacks by the ad hoc Peel Division were disorganized and too small, so it could not hinder the enemy advance. The Dutch Light Division failed to live up to expectations as the army's only mobile formation. The Dutch III Corps, tasked with defending this part of the country but having suffered nearly 20,000 losses of all categories, began to withdraw towards Fortress Holland and hoped for safety.

The rest of 6. Armee, including two panzer corps, with Fort Eben Emael and the lower Albert Canal behind them, headed for the main Allied defences on the Dyle. According to their original plan, Belgian covering forces pulled back in the face of German pressure. They demolished bridges as they went, but German pioneers were right on their tail with pontoon bridges of their own. A few French motorized units ventured east of the Dyle to assist them. The Belgian III Corps withdrew to the dozen fortifications of the stout Liège system, where it could supposedly threaten Bock's left flank or Rundstedt's right. The Belgians planned to make a brief stand on the upper Albert Canal and prepared intermediate positions along the Gete River, to give them a place to pause on their way back to the Dyle Line. On the far right of the Allied defence of Belgium, the French 9e Armée, soon to have the eyes of the world watching it, fumbled to properly occupy its assigned sector.

On that same 11 May, 1re Groupe d'Armées divisions reached the Dyle Line and began digging in. The sacrificial Belgian, French and BEF efforts gave them desperately needed time. Unfortunately for them, there seemed to be little organization or cohesion, as each of the three nationalities did things their own way. But they believed their combined 40 divisions compared favourably to Bock's 30. On their far left, the 7e Armée arrived by train near Brussels and began to march towards Breda in the Netherlands and hoped-for cooperation with the Dutch. Finding northern Brabant lacking any defenders and encountering advanced detachments of 18. Armee probing westwards, the 7e Armée pulled back and left southern Netherlands to its fate.

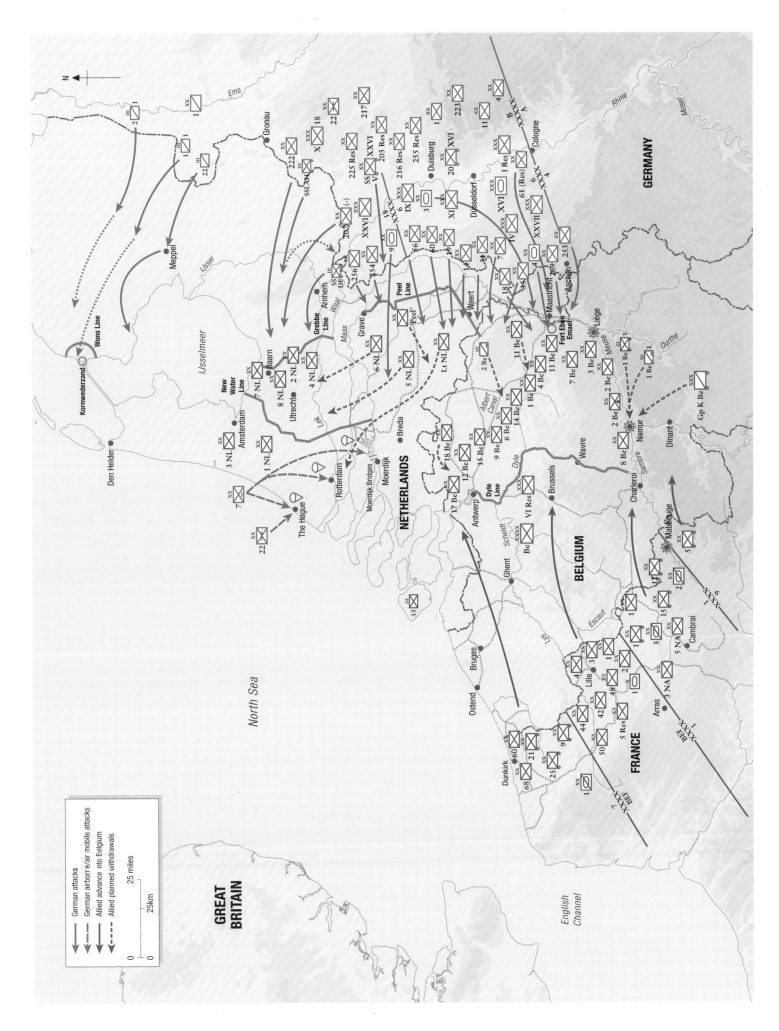

MAP 46: CONQUEST OF THE NETHERLANDS, 12–15 MAY 1940

During the first two days of the war, the Germans had already upset Dutch defensive plans. Airborne units had captured numerous airbases and bridges while panzer, motorized and cavalry forces penetrated deep into the country. The Peel Division manning the Peel Position could not manage to hold out against the 18. Armee for even two days.

During the second and third days of the campaign, German airborne forces along the Waalhaven–Dordrecht–Moerdijk corridor enhanced and hardened their positions to the point where they constituted a solid barrier inside Fortress Holland, far behind the main front. Three Dutch divisions assaulted groupings of paratroopers with minimal lasting effect. To make matters worse in the western Netherlands, Dutch forces around Breda had already abandoned the city and withdrawn into Fortress Holland. When the French 7e Armée arrived in the town, there was no one to link up with. They therefore withdrew back to Belgium on 12 May, pursued by the oncoming 18. Armee.

The Dutch Grebbe Line also posed little more than a minor hindrance to the Germans. The defenders could not execute their flooded lowlands tactic due to the Germans' speed; both armies intermingled. The Dutch had also failed to adequately prepare their troops for fighting in the orchards and woods in this area. Furthermore, with the situation in Fortress Holland already so dire because of the German airborne forces there, the Dutch had no reserves to send to the Grebbe Line. When SS units pierced the south end of the line after less than three days of fighting, the defenders had little choice but to fall back to the weaker New Water Line.

Meanwhile, the invaders' 9. Panzer-Division and SS Verfügungstruppe Division (minus SS-Regiment Der Führer) slipped between the Grebbe Line and the French 7e Armée, now back near Brussels. The SS bore down on Walcheren and Beveland islands, which controlled river traffic leading into the central Netherlands[16].

Meanwhile, the 9. Panzer-Division turned north over the bridges available to it, thanks to the Luftwaffe paratroopers of the 7. Flieger-Division, and towards the edge of Fortress Holland. Here they linked up with airborne forces that had been holding out against Dutch counterattacks for three days, providing much-needed relief and heavy support. Just south of Rotterdam, Dutch troops still held the final Maas Bridge leading into the city. On 14 May, German and Dutch representatives began to parlay the surrender of the bridge's defenders.

Due to miscommunication by both parties, these negotiations dragged on. That same afternoon, unbeknownst to the troops on the ground, 100 He 111 bombers left German airfields to bomb the Dutch holding the bridge. Similarly, aircrews did not know of the pending surrender talks and so bore down on their objectives. The Germans tried by many means to divert or recall the bombers: They made desperate radio calls, ground troops fired Very pistols, and even a Bf 109 from Germany raced to get in front of the He 111 formation to turn it around. Only 43 bombers received the abort message, so 57 dropped their loads into the heart of the city. Although only 100 tons of bombs fell, nearly 1,000 people died, another 78,000 were rendered homeless and 1.1 square miles of the old city were destroyed. The inadvertent bombing of Rotterdam – which, in the heated propaganda battle of war, equated to the attack on Warsaw eight months earlier – represented the last straw for the Netherlands. That same evening of the 14th, the Dutch switched from merely giving up a bridge to surrendering the entire country.

The Germans' airborne attacks compromised Fortress Holland from the war's first minutes. Pockets of paratroopers managed to resist Dutch counterattacks for three to four days, until the ground forces arrived. With relative ease, the Wehrmacht overcame the successive Dutch defensive lines in the centre of the country. Fighting largely ended in the Netherlands on 15 May, except for a small contingent on the islands of Zeeland, which held out until the 17th. Dutch and British ships evacuated the royal family, some government leaders and a few Dutch and Allied soldiers. The government in exile and especially the Royal Dutch Navy continued the war, in particular against the Japanese in the Pacific.

16 At the time of writing (2019), these islands form a peninsula joined to the mainland.

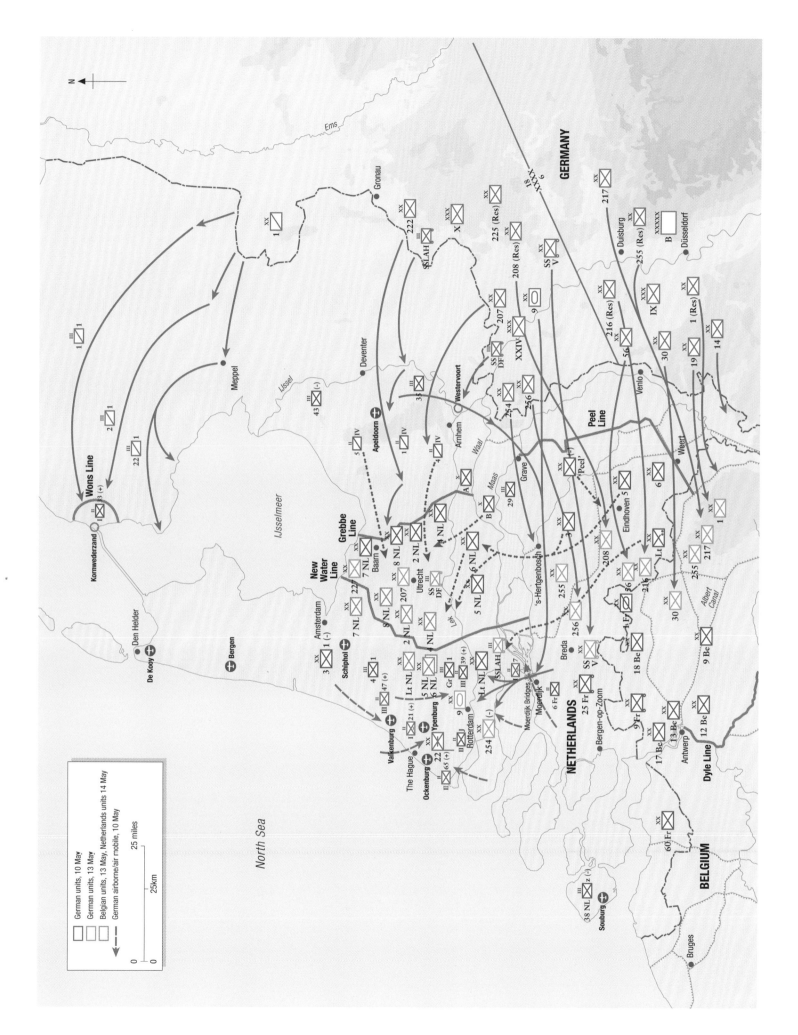

MAP 47: THE APPROACH TO FORT EBEN EMAEL, 10 MAY 1940

Neutrality does not come for free, and Belgium had a long history of fortifying its countryside. Conversely, the Germans also had a legacy of capturing Belgian forts, perhaps most famously when in the very first days of World War I, General Erich Ludendorff captured the Liège fortresses by ruse, when he drove up in a sedan and knocked on the door with his sword hilt, thereby earning the first Pour le Mérite honour of the conflict.

Fort Eben Emael constituted part of the extended Liège fortress zone. In its construction between 1932 and 1935 to guard the confluence of the Meuse/Maas River and Albert Canal, German subcontractors played a large part, and so knew many of its secrets. Reinforced concrete made up most of the fort, and it bristled with cannon and machine guns mounted in concrete emplacements and steel cupolas. Barbed-wire entanglements, moats and anti-tank ditches ringed its pie-shaped exterior. Its longest wall, 990 yards long and 43 yards high, faced the deep Castor cut in the Albert Canal (which opened in 1930). It had a garrison of 1,200, food and water for two months, medical facilities and a self-contained electrical system to generate current for radios, air-conditioning, etc. The fort had two main limitations: Being built into the adjoining terrain, it did not dominate its surroundings and it had only eight anti-aircraft machine guns, a major shortcoming in World War II. The Belgian fortifications had no hope of halting a German invasion, but would delay them long enough to build a credible defence to the rear.

The Germans' main interest was not the fort itself, but the fact that its fire covered three key bridges over the Albert Canal. They wanted to capture the bridges intact to facilitate their westward movement. In *Fall Gelb*, the 6. Armee – in particular, its XVI Panzer-Korps – needed to cross the waterways without delay to keep the pressure on the Allies. With the campaign plans barely a month old, Hitler met Luftwaffe Generalmajor Kurt Student, commander of the 7. Flieger-Division, to discuss the Eben Emael problem. One early decision included use of gliders rather than parachutes, as this way teams would land close together (rather than risk landing widely dispersed by bad weather).

Four groups of 9–11 Ju 52s lifted off from airfields around Cologne at 0430 hours on 10 May, each pulling a DFS 230A glider with ten men inside. Three groups would assault the bridges, while one would take out the fort. As the planes and gliders flew through Dutch airspace, they attracted some air-defence fire, but suffered no losses. Around 35–40 minutes after take-off, the transports and gliders separated. Ten to 15 minutes later, the gliders touched down largely without problems and the paratroopers went to work. The actual assaults are covered on Map 48.

Back in Germany, meanwhile, German Army soldiers moved out to attack across the 15-mile-wide Maastricht appendix between them and Eben Emael. A single Dutch battalion armed with ineffective 20mm anti-tank rifles had the impossible mission of defending the area. Again, the Germans led with special operations forces, in this case commandos dressed as local police on bicycles. The trick failed to deceive the Dutch, who resisted until overcome by German reconnaissance units. A couple of hours later, the Germans had crossed the narrow strip of the Netherlands. They arrived at the Maas just in time to see the bridges demolished by engineer troops. A few hours after that, Maastricht surrendered. German engineering units used ferries to get fresh troops and light vehicles to the western bank, while their comrades began building replacement bridges. By early afternoon, the motorized 10. Schützen-Brigade (4. Panzer-Division) had crossed and set out to relieve the glider troops holding the Albert Canal bridges.

The two German forces linked up at the bridges mid-afternoon. They immediately began attacking the Belgian 4th and 7th Divisions west of the canal. Neither formation gave a good account of itself, considering the few Germans they faced. During the early hours of the 11th, armoured elements of the panzer corps crossed the Maas, joined up with the infantry and set off towards the west. Between the pontoon bridges over the Maas and those captured over the Albert Canal, the Germans regained their mobility. Around 1100 hours that same morning, the garrison of Fort Eben Emael surrendered.

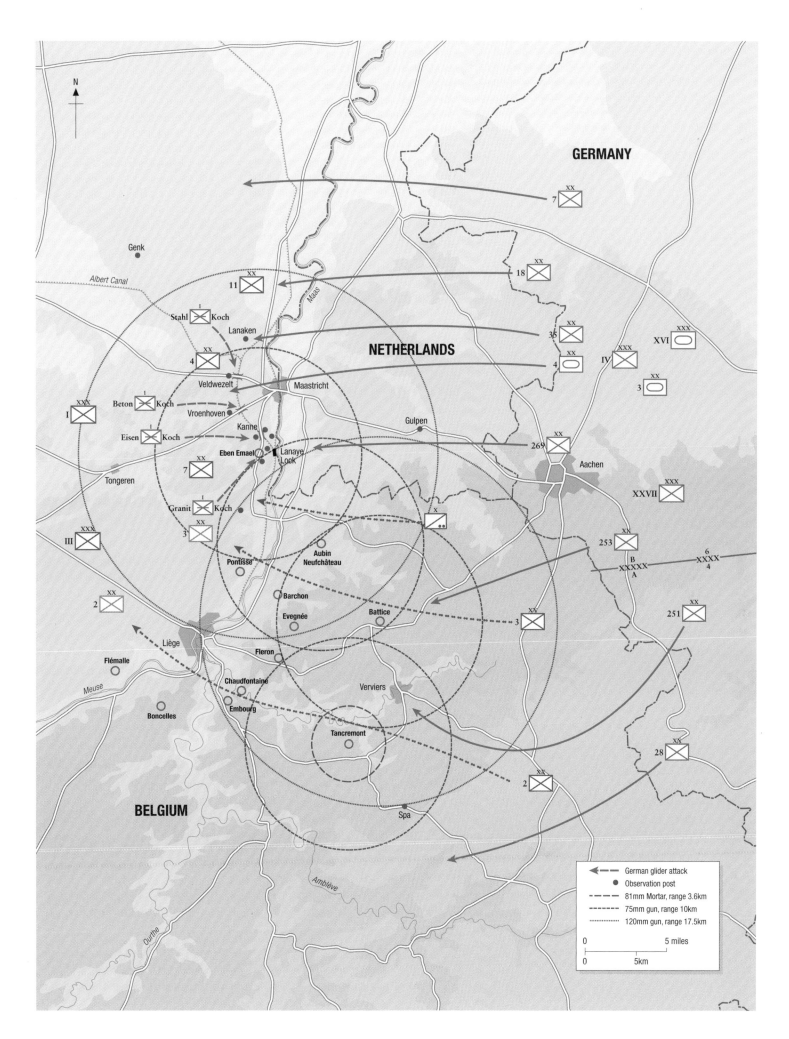

GERMANY

Genk

Albert Canal

NETHERLANDS

11

Stahl | Koch
Lanaken

4

Veldwezelt

Maastricht

Beton | Koch

Vroenhoven

Kanne

Eisen | Koch

Eben Emael

Lanaye Lock

7

Tongeren

Granit | Koch

3

Pontisse

Aubin Neufchâteau

Barchon

Evegnée

Battice

Liège

Fleron

Flémalle

Chaudfontaine

Verviers

Meuse

Boncelles

Embourg

Tancremont

BELGIUM

Spa

Amblève

Ourthe

Gulpen

Aachen

7

18

35

4

IV

3

XVI

269

XXVII

253

A B

XXXXX XXXX 6 4

251

3

2

28

2

Observation post

German glider attack

Observation post

81mm Mortar, range 3.6km

75mm gun, range 10km

120mm gun, range 17.5km

0 _____ 5 miles

0 _____ 5km

MAP 48: CAPTURING FORT EBEN EMAEL, 10 MAY 1940

Although (due to secrecy concerns) the Luftwaffe parachutists did not know the actual objective of their mission until 2130 hours on 9 May, they had been training for six months. The teams had rehearsed and practised against similar fortifications in the Sudetenland. They also tried out specialized weapons, in particular the brand new shaped charge, an innovative chemical energy device for burning holes in steel armour, like that found in Eben Emael's cupolas. The airborne forces did not have to capture the large, well-manned fort (holding 982 men on 10 May), but only incapacitate it until heavier ground troops arrived, so that it could not interfere with traffic over the Maas bridges.

The fort's defenders had a few hours' warning of the pending assault. Unfortunately for them, this was the fifth alarm in six months and it also indicated the wrong type of attack: From the ground, not the air. German gliders arrived at Eben Emael and the three bridges on time and without loss[17]. The paratroopers exited the gliders and fanned out for their group objectives. Surprised and already confused, some defenders fought back, while others quickly surrendered. With each group attacking a specific gun emplacement or cupola, the fort's rooftop saw a flurry of organized chaos. The occasional fake cupola caused some wasted effort and the Germans sustained a few casualties.

For the most part, however, the assault went the Germans' way. In most cases, the shaped-charge explosives worked as intended. Even if they did not completely destroy the weapons inside, the jet created a human killing over-pressure, made the cupola unusable, or ruined the rotating mechanism. In many cases the Belgians abandoned and sealed the cupola and retreated into the bowels of the fort. The fort's machine-gun emplacements, while not the biggest threat, could do plenty of damage against the light airborne troops.

Reducing concrete emplacements was a different matter, since shaped charges had little effect against that material. However, a shaped charge set in a gun embrasure represented just another large explosive. It might only kill one or two and wound a few more, but could fill the

space with smoke and dust or start fires. It also created enough confusion so that hand grenades could be thrown in, or machine-pistol fire could be sprayed through the opening. With the defending crew dead, wounded, or stunned, Germans wearing their protective masks came in. In a few cases, other cupolas or emplacements would fire on the location under attack, but every one of the fort's fighting positions had to fight for its life.

Perhaps half an hour into the assault, the Germans had the top of the fort under control. Another group had arrived as reinforcements and they had suffered only two men killed. With daylight, the Luftwaffe arrived, sure to help against the Belgian counterattack that they expected momentarily. Two He 111s parachuted in canisters of ammunition. From the high ground of the fort, the Germans could see 6. Armee soldiers around the destroyed Maastricht bridges, working hard to get to them.

Meanwhile, at the three bridges, the gliders also landed without serious problems. The local defenders suffered from the same surprise and confusion as their fellows in the fort. The bridge at Kanne, closest to the fort (and under the control of the fort's commander) presented the biggest challenge for the Germans. Gunfire from the fort's outlying blockhouses poured into the assault team on the far bank, and then demolition charges dropped the bridge into the Albert Canal. Girders still above the water could hold individual walking soldiers, but otherwise the bridge was useless. At the other two bridges, the Germans enjoyed more success, at least capturing the crossings intact. At Veldwezelt, a rough landing injured an entire glider load of troops. With the assistance of Luftwaffe close air support and reinforcements that subsequently parachuted into the bridge sites, the airborne forces beat back the infrequent Belgian counterattacks.

The Belgians trapped inside Eben Emael were facing a very difficult situation, with many wounded and little ability to resist. The fort's commander called in friendly artillery on his own rooftop, causing the Germans to seek shelter in abandoned structures. Belgian firing positions in the Castor cutting prevented German ground troops from crossing the Albert Canal until the morning of 11 May. At 1215 hours that day, the fort's bugler sounded the surrender. Essentially, Eben Emael had fallen in 30 minutes to 90 men.

---

17   The leader of the team attacking the fort, Oberleutnant Walter Witzig, did not make it, as the rope towing his glider snapped. He eventually arrived aboard another glider, rejoining his men at 0830 hours.

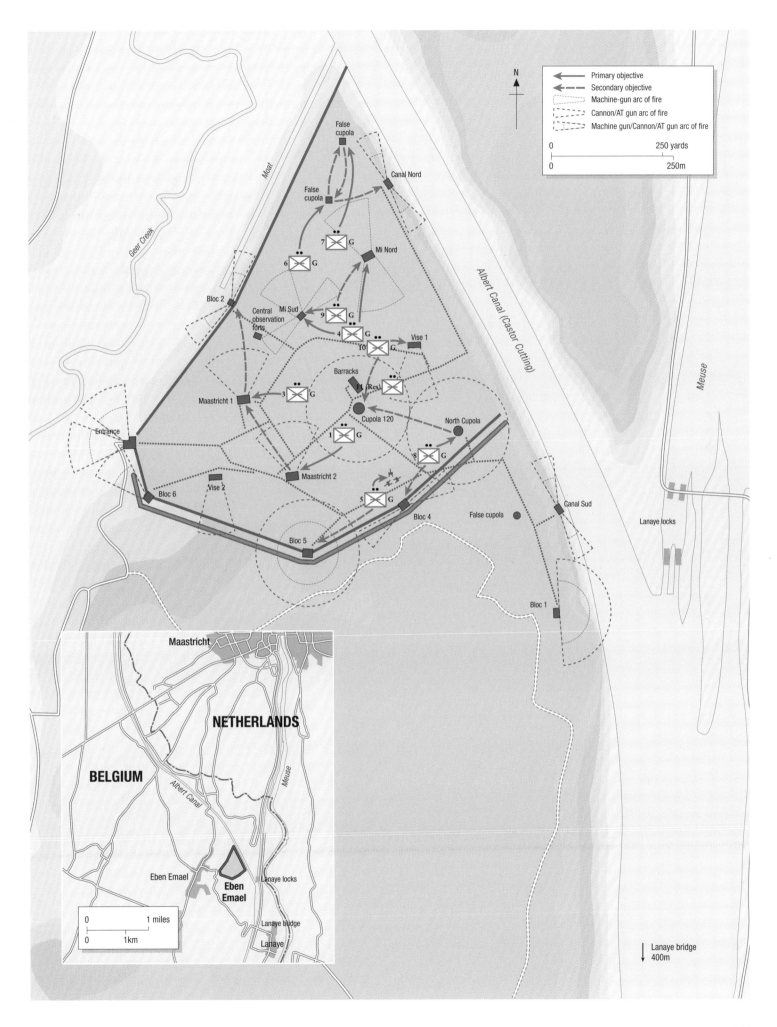

N

←	Primary objective
⇠	Secondary objective
	Machine-gun arc of fire
	Cannon/AT gun arc of fire
	Machine gun/Cannon/AT gun arc of fire

0   250 yards
0   250m

Moat

Geer Creek

False cupola

Canal Nord

False cupola

Mi Nord

7 G

6 G

Bloc 2

Central observation forts

Mi Sud

9 G

4 G

Vise 1

10 G

Barracks

H (Res)

Maastricht 1

3 G

1 G

Cupola 120

North Cupola

8 G

Entrance

Maastricht 2

Vise 2

5 G

Bloc 6

Bloc 4

False cupola

Canal Sud

Lanaye locks

Bloc 5

Albert Canal (Castor Cutting)

Meuse

Bloc 1

Maastricht

NETHERLANDS

BELGIUM

Albert Canal

Meuse

Eben Emael

Eben Emael

Lanaye locks

Lanaye bridge

Lanaye

0   1 miles
0   1km

↓ Lanaye bridge
  400m

113

MAP 49: THE GERMAN INVASION OF CENTRAL BELGIUM, 10–13 MAY 1940

Central Belgium marked the boundary between the two main German army groups, which worked in tandem through this sector of the front. With the Maastricht appendix, Maas and Albert Canal, plus Fort Eben Emael behind them, there would be no major obstacles until they hit the main Allied defences along the Dyle.

The Belgians had never intended to become decisively engaged in the rolling countryside of Limburg and Liège. But neither did they assume that their I Corps would maintain itself in the field barely 36 hours. The corps' two divisions, especially the 4th, had poor reputations, so this turn for the worse did not come as a total surprise. The Allies' primary concern was getting to the Dyle positions (by road, foot and rail) and firmly establishing themselves there, and for this their screening forces to the east had to delay the Germans for a few more days.

One of the first weapons available to the Allies to slow the blitzkrieg was airpower. For millennia, bridges have provided vulnerable chokepoints at which to blunt an enemy's advance. During the first few days of the campaign, French and RAF bombers and close air support aircraft made repeated raids against the numerous bridges in the Maastricht area, critical especially to the XVI Panzer-Korps' manoeuvres. The Germans also understood the bridges' value and susceptibility, so placed large numbers of both army and Luftwaffe Flak gunners near them. German fighters also aggressively patrolled the crossing sites. The Allied air forces took terrible casualties making their attacks and, despite causing little material damage, did contribute to slowing the panzers.

With the disintegration of the I Corps, responsibility for delaying the Germans fell on the various Allied cavalry, armoured car and light mechanized forces such as the Régiment des Chasseurs Ardennais. Luftwaffe reconnaissance and close air support units kept the ground commanders well informed of Allied movements and positions. The reverse, the ability of the Allies' aircraft to observe and attack the German Army, quickly diminished in the face of growing Luftwaffe air superiority. Armed with good intelligence on the enemy, XVI Panzer-Korps' commander General der Kavallerie Erich Hoepner knew exactly how to arrange his forces. Capitalizing on the Germans'

combined-arms skills, he created *Kampfgruppen* (battle groups) of infantry, artillery and panzers, all covered by fighters and supported by Stukas. These infiltrated between the two shoulders of the remaining defence here, the bend in the Gete River near Diest in the north and the fortresses of Liège and Namur in the south. Rivers and adjoining terrain ran parallel to their movement, hindering the Allied defenders. Planning to bar the way of his 824 panzers stood the 2e and 3e French Divisions Légère Mécanique,(Light Mechanized) of the Corps de Cavalerie (520 tanks), about 20 miles in front of the developing Dyle defences.

Advancing on a broad front between Neerhespen and Braives early on 12 May, forward detachments of 4. Panzer-Division came under fire from the French tanks. That afternoon, attack and counterattack followed, with villages near Hannut changing hands often. Around noon on the 13th, German artillery and close air support began softening up the French positions before the infantry and panzers attacked. Battles raged in the area all afternoon, the village of Merdorp saw several vicious tank-vs-tank encounters. By 1500–1600 hours, the Corps de Cavalerie commander Général René Prioux could see that his front had been penetrated, and so ordered his men to withdraw. His tankers launched stalling attacks to allow his infantry to disengage. Belgian refugees fleeing to the south-west hindered both retreat and pursuit.

Early in the morning of the 13th, the 3. and 4. Panzer Divisionen moved out towards Gembloux and the Dyle, where another tank battle erupted. In 48 hours of armoured combat, the French lost 134 tanks to the Germans' 48. Hoepner's men had possession of the battlefield. This earned more than simple bragging rights: His maintenance crews could recover and repair many of the 174 damaged AFVs and return them to battle. In a larger sense, these battles demonstrated what French armour could accomplish in fairly evenly matched contests. German combat experience gained in Poland and close air support probably made the difference around Hannut. However, these two days of fighting beg the question: How might Allied fortunes have improved that spring if they had used their mechanized formations more like Prioux had?

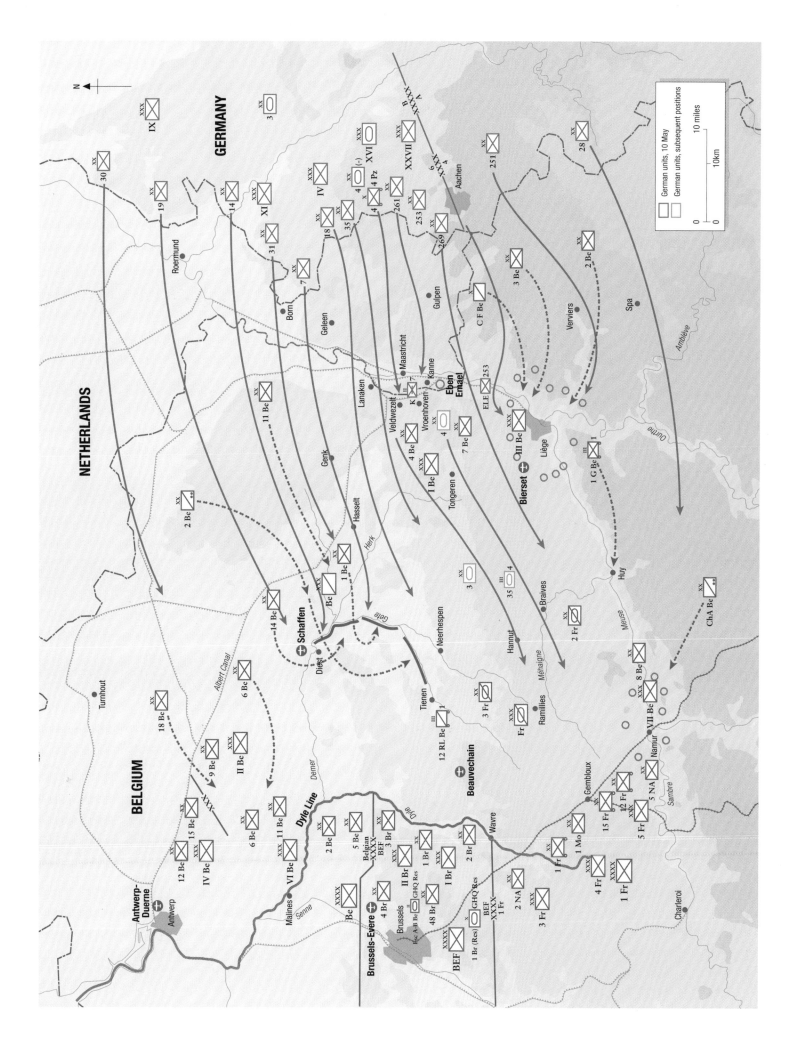

NETHERLANDS

GERMANY

BELGIUM

Antwerp-Duerne

Antwerp

Turnhout

Roermund

Born

Geleen

Gulpen

Aachen

Spa

Verviers

Genk

Hasselt

Maastricht

Kanne

Eben Emael

Liège

Lanaken

Veldwezelt

Vroenhoven

Bierset

Tongeren

Huy

Diest

Schaffen

Tienen

Neerhespen

Hannut

Braives

Malines

Brussels

Brussels-Evere

Wavre

Gembloux

Namur

Ramillies

Beauvechain

Charleroi

Dyle Line

Albert Canal

Gete

Demer

Senne

Dyle

Méhaigne

Meuse

Sambre

Ourthe

Amblève

Herk

N

MAP 50: THE BATTLE OF BELGIUM, 14–21 MAY 1940

Four days into *Fall Gelb*, major problems on the flanks of the Allies' Dyle defensive system appeared: To the north, Fortress Holland stood on the verge of collapse, while in the south Panzergruppe Kleist had crossed the Meuse in force. During the third week of May, the defenders bowed to the inevitable and abandoned the Dyle Line.

With the Germans celebrating their good fortune so far, the Allies tackled the issue of command and control at their top echelons. Gamelin had all but surrendered his generalissimo position, so now a clutch of French generals, a British field marshal, and the Belgian monarch met on the 12th near Mons to decide who would fill the de facto leadership vacuum. At this decisive juncture, the three national contingents preparing to fight for their existence in central Belgium needed someone to coordinate their efforts. In the end, Général Gaston Billotte, commanding the French 1re Groupe d'Armées and a logical choice, got the job, despite his own objections.

The screening mission in front of the main Dyle Line concluded when the Belgian Cavalry Corps gave up the Gete River and withdrew, exposing British and French units to Bock's men bearing down on them. In front of Rundstedt, divisions around Liège pulled back towards Namur, leaving the Liège forts to fend for themselves. The Dyle Line (in the main corresponding to the Belgian Koningshooikt–Wavre or KW Line) ran generally from the Scheldt Estuary north of Antwerp, down the Scheldt and Dyle Rivers, then cross country to Namur. Some 22 Allied divisions manned the first line, although a couple of these had been roughed up during the preceding days' fighting. During the interwar period, the Belgians, not in coordination with Britain or France, built a number of concrete defensive works along the line, plus supporting infrastructure. In the event of war with Germany, they merely assumed that their allies would agree on the wisdom of their plans and fall into position. Lacking time to do much otherwise, and with the Germans fast approaching, they had to make every hour count.

Between 14 and 15 May, around 16 divisions of 6. Armee pulled up opposite the Dyle positions with orders not to allow the Allies to regain their footing following the retreat. Antwerp stood on the wrong side of the Scheldt, so Belgian units falling back in that direction did not gain much defensive benefit from the river or the city. Where the rivers bulged to the east of Brussels, German corps probed to find the army boundaries. Not only were these vulnerable seams administrative, they were national, too. A see-saw battle developed around Wavre between the IV Armee-Korps and French 3e Corps. The fortresses surrounding Namur on the Allies' right did their job of keeping back the Germans.

By 16 May, the Dyle Plan showed its unrealistic and overblown importance for all the world to see. The Allies' primary defensive line and key to their operational plans for years had lasted barely 36 hours. Billotte resolved to abandon the position, but poor communications prevented him from telling his two allies. As much as they regretted leaving their capital, between Antwerp and Brussels the Belgian II and IV corps fell back to the Willebroek Canal. Just like 1914, joining Britain and France in 1940 had not saved this small country. Between Brussels and Namur, the French 3e Corps withdrew to the Charleroi Canal. With the Germans keeping up the pressure, the Allies made temporary pauses along the Senne and Dendre Rivers. Meanwhile, units of the untethered French 7e Armée moved south perpendicular to everyone else, adding to the chaos. The retreat threatened to turn into rout.

Where they could, Allied mechanized forces launched counterattacks to keep the Germans back, the Belgian Cavalry Corps action west of Antwerp being the best example. However, the cause of the disease was at the very top and, on 18 May, Premier Reynaud cashiered Gamelin. The new supreme commander, 73-year-old Général Weygand, said he needed 48 hours to decipher the situation and decide what to do next. However, two days is like a lifetime when trying to counter the blitzkrieg decision cycle. At that same time, Gort visited Billotte and found him a shattered man – perplexed and out of ideas of what to do next.

By 19 May, all three Allied armies had reached the Escaut Line, the combination of the Escaut (Scheldt) River and Terneuzen–Ghent Canal. Here 25 exhausted and, in some cases, heavily attritted Allied divisions ceased withdrawing, faced about and made ready for the next German onslaught. The situation became immeasurably worse on the following day: XIX Panzer-Korps reached the Channel coast near Abbeville. In exactly ten days, Hitler had encircled the cream of the Allied armies – the French 1re Groupe d'Armées, the BEF and the Belgian Army – between the anvil of the English Channel and the hammer of the German Army.

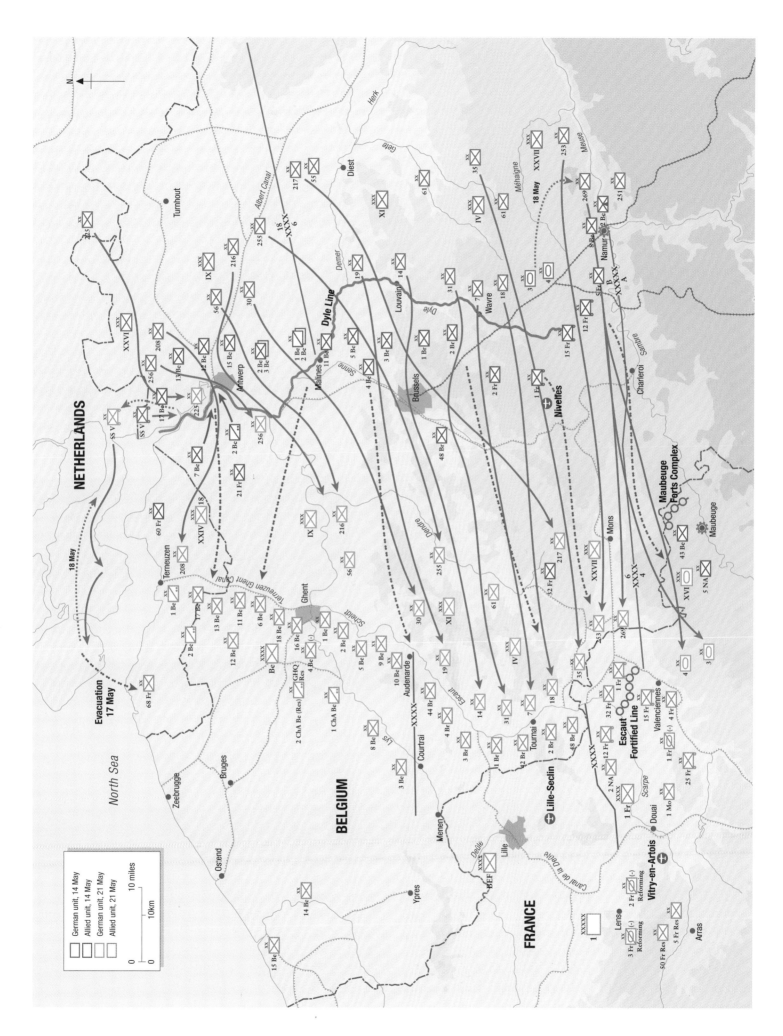

MAP 51: GERMAN MOVEMENTS THROUGH THE ARDENNES FOREST, 10–12 MAY 1940

The single key to the success of the entire *Fall Gelb* sickle-cut operation rested on Panzergruppe Kleist's ability to cross the Ardennes Forest undetected. Allied units advancing into Luxembourg and eastern Belgium to block the Germans, or air interdiction in the steep defiles and narrow roads in the forest would surely complicate the invasion; in the worst-case scenario, they would seriously jeopardize it.

To ensure the success of Heeresgruppe A, the Germans employed a wide array of special tactics, including extensive deception actions, a thick blanket of fighter cover and flak guns and special operations forces. One example of the latter in particular, Operation *Hedderich* early on 10 May, saw 125 volunteers from the 34. Infanterie-Division in 25 Fi 56 liaison aircraft (two passengers each, making numerous round trips) fly to half a dozen places along the French–Luxembourg border to block French units tasked with entering Luxembourg and slowing the invaders. A number of Brandenburger teams also went ahead of the panzers, disarming the Luxembourg gendarmerie. Together, these moves helped delay the French units detailed to move east and set up obstacles to slow the Germans: The 3e Division Légère de Cavalerie and 1re Brigade de Spahis (on horseback). The 3e Division came up from the south towards Esch, but did not aggressively push hard against the 16. Armee, covering Kleist's left. Elsewhere, opposite Heeresgruppe A, scouting elements of the French 2e and 9e Armées tentatively crept forward into south-eastern Belgium.

Across the front, German infantry divisions led the way into Belgium and Luxembourg against light to non-existent opposition. Immediately behind them came Kleist's panzers – working with General der Infanterie Hermann Hoth's XV Panzerkorps immediately to the north – upon which all German hopes rested. Kleist organized the Panzergruppe into highly choreographed echelons stretching back to the vicinity of Frankfurt. His 41,000 vehicles had to negotiate four routes west through the Ardennes, with Guderian's XIX Panzer-Korps in the lead (1., 2. and 10. Panzer Divisionen, totalling 818 panzers), followed by Generalleutnant Georg-Hans Reinhardt's XLI Panzer-Korps (6. and 8. Panzer-Divisionen plus 2. Infanterie Division (mot.), 436 panzers), with XIV Armeekorps (mot.) (13. and 29. Infanterie-Divisionen, securing the group's left flank) bringing up the rear. Hoth had 542 panzers in the 5. and 7. Panzer Divisionen and the 62. Infanterie-Division. The three panzer corps had as their objectives the following Meuse River crossings: Guderian, *Schwerpunkt* of the *Schwerpunkt* – Sedan; Reinhardt – Monthermé; and Hoth – Dinant.

The 2e and 9e Armées had the unenviable job of halting the panzer thrust. Between Sedan and Longuyon stood 2e Armée with six infantry divisions, one light brigade (Chasseurs) and two divisions légère de cavalerie. The 9e Armée defended between Sedan and Namur with seven infantry divisions (one motorized), one cavalry brigade and two divisions légère de cavalerie. Both assumed they occupied easily defended terrain between the Maginot Line and the main defence on the Dyle River. Unfortunately for them, German intelligence had already identified their vulnerable shared boundary, running just north of Sedan. This seam would become the Allies Achilles' heel.

By noon on 10 May, the Germans had passed through Luxembourg and entered into eastern Belgium, but were still deep in the Ardennes. As planned, Belgian and French light screening forces gave way. They probably withdrew too easily and quickly, failing in the main missions of cavalry for centuries: to appreciably slow the enemy; gain intelligence on his strength, dispositions or main attack vectors; and give friendly main defensive forces time to prepare. Lacking motorized transport, the French 11e and 12e Division d'Infantrie moved forward slowly and often without all their artillery and heavy equipment.

By the afternoon of 12 May, advanced detachments of the leading panzer divisions neared the Meuse. Across the front, French units stretched back for miles in long, congested columns. Some divisions only had half their combat troops in position, and then often without their anti-tank or anti-aircraft guns. Compounding their problems, Belgian defensive works along the river fell short of pre-war Belgian promises. Cooperation and command and control between the two Allies were deficient. Late that day, Generalmajor Erwin Rommel's 7. Panzer-Division became the first German unit to cross the Meuse, immediately north of Dinant.

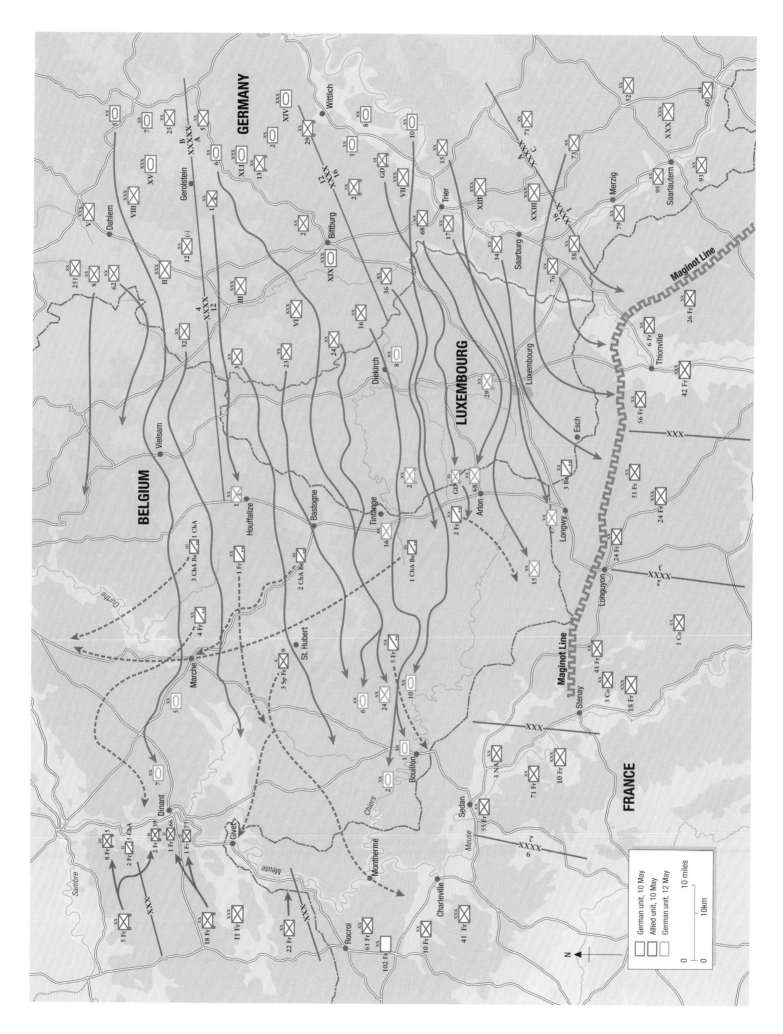

GERMANY

BELGIUM

LUXEMBOURG

FRANCE

Dahlem
Gerolstein
Bittburg
Wittlich
Trier
Saarburg
Merzig
Saarlautern
Thionville
Vielsam
Houffalize
Bastogne
Tintange
Luxembourg
Esch
Marche
St. Hubert
Arlon
Longwy
Longuyon
Diekirch
Stenay
Dinant
Givet
Bouillon
Sedan
Monthermé
Charleville
Rocroi

Ourthe
Sambre
Meuse
Meuse
Chiers

Maginot Line
Maginot Line

N

Legend:
German unit, 10 May
Allied unit, 10 May
German unit, 12 May

10 miles
10km
0

119

MAP 52: THE GERMAN MEUSE RIVER BRIDGEHEADS, 13–15 MAY 1940

Armies in World War II still placed inordinate significance on river defences. We have seen this with the Vistula and Dyle Rivers, but the same would be the case with Dvina, Dnepr, Rapido, Rhine and countless others. In almost every case, the river failed to live up to its decisive reputation. An average golfer could clear the Meuse River at Sedan-Glaire with a 9-iron. Yet in 1940, both sides inflated the importance of the river's value as an obstacle: The Allies as an anchor for their defences, the Germans as a major impediment to their panzer thrust through the Ardennes.

Two days into *Fall Gelb*, the Germans had the worst of the hilly forest behind them. Operationally, the Allies still had not awakened to the danger, while tactically delaying forces had failed to accomplish their mission. A key factor in the calculated gamble of the Manstein plan consisted of putting an entire army of panzers and thousands of vehicles on narrow twisting forest roads, each with countless chokepoints and defiles where a competent defence could have wrecked the entire operation. This did not happen and, on the morning of 12 May, forces of the 4. and 12. Armeen prepared to transition from the rough Ardennes to the more open, rolling countryside of the Meuse Valley.

The Germans approached the Meuse along three main axes. From north to south these were: Hoth's XV Panzer-Korps (5. and 7. Panzer plus 62. Infanterie Divisionen) aiming for the crossing at Dinant; XLI Panzer-Korps (6. and 8. Panzer Divisionen with 2. Infanterie-Division [mot.]) under Reinhardt making for Monthermé; and Guderian's XIX Panzer-Korps (1., 2. and 10. Panzer Divisionen and Infanterie-Regiment Grossdeutschland), attacking towards Sedan. The defenders included the Belgian 1st Chasseurs Ardennais Division screening forwards, and the 4e, 1re and 5e Division Légère de Cavalerie (a mix of horse/motorized) and 3e Brigade de Spahis (all horse, from North Africa) of the 9e Armée behind them.

Early on 12 May, Hoth and Guderian advanced and easily shoved aside the Belgian and French defenders. Reinhardt remained stretched out behind Guderian, still deep in the Ardennes, although his 6. Panzer-Division would soon reach the open. Considering the short distance and relatively constricted terrain encountered so far, along much of the German front, infantry had kept pace with the mechanized formations.

HOTH AT DINANT

The French 11e Corps d'Armée did not have its defences fully established when XV Panzer-Korps hit them on the 12th. As everywhere else, they had badly miscalculated how much time the Germans required, both to reach the river and to make a hasty crossing. Hoth only needed a couple of hours to cover the last dozen miles to the Meuse. North of Dinant,

using the island at Houx late in the day,[18] 5. Panzer-Division gained a small bridgehead, which it held during the night. Between there and Dinant, 7. Panzer-Division assaulted across the river, but the French defenders threw it back. By early on the 13th, both panzer divisions were on the west bank, slightly expanding their bridgeheads. A day later, 7. Panzer-Division had split the seam between the 1re Division Cuirassée and 18e Division d'Infanterie. By the 15th, Hoth's corps had raced down the road to Philippeville. To his left, 32. Infanterie-Division had created its own bridgehead at Givet and beyond.

REINHARDT AT MONTHERMÉ

The XLI Panzer-Korps had enough of 'eating Guderian's dust' and was in the open late on 12 May. Its leading 6. Panzer-Division covered the distance between Luxembourg and the Meuse in just over a day. At Monthermé, the river cuts through a deep gorge and makes a 180-degree turn. Supported by 450 bomber sorties from Flieger-Korps II, and stringing together assault rafts to make an improvised pontoon bridge, on the 13th the 6. Panzer-Division fought its way across against the 102e Division d'Infanterie de Forteresse. In the constricted terrain, the division made slow progress over the 14th. With nowhere to hide, it suffered under intense French artillery fire. Reinhard finally broke out towards the east on 15 May. By that time, marching infantry had caught up on both flanks.

GUDERIAN AT SEDAN

Early on 12 May, XIX Panzer-Korps easily negotiated the small Semois River on either side of Bouillon, scattered the 5e Division Légère de Cavalerie and reached Sedan by evening. As before, the 55e Division d'Infanterie assumed the Germans would need days to bring up artillery and pioneer equipment. But Guderian did not allow his men the luxury of much sleep, and that night made final preparations for a hasty crossing the next day. The 13th began with nearly 600 close air support sorties from Flieger-Korps II and VIII, followed by an hour-long barrage by his corps guns. At 1600 hours, Guderian's main effort, 1. Panzer-Division and Grossdeutschland, hit at Glaire. Two supporting attacks came up river at Wadelincourt (10. Panzer-Division) and downstream at Donchery (2. Panzer-Division). The 1. Panzer-Division's assault enjoyed immediate success, 2. Panzer-Division's less so, while 10. Panzer-Division struggled to get across. The damage had been done, however, right on the boundary of the 9e and 2e Armées. The XIX Panzer-Korps expanded its bridgehead on the 14th and 15th against feeble resistance and uncoordinated counterattacks. Manstein's plan had passed another critical milestone.

---

18 In August 1914, German troops crossed the Meuse at this precise location.

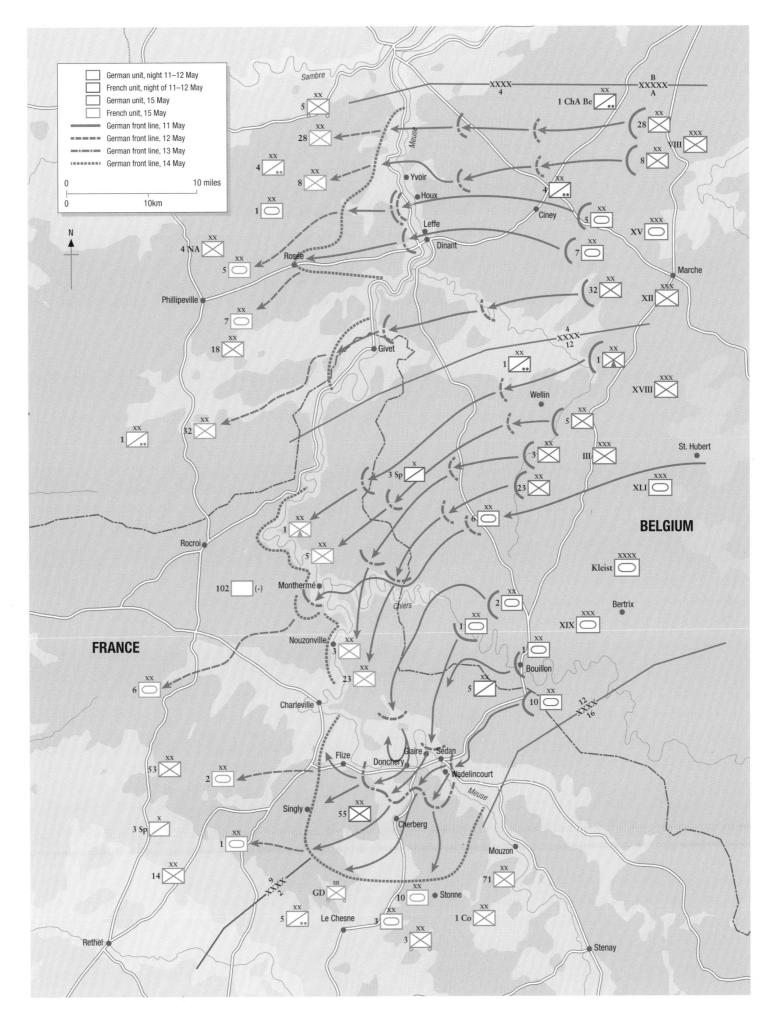

Legend:
- German unit, night 11–12 May
- French unit, night of 11–12 May
- German unit, 15 May
- French unit, 15 May
- German front line, 11 May
- German front line, 12 May
- German front line, 13 May
- German front line, 14 May

0 — 10 miles
0 — 10km

N

Sambre
Meuse

5 XX
28 XX
4 XX
8 XX
1 XX
4 NA XX
5 XX
Rosee
Phillipeville
7 XX
18 XX
1 XX
32 XX
Rocroi

Yvoir
Houx
Leffe
Dinant
Ciney
Givet
Wellin
3 Sp x

1 ChA Be XX
B
XXXXX
A
28 XX
VIII XXX
8 XX
4 XX
5 XX
XV XXX
7 XX
32 XX
XII XXX
Marche
4
XXXX
12
1 XX
XVIII XXX
5 XX
3 XX
III XXX
23 XX
6 XX
XLI XXX
St. Hubert

BELGIUM

Kleist XXXX

1 XX
5 XX
102 (-)
Monthermé
2 XX
1 XX
Chiers
1 XX
Bouillon
XIX XXX
Bertrix

FRANCE

Nouzonville
3 XX
23 XX
6 XX
5 XX
10 XX
12
XXXX
16

Charleville
53 XX
2 XX
Flize
Glaire
Sedan
Donchery
Wadelincourt
Meuse
Singly
55 XX
Cherberg
3 Sp x
1 XX
14 XX
9
XXXX
2
GD III
5 XX
Le Chesne
3 XX
10 XX
Stonne
Mouzon
71 XX
1 Co XX
3 XX
Rethel
Stenay

121

MAP 53: THE GERMAN BREAKOUT, 15–17 MAY 1940

With significant bridgeheads over the Meuse at Dinant and Sedan, and another threatening at Monthermé, Kleist and Hoth were poised to break out into the gently rolling Belgian and French terrain to the west of the river. Into the relatively confined 50-mile-wide gap between Laon and the fortress complex at Maubeuge, Rundstedt crammed seven panzer, three motorized and nine infantry divisions. Against this, the 9e Armée mustered five mechanized, three motorized and ten marching divisions. While this appears to be an even-odds encounter, superior German command and control, concentration of force (especially its mechanized formations) and aviation would make the decisive difference.

The morning of 15 May began with Prime Minister Reynaud telephoning Churchill to exclaim, 'We are beaten. We have lost the Battle. A torrent of tanks is bursting through!'[19]. Wanting a second opinion, the new prime minister called Général d'Armée Alphonse-Joseph Georges, commanding the north-west theatre, who painted a more positive picture. Gamelin sent a telegram admitting to difficulties between Namur and Sedan, but also exuding calmness. The situation on the ground looked much different.

During the night of 14/15 May, the retreating 9e Armée was pulled in every direction with army group, army and corps commanders all having their own ideas of where the army should halt and make its stand. Right or wrong, ultimate blame for the deteriorating defensive situation fell on the commander of the 9e Armée, Général d'Armée André Corap. Georges replaced him late on the 15th, with Général d'Armée Henri Giraud. Giraud did not bring the best reputation with him: His 7e Armée had ceased to exist, getting caught up in the chaos in the southern Netherlands and northern Belgium. Conflicting orders, a new commander and, most of all, the rampaging Germans made the bad conditions worse. But on top of these problems, every road in northern France was clogged with refugees fleeing the fighting, while civilians injured by Luftwaffe attacks competed with wounded soldiers for hospital space.

Whereas the Wehrmacht wielded its panzer and motorized units as an operationally concentrated and unified fist, the French scattered their mechanized formations all over the battlefield. At the base of Kleist's penetration, at Stonne in the 2e Armée area, the 3e Division Cuirassée arrived as part of the 21e Corps d'Armée, sent to threaten Guderian's flank and rear. French command and control, inefficient

dispersal and logistics, in this case refuelling the tanks, delayed the counterattack. Early on 15 May, the French manoeuvre enjoyed some initial success, since German anti-tank guns could not defeat the large Char B tanks. The 10. Panzer-Division and Infanterie-Regiment Grossdeutschland stabilized the situation by afternoon. The XIX Panzer-Korps resumed its advance towards the Montcornet crossroads.

In the centre of the German panzer thrust, Reinhardt finally gained the upper hand at Monthermé. Defending in some of the most favourable terrain along the middle Meuse, the 41e Corps d'Armée held, despite blistering Luftwaffe close air support. The 41e finally began to fall back on the 15th. The 6. Panzer-Division led the pursuit with the 8.Panzer-Division behind it. The 2e Division Cuirassée, arriving variously by rail and road, attempted to blunt the panzers, but was spread out between the Oise and Serre Rivers in regimental packets. That evening, 6. Panzer-Division reached Hirson; 9e Armée headquarters was only 10 miles away at Vervins.

By 16 May, 9e Armée, cut off from its neighbours to the north and south, was evaporating before Giraud's eyes. Orders went out that day to the 2e Division Cuirassée to launch a counterattack at Montcornet (now occupied by the 1., 2. and 6. Panzer Divisions), but these were amended to a defensive mission, much to the frustration of the French tankers. However, the panzers and motorized infantry had advanced too far for the comfort of Hitler, the OKH and army group headquarters. Rundstedt made the initial decision to halt his panzers that morning and his chain of command endorsed the order. With the exception of forward detachments allowed to seize bridgeheads at Landrecies and Moy, the bulk of his panzers were to stand fast until the 18th, when marching infantry theoretically would close the distance. As was their style, commanders like Guderian and Rommel used very liberal definitions of forward detachments to include the bulk of their organizations.

On 17 May, the French launched a counterattack that both sides of the panzer halt debate could use to bolster their argument. That day, the 4e Division Cuirassée – a hastily thrown together, untrained and improvised grouping commanded by Colonel Charles de Gaulle – assaulted Guderian's left north-east of Laon. With the help of Stuka close air support, the threat was brushed aside by afternoon. Cautious leaders used the attack to justify the halt order; aggressive younger panzer generals pointed to de Gaulle's futility to demonstrate that the French Army could no longer mount a serious threat.

19 John Williams, *France: Summer 1940*, Ballantine's: New York, 1969, p. 56

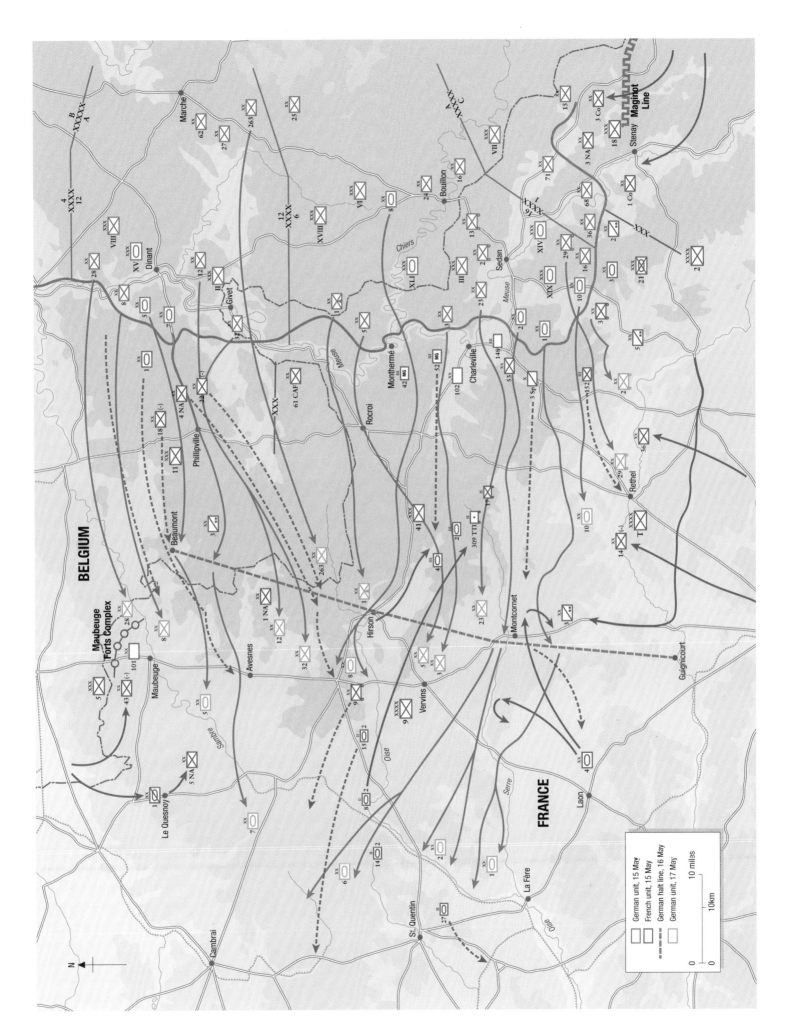

BELGIUM

Marche

25

263

27
62

B
XXXX
A

4
XXXX
12

VIII
28

XV
Dinant

8

5

1

12
XXXX
6

XVIII

VII

8

24
Bouillon

16

VII

C
XXXX

15

3 Co
Maginot
Line

18

Stenay

3 NA

71

68

36
1 Co

2

29

XIV

16

3

2

XXXX

XXXX
2

12

II
Givet

37

263

61 CAF

Meuse

Chiers

Sedan

13

2

XLIX

III

23

Meuse

10

5

21

5

Montcornet

Rethel

36

29
T

14

T

Monthermé

42 MG

52 MG

102

Charleville

148

53

152

2

10

Rocroi

Phillipville

4 NA

11

18

8

3

263

1 NA

12

32

Beaumont

41

2

309 TTI

4

23

3

1

Hirson

8

9

Vervins

9

5

3

Maubeuge
Forts Complex

28

101

5

43

Maubeuge

5

8

Avesnes

5

15

2

8

2

Guignicourt

10

4

Laon

Serre

Le Quesnoy

1

2

5 NA

7

6

14

2

1

6

La Fère

Oise

Cambrai

St. Quentin

27

Oise

N

German unit, 15 May
French unit, 15 May
German halt line, 16 May
German unit, 17 May

10 miles

10km

123

MAP 54: THE DRIVE TO THE SEA, 18–20 MAY 1940

Although some historians make much of the panzer halt orders, arguing that these point to the continued conservatism of the German Army and even Hitler, they had little impact on *Fall Gelb*. Even at this early point in the campaign, the Wehrmacht could have taken a 'rest and relaxation' day and this would not have saved the Allied cause.

In Belgium on 16 May, the Allies began to abandon the Dyle for the Escaut. The OKH ordered 6. Armee not to follow too aggressively; it did not want the Allied armies in Belgium to slip the trap. The BEF had already drifted southward towards Gort's headquarters at Arras. On the 17th, Gort took the 12th, 23rd and 46th Territorial Divisions off 'line of communications' duty (keeping the army's rearward communications open) and sent them to man the front along the Canal du Nord. Together, the BEF would back up the wavering 9e Armée, which had been on the receiving end of Rundstedt's main effort.

By 18 May, German intelligence picked up indications that the Allies had begun to retreat away from Belgium, south over the Somme River and on to a possible escape. This moved Hitler to stop fretting over imaginary Allied attacks against Kleist's left and he had OKH again unleash the panzers towards the Channel. Guderian and Reinhardt received the mission to puncture the canal line. Hoth, soon to be joined by Hoepner, transferred from the 6. to the 4. Armee. The British 12th and 23rd Infantry Divisions, minus most of their artillery, were to hold the line along with two French divisions soon to arrive; unfortunately, their allies never showed up. Seven panzer and three motorized divisions (now including SS-Division Totenkopf) squeezed into a front barely 30 miles wide.

Giraud ordered the 1re Division Légère Mécanique to counterattack into 5. Panzer-Division near the Mormal Forest to blunt Reinhardt, but because it lacked mass, this came to nothing. The French still seemed numb to what the Germans were doing. On the morning of the 18th, Billotte told Georges, 'We are holding everywhere. The withdrawal of the Belgians and British is going according to plan. Giraud is content'[20]. The entire statement is laughable; at the moment Billotte uttered it, Reinhardt's 6. Panzer-Division overran Giraud's headquarters at Le Catelet and the general wandered alone through the night until a

German patrol captured him early the next morning. In the north, Rommel reached the World War I battlefield of Cambrai. Along the Somme, Guderian approached Péronne.

Finally, on 19 May, Gamelin realized that the German plan was not a modernized Schlieffen Plan aiming for Paris, but one seeking to trap the 1re Groupe d'Armées, including the BEF and Belgians, against the Channel. He ordered the 2e and 6e Armées to counterattack at the base of the penetration, near Sedan. He added, 'It is all a matter of time' – the one commodity he did not have. At this late stage he wanted to save the trapped army group by acting 'with extreme audacity',[21] another commodity in very short supply. After doing next-to-nothing to lead his army or save his country, Reynaud cashiered Gamelin and replaced him with Weygand. Reynaud took over the defence portfolio (from Daladier) and made other changes to his government. Gort sensed pending disaster too, and on the same day recommended to London that the BEF retreat either south over the Somme or towards the Channel. Believing reports from Paris, the British cabinet decided to move the BEF to the Somme.

As the politicians pontificated, British soldiers died. After days fighting the 8. Panzer-Division, by the 19th the 70th Infantry Brigade of the 23rd Infantry Division counted 250 men. Guderian hugged the right bank of the Somme. De Gaulle launched another attack from Laon towards Crécy with his ad hoc division of 150 tanks, a smattering of infantry, but almost no artillery. Such manoeuvres are prudent and tactically sound, but de Gaulle's results were predictably meagre.

Then it happened. On 20 May, Guderian's panzer troops began to arrive near the Channel coast. The 2. Panzer-Division made it there first, arriving at Abbeville after covering 56 miles from the Canal du Nord in a single day. Right behind it, its sister 1. Panzer-Division took Amiens and its environs. To the north, the other panzer divisions pulled even with Guderian, although they would not reach the sea until early on the 21st. Twenty miles of German-held territory separated the BEF at Arras from the French south of the Somme. Nearly 420,000 Allied soldiers had been encircled. That dark day, Weygand did not even think of saving them; instead he made diplomatic rounds in Paris.

---

20 Shirer 1971, p. 609

21 Robert Jackson, *Dunkirk*, Playboy Press: New York, 1980, p. 16.

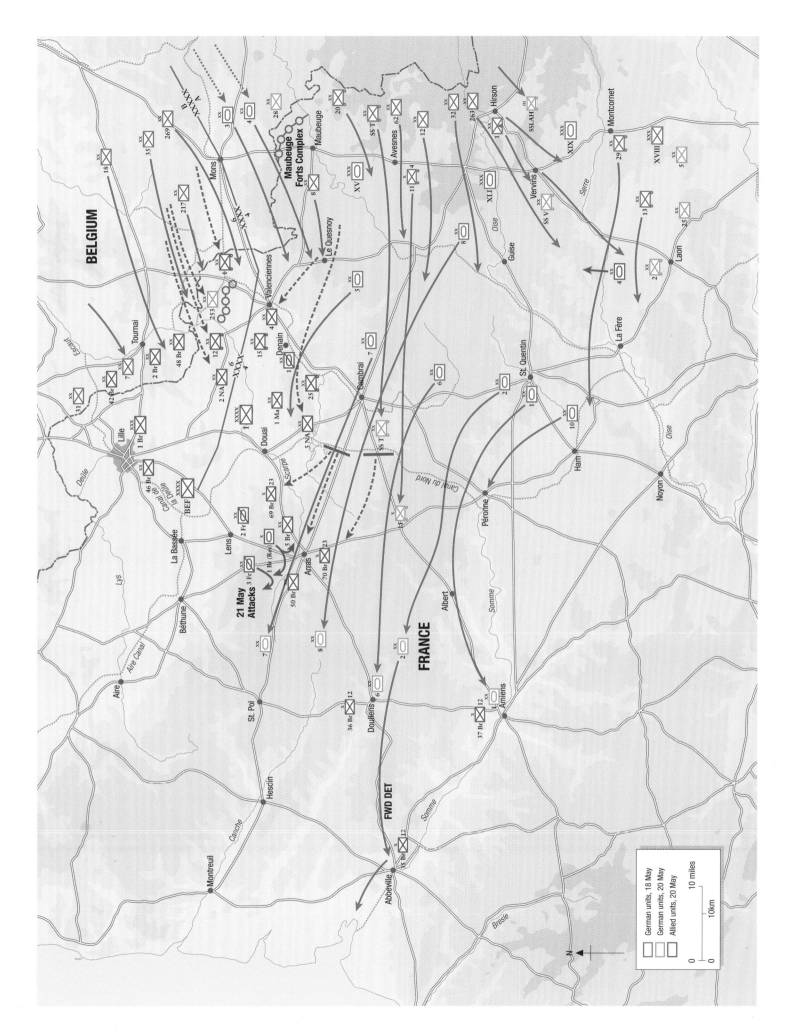

BELGIUM

FRANCE

Maubeuge
Forts Complex

21 May
Attacks

FWD DET

Lille
Tournai
Mons
Maubeuge
Avesnes
Hirson
Montcornet
Valenciennes
Le Quesnoy
Guise
Vervins
Laon
Denain
Cambrai
La Fère
Douai
St Quentin
La Bassée
Lens
Arras
Ham
Noyon
Béthune
Péronne
Aire
Albert
Amiens
St. Pol
Doullens
Hesdin
Abbeville
Montreuil

Escaut
Deûle
Lys
Canal de la Deûle
Scarpe
Canal du Nord
Oise
Serre
Oise
Somme
Somme
Aire Canal
Canche
Bresle

	German units, 18 May
	German units, 20 May
	Allied units, 20 May

0   10 miles
0   10km

125

MAP 55: CLOSING THE DUNKIRK–LILLE POCKET, 22–24 MAY 1940

Général Weygand finally made it to the fighting front two days after taking command. On 21 May, he flew to Ypres, Belgium and met King Leopold, army group commander Billotte and a BEF representative. The 73-year-old's ignorance of the situation made a negative impression on many participants. He blithely resuscitated Gamelin's plan from 54 hours earlier, stating that counterattacks against the panzer corridor's flanks should start 'within a matter of hours'. The BEF (in the pocket) and French (south of the Somme) would attack to cut off the German spearheads while the Belgians would take over defending the encirclement's front. Problems arose immediately, since neither attack force had the necessary strength and King Leopold refused to take on his sacrificial mission. Billotte struck everyone as a thoroughly beaten man; he would die in a car crash before the end of the day.

Another problem with the Gamelin–Weygand plan was the fact that Gort did not attend the Ypres meeting, so there was little BEF buy-in. In fact, the day before, Gort had met with his superiors, who ordered a counterattack for the 21st by BEF forces acting alone if need be. He had two disengaged divisions – the 5th and 50th – plus the 1st Tank Brigade (73 tanks, only 16 of which had cannons) attacking from Arras. The combined unit, 'Frankforce', took its name from the commander of the 5th Infantry Division, Major-General Harold Franklyn. Remnants of the 3e Division Légère Mécanique would assist (60 Souma tanks). From the south, the 2nd Armoured Brigade of the 1st Armoured Division would launch a supporting attack against the Somme bridgehead of 2. Infanterie-Division (mot.) at Flixecourt. Forty miles of Panzergruppe Kleist separated the two British thrusts.

After numerous delays, the attack was launched at 1400 hours, nine hours late. Only a small number of British infantry battalions actually made it to the battlefield. The 1st Tank Brigade was unsuited to leading the counterattack into German panzer and motorized infantry divisions, since it had been created as an infantry support outfit. Rommel's 7. Panzer-Division blocked their way and the two sides traded villages most of the day. The motorized SS-Division Totenkopf did not acquit itself well and some of that unit's panic spread to 7. Panzer-Division. Rommel passed the exaggerated estimates of Allied tanks attacking up his chain of command and suddenly 'hundreds' were bearing down on his outnumbered men. Although in reality the panzer men had the battle well under control, soon Hitler's worries over the security of the panzer thrust were renewed. Reinhardt's 6. and 8. Panzer Divisionen,

attacking along the Aire Canal, had to stop and face east against the supposed threat.

Undeterred by this drama, Guderian worked his way up the coast to Boulogne (22 May) and Calais (23rd), investing both ports and pushing on to Gravelines (24th). Fierce fighting took place around Boulogne that did not always go the Germans' way (partially due to the permanent forts guarding the ports and naval gunfire from ships at sea). One reason for this was air support, as Guderian did not receive the help from the Luftwaffe he had come to expect. Churchill ordered the evacuation of the ports, beginning with Boulogne on the night of 23/24 May. At the same time, German senior leaders from Kleist to Hitler again worried about their overextended lines and Allied counterattacks. For two days, the panzers sat along the Aa Canal.

Now alert to the danger the panzer group posed to the entire Dyle Plan enterprise, Churchill flew to Paris to work out a new plan and, more importantly, buck up his flagging French allies. The prime minister and Weygand failed completely to understand each other about future operations. A supposed assault by eight divisions from Arras towards Cambrai was downgraded in reality to one infantry regiment attacking on the 22nd and then abandoning its small gains that same night. Hoth, now commanding a panzer group much like Kleist's, transitioned to the offensive the next day. Within 24 hours, he had shoved parts of the BEF (now known as Petreforce, after Major-General R.L. Petre) out of Arras and towards Lille[22].

Allied command and control inside the pocket was still a shambles. Rumours abounded. Billotte's replacement, Général Jean Blanchard, lasted only a couple of days and had in turn been replaced by Général Prioux (see Map 49). This turmoil at the top ranks of the trapped armies could only have negative effects. Command posts were full of talk about counterattacks out of and into the pocket by forces that did not exist and according to plans that had not been written. Relief action that had progressed beyond the 'good idea' stage kept being pushed back later and later. All the while, the Germans strengthened their hold on the pocket, both its inner (Dunkirk) and outer (Somme) walls.

---

22 A bone of contention between the British and French that lasted past the war was that the British had abandoned Arras and the remaining French in their zeal to get to the Channel ports and evacuation. This was not true: Gort had moved north-east.

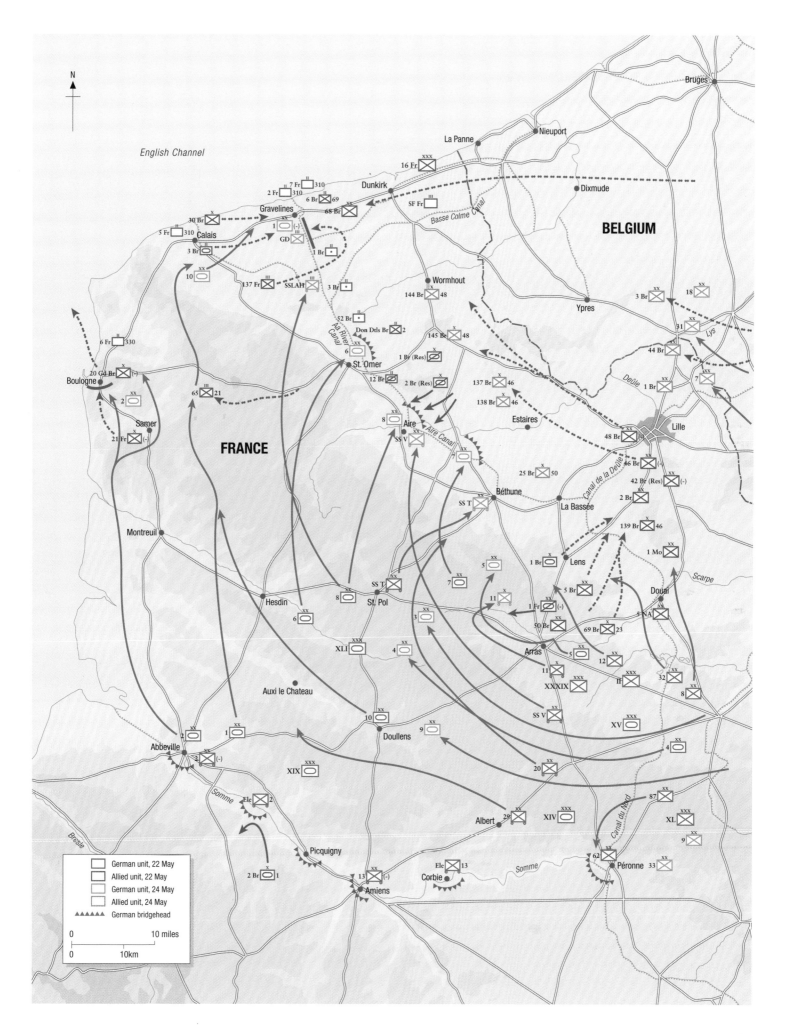

English Channel

BELGIUM

FRANCE

Bruges

Nieuport

La Panne

Dixmude

Dunkirk

16 Fr

Gravelines

7 Fr 310
2 Fr 310
6 Br 69
68 Br
SF Fr

Basse Colme Canal

Calais
5 Fr 310
30 Br
3 Br
1 GD
1 Br

10

137 Fr   SSLAH   3 Br

Wormhout
144 Br 48

Ypres

3 Br   18

31

44 Br

Lys

6 Fr 330

St. Omer
52 Br
Don Dtls Br 2
6
12 Br   2 Br (Res)

Aa River Canal

145 Br 48
1 Br (Res)

137 Br 46
138 Br 46

Estaires

1 Br

7

Deûle

Lille

Boulogne
2
20 Gd Br
65 21

8   Aire
SS V
7

Samer
21 Fr

Aire Canal

Béthune
SS T

La Bassée

25 Br 50

48 Br
46 Br

Canal de la Deûle

42 Br (Res)
2 Br

Montreuil

Hesdin
8   SS T
St. Pol
6

5
7

1 Br
Lens
5 Br

139 Br 46
1 Mo
Douai
8 NA

50 Br
69 Br 23
1 Fr
11

5
12
Arras
11
32
8

Auxi le Chateau

XLI
4

3

XXXIX
SS V
XV

4

Abbeville
1
1
2

XIX

Doullens
10
9

20

Somme
Ele 2

XIV
87
XL
9

Bresle

Picquigny

Albert
29

62
Péronne 33

Corbie
Ele 13

Somme

2 Br 1

13
Amiens

	German unit, 22 May
	Allied unit, 22 May
	German unit, 24 May
	Allied unit, 24 May
▲▲▲▲	German bridgehead

0   10 miles
0   10km

127

MAP 56: CLOSING IN ON DUNKIRK, 26–28 MAY 1940

Days too late, the Allies had awoken to the danger facing their forces in Belgium carrying out the Dyle Plan. In the intervening half-dozen days, they had initiated a series of ineffectual partial solutions, opportunities missed and bungled, or weakening counterattacks. Their comrades outside the pocket stood by passively, as if they realized there could be but one outcome to the ongoing battle. The new 3e Groupe d'Armées, organizing the Somme Line, could not even reduce the German bridgeheads on the river's left bank, much less attack across it to relieve the encirclement (including de Gaulle's 4e Division Cuirassée putting in another appearance at Abbeville). Especially during the previous week, the commander of the principal French army group and each of the armies in the thick of the fighting in Belgium and northern France had changed a number of times, exacerbating the already terrible Allied situation. Even the British were not immune, on 25 May replacing Chief of the Imperial General Staff Field Marshal Edmund Ironside with General John Dill. All the while, Wehrmacht forces increased the mortal danger to the three remaining combatants.

The map here shows where Rundstedt's *Schwerpunkt* and Bock's supporting effort came together. On 25 May, Allied commanders inside the pocket had decided to make their stand along the Aa Canal, Lys River and the Yser River/Canal de Dérivation to create a secure bridgehead around Dunkirk. For what it was worth, Weygand approved. By the 26th, the British cabinet, Weygand and other senior Allied leaders began to consider an evacuation from Dunkirk; no relief counteroffensive was coming to the rescue. They did not bother to tell the Belgians. The Germans had their problems as well. Even though they generally enjoyed the upper hand, two weeks of constant combat had driven down ready rates for many formations. Stukas operating out of bases near St. Quentin could barely reach the Channel ports and still have much flying time remaining for their close air support missions.

A bit of good news for the Germans arrived in the form of 18. Armee, free to join the fighting in Belgium now that the Netherlands had surrendered. Likewise, King Leopold's strong desire to defend his last toehold around Ghent (off map outside the Dunkirk 'bridgehead'), simultaneously benefited the Germans and frustrated the British and French. The king wanted Gort to shift some elements in his direction, but the BEF had no troops to spare for this task. Besides, on 26 May, the British embarked on Operation *Dynamo*, the evacuation of Dunkirk.

The second halt order having now been lifted, the Germans re-exerted the pressure on 27 May. On that day, along the pocket's western edge, they crossed the Aa Canal in strength all along the front. To the east, they pushed north from Courtrai towards Bruges, threatening to completely cut off Leopold and Ghent. In the centre, Gort had no intention of stopping on the Lys, despite the fact that it had been the agreed-upon line just 48 hours earlier. With Guderian, Reinhardt and Hoth pressing against Bergues, Cassel and Eecke and 6.Armee attacking from Ypres, the Lys River could only be considered a small death trap within a larger *Kessel*. Half the Allied divisions and brigades inside the encirclement were south and west of Ypres. On the 27th and 28th, they began a mass exodus towards Dunkirk. They did not even stop in the intermediate positions that had been prepared for them.

Earlier that day, Weygand flew into the pocket for a meeting at Cassel to discuss future plans. Representatives of the Allied armies and navies met and decided on a perimeter around Dunkirk they believed could withstand German attacks. A major concern was the effect of Luftwaffe bombing on such a small, crowded space. Around noon, Leopold informed Gort of his intent to surrender and, later that day, he sent his deputy chief of staff to inquire of the Germans about terms. The invaders responded: Unconditional surrender.

Belgium surrendered at 0400 hours on 28 May. British and French divisions had to rush east to fill the gap left by the departing Belgians. By now, most Allied units were heading for the Dunkirk perimeter, just as the Germans began to pull their mechanized forces out of the fighting in preparation for their assault south of the Somme. By the end of 30 May, the 9. Panzer-Division and eight infantry divisions had closed in on the Allied units establishing their defences.

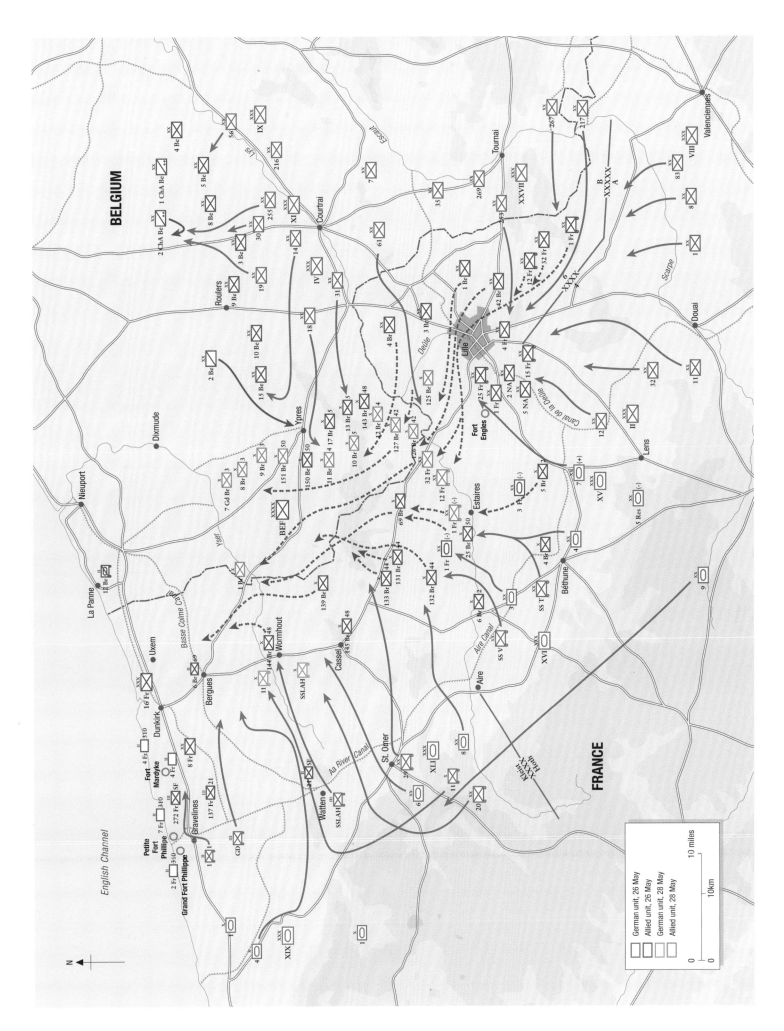

MAPS 57 AND 58: THE GERMAN CAPTURE OF DUNKIRK AND THE ALLIED EVACUATION, 2–4 JUNE 1940

Conducting a fighting withdrawal in the face of an attacking enemy is very difficult. Having to cross 16 miles of open sea added to the challenge. Operation *Dynamo* included all the complexities of any tri-service operation, all under the guns of the Wehrmacht. The BEF would hold the perimeter with its French allies. The Royal Navy would coordinate its warships, plus civilian British, French, Belgian and Dutch boats of all types. The RAF would provide air cover against the Luftwaffe.

The Germans suffered from a conspicuous lack of overall command and control in their own operations. Hitler did not distinguish between political and military objectives. The OKH and the two army groups did not have a unified plan. The Luftwaffe had no experience with this kind of operation and was at the end of an exhausting three-week campaign. On top of these problems, the entire Wehrmacht now shifted focus to the conquest of France, the upcoming *Fall Rot*. Its reaction to *Dynamo* would be improvised on a day-to-day basis, crippling its effectiveness.

Map 57: The Germans take Dunkirk

The OKH could tell that its command and control for the Dunkirk operation had serious flaws, and so on 30 May, it gave 18. Armee overall responsibility. Behind a semicircle of canals, the Allies waited for the assault. On 1 June, the Germans launched attacks all along the perimeter, which the British and French parried with local counterattacks and shifting reserves. A day earlier, the British managed to evacuate 68,000 troops, their biggest tally of *Dynamo,* but a drain on the number of troops able to resist the Germans.

On 2 June, the Germans stepped up their attacks all around the front, while the defenders (minus 64,000 soldiers removed on the 1st) struggled to hold them back. By night, the attackers had crossed the Bergues–Furnes Canal in strength and captured the villages of Spycker and Bergues. They were now within 4 miles of Dunkirk, which placed the evacuation beaches well within their artillery range. That day, the final 24,000 soldiers of the BEF departed, leaving the 12e, 32e, and 68e Divisions under 16e Corps d'Armée still in and around Dunkirk.

From late on 2 June through to early on the 4th, the French simultaneously defended the perimeter and evacuated their own forces. The Germans stood a mere 1–2 miles from the beaches, pouring fire into the defenders, waiting evacuees and ships. More than 53,000 Frenchmen departed by 0200 hours on the 4th, when the last vessel left. At 0900 hours that day, Général de Division André Beaufre,

commander of the 68e Division, surrendered at the head of approximately 40,000 troops. About 6,000 of their comrades died making it possible for the rest to escape.

Map 58: The evacuation of Dunkirk

Although there is nothing glorious about quitting the battlefield, Operation *Dynamo* represents military organization under difficult conditions at its best. Vice Admiral Bertram Ramsay, Flag Officer, Dover, with extensive experience in the Channel, managed the operation. With the Royal Navy's worldwide commitments and the Norwegian evacuation in high gear, civilian craft augmented the naval ones. Ramsay set up three shipping routes, X, Y and Z, considering undersea obstacles, minefields, exposure to Luftwaffe attacks, and the coastline, now lined with German artillery ranging 10 miles into the water. He planned to avoid the actual port, already damaged by bombardment, and evacuate from the beaches, especially the 1,400-yard long (but 2-yard wide) wood and stone 'east mole'.

Many BEF soldiers, mostly wounded, had been evacuated by the time *Dynamo* began late on 26 May. Navy Captain William Tennant controlled the embarkation. Chaos ruled in the town of Dunkirk. It was filled with shattered military formations and countless individual soldiers, who just wanted to survive. Depending on weather, time of day, smoke from the burning town, or RAF activity, the Luftwaffe either made life hell on the beaches and on the vessels, or else was nowhere to be seen. On some days, the Luftwaffe could not arrive until mid-afternoon. At times, hundreds of craft were at sea, en route to or from Dunkirk. The evacuations went on round the clock. Groundings, collisions and the like hurt the evacuation more than enemy action.

On 30 May, the Germans finally realized what was happening, so reorganized their efforts. However, by then the Allies had streamlined the operation and reached record numbers of troops evacuated, despite the increased German emphasis. The Germans damaged and sank many craft, but even more got through. Ultimately, *Dynamo* evacuated about 350,000 Allied soldiers, 225,000 of them British. The Luftwaffe lost approximately 250 aircraft over the entire area (130 over Dunkirk), while the RAF lost about 180. Of nearly 850 vessels involved, almost 250 were sunk, including 60 large ships (destroyers, minesweepers and ferries). *Dynamo* was cause for mixed-emotion celebrating among the Allies, but along with German complacency, contributed to downgrading *Fall Gelb* from a decisive to an 'ordinary' victory.

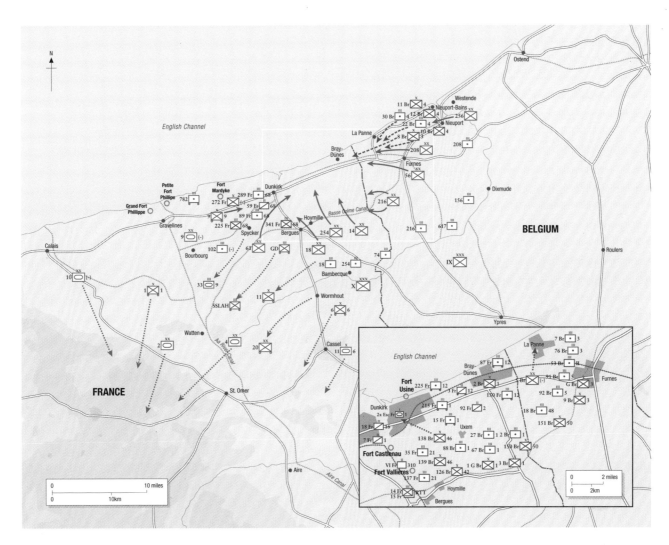

MAP 57

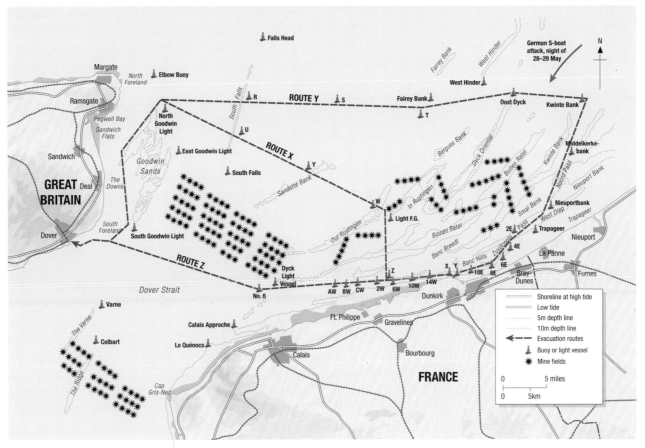

MAP 58

MAP 59: 4 JUNE 1940 – THE EVE OF *FALL ROT*

Few at the time would consider *Fall Gelb* anything other than an unqualified success. Despite Operation *Dynamo*'s silver lining appearance, a third of a million soldiers fleeing the Continent, minus their heavy weapons and equipment, can only be seen as a massive failure. As we know now, the unsatisfactory conclusion to *Fall Gelb* represents a golden opportunity missed for the Germans, and *Dynamo* a tremendous stroke of good fortune for the Allies.

But as *Dynamo* drew to a conclusion on 4 June, the world's attention focused on the new front separating the Wehrmacht from the French along the Somme, Oise and Aisne Rivers and the Maginot Line. During the second half of May, while the Germans disgraced the best of the Allied armies in Artois, Gamelin basically did nothing with the rest of the French military. The small and uncoordinated attacks against Kleist's left flank and bridgeheads accomplished little besides causing a temporary nuisance.

The Allies' quantitative superiority in divisions and armour on 10 May had vanished by 4 June. In addition, the Germans' qualitative superiority in command and control, doctrine and fighting spirit was unquestionable. Posterity may wonder if, in view of these harsh realities of the time, any French plan would have succeeded. Weygand could be fairly sure that the Maginot Line would still hold indefinitely, but his best concept for the coming Battle of France consisted of fighting a static defence along the chain of rivers. German success along the Meuse, Dyle and Escaut had already demolished the river-line defence gambit, but the generalissimo held fast to that course of action[23].

Manning the 200-mile front between the end of the Maginot Line near Longuyon and the Channel, Weygand had 43 divisions under the newly organized and untried 3e Groupe d'Armées. The 3e Groupe d'Armées had begun the war where the French, German and Swiss frontiers meet. The three Divisions Cuirassée and three Divisions Légère de Cavalerie backing up the first line were broken remnants of their pre-war selves, with one-third to one-quarter of their normal AFV

establishment. The entire French Army had 1,200 tanks remaining, scattered around the country. The absence of mobile formations is one reason why the French eschewed a mobile defence, although a few, such as de Gaulle, disingenuously called for more 'manoeuvre and manoeuvre'. To beef up what all expected to be the main fighting along the three rivers, the French stripped their defences opposite the Rhine and Alpine fronts. A small and reinforced fragment of the BEF, including the 1st Armoured Division, held the far-left flank along the Channel coast. Backing up the Maginot Line stood 18 divisions (12 regular and six colonial, fortress, etc.) of the 2e Groupe d'Armées, none of them mechanized. Perhaps hoping for another miracle, Weygand ordered a second line established along the Seine and Marne Rivers. The Armée de l'Air was severely depleted and the defenders could count on only minimal support from the RAF.

Rundstedt and Bock's reoriented army groups counted about 90 divisions, including all ten panzer and four and a half motorized. Each now had a panzer group – Guderian had been elevated to co-equal status with Kleist (XIX, XXXIX and XLI Panzer-Korps). The army groups and their mechanized teams would attack on either side of Paris. Kleist would head for the Atlantic coast, Guderian for Reims and the rear of the Maginot Line; Hoth retained his semi-independence, aiming for Cherbourg. This operational manoeuvre would split the French into three isolated parts. German forces facing the Maginot Line, Heeresgruppe C, would finally get into action with its *Bär* (Bear) and *Tiger* attack plans. The Germans took particular care to rest and rehabilitate the panzer divisions, which had attacked over 300 miles for *Gelb* and then redeployed between 100 and 150 more for *Rot*. After battlefield recovery and repairs, Halder estimated 70 per cent of the panzers would be ready for the Battle of France. The Luftwaffe had also suffered from maintenance problems and combat losses, so needed time to regain its strength.

The Germans were at the top of their game and anticipated a quick campaign. In Paris, however, Reynaud again reshuffled his cabinet to get rid of defeatists. His actions at this critical juncture alienated Weygand and another powerful force in French politics, World War I hero and Deputy Prime Minister Marshal Pétain.

---

23 The French were not alone in an anachronistic faith in the defensive value of rivers. Every army made the same mistake at one point or another.

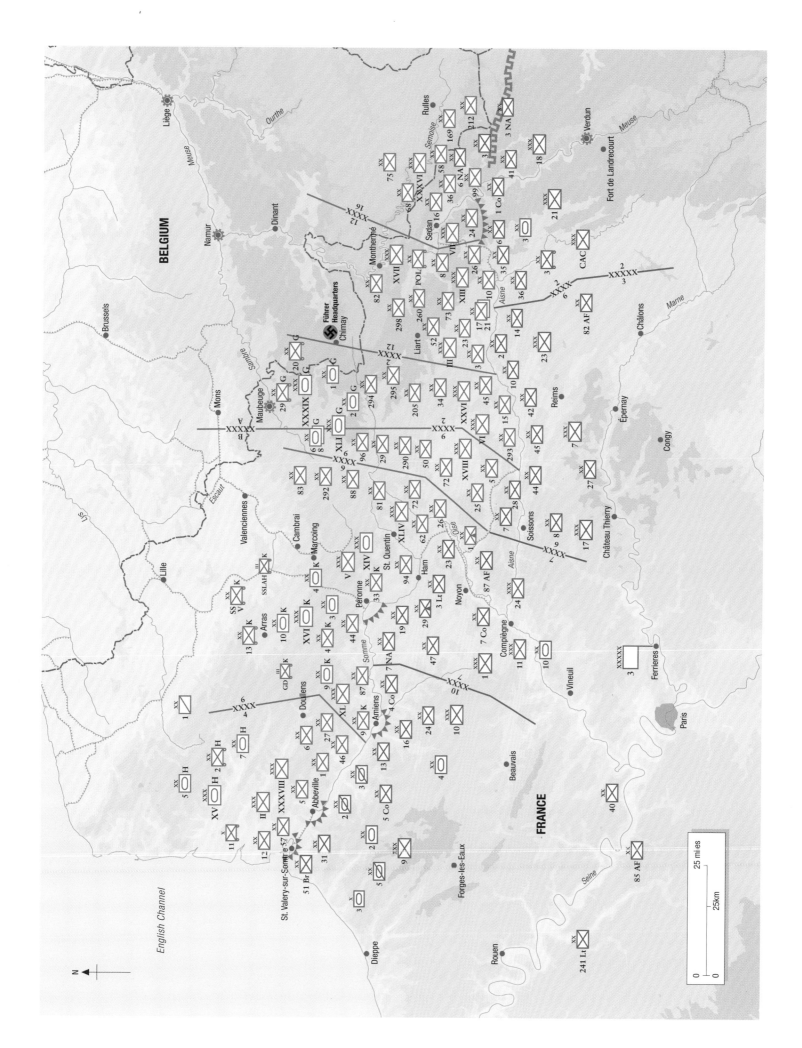

English Channel

BELGIUM

FRANCE

Liège

Namur

Dinant

Brussels

Mons

Valenciennes

Lille

Cambrai

Marcoing

Arras

Doullens

Abbeville

St. Valery-sur-Somme

Dieppe

Rouen

Forges-les-Eaux

Beauvais

Paris

Vineuil

Ferrieres

Compiègne

Noyon

Soissons

Château Thierry

Reims

Épernay

Congy

Châlons

Verdun

Fort de Landrecourt

Sedan

Monthermé

Chimay

Maubeuge

St. Quentin

Péronne

Ham

Amiens

Rulles

Führer
Headquarters

Ourthe

Meuse

Semois

Sambre

Escaut

Lys

Somme

Oise

Aisne

Aisne

Marne

Seine

25 miles

25km

N

MAPS 60 AND 61: OVERCOMING THE SOMME AND OISE–AISNE RIVERS, 5–7 JUNE 1940

The modern armies of World War II, with their sophisticated bridging equipment, motorized boats and close air support delivering the 1940s version of precision munitions, barely paused at rivers. So it was with *Fall Rot,* which began early on 5 June with Bock and Heeresgruppe B in the west, and four days later with Rundstedt's Heeresgruppe A to the east.

The Wehrmacht did not waste any time between concluding *Gelb* and starting *Rot.* The offensive began around dawn with a massive air and artillery barrage along the 120-mile front between the Channel and Laon. Despite earlier losses, the Luftwaffe could still commit 200 Stukas and 700 bombers to the battle, escorted by more than 500 Bf 109s. However, *Fall Rot* did not start in a uniform manner. Because some armies were more ready than others, it began in a staggered fashion.

Map 60: Overcoming the Somme, 5–7 June 1940

The 4. Armee attacked the so-called Weygand Line first between the Channel and Amiens, because the 6. and 9. Armeen told Bock they were not ready. Considering all of the German advantages, the Allies gave the impression of doing well on the first day, limiting the attackers to 5-mile gains out of their St. Valery and Abbeville bridgeheads. In between these two locales, Hoth's 5. and 7. Panzer Divisionen made their own hard-earned crossings. Further upriver, the 6. Armee infantry stayed put, but armour of the XIV and XVI Panzer-Korps passed through them and into the French positions. The defenders generally held their ground.

By the second day of the offensive, things had dramatically improved for the Germans. In the far west, the British 51st Highland Division gave up any pretense of holding the Somme and began to fall back to the smaller Bresle River. This move infuriated Weygand, who suspected British perfidy. The two divisions of Hoth's XV Panzer-Korps joined forces and moved south with almost no French in front of them to bar

the way. In fact, they were running down the boundary dividing the 9e and 10e Corps d'Armée, while Manstein's XXXVIII Armee-Korps covered the panzers' left. Attacking out of the Peronne bridgehead, the XVI Panzer-Korps also seemed to have achieved a breakthrough. On the evening of the 6th, Weygand authorized the 3e Groupe d'Armées to give up the Somme. By 7 May, both Hoth and Hoepner were unopposed and in the open countryside. Having used, perhaps imprudently, the 2e Division Légère de Cavalerie to man the Somme defences, the British 1st Armoured Division was the only Allied mobile division uncommitted to move against the panzers (and it was far from the fighting at that moment). Having put up a stout defence against unfavourable odds for three days, the French infantry could expect little help in the form of a mechanized counterattack.

Map 61: Overcoming the Oise–Aisne network, 5–6 June 1940

Slightly to the east, the terrain on this map shows a jumble of rivers and canals that definitely favoured the defenders. A thin curtain of infantry regiments (many of them colonial, Foreign Legion, or training troops) held the line. The area represented a backwater of sorts in Bock's concept for *Fall Rot,* consisting of attacks only by marching infantry divisions on his far-eastern flank. When the offensive began, the French enjoyed some early success on the right and left. However, the XVIII Armee-Korps in the centre made good progress crossing the canal, supported by heavy artillery and Luftwaffe close air support. On 6 June, as it drove on Soissons, both the 6e and 7e Armées had to fall back to the Aisne to maintain some sort of defensive cohesion. The 7e Armée was also being assaulted to its west by Kleist's panzers (Map 60). When engineers started demolishing the Oise River bridges before French troops had crossed them, it hindered the withdrawal of the 7e Armée. By 7 June, the middle of the Aisne Line looked no more viable a place to anchor a defence than any other river or canal.

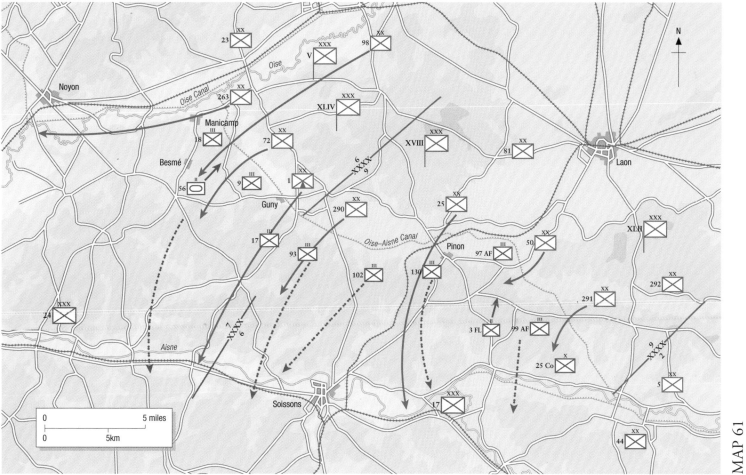

MAP 60

German unit, 5 June

German unit, 7 June

0		10 miles
0		10km

Auxi le Chateau

Doullens

Abbeville

154 Br   153 Br   152 Br

Bresle

Gamaches

Picquigny

Albert

Corbie

Somme

Péronne

Amiens

Oresmaux

Aumale

SS
V

Roye

Ham

Forges-les-Eaux

Noyon

Oise

Noyon

Oise

Oise Canal

Manicamp

Besmé

Guny

Oise–Aisne Canal

Pinon

Laon

Aisne

Soissons

MAP 61

0		5 miles
0		5km

MAP 62: THE GERMAN ENCIRCLEMENT OF THE 2e GROUPE D'ARMÉES, 10–20 JUNE 1940

The next stage of the Battle of France began on 9 June, when Heeresgruppe A joined the offensive. (Heeresgruppe C still had not completed its preparations.) This manoeuvre would outflank the Maginot Line, which had already been compromised: Less than a week into *Gelb,* the Germans had captured the westernmost Fort La Ferté in a three-day battle (in which they suffered surprisingly few casualties), and the French high command had been steadily removing the army units needed to back up the line, sending them west to the scene of the main fighting. These two events were interconnected, since the battle of Fort La Ferté proved that the Maginot Line required substantial outside help if it was to accomplish its mission.

Rundstedt's men moved out at 0630 hours on the 9th along the western two-thirds of its front; they did not directly challenge the Maginot Line. The newly organized Panzergruppe Guderian began the offensive by attacking dangerously close to the seam between the 2e and 3e Groupes d'Armées (6e and 2e Armées). From assembly areas near Sedan, site of the panzer general's triumph a month earlier, it led the way south. By evening, it had two small bridgeheads over the Aisne west of Rethel, off the adjacent map to the west. The French promptly began withdrawing towards the Marne, so to the Germans it looked doubtful that the defence could maintain a continuous front. With this assessment in mind, the OKH transferred parts of Kleist's panzers to Rundstedt to exploit the developing situation. Resistance during the first two days of *Fall Rot* was very determined, more so than at many points in May, when it would have really mattered.

As the French retreated from the Aisne to the Marne, they uncovered the western end of the Maginot Line. Therefore, on 11 June, 16. Armee's divisions began to swing through gaps in the fortress line between the subdued Fort La Ferté and Longuyon. On that day, Weygand decided to withdraw the bulk of his forces, leaving the Maginot Line to its fate. Over the next six days, the Germans advanced as far as Metz and St. Mihiel. Days later, and nearly 60 miles along the Maginot Line to the south-east, Heeresgruppe C sprang into action with Operation *Tiger.* Starting on 14 June (the day Paris surrendered), its 1. Armee created a breakthrough four divisions wide (the 258., 93., 268. and 75.) from Faulquemont to Sarre-Union. Up to that point, other troops of Heeresgruppe C had been attempting to take out fortresses with mixed results, so an order went out cancelling any more of the costly attacks. By now, the line had lost much of its original usefulness anyway.

In fact, by the third week of June, the Germans had penetrated the Maginot Line in numerous places. On the 15th, 7. Armee launched its own attack across the Rhine, Operation *Kleiner Bär.* Somewhat compensating for the low-quality infantry divisions participating, 170mm and 240mm guns, 240mm and 280mm railway artillery, plus 305mm and 355mm howitzers provided support. Within 24 hours, the Germans had five divisions across the wide river against a selection of even weaker French units. By the 21st, they had captured a lodgement 25-miles deep. The conquest (or reconquest, according to the Nazis) of Alsace-Lorraine mattered more politically than it did militarily.

The final nail in the coffin of the 2e Groupe d'Armées came from the south-west. During the intervening week, Panzergruppe Guderian had worked its way up the Marne Valley with four panzer and three motorized infantry divisions. It had studiously avoided centres of French resistance. At Juniville (off the map, to the west) the 1. Panzer-Division received a nasty surprise in the form of a counterattack by the 1re Division Cuirassée, which took out nearly 100 German AFVs. On 11 June, Panzergruppe Kleist had redeployed to Rundstedt's army group and headed south to Guderian's right. By mid-month, Weygand's men were trying to hold a jagged line that crossed central France, and Pétain had replaced Reynaud as prime minister.

Guderian kept driving south. On 17 June, his units reached Pontarlier on the Swiss border (off the map to the south), completing the official encirclement of the 2e Groupe d'Armées. The XLI Panzer-Korps sealed the west of the pocket, while XIX Panzer-Korps exited the bottom of the map, curved around and re-entered from the south. Heeresgruppe A linked up with Heeresgruppe C (7. Armee) on the 19th. The two army groups had cooperated to trap the 3e, 5e and 8e Armées plus the Maginot Line garrisons, totalling 400,000 men. Unsurprisingly, Weygand ordered the encircled formations to break out. This plan had little prospect of success given the German strengths and French weaknesses. Starting on 20 June, the entrapped French soldiers began surrendering.

MAP 63: THE FALL OF PARIS, 10–14 MAY 1940

During the final stages of the 1870–71 Franco-Prussian War, approximately 23,000 artillery shells hit Paris, causing considerable damage. In World War I, artillery, bombers and Zeppelins bombarded the city, to much less effect. A great question of World War II (twice – in 1944, too) was what would become of the beautiful metropolis.

Without Paris even playing a role, *Fall Gelb* had de facto defeated France in three weeks and, if there were any doubts, *Fall Rot* erased those within a single week. The French capital had not been attacked, let alone captured[24]. The *Fall Rot* plan was to attack on either side of Paris, thus separating it from the mass of the 2e and 3e Groupes d'Armées. According to Weygand, fighting a mobile defence in the 90 per cent of France not yet occupied during *Fall Gelb* was not possible. The dearth of remaining mechanized formations ruled out any resistance other than a last-ditch fight on the rivers to the north of Paris. Weygand knew that if the Wehrmacht reached the Seine, they could take the city.

Four days after the beginning of *Fall Rot,* artillery fire could be heard in Paris, and Weygand created the Armée de Paris. The military governor of Paris, Général Pierre Héring, assumed the new army would defend the capital until the last. On 10 June, Italy declared war on France, by which time the Germans had crossed the lower Seine in two places. That day, they had the city surrounded in a semicircle to the north, and the French government left for Tours. On the 10th, Weygand

decided to declare Paris an open city; it took him 48 hours to tell Héring, who informed Parisians on the 13th. Ten German infantry divisions kept up the pressure, as the defenders steadily fell back, not into but around the capital and to the south. With rumours of the open city declaration starting to circulate on the 12th, the stream of refugees fleeing the city turned into a flood.

At that point, the Germans demanded a quick surrender of Paris. The first advanced detachments of the 9. Infanterie-Division began to arrive in the suburbs on the evening of 13 June, around the same time as the German officer detailed to negotiate the surrender arrived in St. Denis. Capitulation discussions took place in the early hours of the 14th. At 0600 hours, Héring's replacement, Général Henri Dentz, met with Generalmajor Bogislav von Studnitz, commander of the 87. Infanterie-Division, to sign the pertinent documents. The papers stipulated no resistance by soldiers or civilians and no destruction or sabotage of bridges or services like water, electricity and communications facilities. The French did burn some of the city's oil supplies, but Parisian industry, the mass of all French industry, and firms like Renault and Schneider-Creuzot, fell into the invaders' hands.

Early on 14 June, the sound of marching German infantry filled Paris. By 0900 hours, the Wehrmacht battle flag fluttered under the Arc de Triomphe, soon the site of a victory parade by the 8. and 28. Infanterie Divisionen. The 18. Armee took possession of the city, which now gave every indication of being abandoned. Swastika flags flew everywhere, while on the normally bustling streets, only German military vehicles could be seen. It was the beginning of a dreadful four-year occupation.

---

24 A fact, similar to that of Warsaw the year before, that historians would do well to remember when considering Moscow a year later.

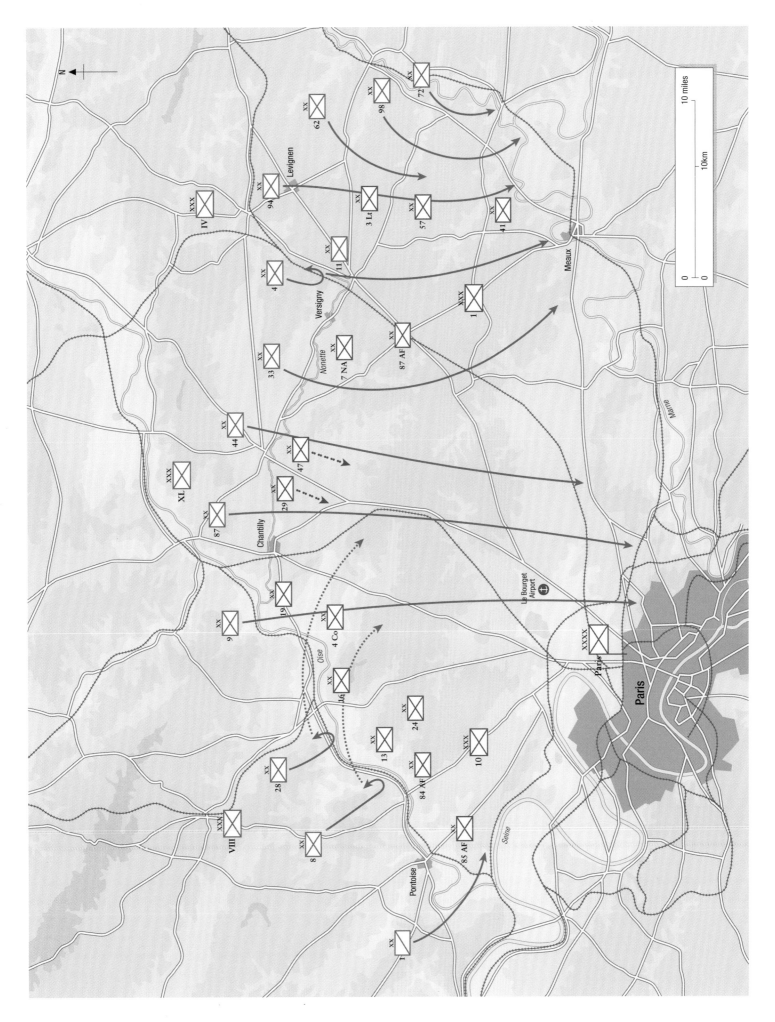

MAP 64: THE CONQUEST OF NORTH-WEST FRANCE, 15–30 JUNE 1940

In the first half of June 1940, *Fall Rot* had overthrown the Weygand Line, outflanked and pierced the Maginot Line, captured Paris, eliminated the British presence on the Continent and worn down the weary remnants of the once proud French military. By mid-month, Prime Minister Reynaud was out and a new, anti-war party led by the new premier Pétain was in. The French government fled first to Tours and then to Bordeaux on the 14th[25]. Three days later, it made the first moves towards an armistice. On the 18th, Hitler and Mussolini met to discuss the fate of France, while Britain's main concern was the disposition of the French fleet.

Heeresgruppe A concentrated on the encirclement of the 2e Groupe d'Armées around Alsace-Lorraine and the Vosges Mountains and pushing down the Rhône River. Heeresgruppe B meanwhile fanned out across north-west France against the 3e Groupe d'Armées. Most German mechanized forces, except the XV Panzer-Korps, had been sent east, so Hoth's men headed for distant Normandy and Brittany. German marching infantry occupied the centre of France against little resistance and no organized defence. Roadsides were strewn with discarded weapons and entire regiments refused to fight. No Frenchman wanted to be the last to die in a forlorn, lost cause. No German soldier wanted to be the last to die in the anticlimactic pursuit against a beaten enemy. The Luftwaffe dropped leaflets urging the French to surrender, while many commanders restricted their troops to their barracks to save them from unnecessary death. On 18 June, all communities over a population of 20,000 were declared open towns, so most gave up without a shot. The Wehrmacht pushed south on refugee-clogged roads without much enthusiasm. The Third Reich turned its attention to the expected showdown with Great Britain.

On 19 June, Pétain's government asked the Spanish ambassador to France, José Félix de Lequerica, to act as intermediary for the peace process. It also decided that Général Charles Huntziger would represent France at the surrender, so sent him and a ten-car convoy upstream to Paris against the river of refugees. The delegation was shocked by the disgraced state of the French military they saw on the road. They travelled north all day on the 20th and arrived in Paris early on the 21st. They immediately drove the final 50 miles to Compiègne, site of the November 1918 Armistice, where Hitler and top Nazis and Wehrmacht leaders awaited them. Salutes were exchanged but no handshakes. General Keitel began to read the surrender documents, Hitler barely stayed long enough to hear the preamble. Germany took over the northern 60 per cent of France, including the Atlantic coast. It left unoccupied the poorest southern 40 per cent, under the new collaborationist Vichy regime. The Germans prudently left the French Empire and fleet to Vichy. The ceasefire took effect at 0035 hours on 25 June, a day of national mourning in France. As the Germans had arrived in Bordeaux, Pétain's government left for Clermont-Ferrand and then eventually Vichy.

---

25 The French Third Republic officially ended on 10 June, so from that point onwards the nation was known as the French State.

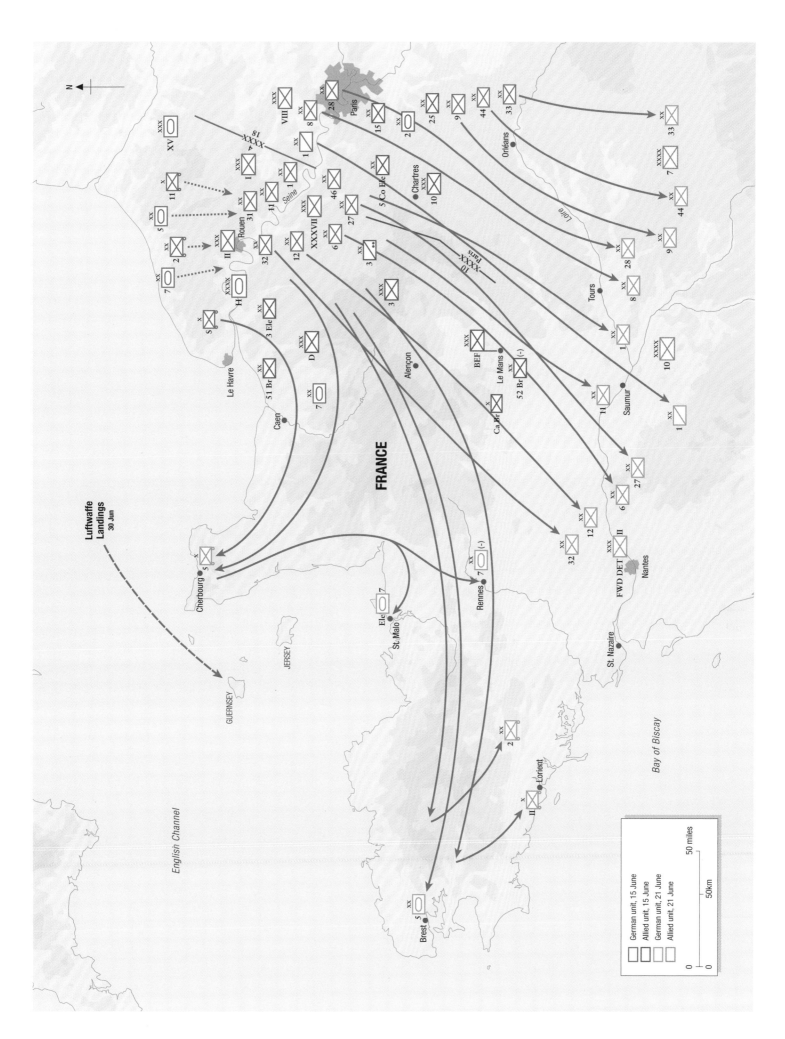

Luftwaffe Landings
30 Jun

FRANCE

English Channel

JERSEY

GUERNSEY

Bay of Biscay

Le Havre

Caen

Cherbourg

St. Malo

Brest

Lorient

St. Nazaire

Nantes

Rennes

Alençon

Le Mans

Saumur

Tours

Orléans

Chartres

Paris

Rouen

Seine

Loire

	German unit, 15 June
	Allied unit, 15 June
	German unit, 21 June
	Allied unit, 21 June

50 miles

50km

141

MAP 65: THE ITALIAN ALPINE FRONT, 20–22 JUNE 1940

The German success in *Fall Gelb* had surprised Mussolini as it had the rest of the world. Barely nine months earlier, he had told Hitler he could not possibly join the war without substantial German materiel and resources. The weeks leading up to Dunkirk changed all that. Even before *Fall Rot* began, the Duce told his chief of staff that Italy needed several thousand dead if it wanted a seat at the peace table. On 10 June, he declared war on the Allies.

For the first few days of the war, both sides traded air raids; severe weather over the Alps provided the best air defence for the non-blacked-out northern Italian cities. On 18 June, days after the fall of Paris and with French defeat a formality, Hitler took time off from the war to go to Munich to meet Mussolini. He told the Duce that Italy would not get any French colonial possessions from him. It would have to earn whatever it could get from a defeated France the old fashioned way: Conquest in war. Italy's ultimate objective was Marseille.

More than 30 Italian divisions, under the overall command of Army Group West under Crown Prince Umberto, faced off against 200,000 French holding the Western Alps in six divisions. Commander of the defending Armée des Alpes likewise had to contend with German units racing southwards, down the Rhône Valley. The Mayor of Lyon had just declared his city open also, allowing the Wehrmacht to use its valuable bridges.

It took the Italian Army ten days to get ready and on 20 June it attacked across the mountain passes[26]. Aided by deep snow and bad weather, the skeleton defences limited the Italians to small gains; even

the 'elite' Alpine divisions were stymied. In the much nicer climate along the Mediterranean coast, an entire Italian corps could barely advance 3 miles against the French outpost line guarding Menton. On the second day of fighting, Italian and French forts (the Little Maginot Line) traded shots in the high mountains. The Italians requested that the Germans speed up their march down the Rhône to put pressure on the French rear. Chief of staff Halder had no enthusiasm for such 'trickery'. The whole Alpine enterprise humiliated Mussolini. On the third day, 22 June, the First Army finally captured Menton. At the same time, however, France surrendered to Hitler, so fighting in the Alps died down. Italy and France signed an armistice on the 24th. At a cost of 631 dead and 2,361 wounded, Italy occupied Nice and a slice of the Savoy Alps. France suffered 79 dead. Through the US ambassador in Berlin, the Italian ambassador inquired about peace with Britain. The British rejected these peace feelers.

Mussolini's two-week war had earned him little besides international disgrace. His military had performed dismally and he knew it. Hitler wanted to avoid French diplomatic humiliation alongside the military one, so to the Duce's frustration, he allowed the Vichy regime to keep its empire. Italy's demonstrated weakness, not the Führer's intransigence, caused Mussolini to meekly acquiesce to the new order. Hitler had hoped that Mussolini could at least manage Axis affairs in the central Mediterranean, but this was not to be. On 23 October 1940, the Führer met Spanish dictator Francisco Franco at the Bay of Biscay port of Hendaye, to sell him the idea that the three fascist states (the third being Vichy France) would cooperate in that region. As usual, Hitler's unfamiliarity with the world outside of Germany's immediate neighbourhood failed him. France, Spain and 'Italy' had been competing in the Mediterranean for centuries and would not reverse that trend just for him.

26   The original start date of the offensive was 23 June. The Italians moved the operation forward by three days after hearing of preliminary French efforts at peace with the Germans.

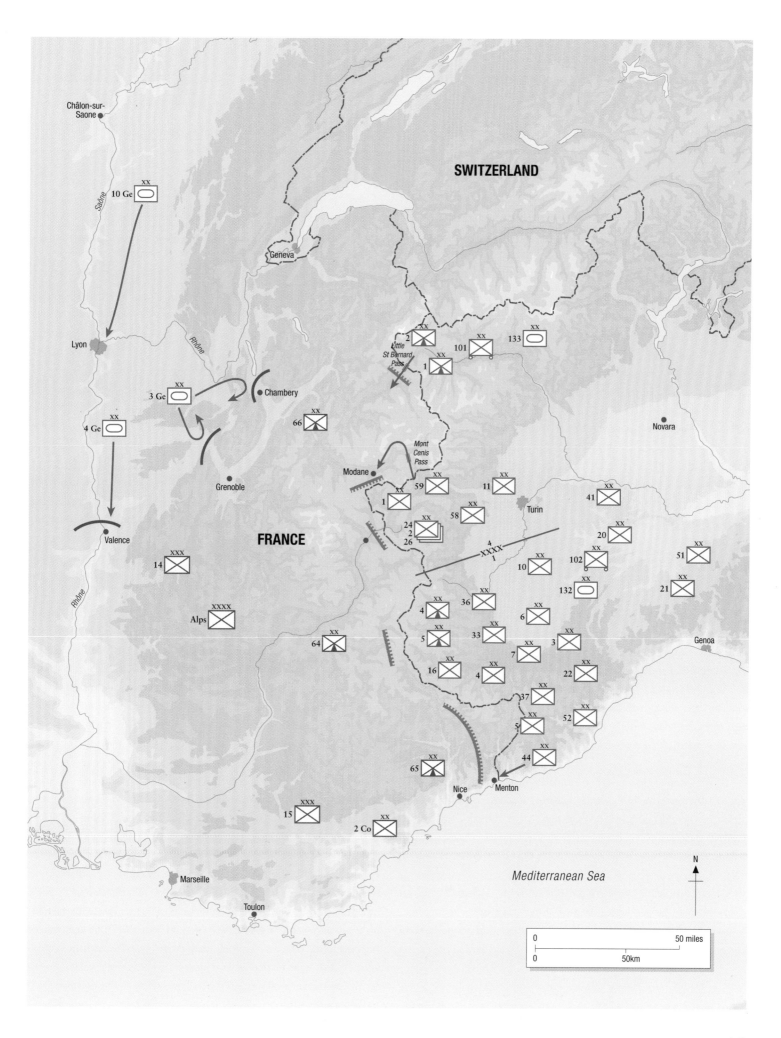

SWITZERLAND

Châlon-sur-Saone

Saône

10 Ge

Geneva

Lyon

Rhône

Little St Bernard Pass

2

101

133

1

3 Ge

Chambery

4 Ge

66

Novara

Mont Cenis Pass

Modane

59

11

41

Valence

1

58

Turin

20

FRANCE

24
2
26

4
1

XXXX

51

14

10

102

132

21

Alps

XXXX

36

4

6

64

5

33

7

3

Genoa

16

4

22

37

65

5

44

52

Nice

Menton

15

2 Co

Mediterranean Sea

N

Marseille

Toulon

0   50 miles

0   50km

143

MAP 66: AERIAL OPERATIONS DURING THE WESTERN CAMPAIGN

On 2 September 1939, between the time Hitler invaded Poland and the Allies declared war, the RAF began to deploy ten squadrons of bombers to France. For the next eight months, the two sides skirmished in the air over their frontiers and adjoining seas. As in Poland, the Germans employed six *Flieger-Korps* in two *Luftflotten* for *Fall Gelb* against the West – *c.*2,800 combat aircraft (approximate numbers were: 1,200 bombers, 350 Stukas, 1,000 Bf 109s and 250 Bf 110s). The Allies had considerably fewer planes: 400 RAF aircraft of all types and perhaps 2,000 French machines near the front (400 bombers, 800–1,000 fighters, plus 400 scouting, observation and reconnaissance models). They had nothing comparable to the Stuka, flying artillery used in tactical and operational roles. Additionally, German Flak would make these statistics even more lopsided.

The Luftwaffe opened the Western campaign with attacks all along the front. The Allies' aerial plan, in hindsight a poor one, was to save its air power for late in the campaign when it would be more decisive. As part of the German deception plan, fighters covered the Ardennes in an effort to keep prying Allied eyes from discovering Kleist's panzers executing Manstein's plan. Therefore, the Netherlands and Belgium took the brunt of the attacks during the first two days. The Luftflotte hit Fortress Holland particularly hard early on 10 May, paving the way for nearly 475 Ju 52s flying in paratroopers and air-transportable soldiers. The 50 or so modern Dutch fighters tried to cover the fighting over the Grebbe and other defensive lines. The raid by 54 He 111s against Rotterdam on the 14th (see Map 46) hastened the Netherlands' exit from the war.

Before the sun rose on 10 May, Belgium lost 53 of its 179 operational aircraft destroyed on the ground. German close air support aircraft, including Richthofen's new Flieger-Korps VIII, not yet needed over the Ardennes, threw their weight behind Hoepner's panzers. Allied bombers were powerless to stop him from breaking out into the central Belgian plain, despite near-suicidal attacks. In the swirling tank battles on the 13th and 14th near Gembloux on the Dyle Line, Luftwaffe close air support helped tip the balance in the Germans' favour.

On what was soon to be the main front in France, the Luftwaffe did not wait for Kleist to emerge from the Ardennes in order to get to work. On the campaign's first day, it attacked airfields at Dijon, Lyon, Metz, Nancy, Romilly and Reims (the last named surrounded by about ten Allied airstrips). Thirty British Advanced Air Striking Force (AASF) Blenheim bombers were destroyed in one raid, along with their fuel depot. In the three days leading up to Kleist's breakout, the RAF in this sector lost half of its 200 machines. After transiting the Ardennes, the panzers stood ready to negotiate the Meuse River and Richthofen's Flieger-Korps VIII shifted south to join Flieger-Korps II. Kampfgeschwader (KG) 76 and KG 77 plus Stukas of Stukageschwader (StG) 51 assisted Hoth against Dinant in the north. Kampfgeschwader 2 and KG 3 and StG 77 flew in support of Guderian to the south, the Stukas contributing 180 sorties that day. Meanwhile, Flak and Messerschmitts downed 30 RAF Fairey Battles and damaged ten more. In the centre, StG 76 flew 500 sorties for Reinhardt at Monthermé.

Having helped the panzers cross the Meuse, the Luftwaffe once again turned on the Allies' air bases, forcing the latter to basically abandon northern France. With very few Allied attacks on the German homeland to defend against, Luftwaffe fighters could concentrate on supporting the ground troops. The RAF could see the writing on the wall and began withdrawing smashed AASF formations back to Britain. The French railway system also came under sustained aerial attacks. Between 15 and 20 May, Flieger-Korps VIII provided Rundstedt flying artillery support right up the English Channel. On the 21st, StG 2 came to the aid of Rommel near Arras, fending off BEF counterattacks there. At that point, the Messerschmitts and Stukas had reached their maximum range, but Richthofen did not believe he had the luxury of time to jump his bases into France. They had farther to fly than the defending Hurricanes and Spitfires flying out of south-east England. Not wanting the army to get all the credit for destroying the Allied armies at Dunkirk, Hitler gave that mission to Göring. However, Luftwaffe woes over the evacuation beaches (see Maps 57 and 58) were harbingers of what was to come during the Battle of Britain.

Commencing 5 June, the two *Luftflotten* turned south over the Somme with Bock and Rundstedt. The RAF had practically abandoned France, except for 100 aircraft left behind, while the Armée de l'Air was in a shambles. Technically, it had more planes available than on 10 May, but perhaps only 600 were operational. It tried to influence *Fall Rot* until about 9 June, but then withdrew to southern France. Over the following two days, a dozen RAF bombers launched nuisance raids against Turin and Genoa to welcome Mussolini to the war. German aircraft losses during the campaign amounted to 1,428 destroyed and 488 damaged.

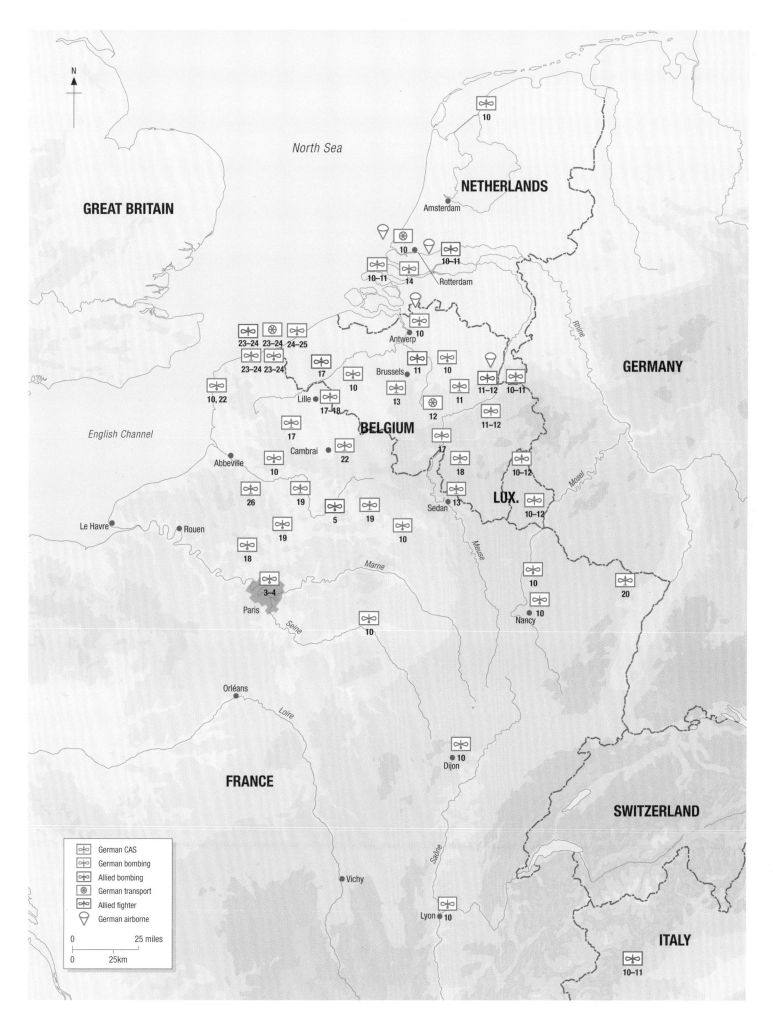

North Sea

GREAT BRITAIN

NETHERLANDS

Amsterdam

10

10–11

10

10–11

14

Rotterdam

Antwerp

10

GERMANY

23–24 23–24 24–25

23–24 23–24

17

Brussels   11   10

11–12 10–11

BELGIUM

10

13

11

12

English Channel

10, 22

Lille

17–18

11–12

17

Cambrai

22

17

18

10–12

LUX.

Abbeville

10

Sedan 13

10–12

26   19

19

Le Havre

Rouen

5

19

10

20

18

10

Nancy 10

3–4

Paris

Marne

Meuse

Mosel

Rhine

Orléans

Loire

Seine

10

FRANCE

10

Dijon

SWITZERLAND

Saône

Vichy

Lyon 10

ITALY

10–11

German CAS

German bombing

Allied bombing

German transport

Allied fighter

German airborne

0   25 miles

0   25km

145

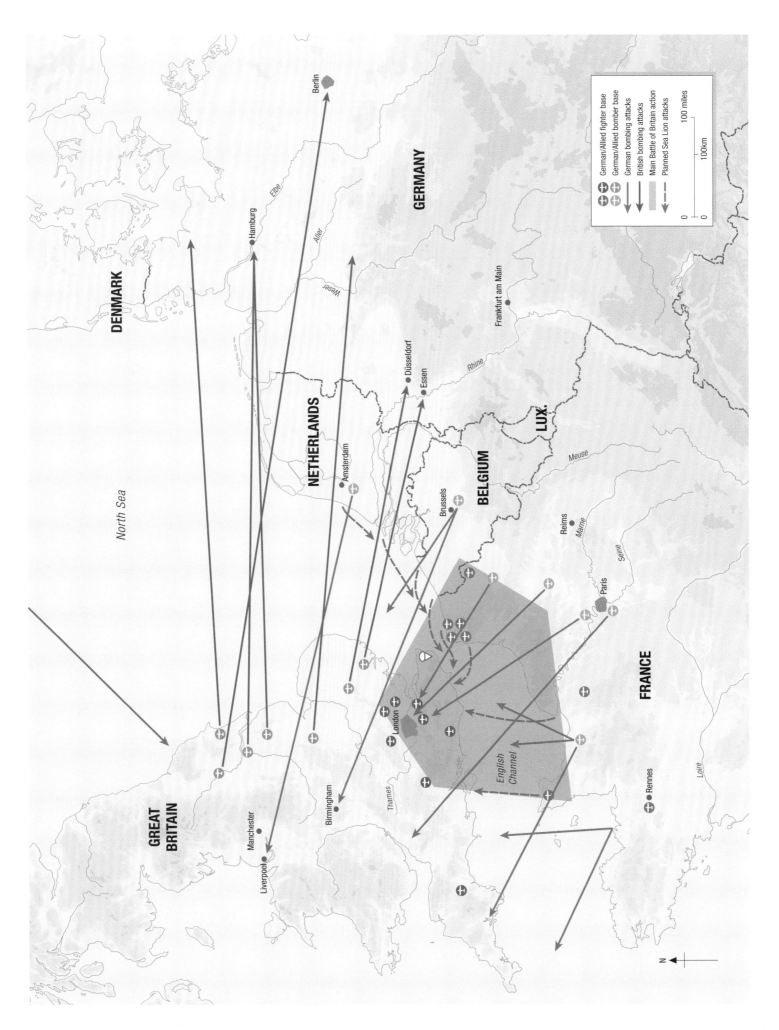

CHAPTER 6:
THE AIR WAR OVER BRITAIN AND GERMANY

The militarization of the skies had matured by the end of the Great War and air power theorists came into their own during the interwar period. As discussed in Chapter 1, the European powers and the United States each had their own air power philosophies, doctrines and equipment. Hitler's first three campaigns in 1939–40 only bolstered enthusiasm for aerial operations and gave exaggerated pictures of their possibilities. This was especially true in the realm of 'strategic bombing' – terror attacks against civilian targets such as large cities. Both sides looked at the attacks launched against the largely undefended and relatively close (to Germany) Warsaw and Rotterdam, and drew the wrong conclusions. From today's perspective, we can see that observers at the time blew the effects of one week's concentrated bombing (Warsaw) or even one raid by 54 medium bombers (Rotterdam) completely out of proportion.

This chapter covers the aerial struggles known as the Battle of Britain, the Blitz and the early stages of the Battle for Germany in three sections. First, Hitler tried to subdue Britain from the air, initially by destroying the RAF, and later by terrorizing the civilian population. Second, when this failed, he toyed with the idea of invading Great Britain, so we will briefly look at his Operation *Seelöwe* (*Sea Lion*) and Britain's defensive measures. Finally, the RAF turned on Germany and tried to destroy the Third Reich from the air.

Hitler's understanding of the wider world and even the rudiments of strategy have already been challenged earlier in this work. His high command, especially when it exceeded the comfort zone of armies and land operations, was likewise out of its element when confronting naval, aerial, economic, or diplomatic problems. Hitler therefore somehow assumed that the fall of France alone would be enough to drive Britain from the war. This faulty logic contributed to his permitting the BEF to escape from Dunkirk, when his army could have captured and/or destroyed most of it instead. When Britain did not capitulate just because its French ally did, the Führer had no plan B. In the absence of any better options, eventually Germany settled on a combined air and sea campaign against Great Britain.

Before the war, both Germany and Britain assumed a future conflict between them would be fought in the air. While Great Britain made concrete moves to prepare, Germany's arrangements were mainly in the category of wishful thinking. By inclination and personality, Hitler had no patience for this sort of warfare, so his heart was never in the enterprise. Besides, his small navy had been ravaged during the Norwegian campaign, while war in the West had betrayed numerous limitations within the Luftwaffe. In early July 1940, with little strategic bombing doctrine, undersized aircraft and only a flimsy plan, the Luftwaffe began attacking Britain. In its defence, German resources and industry could never have created serious and sustained aerial or naval over-the-water threats, while the Wehrmacht had given little thought to such operations.

After less than a week of limited raids on Britain, Hitler realized the aerial and naval gambit alone would not knock Great Britain out of the war. Therefore, on 16 July, he issued his Directive No. 16 concerning the air and amphibious assault on the 'English motherland'. Three days later, he gave a speech to the Reichstag (naturally, packed with Wehrmacht top brass and deputies from the Nazi Party, the only lawful political party in the country), which has since become known as his 'Last Appeal to Reason'. In reality a rambling and arrogant surrender demand, Churchill immediately rejected it. Hitler now had no alternative other than to continue the attacks for which he, the Wehrmacht and Germany were neither prepared nor qualified to prosecute.

For years, Germany had been building the wrong air force and aircraft for this type of war. Göring, a good man in the political knife fights during the Nazis' rise to power, was a poor leader and manager. Losses in Poland, Norway and the West had cost the Luftwaffe dearly. Meanwhile, the RAF enjoyed a combination of advantages. By the late 1930s, it had new monoplane fighters already entering service or about to come online and its aviation industry would soon out-build Germany's. It expended effort on perfecting radar and developed a command and control network par excellence, the Dowding System. To France's dismay, Britain began to pull its AASF off the Continent before Dunkirk and did not send many aviation assets there afterwards. The RAF created a reserve backup to provide a continuous stream of pilots and aircraft (although losses would severely test this). By the start of the Battle of Britain, its pilot corps represented a 'miniature United Nations' made up of volunteers from the dominions plus Czech, Polish, Norwegian, Belgian, French and American men.

Phase I of the Battle of Britain was the *Kanalkampf* (Channel Battle, 10 July–12 August), with which the Luftwaffe wanted to clear the Royal Navy and merchant shipping from the Channel, destroy the RAF and generally create preconditions for Operation *Seelöwe* (Sea Lion, invasion of the British isles), scheduled for any time after mid-August. Problems with slow Stukas, unescorted bombers and too few fighters with too little range quickly became obvious. Despite some teething problems with the Dowding System, the RAF came out on top in most engagements against the Luftwaffe. The bombing raids that did get through were not crippling. Weather played, and would continue to play, a critical role; it significantly curtailed flying on some days, while on others planes could not get airborne before noon. This deprived the Luftwaffe of much-needed momentum and gave the RAF equally needed pauses with which to recover a little.

Phase II began with *Adlertag* (Eagle Day, 13 August) and ran until the 23rd. Supposedly the Luftwaffe's main effort, poor weather caused a two-day delay; but then the Germans concentrated on Fighter Command aerodromes and radar stations. After four days of intensive operations, poor weather again intervened, breaking German momentum. Partially based on weak intelligence reports, complicated by exaggerated Luftwaffe claims of RAF planes shot down, Göring changed tactics after a disappointing ten days.

The third and final phase of the Battle of Britain started on 24 August. The Luftwaffe's plan was to escort a smaller bomber force with massive numbers of fighters: Bait RAF interceptors with the first, and then destroy them with the second. The German tactic began to bear fruit, with the two sides' losses approaching near parity. The resulting pressure caused fissures in Fighter Command's top echelons, with leaders of No. 11 and No. 12 Groups turning on each other. On 6 September, just when things appeared to be at their worst for the defenders, Hitler and Göring again changed tactics away from attacking Fighter Command. This adjustment reflected both Göring's weak leadership and management style, as well as the immaturity of Germany's warfighting abilities when not involved on land. They were basically unable to accurately see or understand the results of their efforts.

The Luftwaffe had been bombing British cities since June, but on 7 September, the official start date of the Blitz, it shifted to bombing London in earnest. Raids by many hundreds of bombers escorted by many hundreds of fighters dropped many hundreds of tons of bombs all over Britain, causing mass casualties each day. However, operationally this represented a new set of target priorities (cities, dock installations and civilian morale) before the earlier set of targets had been eliminated (Fighter Command, airfields and radar). German losses mounted, both in absolute numbers and as a proportion of RAF losses. After ten days it became clear to Hitler, if not Göring, that he could not beat Great Britain in 1940, so he called off *Seelöwe*. The size of the raids increased until 15 October, but then began to dwindle. The Germans again changed target priorities in mid-November, this time to provincial cities, mostly in the south of England. From then until the end of February 1941, the Germans scattered their attacks all over the country. Thereafter, raids trailed off until May, at which point most Luftwaffe units transferred east for Operation *Barbarossa*.

This chapter also briefly covers *Seelöwe*, a source of much interest to amateurs curious about World War II. The German invasion of Great Britain is the second great 'what if' of 1940, after speculation about 'what if' Hitler had not made a hash of Dunkirk. By August and September, the Battle of Britain had not knocked out the RAF, the Royal Navy persisted unbowed, the U-boats had not strangled Britain, and the nation's morale remained high. Especially in view of the tremendous aerial, naval and logistical effort required to make Operation *Neptune* a success in June 1944, we can see that *Seelöwe* never stood a chance. Nevertheless, the Germans did plan for the operation, which in early September the British believed could come any day, and so maps of this are included here.

Finally, beginning in the spring of 1940, the RAF's Bomber Command began to seriously target the German homeland. Between the defeat of France and the expansion of the North African sideshow after February 1941, Churchill wanted to take the war to the Third Reich. Bombing raids seemed like the best way to do this, as well as to justify the huge interwar expenditures on bombers and bombing. The arrival of the four-engined Stirling and Halifax bombers in the winter of 1941 (with bomb loads of 6–7 tons and respective ranges of 600 and 1,200 miles) made this possible. However, the RAF soon found out what the Luftwaffe already knew: Daylight raids were costly and, indeed, the bomber did not 'always get through'. By mid-1941, the British had given up on so-called 'precision' daytime attacks against military, industrial and infrastructure targets. They shifted to area attacks at night, with the unabashed purpose of destroying cities and terrorizing civilians. Throughout the year, these attacks frequently failed to have significant effects and often suffered more aircrew lost than they killed Germans on the ground.

MAP 68: RAF FIGHTER COMMAND DEPLOYMENT AND THE DOWDING SYSTEM

Just in time, around 1936, Great Britain awoke to the realization that a future air war with Germany would require more than taking the offensive with bombers. That year, the RAF created Fighter Command under Air Marshal Sir Hugh Dowding, an early and energetic advocate of modern monoplane fighters, radar and other new technological advances. The British scheme of radar-controlled interception begun in 1938, better known as the Dowding System, ranks as his greatest aerial command and control innovation. This integrated network of radar stations, volunteer observers, buried telephone lines, centralized sector stations and decentralized fighter bases, along with prodigious fighter-plane production and repair efforts, plus pilot rescue and replacement training, defeated the Luftwaffe in the summer of 1940.

In the Western campaign, the RAF had lost nearly 450 fighters and 400 aircrew killed, missing and captured. During the first five months of 1940, Dowding had to work hard against the wishes of politicians to keep more crew and planes from being sent to Norway or France to fight for lost causes. The good news for the RAF was that, under Lord Max Beaverbrook, British factories were cranking out between 100 and 150 fighters per week, outstripping German production by 137 per cent for the year. By the end of the Dunkirk episode, Dowding had 446 fighters, 331 of which were modern aircraft.

Fighter Command divided Great Britain into four group areas, each with subordinate sector stations and fighter squadrons. Dowding directed Fighter Command operations from the 'filter room' at his headquarters at Bentley Priory near RAF Stanmore. Input came from radar, plus human observers and listening posts. Chain Home (the codename for the radar) used technology barely five years old in 1940 and came in two varieties: Low (above 500ft altitude) and High (above 15,000ft). Organized as No. 60 Group, military, auxiliary (Women's Auxiliary Air Force, WAAF) and civilian radar operators were directly under Dowding. Operators worked in a hut below the 300ft-tall antennae, monitored cathode-ray tubes and phoned their findings into the filter room. Observers corroborated their information. Operations room staff then vectored fighters towards the incoming raiders. Ultra intercepts of deciphered German codes also provided valuable intelligence.

Pre-war tests had demonstrated the debilitating effects of 'too much information' coming into the Dowding System, alternately confusing and overwhelming decision-making. Therefore, Dowding streamlined the process and refined the definition of which data was essential for intercept. He standardized operations rooms at Fighter Command and at group and sector stations. He built the system so that groups and sectors could easily transfer squadrons as the situation demanded. With these brains and eyes, Fighter Command's weapons – the fighters – had around 15 minutes to scramble and get airborne in preparation for Luftwaffe attacks assembling over Belgium and northern France. Dowding had full responsibility for Britain's air defence: In addition to Fighter Command and radar, he controlled Anti-Aircraft (AA) Command (artillery and searchlights), the Observer Corps and Balloon Command.

The fighters were organized into squadrons of a dozen planes or so, based one, two, three, or sometimes four per aerodrome. Taking into account the limited range of Luftwaffe planes, Kent and Sussex housed most bases. Hawker Hurricane Mk Is represented the most numerous RAF fighter in the summer of 1940, making up 29 squadrons, and also accounted for the most kills. Britain's first monoplane interceptor, mounting eight .303in. machine guns in the wings, entered service in the closing days of 1937. Supermarine Spitfires arrived in the RAF inventory 18 months after the Hurricane, and filled 19 squadrons. These mounted the same armament, but had many upgrades. Although Spitfire Mk I and IIs and Messerschmidt Bf 109s had different strengths and weaknesses, they are generally considered evenly matched. Boulton Paul Defiant Mk Is, with a turret mounting four machine guns, could have devastating effects on German bombers or unsuspecting fighters. Bristol Blenheims, modified light bombers, served effectively as night fighters.

Dowding also had to develop an effective doctrine for fighter vs fighter combat; previously the RAF had only thought in terms of fighter vs bomber (since 'the bomber would always get through', the theory was that German bombers would not be escorted). They also used the 'vic' or 'V' formation of three aircraft, inferior to the German model described in the next map, but supposedly more effective against the unescorted bombers they expected to encounter. RAF pilots did have certain advantages, however: British pilots defending their homes alongside foreign pilots avenging Nazi conquest of theirs, were fighting above their own bases, which meant that many pilots shot down over England could land by parachute, catch a ride to an airfield and then be airborne again later the same day.

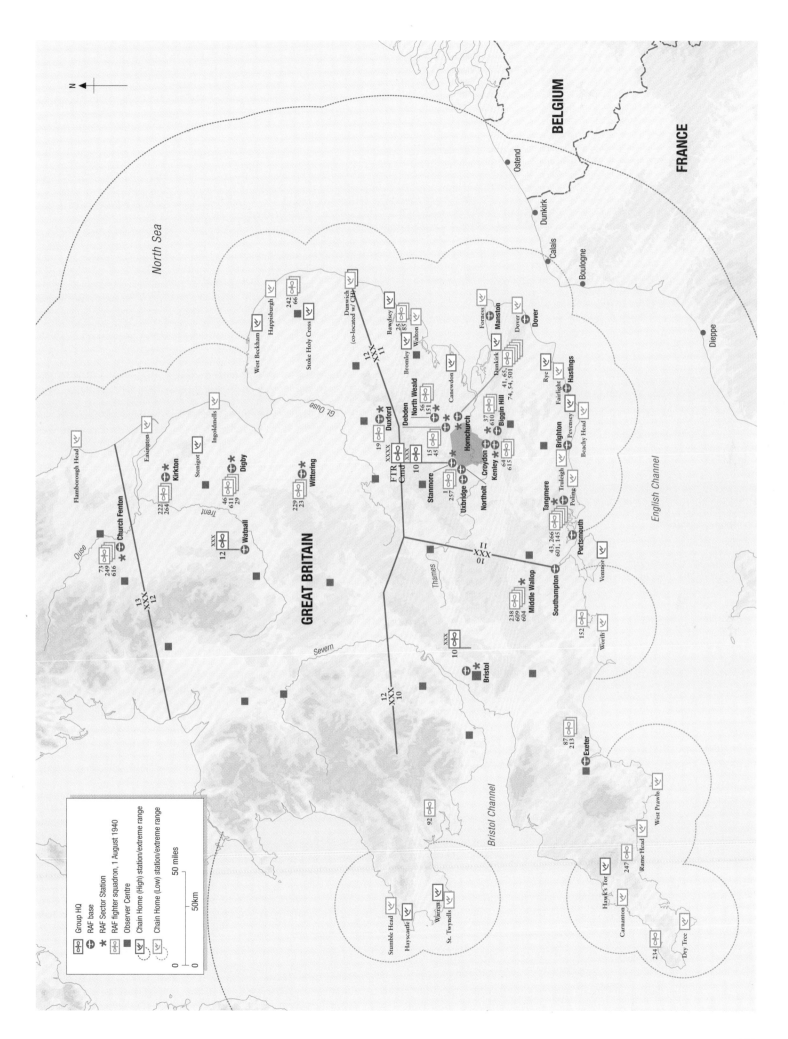

N

North Sea

BELGIUM

FRANCE

Ostend

Dunkirk

Calais

Boulogne

Dieppe

GREAT BRITAIN

Happisburgh

242
66

West Beckham

Stoke Holy Cross

Dunwich
(co-located w/ CH)

Bawdsey

12
XXX
11

25
85

Bromley

Walton

North Weald

56
151

Debden

Forness

Manston

Dover

Dover

Canewdon

Dunkirk

41, 65, 501

74, 54, 501

Rye

Hastings

37
610

Biggin Hill

Fairlight

Pevensey

Beachy Head

Flamborough Head

Easington

Kirkton

222
264

Ingoldmells

Stenigot

Digby

46
611
29

Duxford

19

Wittering

229
23

Church Fenton

73
249
616

Ouse

Trent

Watnall

12

FTR
Cmd

XXX

15
45

Stanmore

1
257

Uxbridge

Northolt

Hornchurch

Croydon

64
615

Kenley

Brighton

13
XXX
12

12
XXX
10

Severn

Thames

10
XXX
11

Tangmere

43, 266
601, 145

Truleigh

Poling

Portsmouth

152

Worth

Ventnor

Middle Wallop

238
609
604

Southampton

10
XXX

Bristol Channel

Bristol

92

Exeter

87
213

Stumble Head

Hayscastle

Warren

St. Twynells

Hawk's Tor

Carmanton

234

Dry Tree

Rame Head

West Prawle

English Channel

Gt. Ouse

Legend:
- Group HQ
- RAF base
- RAF Sector Station
- RAF fighter squadron, 1 August 1940
- Observer Centre
- Chain Home (High) station/extreme range
- Chain Home (Low) station/extreme range

0   50 miles
0   50km

151

MAP 69: THE LUFTWAFFE DEPLOYMENT

For years, the Luftwaffe had also prepared for the upcoming Battle of Britain, just not as well as the RAF. One of the secrets to the success of the blitzkrieg had been the synergistic effects of the Wehrmacht's various elements all working together to overwhelm the enemy. Now the Luftwaffe would go it alone against the island nation, with some assistance from the Kriegsmarine, but none from the Heer (Army). Also, despite the seemingly decisive nature of the German victory in the Western campaign, they suffered nearly 1,500 aircraft lost to all causes and an additional 500 damaged during those six weeks.

Leading the German efforts would be Göring, with his gregarious personality the polar opposite of 'Stuffy' Dowding. By 1939, Göring had created the world's most effective and well-rounded air force. A decorated World War I ace, he favoured fighters, supposedly a benefit in the upcoming battle against the RAF. But in the Nazi 'Führer state', his sometimes incorrect, dilettantish notions were not subject to challenge (as was also the case with Hitler). This led to constantly changing priorities. Key subordinates, often former army officers like Kesselring and Richthofen, were close air support experts and probably not well suited to the Battle of Britain.

A number of problem areas within the Luftwaffe have already been mentioned, such as comparatively weak industrial output, small, short-range aircraft and losses in earlier campaigns. Additionally, vague objectives from the highest echelons of the Reich, inexperience in purely air force vs air force operations, the relatively immature infrastructure of Belgium and northern France, lower octane fuel and terrible intelligence on the enemy all added to the challenges. Of these, the undervaluing of military intelligence hamstrung all segments of the Wehrmacht for the entirety of World War II.

Starting with the Spanish Civil War, the Luftwaffe perfected the superior two-plane *Rotte* (lead pilot plus wingman) and four-plane *Schwarm* (two *Rotten*) tactical arrangements. As opposed to RAF pilots altruistically defending their homeland, Luftwaffe pilots were motivated by personal glory as competing high-scoring individual aces. German aerial gunnery training was also considered better than the British.

Germany's principal fighter, the Bf 109 – especially up-gunned 'F' models – possessed offsetting advantages compared to the Spitfire. Germany's other fighter, the twin-engine Bf 110, is incorrectly maligned in most traditional Battle of Britain histories. Just as fast as Spitfires, and able to turn like a 109, it had two cannons and four machine guns

concentrated in the nose, which could fire for 20 seconds (compared to 16 seconds for the 'Spit' and 9 for the 109). In 'free hunting' missions the 110 was better than its single-engine competition and only suffered when tied to bombers for escort missions; through September 1940, the Luftwaffe's highest scoring formation flew *Zerstörers*.

German bombers were uniformly suspect, except for the fast and accurate Ju 88 (with its 2,500kg bombload). All had only a few small guns for defence. The Stuka was slow, lacked manoeuverability and had only two small guns firing forward. Elderly Do 17s carried roughly half the bombload of British Hampdens. The Luftwaffe's main bomber, the rugged He 111, compared favourably to British Wellingtons and carried 2,000kg of ordnance. In early missions against Operation *Dynamo* over Dunkirk, it became obvious that Luftwaffe bombers of all types needed fighter escorts when facing the RAF. Therefore, with Bf 109s able to loiter over London for only 10–15 minutes (as shown in the range arcs on this map), during the Battle of Britain this mission fell principally to the 110s.

During June and July, the Luftwaffe concentrated on making good losses from the Western campaign and improving sometimes primitive airstrips in Belgium and north-west France; this was the last of its many redeployments since launching *Fall Gelb*. Two *Luftflotten* – 2. and 3. – would carry the Luftwaffe's main load, with help from 5. Luftflotte in Denmark and southern Norway. Göring concentrated most single-seat fighters under the command of Jagdfliegerführer 2. and 3. New phone and telex lines had to be laid, hangars built and spare parts accumulated. Weather reporting infrastructure had to be created, assisted by U-boats, fishing trawlers, or even very long range Fw 200 Condors flying west of the British Isles between France and Norway.

All of the Wehrmacht, from the OKW and Oberkommando der Luftwaffe (OKL) down, recognized from the start that destroying the RAF and gaining air superiority over the British Isles held the key to future success in the West. Göring issued his disjointed, vaguely worded, poorly thought-out operational order 'General Directive for the Luftwaffe War against England' on 30 June. What the Germans failed to understand was that Fighter Command was their main enemy, not Bomber Command, Coastal Command, nor the British aviation industry. Granted, no other air force had attempted such an ambitious operation in the short history of aerial warfare. But the way that the Germans prosecuted the Battle of Britain and the Blitz gave them very slim chances of success, if any.

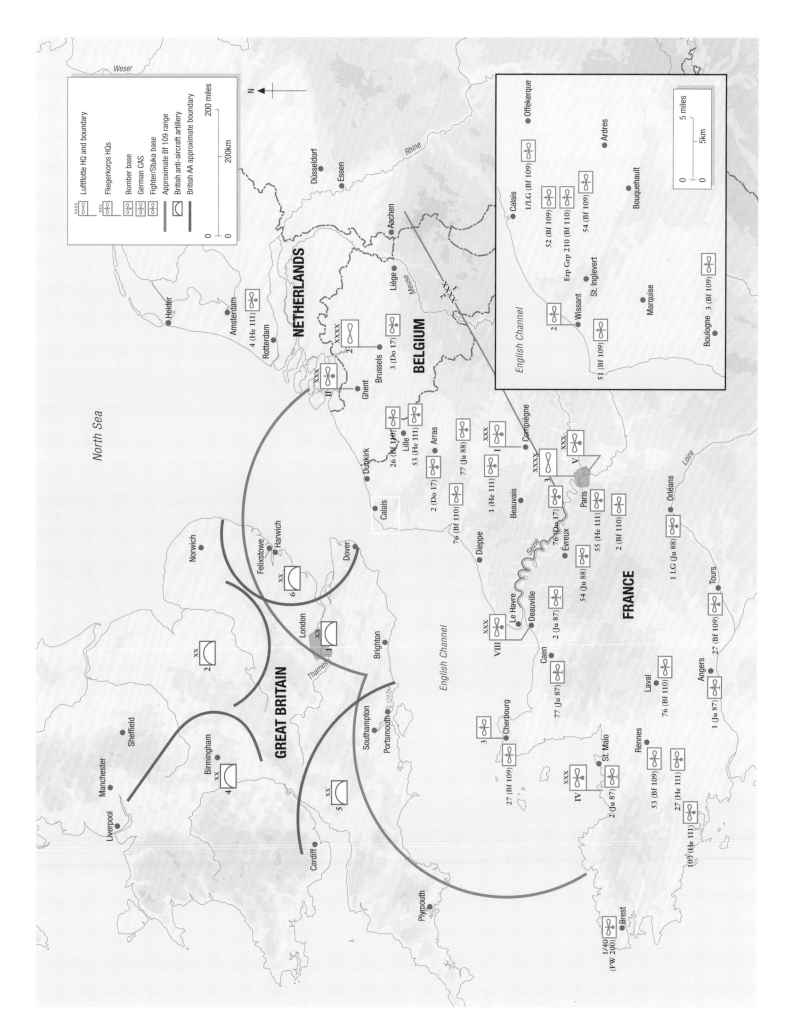

Map legend

- Luftflotte HQ and boundary
- Fliegerkorps HQs
- Bomber base
- German CAS
- Fighter/Stuka base
- Approximate Bf 109 range
- British anti-aircraft artillery
- British AA approximate boundary

N

200 miles
200km

Weser

North Sea

NETHERLANDS

Helder
Amsterdam
Rotterdam
4 (He 111)

Düsseldorf
Essen

Rhine

Liège
Aachen
Meuse

XXXX
2

XXX
II

Ghent
Brussels
3 (Do 17)

BELGIUM

26 (Bf 110)
Lille
53 (He 111)
Arras
77 (Ju 88)
XXX
I
Compiègne

XXXX
3

XXX
V

Dunkirk
2 (Do 17)
76 (Bf 110)
1 (He 111)
Beauvais

Calais

Dieppe
Seine
76 (Do 17)
Évreux
55 (He 111)
Paris
2 (Bf 110)

54 (Ju 88)

FRANCE

Orléans
Loire

GREAT BRITAIN

Norwich
Felixstowe
Harwich
XX
6
Dover

London
XX
1
Thames

XX
2

Brighton

Southampton
Portsmouth

Sheffield
Manchester
Liverpool
Birmingham
XX
4
XX
5

Cardiff

Plymouth

Brest
1/40
(FW 200)

English Channel

Le Havre
Deauville
2 (Ju 87)
XXX
VIII

Caen
77 (Ju 87)

Cherbourg
3

St. Malo
27 (Bf 109)
2 (Ju 87)
XXX
IV

Rennes
53 (Bf 109)
27 (He 111)

Laval
76 (Bf 110)

Angers
1 (Ju 87)
27 (Bf 109)

Tours
1 LG (Ju 88)

105 (He 111)

Inset map

5 miles
5km

0   0

Offekerque
Calais
1/LG (Bf 109)
52 (Bf 109)
Erp Grp 210 (Bf 110)
54 (Bf 110)

Ardres
Bouquehault

St. Inglevert
Wissant
2

Marquise

Boulogne 3 (Bf 109)
51 (Bf 109)

English Channel

153

MAP 70: *KANALKAMPF*, 1 JULY–12 AUGUST 1940

Granted, following their victory in north-west Europe, the Germans wanted to strike quickly against Great Britain. However, the aerial assault saw none of the discussions, war games and other extensive staff work that would usually precede a German military operation. Kesselring, commanding 2. Luftflotte, had responsibility for half of the coming attacks, yet, as he wrote in his post-war memoirs, 'I was even left in the dark about the relations of the current air raids on England and the invasion plan; no orders were issued to the Chiefs of Air Commands. No definitive instructions were given about what my air fleet had to expect in the way of tactical assignments or what provision had been made for cooperation of army or navy.'[27]

According to Göring's 30 June directive, his air force had a number of missions: 1. Gain air superiority through attacks on the RAF and the British aero-industry; 2. Prepare the way for a cross-Channel invasion by attacks against the Royal Navy and Bomber Command; 3. Bomb British ports and Channel shipping; and 4. Terrorize the British civilian population, especially in large cities. A by-product of all four tasks was 5. Draw Fighter Command into the air, where the Luftwaffe could destroy it. Göring thought that by attacking the south-east of England, he could accomplish all of these missions. He made Oberst Johannes Fink, commander of KG 2, the *Kanalkampfführer*, while Oberst Theo Osterkamp, commander of Jagdgeschwader (JG) 51, led the fighter support. Stukas from Flieger-Korps VIII (3. Luftflotte) would add valuable assistance. Before the first sorties, we can already see a fatal dilution of effort among too many objectives and no clear lines of responsibility between the two *Luftflotten*.

The *Kanalkampf* complicated Dowding's job for a number of reasons. First, Luftwaffe forces attacking the Channel assembled farther inland, beyond the range of his radar. Fighting over the Channel evenly divided the distance Spitfires and Messerschmitts had to fly, eliminating a key RAF advantage. Furthermore, aircrew shot down over the water could not just catch a train back to their squadrons, cancelling another big plus that his aviators had. Mainly, however, he worried about weakening Fighter Command through missions of secondary importance. This did not create many friends for Dowding at the Admiralty or within the merchant fleet.

Although 10 July is often considered the start date of the Battle of Britain, the Luftwaffe began attacking convoys and ports on the 1st. Fink and Osterkamp spent the first days of July probing the skies over the Channel and south-east England, to judge British reaction times and the effectiveness of Dowding's system. One 4 July attack against convoy OA178 off Portland (without fighter cover) tested Dowding's ideas about protecting Channel shipping. Two *Gruppen* of StG 2 sank four vessels (15,856 tons, including the auxiliary anti-aircraft ship HMS *Foyle Bank*) and damaged nine others (40,286 tons), some very badly. Churchill immediately ordered the direct escort of all convoys. That same day, Stukas attacked Portsmouth and sank two and damaged three merchantmen. Between the two raids Richthofen lost one dive-bomber. Those numbers were clearly an anomaly, however. Between 10 and 13 July, Luftwaffe:RAF losses stood at 40:29. It was at this time that Bf 110s were ordered to close escort duties, seriously cutting into their effectiveness.

By 24 July, the Germans had set up their own Freya radars at Cap Blanc Nez, south-west of Calais, with 'visibility' on British convoys from the Thames Estuary to Cherbourg. By the end of the month, the Royal Navy had practically abandoned the Channel except in case of invasion. July had cost Britain 48 merchant vessels and 14 naval craft, including four destroyers sunk. Even so, the RAF maintained a 184:160 advantage in kills.

At this point, the Luftwaffe began to prepare in earnest for its large-scale Operation *Adlerangriff* (Eagle Attack), which, thanks to Ultra signals intelligence, Dowding knew was coming. The Germans switched to raiding airfields and radar stations in Kent. Chain Home masts at Dover, Rye, Pevensey and Ventnor (on the Isle of Wight, which was put out of action for three days) sustained damage, creating a 160-mile gap in radar coverage on the eve of Göring's main effort. One last notable convoy attack took place between Beachy Head and the Isle of Wight over 7–8 August. Convoy CW9 'Peewit' (21 ships, totalling 70,000 tons) was first set upon by E-boats at night, sinking two merchantmen and damaging another. Stukas hit the convoy on the next day, as 150 fighters tangled overhead; four ships went down, while seven more took a beating. Only four Peewit ships had escaped damage. A dozen RAF pilots died in 13 Hurricanes and one Spitfire. The Germans lost eight Bf 109s, one Bf 110 and seven Stukas. Also shown on this map are British Army deployments during the immediate post-Dunkirk period.

---

27 Albert Kesselring, *The Memoirs of Field Marshal Kesselring*, Presidio Press: Novato, CA, 1989, p. 67. Perhaps he should have had more curiosity.

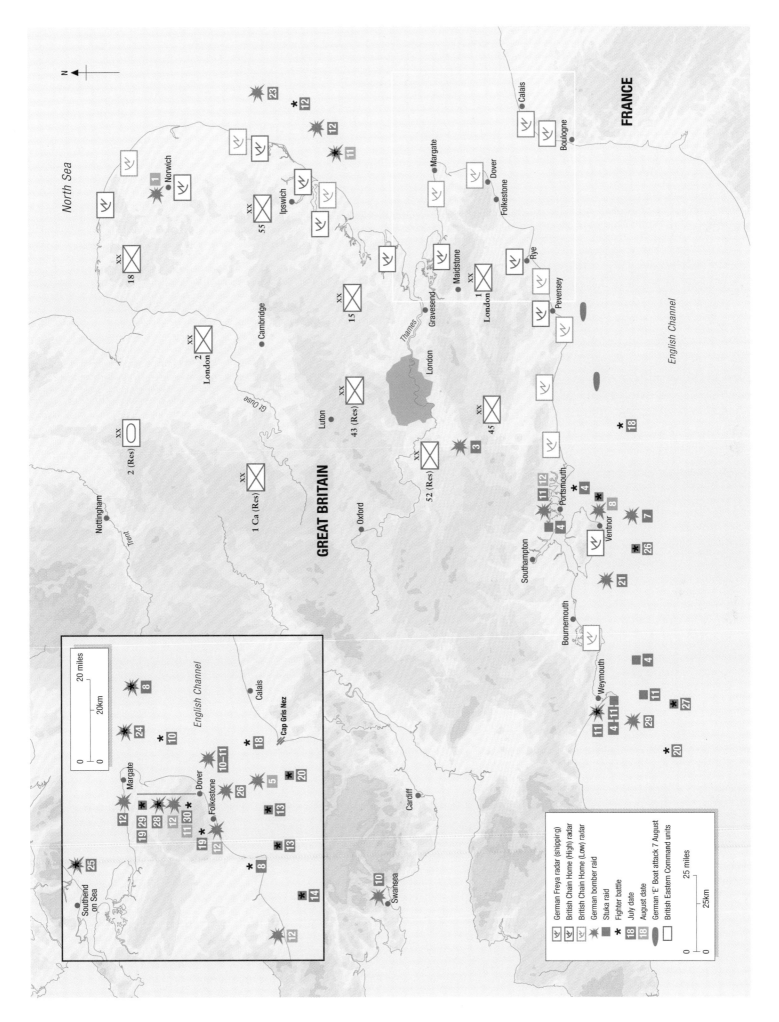

North Sea

N

Norwich

Ipswich

XX
55

XX
18

XX
2
London

XX
2 (Res)

Nottingham

Trent

Cambridge

R. Ouse

Luton

XX
43 (Res)

London

XX
15

Gravesend

Maidstone

London

XX
1

Margate

Dover

Folkestone

Rye

Pevensey

Thames

XX
52 (Res)

Oxford

XX
45

XX
1 Ca (Res)

GREAT BRITAIN

3

Portsmouth
11 12
4
Ventnor
8
7
4

Southampton

21

Bournemouth

Weymouth
4
11
4–11
11
29
27
20

English Channel

FRANCE

Calais

Boulogne

English Channel

Southend
on Sea
25

Margate
12
29
28
12
30
19
19 12
11
8
14
12

Dover
26
5
20
10–11
13
13
13

Folkestone

Cap Gris Nez

Calais

24
8
10
18

0   20km
0   20 miles

German Freya radar (shipping)
British Chain Home (High) radar
British Chain Home (Low) radar
German bomber raid
Stuka raid
Fighter battle
July date   18
August date   18
German 'E' Boat attack 7 August
British Eastern Command units

0   25km
0   25 miles

155

MAP 71: THE BATTLE OF BRITAIN (I), 13–23 AUGUST 1940

The Luftwaffe's *Kanalkampf* had accomplished little besides once again showing the Stuka's vulnerabilities in the face of RAF fighters. The British mainly rerouted their Channel convoys and honed their air intercept skills.

Germany's next phase in its campaign to defeat Britain from the air was *Adlerangriff* (Eagle Attack) against Fighter Command, launched on *Adlertag* (Eagle Day), 13 August. For all his faults, Göring was no idiot and he had good men in command and staff positions, but none of them knew how to make *Adlerangriff* work. Imbued with a fateful combination of blitzkrieg thinking (hit the enemy hard enough and fast enough and he will be defeated) and victory disease, they had no real plan other than a list of targets. First, they did not have any good intelligence regarding anything going on in Britain – either before or during the campaign: How many planes the RAF had, how many planes British industry could produce, or how radar or the Dowding System worked. They did not understand that the upcoming struggle would be one of attrition, lacking both a decisive battle lasting a couple days or a single dramatic manoeuvre. Neither did they have the patience for this sort of fight, so constantly changed emphasis. *Adlerangriff* supposedly had as its *Schwerpunkt* the defeat of Fighter Command, but Hitler and Göring diluted this main effort with many supporting orders: Continue attacks on convoys and the Royal Navy, disrupt the British aviation industry and terror-bomb random cities – all under the general rubric of preparing for *Seelöwe*.[28]

As intended, the Germans would prevail with *Adlerangriff* just as they had done elsewhere so far during the war, through superior élan and willpower, plus overwhelming strength at the critical point (and a healthy serving of enemy mistakes). Perhaps nothing betrays the weaknesses of their attitude better than their thinking about the Dowding System. It would provide an essential service for the Luftwaffe: Bring Fighter Command to the Germans, where they could destroy it in aerial combat.

Adlertag began with uncooperative weather, poor communications, and errors that would hamstring the entire Luftwaffe campaign. A *Gruppe* of 74 Do 17s (an aircraft past its prime) did not get the message that, because of the weather, the German commanders had postponed the raid. The bombers therefore kept going without escort, got bounced by a succession of Hurricane and Spitfire squadrons (nos. 111, 151 and 74) and then bombed a Coastal Command airfield at Eastchurch. Without harming Fighter Command, III./KG 2 lost five bombers shot down and five more that returned to base so full of holes they never flew again. Another raid that same day against the Isle of Wight fizzled out for quite the opposite reason: Poor weather forced the KG 54 bombers to turn back, while its I./JG 2 fighter escort continued on uselessly. The weather cleared that afternoon (a common occurrence) and the Luftwaffe managed to launch some successful, coordinated attacks. However, it lost nearly twice the number of planes as the RAF[29]. In a much more telling statistic, it lost more than four times as many crewmen, 52:11.

The Luftwaffe launched many attacks on 15 August, the de facto *Adlertag* and destined to become its 'Black Thursday'. Once the morning weather improved, level bombers, Stukas and even fighters attacked targets all over south-east England. They caused damage to numerous RAF aerodromes, some of it extensive, and put a couple of radar stations out of action by bombing the local power grid. Dozens of RAF fighter squadrons rose to intercept them. On this day, 5. Luftflotte in Scandinavia made its disastrous attack against the north of England and Scotland. Even the newer, faster Ju 88s proved to be no match for Spitfires after all. With an aircrew losses differential of 128:11 that day, the Luftwaffe would never prevail at this rate.

Fighter Command had its own 'Hardest Day' on 18 August. Early on, its radar picked up the largest attacking formations it had yet seen, and Dowding alerted every No. 11 Group squadron. In some raids, escorts outnumbered bombers almost 3:1. Sector stations at Biggin Hill and Kenley came under heavy assault. Bombers and Stukas also pounded airfields and radar stations in the Southampton area, but these mainly belonged to the Fleet Air Arm and Coastal Command. German intelligence had been telling Göring that his attacks were decimating the RAF (seemingly confirmed by pilot claims) and he had passed along this false assessment to his men. Combat over England told a different story. Stuka losses had become so prohibitive that they flew no more in this battle (they would be saved for *Seelöwe*). Comparative aircrew losses again reached an unsustainable rate that day, 97:10. Poor weather over the next few days gave the Germans a pause in which to rethink the campaign.

---

28 The neophyte Germans were certainly not unique in this regard. Even with the benefit of observing Luftwaffe mistakes, plus allegedly superior leaders, doctrine and weapons, years later the Allied Combined Bomber Offensive repeated many of these same errors.

29 Although Germany and Great Britain were modern nations with extensive military bureaucracies, the Battle of Britain scholarship suffers from terrible record keeping. No two sources agree on key facts, such as crew and aircraft losses or RAF aircraft destroyed on the ground. I have averaged reliable sources for my figures.

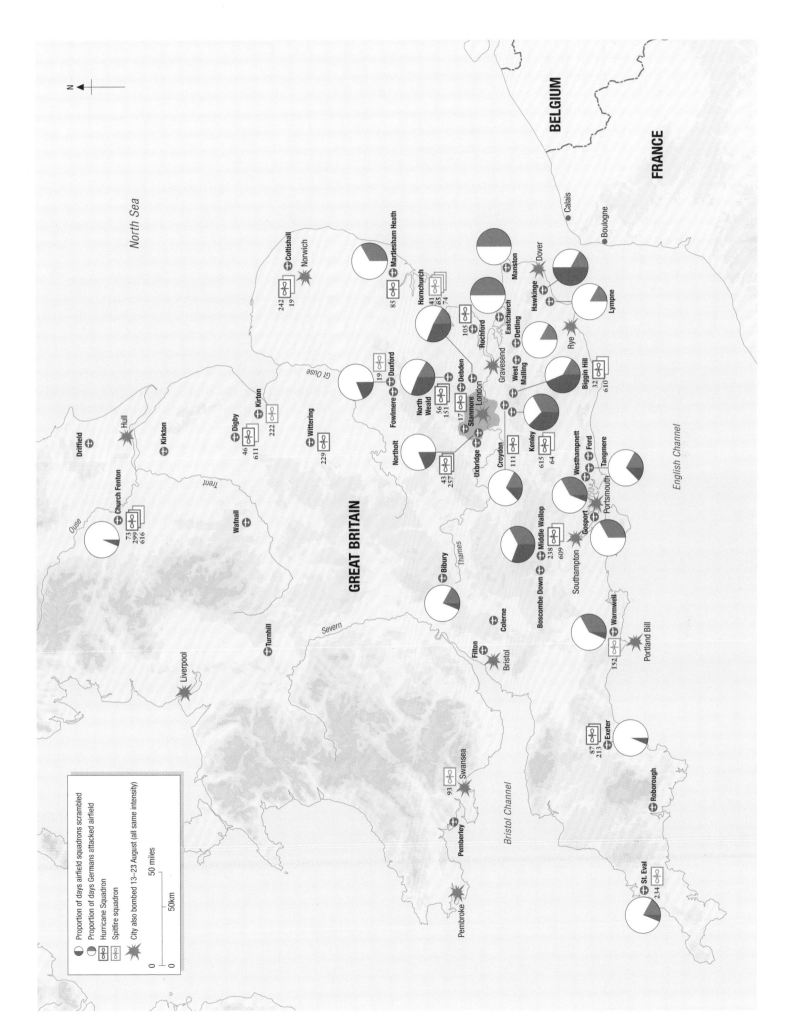

BELGIUM

FRANCE

North Sea

GREAT BRITAIN

English Channel

Bristol Channel

Severn

Thames

Trent

Ouse

Gt Ouse

Calais

Boulogne

Dover

Manston
Hawkinge
Lympne
Rye
Eastchurch
Detling
West Malling
Biggin Hill
Kenley
Rochford
Gravesend
Hornchurch
London
Stanmore
Uxbridge
Croydon
Debden
North Weald
Fowlmere
Duxford
Martlesham Heath
Coltishall
Norwich
Northolt
Wittering
Digby
Kirton
Kirton
Hull
Driffield
Church Fenton
Watnall
Turnhill
Liverpool
Bristol
Filton
Colerne
Boscombe Down
Middle Wallop
Bibury
Southampton
Gosport
Portsmouth
Ford
Westhampnett
Tangmere
Warmwell
Portland Bill
Exeter
Roborough
St. Eval
Pembroke
Pemberley
Swansea

242
19

85

41
65
74

105

19

56
151

17

43
257

46
611

222

229

111

615
64

610

32

238
609

152

87
213

93

2
34

73
299
616

Legend

⦿ Proportion of days airfield squadrons scrambled
◒ Proportion of days Germans attacked airfield
Hurricane Squadron
Spitfire squadron
✹ City also bombed 13–23 August (all same intensity)

0   50 miles
0   50km

N

157

MAP 72: THE BATTLE OF BRITAIN (II), 24 AUGUST–6 SEPTEMBER 1940

On 19 August, in response to *Adlerangriff's* twin handicaps (mediocre results and debilitating losses of men and machines), Reichsmarschall Göring convened a leadership conference. The former fighter ace wanted the fighters to have the freedom to hunt. His senior generals, especially the *Luftflotten* commanders, argued for close escorts; they prevailed[30]. The group also decided on a new tactic, henceforth: 2. Luftflotte, with many fighters but fewer bombers, would continue its war against Fighter Command; 3. Luftflotte would switch to bombing the British aviation industry, its cities and other air bases. These decisions formalized the dilution of *Adlerangriff*. Meanwhile, Fighter Command hummed. Dowding had excellent inputs thanks to Ultra intelligence and radar operators who learned to read the Luftwaffe. His filter room at Bentley Priory and the group sector stations provided the process. Fighters vectoring towards Göring's formations were the outputs.

With this new plan, the Germans renewed their offensive on 24 August against four aerodromes and the Portsmouth and Southampton area. With the emphasis on escorts, bomber losses declined, while fighter losses increased. Some 2. Luftflotte bombers inadvertently hit London that night, ranking as the most important event that day. In retaliation, Churchill ordered a raid on Berlin the next night. Although the attack only killed seven Berliners, as Churchill had anticipated, Hitler flew into a rage. The Führer soon derailed Operation *Adlerangriff* to the point where it could not possibly succeed.

The Luftwaffe's new 'fighter stream' tactic failed to meet expectations, angering Göring. Escorts now often outnumbered bombers 8:1. But the *Jägers*, even in huge escorting formations, could not bring down Fighter Command machines in sufficient numbers: On the 28th, 576 fighter sorties brought down 'only' 15 RAF fighters, while on the next day, 700 sorties tallied up the same score. Huge numbers of fighter sorties per day exhausted the pilots and led to massive casualties; many *Jagdgeschwadern* stood at 50 per cent strength. Göring railed against the Bf 109 units and decided to put more emphasis on the *Zerstörers*[31]. Despite these statistics, bombers escorted at a 10:1 rate did get through to their targets. Tracking the huge formations exhausted Dowding's

radar operators and controllers. Worst of all, RAF pilot losses took their toll: The number of fighter pilots available at the end of July was 1,430, in mid-August 1,020, and in early September 840.

Tensions wore down the RAF. A debate developed between 'small wing' (immediate, forward defence) advocates Dowding and No. 11 Group Commander Air Vice Marshal Keith Parks versus those favouring the 'big wing' (large formations) in the Air Ministry and No. 12 Group Commander Air Vice Marshal Trafford Leigh-Mallory. An even more fateful debate sprung up among the Germans, however. Spurred on by his OKW chief of operations, General der Artillerie Alfred Jodl, Hitler wanted to shift to further bombing of London. Kesselring at 2. Luftflotte, Richthofen at Flieger-Korps VIII and Luftwaffe chief of staff General der Flieger Hans Jeschonnek agreed. Göring and 3. Luftflotte commander Generalfeldmarschall Hugo Sperrle wanted to keep up the pressure on Fighter Command, lest it rebound if given a break. For once, Göring was right.

Kesselring kept his men flying against Britain. He did not know it, but they were coming close to overwhelming Fighter Command, which would suffer a net loss of nearly 200 fighters during the period depicted here: 466 destroyed or damaged against only 269 new and repaired. He had concentrated on No. 11 Group with telling effect. Fighter Command was on the ropes. Then, on 4 September, Göring ill advisedly changed target priority again, now aiming at aircraft factories. Two days after that, the entire complexion of the Battle of Britain changed. As we know, on 6 September, Hitler removed most restrictions against bombing London and the Battle of Britain morphed into the Blitz.

Fighter Command, Churchill's 'few', won the Battle of Britain, with the pilots and organization of Park's No. 11 Group its critical element. Aircraft combat losses per month seemed to favour the British (Luftwaffe:RAF): July, 186:142; August, 585:367; September, 446:389; in total, 1,217:898[32]. But German losses were shared by fighters and bombers, while most RAF losses were fighters. German inexperience and impatience hurt them as much as the losses. When on 6 September, they added 'break British morale' to the Luftwaffe's existing three missions – gain air superiority, prepare the way for *Seelöwe*, destroy British means of resisting the invasion – it was too much. Not that it mattered much in the days before the Battle of Britain attained its near-mythical status. There was always little danger that Great Britain could have been invaded. Hitler had cared little for the air war's outcome back in July, and did not care any more about it in September.

---

30 In the winter of 1944, the US Army Air Forces bombing Germany had the same debate. However, Lieutenant-General Jimmy Doolittle made the opposite decision and destroyed the Luftwaffe as a result.

31 Bf 110s received a poor reputation for their activities during the Battle of Britain, mainly while closely escorting bombers. In fact, the best Bf 110 unit, III./Zerstörergeschwader (ZG) 26, had 70 kills to six losses; for the best Bf 109 unit, III./JG 26 that ratio was 70:15. Bf 110s, which made up 20 per cent of the Luftwaffe's fighter forces, scored 28 per cent of its kills.

32 During the same three-month period, Beaverbrook's repair shops returned 247 'destroyed' planes to service.

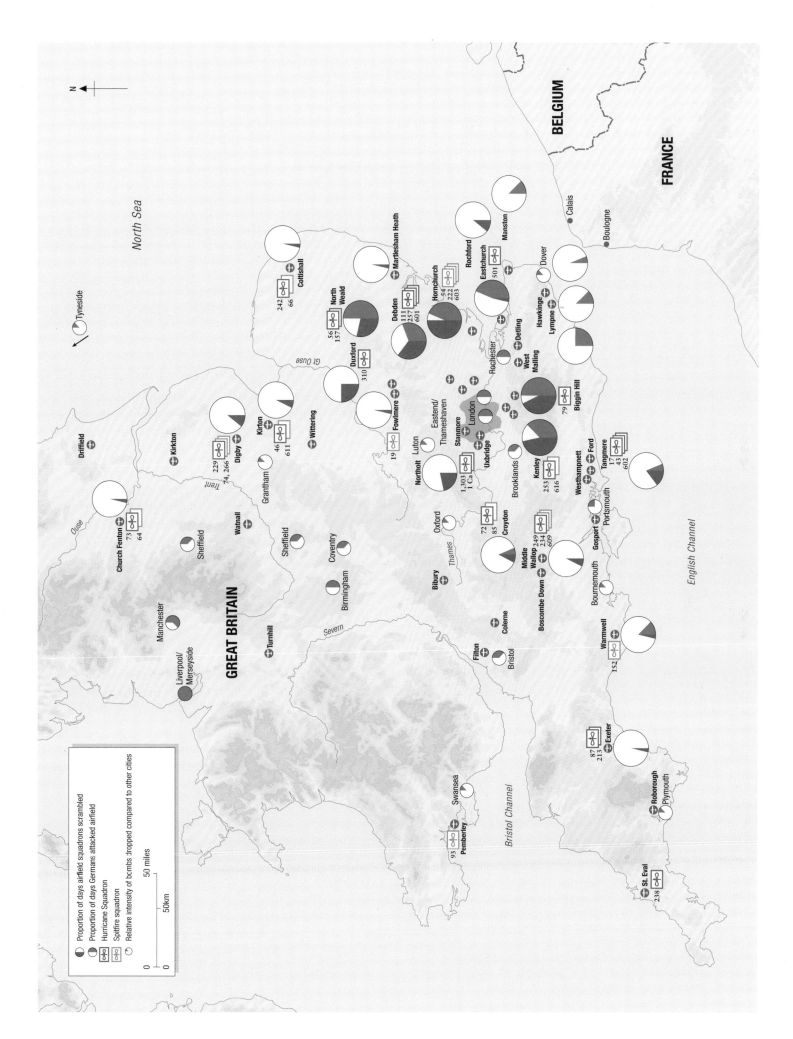

N

North Sea

BELGIUM

FRANCE

Calais

Boulogne

GREAT BRITAIN

Tyneside

Drifield

Church Fenton
73
64

Kirkton

Cottishall
242
66

Digby
74, 266
229

Kirton
46
611

North Weald
56
157

Martlesham Heath

Debden
111
257
601

Hornchurch
54
222
603

Rochford

Manston

Eastchurch
501

Dover

Hawkinge
Lympne
602

Duxford
310

Wittering

Fowlmere
19

Grantham

Watnall

Sheffield

Coventry

Birmingham

Manchester

Liverpool/
Merseyside

Turnhill

Detling

Rochester

West Malling

Biggin Hill
79

Kenley
253
616

Croydon
72
85

Uxbridge
1,303
1 Ca

Northolt

Stanmore

London

Eastend/
Thameshaven

Luton

Oxford

Bibury

Middle Wallop
249
234
609

Brooklands

Westhampnett
Ford

Gosport
Portsmouth

Tangmere
17
43
602

Bournemouth

Boscombe Down

Colerne

Filton

Bristol

Warmwell
152

Exeter
87
213

Swansea

Pemberley
93

St. Eval
238

Roborough
Plymouth

Severn

Thames

Trent

Ouse

Gt Ouse

English Channel

Bristol Channel

Proportion of days airfield squadrons scrambled
Proportion of days Germans attacked airfield
Hurricane Squadron
Spitfire squadron
Relative intensity of bombs dropped compared to other cities

0   50km
0   50 miles

159

MAP 73: THE BLITZ OVER BRITAIN, 7 SEPTEMBER 1940–SPRING 1941

The Luftwaffe began intentionally and routinely bombing British cities around the time of Dunkirk. During the summer of 1940, it did so more frequently to weaken the British aviation industry, disrupt infrastructure that might interfere with *Seelöwe* and also to terrorize the civilian population into surrendering. Perhaps believing apocalyptic pre-war fiction and propaganda about bombing cities, or overestimating the effects of single, relatively small raids (certainly by the standards of 1944–45) on Guernica and Rotterdam, and relatively brief assaults lasting a couple weeks such as against Warsaw, or just wishful thinking about their own power and British weakness, the Germans overestimated by a long way the impact of bombing Britain into submission.

By early September, it had become clear to most observers that during the Battle of Britain, the Luftwaffe had failed to knock out Fighter Command, or come close to preparing the way for *Seelöwe*. On the 7th, bombing British cities became a Luftwaffe operation in itself, not simply an adjunct to other goals. Historians consider that the Battle of Britain and the supposed threat of invasion, lingered for another week, but the bombing of British cities – the Blitz – became the Luftwaffe's focus. For eight months, it went through a number of stages, including concentrating on London (September–November 1940), bombing provincial cities (November–February 1941) and hitting port cities until petering out in preparation for Operation *Barbarossa* (February–May 1941)

Hitler issued an order on 5 September for 'disruptive attacks on the population and air defences of major British cities, including London, by day and night'. There are three interconnected reasons why he lifted his earlier prohibition against terror bombing and began the Blitz: 1. The Luftwaffe assumed the accelerated destruction of the RAF drawn into defensive combat; 2. The Wehrmacht wanted to paralyse the British government on the eve of *Seelöwe* (in addition to terrorizing the civilian populace); 3. The Führer retaliated for the RAF bombing raid on Berlin on 24–25 August. The Germans had to take a practical consideration into account as well: with their failure over the preceding two months, the numerical imbalance was more extreme than ever. To these I would add that Hitler had lost patience with earlier tactics that had not worked, so could think of no better option.

The earliest manifestation of Germany's new tactic occurred on

7 September, with the first massive raid on London (see Map 74). The move surprised Fighter Command, but it did not take Dowding long to discern Göring's change of plans and adjust. As the Germans intended, the bombing raids with their massive fighter escorts did bring up RAF fighters, and losses mounted on both sides. But within about a fortnight, Göring blinked; on the 20th, he changed tactics again, switching to nighttime attacks[33]. Four days later, he made yet another change, to attacking the British aero-industry. Because of surprise and other factors, each change of tactics usually brought a day or two of success before the RAF figured out the new threat and made its own adjustments.

The Luftwaffe made its last daylight attack on London on 30 September and, that night, it hit Liverpool, Birmingham and Coventry. Attacks on aircraft factories centred on Southampton and Bristol. During October, the Germans launched 9,911 sorties against the British Isles, over half of them on London. That month's attacks killed 6,334 Britons and injured a further 8,695. London remained the principal target through mid-November, with 200 bombers hitting Britain every night except one. In two months, the Luftwaffe had dropped 13,000 tons of high-explosive bombs plus nearly 1 million incendiaries. Its combat losses remained at an acceptable 1 per cent.

Halfway through November, the Germans switched to bombing provincial cities (the adjacent map does not show all the bombing raids). Between then and the end of February 1941, they hit 14 port cities, nine inland industrial centres and London. The Germans lost only 75 planes to combat. On the urging of Admiral Raeder, Hitler changed target priority again. Between mid-February and mid-May, the Luftwaffe concentrated on port cities again; 46 of there were bombed, compared to seven raids against inland cities. In reality, by October and November, the issue had been decided in Britain's favour.

Also shown on this map is Mussolini's contribution to the Blitz, the Italian Air Corps (Corpo Aereo Italiano). It consisted of 80 Fiat BR.20 medium bombers, 48 Fiat G.50 monoplane fighters and 50 Fiat CR.42 biplane fighters. The Italians made their first raid on the night of 24/25 October. For the next few weeks, they made about a dozen attacks against coastal cities, with minimal effects.

---

33 Göring had already tired of the daily grind and took leave, starting on the 14th.

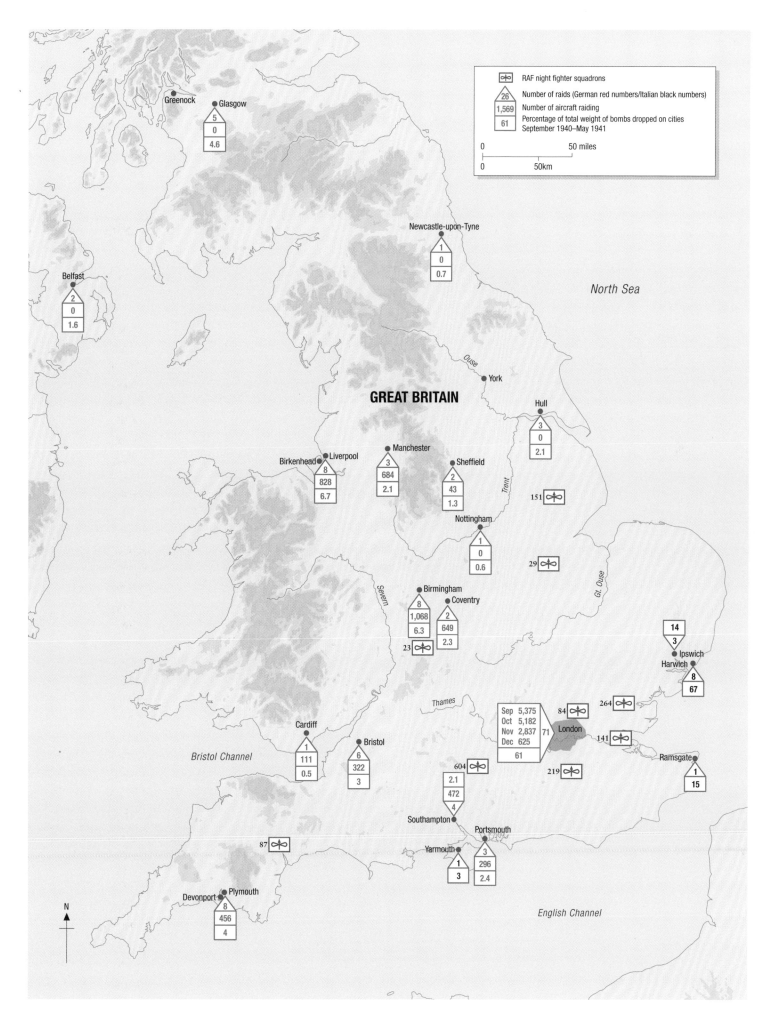

RAF night fighter squadrons

26 Number of raids (German red numbers/Italian black numbers)
1,569 Number of aircraft raiding
61 Percentage of total weight of bombs dropped on cities
September 1940–May 1941

0   50 miles
0   50km

North Sea

Greenock
Glasgow
5
0
4.6

Belfast
2
0
1.6

Newcastle-upon-Tyne
1
0
0.7

GREAT BRITAIN

York

Ouse

Hull
3
0
2.1

Manchester
Birkenhead Liverpool
8
828
6.7

3
684
2.1

Sheffield
2
43
1.3

Trent

151

Nottingham
1
0
0.6

29

Birmingham
8
1,068
6.3

Coventry
2
649
2.3

23

Gt. Ouse

14
3

Ipswich

Harwich
8
67

Severn

Thames

Sep 5,375
Oct 5,182
Nov 2,837
Dec 625
61

84

London

71

264

141

Cardiff
1
111
0.5

Bristol
6
322
3

604

2.1

219

Ramsgate
1
15

Bristol Channel

Southampton
472
4

Portsmouth

87

Yarmouth
1
3

3
296
2.4

Devonport Plymouth
8
456
4

English Channel

N

161

MAP 74: THE BLITZ OVER LONDON, 7 SEPTEMBER 1940–WINTER 1941

London was clearly the big prize in any bombing campaign against Great Britain. Long the most populous city on the globe, it was also capital of a worldwide empire, headquarters of the British military, a commercial and industrial powerhouse and the transportation hub of the nation. It lay tantalizingly close to north-west France. London loomed large from the beginning of Germany's new plan to switch from defeating Fighter Command and preparing south-east England for invasion, to terrorizing the British civilian population. The Luftwaffe warmed up with small nighttime raids against London on 4 and 5 September.

On 7 September, Chain Home operators saw nearly 1,000 German aircraft (343 bombers and 642 fighters, covering 800 square miles of airspace) heading for England, and assumed these intended on bombing RAF airfields as usual. However, the armada made straight for London, mainly bombing wharves and warehouses in its docklands, but also hitting residential areas. For more than 90 minutes, they dropped 300 tons of bombs, which killed about 1,000 Londoners. Göring watched from the French coast, claiming to be in personal command of the assault. In the midst of the Park and Leigh-Mallory spat, Fighter Command barely made an appearance until the Germans departed. Eventually, 21 RAF squadrons scrambled to intercept; Luftwaffe: RAF losses were in a ratio of 41:28. That night, 300 more bombers returned to the capital, dropped another 300 tons of high-explosives plus 13,000 incendiaries, which killed an additional 1,000 people. Approximately 260 anti-aircraft guns lit up the skies and two Blenheim night fighter squadrons rose to meet the threat, all to no effect. The severity of the assault convinced the British high command that *Seelöwe* was imminent.

Fires still burned out of control throughout London on the morning of 8 September. Once again, however, bad weather intervened to ground the Luftwaffe and break its momentum. That day, Göring resumed attacking airfields in Essex and Kent, although 200 bombers returned to London that night, with those attacks lasting nine hours. The raid witnessed another change in emphasis, as the target list expanded from just the docks to the rest of the city. As much as they could with their poor bomb-aiming technology, the Germans concentrated on train stations and railway lines. Unfortunately for the city, RAF defences again failed to significantly hinder the bombers. The Luftwaffe returned for 76 consecutive nights, failing to attack only on 2 November, when bad weather grounded its planes.

Dowding's fighters were ready for September 9. South of London, No. 11 Group disrupted two waves of 100 heavily escorted bombers each, forcing one to scatter its bombs over the city, suburbs and countryside, while the other diverted towards Coventry. To the north,

No. 12 Group did not contribute as it should have, exacerbating conflict at Fighter Command's top echelons. The fighters shot down 28 bombers at a cost of 19 of their own. Around 200 bombers bombed the city that night, killing about 400 and injuring 1,400 others. With lunar and tidal conditions considered ideal for an amphibious landing through the 10th, the entire country was still on edge. The state of British morale remained the great unknown factor – for both sides.

For the next two months, the bombing campaign continued. Buckingham Place and Downing Street took some hits, spreading the misery to all sectors of London society. The RAF expanded London's defences with more guns, searchlights and balloons; this drove the Germans higher and made bombing even more inaccurate, but otherwise accomplished little. Fighter Command continued to experience leadership challenges with No. 11 Group defending forward (i.e. around Canterbury) using small groups, typically pairs of squadrons, while No. 12 Group preferred many squadrons in 'big wings'. The Luftwaffe responded with new technology, like delayed-action bombs (some weighing a ton), which buried themselves into the ground and exploded later. They also experimented with either jamming the Chain Home radars or flying above their maximum effective altitude of 20,000ft. Even escorted by hundreds of Messerschmitts, attacks by corresponding numbers of hundreds of Hurricanes and Spitfires shot down bombers in unacceptable numbers. Forced more and more into the escort role, German fighters were falling, too. By mid-September, the Luftwaffe had largely discontinued daylight raids over London[34].

By the end of September, the Luftwaffe's attacks against London had become both costly and ineffective. Hitler 'temporarily' delayed *Seelöwe*, which would soon be cancelled altogether. Göring ordered the last big daytime raid against London during the final days of September. The Luftwaffe had launched 7,260 sorties that killed 6,954 and injured 10,615. It lost 433 aircraft to Fighter Command's 242. Around that time, RAF night-fighters with new interceptor radar arrived. The Germans flew higher and higher, at times reaching 30,000ft. The Blitz dragged on through the autumn and then, in greatly reduced form, into winter and finally spring. Like the Battle of Britain, it had failed to accomplish any of its assigned missions, while greatly weakening the Luftwaffe. Soon, the Blitz was revealed to be the poor relation of Bomber Command's attacks on Germany, which were ramping up at the same time.

---

34 Ever since, in Great Britain 15 September has been celebrated as Battle of Britain Day.

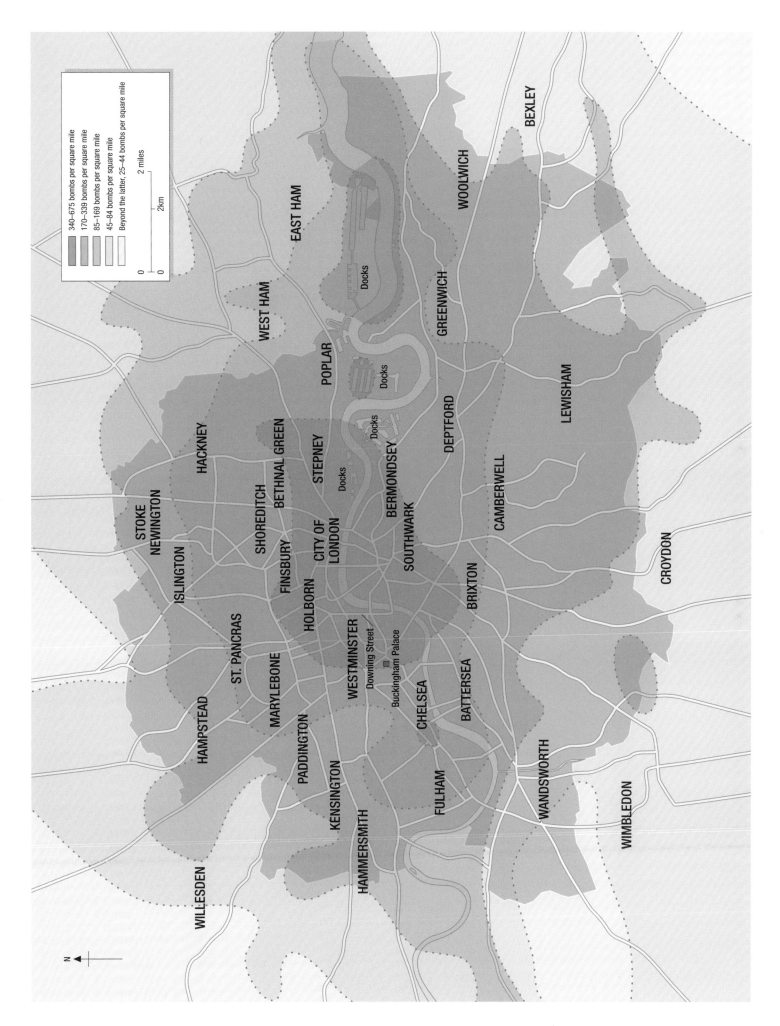

WILLESDEN

HAMPSTEAD

STOKE
NEWINGTON

ISLINGTON

ST. PANCRAS

MARYLEBONE

PADDINGTON

KENSINGTON

HAMMERSMITH

WEST HAM

EAST HAM

HACKNEY

SHOREDITCH

BETHNAL GREEN

FINSBURY

CITY OF
LONDON

HOLBORN

WESTMINSTER

Downing Street

Buckingham Palace

CHELSEA

FULHAM

BATTERSEA

POPLAR

Docks

Docks

STEPNEY

Docks

Docks

SOUTHWARK

BERMONDSEY

GREENWICH

DEPTFORD

CAMBERWELL

BRIXTON

WANDSWORTH

WIMBLEDON

WOOLWICH

BEXLEY

LEWISHAM

CROYDON

340–675 bombs per square mile
170–339 bombs per square mile
85–169 bombs per square mile
45–84 bombs per square mile
Beyond the latter, 25–44 bombs per square mile

0   2km
0   2 miles

N

163

MAPS 75 AND 76: THE DEFENCE OF GREAT BRITAIN, 1940

It is probably not much of an exaggeration to say that Hitler saved Great Britain a good deal of trouble by allowing the BEF to escape from Dunkirk. Those 300,000 trained veteran British and Allied troops in all likelihood spared the Churchill government and made the Germans think twice about invading the British Isles. Without resorting to fiction, the historical summer of 1940 had enough dangers; the Germans made legitimate plans for *Seelöwe,* at more than one point the Battle of Britain could have gone Hitler's way, and through mid-September the British believed that their islands could be invaded any time.

Map 75: The Royal Navy: Britain's traditional first line of defence

Despite its worldwide commitments, in 1940 the Royal Navy would team up with the RAF to ensure any Nazi invasion never reached British soil. In close proximity to the English Channel, light cruisers and destroyers, the latter in many cases stripped from convoy escort duty and at times numbering 36 vessels, stood by for immediate action. Submarines and motor torpedo boats, in conjunction with minefields and shore guns, augmented these light surface units. Further north, the battleships and heavy cruisers of the Home Fleet prepared to sail southwards and fight in the narrow confines of the Channel if absolutely necessary. Above flew the Fleet Air Arm and Coastal Command, the latter being RAF planes under Royal Navy operational control.

The waters around the British Isles had long been divided into Naval Command areas. Coastal Command Group boundaries generally corresponded to the naval sectors. Throughout the late summer of 1940, both organizations kept up constant coverage of air and sea patrols. These were augmented by Ultra intercepts of Enigma traffic, intelligence from reconnaissance flights over ports in German-occupied Europe, as well as reports from spies and resistance movements springing up all over the Continent. As September approached, and, with it, the increased assumption of a German invasion, heavy units transferred from Scapa Flow to Rosyth and Portsmouth. We have to conclude that the Germans would have had a very difficult time crossing the Channel against the Royal Navy.

Map 76: The British Army's deployment in anticipation of Seelöwe

The sparse British Army deployments in south-east England around the time of Dunkirk are shown on Map 70. One of the little-known logistical feats associated with *Dynamo* is the distribution of the 300,000 rescued soldiers from the Dover ports to various assembly areas around Britain. Weeks later, a further 215,000 were evacuated from southern France as part of Operation *Ariel.* Thereafter, the government and War Office, through GHQ Home Forces, integrated these men saved from the Continent into the units shown adjacent. The army also grew in size thanks to a flood of new recruits in 1940: 310,000 men had gone into uniform between January and March, 425,000 followed from April to June, and 460,000 joined from July to September. By July 1, the services had absorbed more than half of British males aged between 20 and 25, and more than one-fifth of the entire male population between 16 and 4035. The dominions also contributed numerous divisions. By mid-summer, 1.5 million part-time enthusiasts of the Local Defence Volunteers (created on 14 May, soon renamed the Home Guard, and often armed mainly with improvised weapons, e.g. Molotov cocktails) supported the troops, watched the coastline, manned roadblocks and rounded-up downed Luftwaffe aircrew, among other duties.

General Claude Auchinleck, head of Southern Command facing the Channel, planned to meet any Germans on the beaches and destroy them there. Having left most of the army's artillery, tanks and heavy equipment on the Continent, conducting a mobile defence would be hard, but the British would try this against any breakthroughs the Germans might achieve. That summer, the British had approximately 250 tanks, probably more than the Germans could have ever shipped across the Channel. By that point, the nation's ordnance factories were working at top speed, to the point where they would outpace their German competition within a year. Since the British Army had been largely de-motorized at Dunkirk, it concentrated on a static defence, including various 'stop lines' and coastal fortifications. By August, the situation had improved, with trained men, new equipment and ammunition purchased from the USA. British tactics thereafter centred on holding towns and other built-up areas with all-round defences.

35 Agnus Calder, *The People's War,* Ace Books: New York, 1972, p. 138.

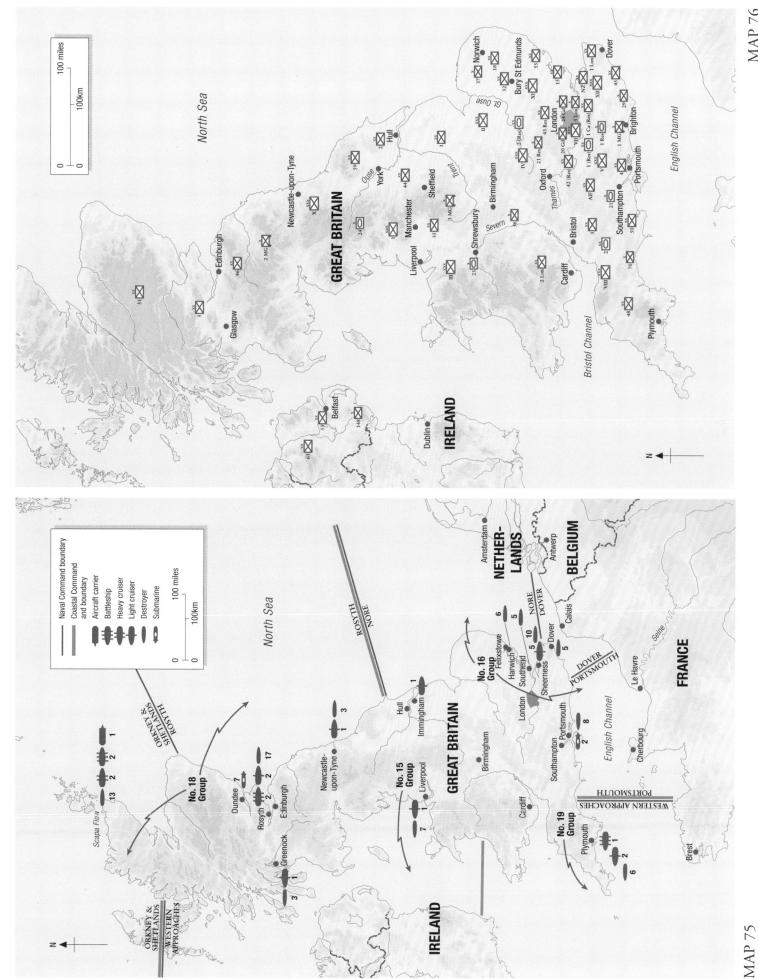

MAP 76

North Sea

GREAT BRITAIN

Norwich

Bury St Edmunds

Dover

Newcastle-upon-Tyne

Edinburgh

Glasgow

Hull

York

Sheffield

Manchester

Birmingham

Liverpool

Shrewsbury

Oxford

London

Brighton

Bristol

Cardiff

Southampton

Portsmouth

Plymouth

Belfast

Dublin

IRELAND

English Channel

Bristol Channel

Ouse

Gt. Ouse

Trent

Thames

Severn

100 miles

100km

0

N

North Sea

NETHER-LANDS

Amsterdam

Antwerp

BELGIUM

Calais

FRANCE

Le Havre

Cherbourg

Brest

ROSYTH

NORE

ORKNEY & SHETLANDS

ROSYTH

ORKNEY & SHETLANDS

WESTERN APPROACHES

WESTERN APPROACHES

PORTSMOUTH

PORTSMOUTH

NORE

DOVER

DOVER

PORTSMOUTH

Scapa Flow

No. 18 Group

Dundee

Rosyth

Edinburgh

Greenock

Newcastle-upon-Tyne

Hull

Immingham

No. 15 Group

Liverpool

No. 16 Group

Felixstowe

Harwich

Southend

Sheerness

Dover

London

Southampton

Portsmouth

Birmingham

Cardiff

No. 19 Group

Plymouth

Saine

Naval Command boundary

Coastal Command and boundary

Aircraft carrier

Battleship

Heavy cruiser

Light cruiser

Destroyer

Submarine

100 miles

100km

0

0

N

MAP 75

165

MAP 77: THE GERMAN PLANS FOR OPERATION *SEELÖWE*

Three-quarters of a century after the fact, we know that a successful German invasion of Great Britain has been relegated to counterfactual historical fiction. No segment of the Wehrmacht was prepared: The Heer had given no thought to large-scale amphibious operations, the Kriegsmarine was woefully inadequate and the Luftwaffe had failed in its grandiose *Adlerangriff.* Any form of *Seelöwe* launched in the summer of 1940 would have been doomed to failure. Nevertheless, Germany did make extensive preparations for the assault.

Nine months before the supposed attack date, in November 1939, Kriegsmarine commander Raeder instructed his naval staff to make a preliminary study. A month later, the Heer and Luftwaffe began to give some thought to the matter. By January 1940, all three services were logjammed on the idea, each blaming the other for poor planning and wrong preparations. By late May, with the Heer and Luftwaffe having their way in north-west Europe, the naval staff had little to do but wanted to claim some contribution, so developed new studies and plans. By early July, Wehrmacht planning accelerated and Hitler also started thinking about an invasion; he issued a Führer Directive on *Seelöwe* on 16 July. Three days later, he made his 'last appeal to reason' speech, which Britain rejected out of hand. Vacuous words had accomplished nothing, so reluctantly, he would have to resort to action.

German staff work immediately began to demonstrate critical failures that would bedevil Wehrmacht operations through operations *Barbarossa, Blau* and beyond. The three services were not prone to cooperating and would rather point fingers, while the OKW was not the organ to engender unity of action. In the case of *Seelöwe*, the Heer's 'wide front' wishes conflicted with the Kriegsmarine's 'narrow front' capabilities. Operations staff dominated the process to the neglect of all other considerations: Personnel, intelligence and logistics sections simply had to make the invasion work, because Hitler and senior commanders wanted it to work. They had little accurate intelligence on any aspect of British land, sea, or air defences or preparations. They sanguinely assumed they could get an invasion forces across the Channel in sufficient numbers and with enough weaponry, ammunition and equipment to succeed. They had no proper amphibious landing craft, so river barges of the type found on the Rhine would be towed across by tugs[36]. When they could not surmount problems, such as British

naval and aerial superiority, these were simply wished away. Raeder, commanding one heavy (*Admiral Hipper*) and two light cruisers, half a dozen destroyers and several U-boats, first saw the impossibility of *Seelöwe.* The Wehrmacht blithely went ahead with its plans, despite the very real prospect of tens of thousands of German soldiers drowning at sea as the Royal Navy slaughtered the barges.

Rundstedt, now a field marshal, commanded the *Schwerpunkt.* Six divisions of his 16. Armee would embark from ports between Rotterdam and Calais, and land at Hythe, Rye, Hastings and Eastbourne. Four divisions from the 9. Armee from ports between Boulogne and Le Havre would come ashore between Brighton and Worthing. The 7. Flieger-Division would parachute in to help secure the right shoulder of the XIII Armee-Korps. Bock would possibly enter the action a week later with three divisions belonging to the reserve 6. Armee on the Cherbourg Peninsula, putting ashore in Lyme Bay. Dover would be taken from the landward side, giving the attackers a major port.

The OKW believed it could somehow safely land 90,000 men from 11 divisions in the first wave, and a further 170,000 over the next three days. Divisional headquarters and two regiments usually made up the first wave, with the third regiment coming in second. After these initial landings, six panzer and three motorized infantry divisions would miraculously get to England. In all, the Germans believed they could get 39 divisions across the Channel in a couple of weeks. They planned to have taken London and won the war within one month[37].

After the war, in the face of German liabilities and British strengths, Rundstedt and other senior generals voiced their scepticism about *Seelöwe* to Nürnberg interrogators. Many considered the talk of invasion merely Hitler's bluff. Put simply, the Third Reich in 1940 had none of the Allies' 1944 strategic dominance, maritime advantages, or air superiority. Throughout August, the Wehrmacht went through the motions and applied some solutions to the invasion's problems, but Hitler did not really care. The strongest indication of this was his decision on 31 July to attack the USSR and therefore defeat Great Britain indirectly.

---

36 Meanwhile, as invasion barges were assembled in Dutch, Belgian and French ports (and were damaged and sunk in large numbers by RAF raids), river traffic was severely curtailed, hurting German industry greatly.

37 For comparison, in their massive, well-planned, well-resourced and successful D-Day invasion, the number of Allied divisions landing in Normandy were as follows: First three days, 14; first week, 19; first two weeks, 21; and by the end of June 1944, 28.

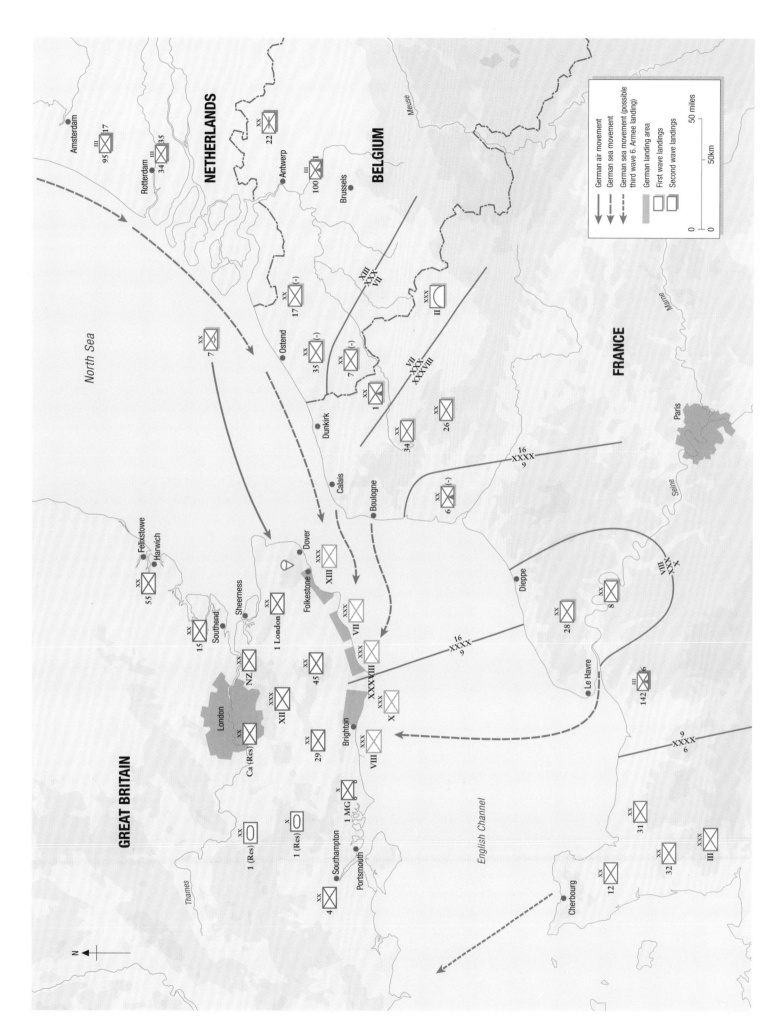

NETHERLANDS

Amsterdam

III 17
95

Rotterdam III 35
34

XX 22
Antwerp

III 1
100
Brussels

BELGIUM

North Sea

XIII
XXX
VII

XX 17
(-)
Ostend

XXX II

VII
XXXVIII
XX 35
(-)

XX 7
(-)

FRANCE

Meuse

Marne

Dunkirk

XX 1

XX 34

XX 26

Calais

Boulogne

XXXX 16
9

XX 6
(-)

Seine

Paris

Felixstowe
Harwich

XX 55

Dover

XXX XIII

XX 15

Sheerness
Southend

XX 1 London

Folkestone

XXX VII

XXX
XXXVIII

XX 45

Dieppe

Le Havre

VIII
XXX X

XX 28

III 142 6

GREAT BRITAIN

London

XX Ca (Res)

XXX XII

XX NZ

XX 29

Brighton

XXX X

XXX
VIII

XXXX 16
9

Thames

XX 1 (Res)

X 1 (Res)

X 1 MG

Southampton

Portsmouth

XX 4

English Channel

XXXX 9
6

XX 31

XX 12

XXX III

Cherbourg

XX 32

N

GREAT BRITAIN

Legend:
- German air movement
- German sea movement
- German sea movement (possible third wave 6. Armee landing)
- German landing area
- First wave landings
- Second wave landings

50 miles
50km

167

MAP 78: THE RAF BOMBING OF GERMANY (I), 1939–40

The British had long considered bombing Germany a viable tactic in a future war. Until the late 1930s, however, it did not have the necessary doctrine or equipment. Untested but expensive bomber forces became an easy target in interwar political skirmishes. Starting in 1937, a new generation of twin-engine bombers appeared: The Handley Page Hampden, then the Vickers Wellington the following year. With these models, the new Bomber Command solved the problems of sufficient range and meaningful bomb load, although not those of exact navigation, accurate bomb aiming, protection against enemy fighters, or crew comfort. When the war began, it had a first-line strength of 500 bombers, perhaps 300 of them medium types. When Canadian Lord Beaverbrook took over aircraft production, this situation began to improve markedly.

With war declared in 1939, the RAF (and the French Armée de l'Air) began a limited air campaign against Germany. At that point, the Luftwaffe still held a significant psychological propaganda advantage, so the Allies were loath to use their actual superiority. Through May 1940, the British cabinet permitted the bombing of Germany, but only against purely military and naval targets. The results were meagre: Of 29 bombers sent on 4 September 1939 to bomb Kriegsmarine bases at Wilhelmshaven and Brunsbüttel, ten returned to base without dropping their bombs, three almost bombed Royal Navy vessels instead, and one bombed neutral Denmark (110 miles off course), while Luftwaffe fighters shot down seven. During a raid on the same target on 18 December, Messerschmitts downed 12 of 22 Wellingtons. Overall losses during daylight raids stood at 20 per cent, while photo-reconnaissance of bombed locales showed little or no damage inflicted. The RAF had to completely rethink its plans and 'the bomber will always get through' mentality. In the meantime, it settled on dropping leaflets over German cities.

The situation drastically changed with Germany's campaign in the West in the spring of 1940. Four days after Hitler's invasion began, more than 90 RAF bombers hit oil, rail and industrial targets along the Rhine. As before, damage was limited. During that spring, the priority of the RAF, and even Bomber Command, was staving off defeat in France, assisting at Dunkirk and breaking up the *Seelöwe* invasion fleet. In the summer, the RAF retaliated for the Luftwaffe's Battle of Britain attacks, while concentrating on the German oil industry (in accordance with a 4 July directive). These culminated on the night of 25/26 August, when 95 bombers hit Berlin (at the bombers' extreme range). The intended targets were military and industrial, but inaccuracy caused many bombs to fall on civilian residential areas. This raid prompted Hitler to switch to bombing London a week later. At this point, both nations took the gloves off with their bomber forces, and now any target was fair game.

Bombing German cities accelerated that autumn, with the RAF switching more and more to night operations to preserve its strength (losses averaged closer to 3 per cent). Berlin, northern port cities and industrial sites along the Rhine and in the Ruhr came under steady assault. Bomber Command even hit Munich on 8 November, during Hitler's annual celebration of his 1923 Putsch. One particularly large raid came on 19 December, part of the larger Operation *Abigail* and the evolving 'area bombing' campaign directed by Churchill's cabinet: 134 Wellingtons attacked Mannheim, 103 of which actually reached their target (76 per cent, with ten losses). However, constantly changing British priorities reduced Bomber Command's effectiveness, as did even greater inaccuracy experienced in the dark. As noted earlier, constantly changing priorities plagued both sides during the entire war.

Bomber Command's operational rates meant that 20–30 aircraft carried out a normal raid. Problems with bad weather, poor navigation and landing accidents caused the RAF most problems, and gave the Germans most cause for relief. The Germans had only lately awakened to modern air-defence requirements, including passive civil defence measures. While individually the German Freya radars were superior to British Chain Home models, through 1940 they were not networked like the Dowding System to command and control, fighters and Flak, and so lacked the same synergistic effect.

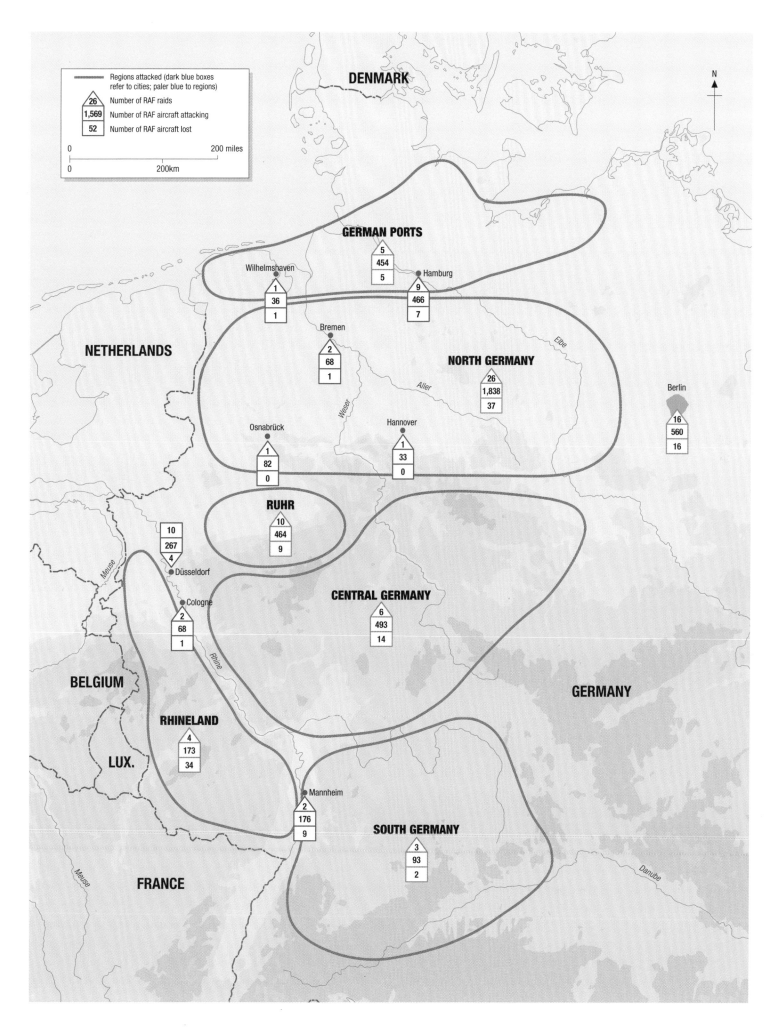

DENMARK

N

Regions attacked (dark blue boxes
refer to cities; paler blue to regions)

26 Number of RAF raids

1,569 Number of RAF aircraft attacking

52 Number of RAF aircraft lost

0 — 200 miles
0 — 200km

GERMAN PORTS

5
454
5

Wilhelmshaven

1
36
1

9
466
7

Hamburg

NETHERLANDS

Bremen
2
68
1

Elbe

Aller

Weser

NORTH GERMANY

26
1,838
37

Berlin

16
560
16

Osnabrück
1
82
0

Hannover
1
33
0

RUHR

10
464
9

10
267
4

Düsseldorf

Meuse

Cologne
2
68
1

Rhine

CENTRAL GERMANY

6
493
14

BELGIUM

GERMANY

RHINELAND

4
173
34

LUX.

Mannheim
2
176
9

SOUTH GERMANY

3
93
2

Meuse

Danube

FRANCE

MAP 79: THE RAF BOMBING OF GERMANY, 1941 (II)

The bombing raids of late 1940 achieved little, but cost much – a fact that Bomber Command concealed from higher authorities. At the same time, German industry was almost immune to the type of destruction the RAF wanted; facilities were dispersed (now throughout France and the Low Countries as well), while trade with Sweden and the USSR was booming and largely negating the Royal Navy's blockade. Post-bombing photo-reconnaissance continued to betray Bomber Command claims, with German plants usually continuing to operate at full capacity. Finally, new men in top positions in the RAF, plus an extensive white paper on bombing effectiveness, demanded a solution to the problem of night operations. Pre-war and early-war predictions of 'precision' daylight bombing of industry, infrastructure and military targets were clearly open to challenge; for night missions, they were demolished. By early 1941, Britain's national leadership had to decide whether to give up the illusion of precision daylight bombing and settle for indiscriminate terror bombing of cities, in general too big to miss. The British railed against the Germans' bombing of cities and civilian targets while doing the exact same thing themselves.

Bomber Command was not quite ready to give up on bombing industry. With heavier Stirling, Halifax and Manchester bombers coming online, on 15 January 1941, the Air Staff directed it to concentrate on 17 German oil-producing facilities for the next four months. For a number of reasons, the 'Oil Plan' never got going, further diminishing the precision argument and making the bombing of cities a future certainty. One key reason for this was that in early 1941, the Third Reich was not short of oil, thanks to Romania and the Soviet Union. With the Oil Plan dying a slow death, on 9 July Air Staff directed a new tactic, the 'Transportation Plan'. It aimed at Germany's infrastructure (specifically six cities and seven chokepoints) under the assumption that such a move would impact the entire war effort, hurting worker morale as collateral damage.

A month later, a group of British scientists issued the Butt Report which further damned the entire bombing offensive. It revealed the abysmal state of nighttime navigation and bomb aiming. Exact results varied depending on the target, weather, German defences, etc., but only one-third of bombs dropped impacted within 5 miles of the intended target. Morale within Bomber Command hit rock bottom. Its main response was to request a force of 4,000 bombers. Not only was that number beyond Britain's capacity, but, as Churchill pointed out, the problem was not numbers, but accuracy.

With Hitler's invasion of the Soviet Union, in the summer of 1941, Bomber Command believed it could go back to daylight bombing with 'Circus' raids, now with fighter escorts. Its twin assumptions were, firstly, that most German fighters were now concentrated in the East and that, secondly, in daytime it could regain a modicum of accuracy. Unfortunately for Bomber Command, it turned out that plenty of Luftwaffe fighters remained in the West. Additionally, Spitfires, even operating at maximum range, could barely reach the German border, a reverse of the Bf 109s' dilemma during the Battle of Britain. Additionally, new Fw 190 fighters just arriving easily mastered the Spitfire Mk. Vs. Furthermore, the Luftwaffe could pick and choose its battles and so could not be drawn into unfavourable combat. Finally, accuracy did not dramatically increase. New bombers did not always live up to expectations, either. For example, the Stirling flew too slow and too low. To make matters worse, Bomber Command still did not have the numbers of bombers it thought necessary to achieve its assigned missions. Quantity does not always trump quality.

Many attacks did make a large impact, however. A raid on Berlin during the night of 9/10 April hit the heart of the city, causing great damage along the Unter den Linden boulevard. The next night, an attack on the naval base at Brest, France, hit the battlecruiser *Gneisenau* with four bombs, meaning she and sistership *Scharnhorst* would be unavailable to sail with *Bismarck* the following month. In June, bombers caused significant damage to the Focke-Wulf factory in Bremen, temporarily closing the Fw 190 assembly line. However, these successes were the exception rather than the rule. A disastrous attack on Berlin over the night of 7/8 November (with 9 per cent losses) settled the debate in favour of future terror bombing of German cities.

Bomber Command had dropped 35,000 tons of bombs on Germany during 1941. However, by the end of the year, it had lost 7,448 aircrew to date (killed or made POWs) in the 27-month war. The good news, however, was the arrival of a new commander, Air Marshal Arthur Harris, whose name would be associated with the command for the remainder of the war: 'Bomber' Harris. On the other side of the front, the Luftwaffe developed its night-fighting capabilities. The Dowding System-like Kammhuber Line covered approaches over the North Sea; German industry created an aircraft-mounted night-fighting radar; Bf 110s found a new role in which to excel; and Luftwaffe generals were beginning to both understand the bombing danger to Germany and take steps to challenge the threat.

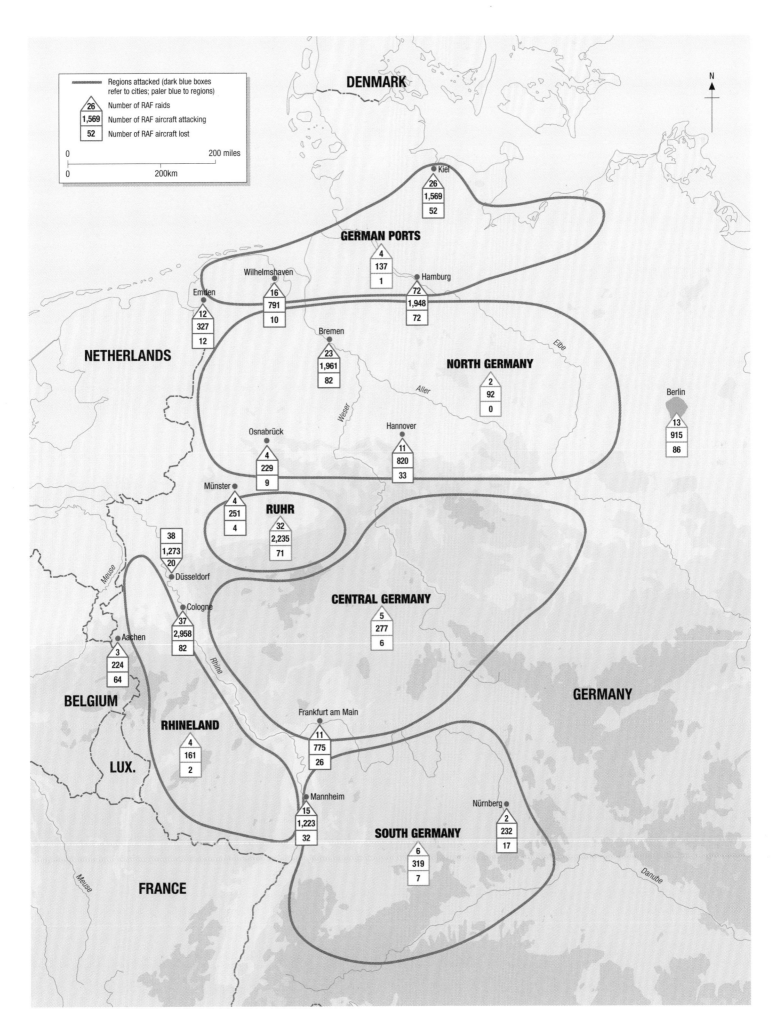

DENMARK

Regions attacked (dark blue boxes
refer to cities; paler blue to regions)

26 Number of RAF raids

1,569 Number of RAF aircraft attacking

52 Number of RAF aircraft lost

0 — 200 miles
0 — 200km

N

Kiel
26
1,569
52

GERMAN PORTS
4
137
1

Hamburg
72
1,948
72

Wilhelmshaven
16
791
10

Emden
12
327
12

NETHERLANDS

Bremen
23
1,961
82

NORTH GERMANY
2
92
0

Berlin
13
915
86

Elbe

Weser

Aller

Osnabrück
4
229
9

Hannover
11
820
33

Münster
4
251
4

RUHR
32
2,235
71

38
1,273
20

Düsseldorf

CENTRAL GERMANY
5
277
6

Cologne
37
2,958
82

Aachen
3
224
64

BELGIUM

Rhine

GERMANY

RHINELAND
4
161
2

LUX.

Frankfurt am Main
11
775
26

Mannheim
15
1,223
32

Nürnberg
2
232
17

SOUTH GERMANY
6
319
7

Meuse

FRANCE

Danube

171

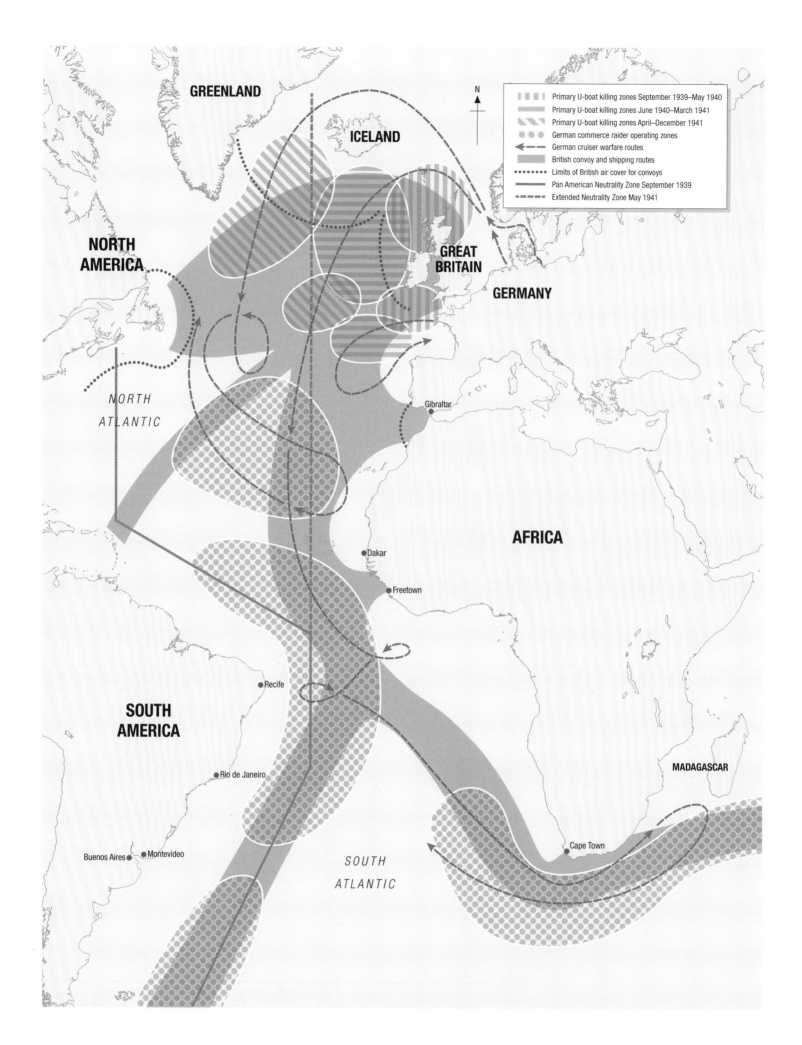

GREENLAND

ICELAND

NORTH
AMERICA

GREAT
BRITAIN

GERMANY

Gibraltar

NORTH
ATLANTIC

AFRICA

Dakar

Freetown

SOUTH
AMERICA

Recife

MADAGASCAR

Rio de Janeiro

Cape Town

Buenos Aires   Montevideo

SOUTH
ATLANTIC

▢▢▢	Primary U-boat killing zones September 1939–May 1940
▤▤▤	Primary U-boat killing zones June 1940–March 1941
▨▨▨	Primary U-boat killing zones April–December 1941
●●●	German commerce raider operating zones
◀– – –	German cruiser warfare routes
▬▬▬	British convoy and shipping routes
•••••	Limits of British air cover for convoys
———	Pan American Neutrality Zone September 1939
–·–·–	Extended Neutrality Zone May 1941

CHAPTER 7:
THE NAVAL WAR

In World War II, naval operations existed on the periphery of the European Theatre. Due to the early exit of France, most of the naval war took place between Britain and Germany. These two combatants were very unevenly matched, the maritime equivalent of the German and Polish armies. Hitler had little appreciation for, or understanding of, the wider world beyond Europe and could not be bothered to learn about naval warfare. The Kriegsmarine had none of the advantages of the Heer (buoyed by the Prussian/German tradition of being a Continental power), or the Luftwaffe (a mid-century technological wonder led by the 'second man of the Reich'). Commander-in-Chief Admiral Erich Raeder would have to fight a poor man's war. When, in November 1937, Hitler told his service chiefs he would be going to war soon, the Kriegsmarine came out the big loser; the grandiose and unrealistic (for a relatively small, resource-poor country starting from zero because of Versailles Treaty limitations) 'Plan Z' would now probably never see the light of day. In the ultimate test of the Kriegsmarine in either world war – defeating or invading Britain – Hitler's version completely failed. Also, the Royal Navy was just too large and too good. Furthermore, the new navy's doctrine, which allegedly corrected the mistakes of World War I, actually represented little more than a tidied-up version of that from 1917. Even without 20/20 hindsight, it can be seen that without a large and balanced fleet, plus a worldwide network of bases or allies, German maritime strategy remained constrained. At the bottom of the Wehrmacht's priority list, in a come-as-you-are war, the Kriegsmarine would show up short.

Raeder did not have the large battlefleet Tirpitz had in 1914, so *guerre de course* (commerce raiding) represented his only real option. When the war began, he had only six all-ocean, all-weather warships: Three panzer ships, two battlecruisers and one heavy cruiser. Thereafter, other heavy units would trickle into the fleet at irregular intervals, but between sinkings and battle damage, wartime new construction never kept up. U-boats, Germany's main naval hope for both world wars, were available only in a fraction of the numbers required (only 17 were at sea on 3 September 1939, having secretly slipped into the Atlantic during the last week of August). For the first nine months of World War II, the French Navy alone was more than a match for the Kriegsmarine. Raeder believed that with an active and aggressive plan, his fleet – equipped with ships considered individually better than the enemy's – could make a positive contribution to Hitler's upcoming war. Unfortunately for them, however, the Germans had learned little about maritime and naval war between 1914 and 1939. In neither 20th-century global conflict did they have the wherewithal to prevail in a 'tonnage war' against the British Empire.

During World War II, both sides would recreate their blockades of 1914–18. The Royal Navy's job would be much more difficult in 1939, because of Hitler's deal with Stalin. However, in the last four months of 1939, it did intercept more than half a million tons of supplies destined for Germany. The Kriegsmarine's anti-commerce war had three main missions: Sink Allied merchantmen, disrupt shipping routes and overwhelm the Royal Navy's resources. Initially, the U-boats would have it easier, thanks to British forgetfulness concerning successful techniques learned in the Great War, mainly the proper use of ASDIC (similar to sonar) and depth charges. While the Royal Navy relearned the benefits of convoys and increased its inventory of destroyers and corvettes, it narrowed the air cover and escort gaps in the mid-Atlantic (initially escorts could only reach 600 miles west of Ireland). In World War II, it had the active support of the USA, which increasingly kept watch over the western Atlantic. The Germans once again fought their U-boats, individually at least, in a very clever and courageous manner. Thanks largely to long hours of darkness in the northern winter, over the first nine months of the war, most of their victims went down around the British Isles and in the North Sea.

The situation improved a little in May 1940, and then markedly in June, with the addition of Norwegian and French bases. U-boats could reach their preferred hunting grounds relatively quickly and safely. Thereafter, British shipping absolutely had to enter the Irish Sea from the north. The mass of U-boat sinkings migrated west to the central Atlantic and the area below Greenland and Iceland (the quickest and shortest route between North America and Great Britain). For the next nine months, U-boat operations remained mostly individual combats, although Konteradmiral Karl Dönitz began to experiment with wolf packs. However, during this critical period in Britain's struggle for survival, only once, in June 1940, did U-boat tonnage sunk exceed half a million tons. It turned out that Britain's ability to both absorb damage and launch new construction was greater than either side knew.

The spring of 1941 ushered in a new era of nighttime *Rudeltaktik* (wolf packs), where any number of U-boats worked together in a certain area. U-boat headquarters ashore tried to manage them over the radio, a serious liability once the British deciphered encoded Enigma traffic. During the second quarter of 1941, the number of deployed submarines finally passed 50, the quantity Raeder believed necessary to win the war from the very start, 18 months earlier. Around the time of *Barbarossa*, the USA extended its neutrality zone many degrees of longitude to the east, again helping the British. Sinkings by U-boats went up, but so did

U-boat losses. Signs of success were deceptive. Despite obvious pain caused to Great Britain, there were never enough U-boats – either in absolute numbers or simply on patrol – while submarines on hand had limited range, Luftwaffe aerial reconnaissance was episodic at best, and British countermeasures (especially radar) improved apace with German enhancements. This trend had become obvious to both sides by the last quarter of 1941, by which time it was too late for the Germans to make corrections. At that point, whatever balance between surface, submarine and air that the pre-war Kriegsmarine might have had vanished, leaving the job of blockading Britain exclusively to the submarine forces. In the end, the U-boat campaign never even slowed British industry, let alone starved the country into submission.

The Kriegsmarine's cruiser war grabbed major headlines. Hitler suspected he might be at war by late August 1939, so the navy dispatched two panzer ships ahead of time, and sprinkled supply ships and tankers across the Atlantic for the necessary rendezvous. These diesel-powered ships had the perfect range for this type of mission and, for the most part, lived up to their 'outrun what they couldn't outgun' motto. After running amok for three months, *Admiral Graf Spee* famously ran out of luck in December off the coast of Montevideo. Other warships – *Deutschland* (*Lützow*), *Scharnhorst*, *Gneisenau* and *Admiral Hipper* all went on raids of varying success, as eventually did *Bismarck* and *Prinz Eugen*. *Admiral Scheer* made it home after a very successful war cruise. All of these ships had to do double duty, also as traditional men-of-war in more conventional operations, and the first four named immediately above suffered damage during *Weserübung* or in RAF bombing raids while sitting in port at Brest. The loss of *Bismarck* in May 1941 marked the end of major surface units raiding Atlantic commerce; thereafter the vessels moved to Norway in order to interdict shipping headed for the USSR's Arctic Ocean ports.

The third leg of the Germans' anti-shipping campaign comprised commerce raiders or *Hilfskreuzers* (auxiliary cruisers). These were standard merchantmen converted into disguised killers with guns, torpedoes and even reconnaissance aircraft. They lurked around normal shipping lanes, constantly and surreptitiously repainting and reflagging themselves to avoid detection. They mainly used deception to approach unsuspecting ships doing business with Great Britain, and captured or sank them. They occasionally worked in tandem with warships and U-boats attacking commerce in the same seas. Between March 1940 (when the first one set sail) until the end of 1941, these raiders sank 891,980 tons of Allied shipping. This was a good return on a minimal investment, but again, not enough to make a significant impact on Great Britain.

MAP 81: BRITISH CONVOYS AND PROTECTIVE MEASURES, 1939–41

On 30 January 1939, the British Admiralty issued its war plan for the early stages of a possible future conflict. It correctly anticipated fighting both Germany and Italy, and adopted a defensive strategy with three principal parts: 1. Defend seaborne trade in home waters and the Atlantic from German attacks; 2. Defend trade in the Mediterranean Sea and Indian Ocean from the Italians. 3. Blockade both potential enemy nations. Heavy units of the Home Fleet were stationed at Scapa Flow, Rosyth and Portland. Lighter anti-submarine forces were based at Plymouth, Portsmouth, the Nore and Rosyth. According to knowledge at the time, this represented a strong enough ring around the British Isles.

The massive and powerful Royal Navy had not prepared well for the coming battle, however. It assumed that Germany would not again employ unrestricted submarine warfare as in 1917. This was in part due to the fact that in March 1936, Hitler signed the London Submarine Protocol, which forbade sinking merchantmen without warning and a number of other restrictions. Aside from this huge failure to correctly judge Hitler's nature, old-fashioned 'battleship admirals' fixated on the German surface fleet instead of the U-boats. Orders placed for five battleships, six carriers and 19 heavy cruisers from 1936 to 1939 reflected this emphasis. Only in 1939 did the Admiralty recognize the growing undersea threat and order 56 *Flower*-class corvettes.

During the first week of September, the British reintroduced a convoy system of sorts, since fast and slow ships often sailed alone. Royal Navy destroyers could escort such convoys as existed only 'so far'. Until July 1940, the Admiralty determined this distance for ships heading west as longitude 15° W. After U-boats started sailing out of the Bay of Biscay ports, the escort line shifted west to 17°, then to 19° (October 1940) and finally to 35° (April 1941) To take advantage of improvements in aviation since 1918 and to bring the war to the U-boats, the Royal Navy created two hunting groups, each consisting of one carrier and four destroyers. This plan ended in disaster on 17 September, when *U-29* sank HMS *Courageous* in the Bristol Channel. The Navy promptly disbanded the hunting groups and returned the other carrier, HMS *Ark Royal,* to the battle fleet.

Convoys represented the best protection for merchant shipping. In the early stages of the war, however, they only included British and dominion ships. A large percentage of Britain's maritime commerce came and went aboard non-combatant or neutral bottoms, and these ships often sailed individually. Escorts for convoys were in short supply

due the paucity of vessels mentioned above, the large number of convoys coming and going to widely separated ports, and all the other demands placed on the Navy. Additionally, many smaller vessels lacked the endurance (i.e., the operating radius) to venture far into the ocean. The fact that it took Mussolini nine months to join the Axis war effort made things simpler in the Mediterranean, where the French were keen to safely transport colonial troops from Africa to France. Old World War I-era destroyers were pressed into service and armed merchant cruisers often sailed with convoys, though the latter had limited utility against U-boats.

The fall of France complicated matters beyond simply removing French escorts from the equation and giving U-boats ideal bases on the Bay of Biscay (which even smaller 500-ton models could effectively use). Less than a week into the Western campaign, the Admiralty closed the Mediterranean to normal shipping. The trip around the Cape of Good Hope not only added thousands of miles to shipping routes, but it forced merchantmen into the South Atlantic, which would soon be full of prowling Germans.

The earlier fall of Denmark somewhat offset this problem. On 10 May 1940, in one of Churchill's first actions as prime minister, Britain occupied the Danish dependencies of Iceland and the Faroe Islands. It took nearly a year to turn these islands into proper air and naval bases, but when they became operational in the spring of 1941, they greatly increased British air coverage over the Atlantic. The completion of new bases in Canadian Nova Scotia and the establishment of its Newfoundland Escort Force, both around this time, also helped immensely. American President Franklin D. Roosevelt did what he could, given domestic political handicaps, principally anti-war isolationism. As soon as war broke out in Europe, he established the Pan-American Neutrality Zone and empowered the US Navy to defend the east coast of the western hemisphere. On 18 April 1941, he expanded the zone to 26° W, practically to Iceland, where it overlapped the new British escort limits. In September 1940, he initiated the Lend-Lease Programme, which gifted 50 old World War I destroyers to Great Britain, overhauled and modernized by the USA. He also demonstrated wide latitude in declaring which bodies of water were or were not 'combat zones', for example, allowing American ships to carry supplies all the way to British-held Egypt. On 7 July 1941, Roosevelt also sent US troops to Iceland to free up the British garrison for duty elsewhere.

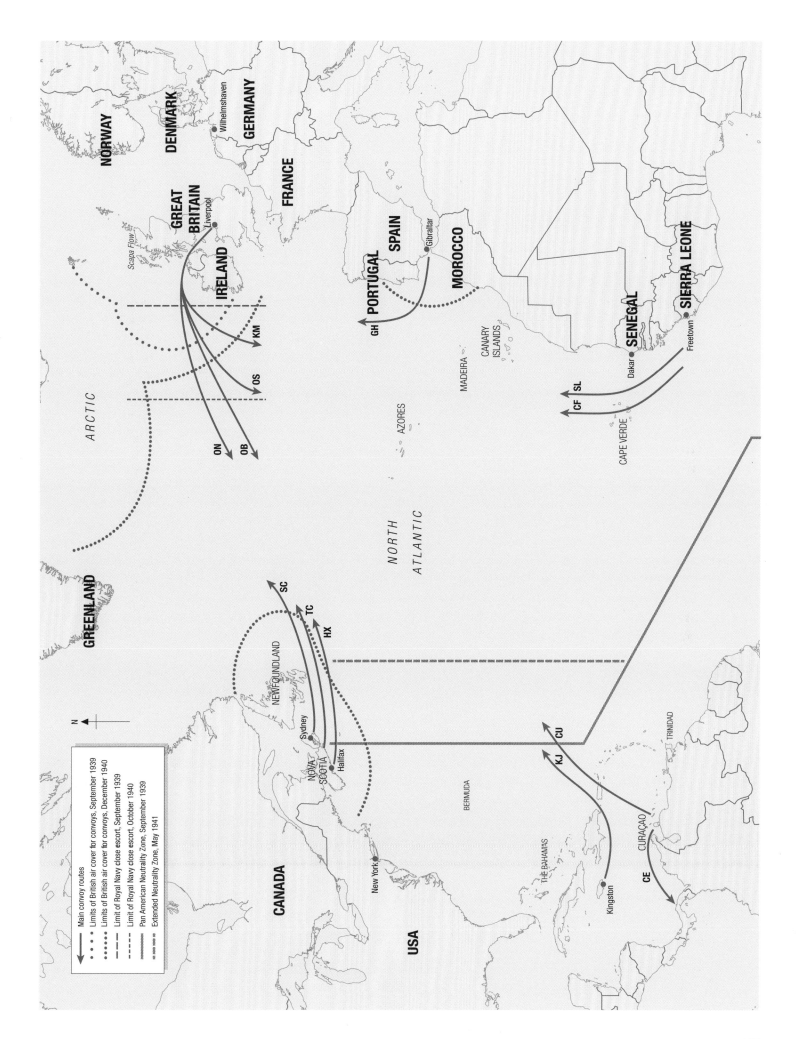

NORWAY

DENMARK

GERMANY
• Wilhelmshaven

Scapa Flow

GREAT BRITAIN
• Liverpool

IRELAND

FRANCE

PORTUGAL
SPAIN
• Gibraltar
MOROCCO

GH

CANARY ISLANDS

MADEIRA

AZORES

SENEGAL
• Dakar

SIERRA LEONE
• Freetown

SL
CF

CAPE VERDE

KM
OS
ON
OB

ARCTIC

NORTH ATLANTIC

GREENLAND

SC
TC
HX

NEWFOUNDLAND

Sydney •
NOVA SCOTIA
Halifax •

CANADA

New York •

THE BAHAMAS

BERMUDA

CURAÇAO

Kingston •
CE

KJ
CU

TRINIDAD

USA

N

Main convoy routes
Limits of British air cover for convoys, September 1939
Limits of British air cover for convoys, December 1940
Limit of Royal Navy close escort, September 1939
Limit of Royal Navy close escort, October 1940
Pan American Neutrality Zone, September 1939
Extended Neutrality Zone, May 1941

177

MAP 82: U-BOAT OPERATIONS (I), SEPTEMBER 1939–MARCH 1941

During the interwar years, German submarine designers kept current with technology in the Netherlands, which in turn designed boats for Finland and Turkey. The Kriegsmarine's new vessels *U-1* through to *U-26* were based on these models. By September 1935, its first U-boat flotilla was ready under Kapitän zur See Dönitz. Although not publicized, submarines took part in the 1936 remilitarization of the Rhineland, the 1938 Sudeten Crisis and the 1939 occupation of Memel. In their spring 1939 training cruise, U-boats sailed as far as Lisbon. Around this time, Dönitz experimented with wolf packs in naval wargames.

Approximately a dozen days before the invasion of Poland, 17 seagoing U-boats began to slip into their North Atlantic patrol areas[38]. This number represented 77 per cent of the larger medium- and long-endurance boats Dönitz had at the time, but only a third of the desired number. Smaller models took up positions in the North Sea or laid mines near ports on the east coast of Great Britain. When, on 3 September, Dönitz learned that Britain and France had declared war, he sent orders to his captains to commence 'war on merchant shipping'. Just hours later, *U-30* sank the liner SS *Athenia*. Reminiscent of early World War I, Hitler quickly issued his own restrictive 'no passenger liners' order. With a few exceptions, warships, merchantmen with surface or aerial escort and ships offering resistance were still fair game. It took only a couple of weeks for other restrictions to fall one by one: U-boats could now attack ships using radios and darkened ships near British or French ports, while Germany declared that the prize law no longer applied to the North Sea. By mid-November, Hitler had removed all restrictions, and now Dönitz, promoted to *Konteradmiral* (rear admiral), issued these instructions:

> Rescue no one and take no one with you. Have no care for ships' boats. Weather conditions and proximity to land are of no account. Care only for your own boat and strive to achieve the next success as soon as possible! We must be hard in this war. The enemy started this war to destroy us, nothing else matters[39].

By the end of 1939, Dönitz's submarines had sunk 114 ships, totalling 421,156 tons, at a cost of nine U-boats. Hitler, Raeder and Dönitz considered these numbers acceptable, especially when considering all the boats scheduled to join the fleet in the next 12–15 months. In addition to *Courageous*, *U-47* sank the battleship HMS *Royal Oak* inside Scapa Flow. What amounted to unrestricted submarine warfare took the Royal Navy by surprise. But after four months, Dönitz had many problems. Actual combat conditions far surpassed those of peacetime training, while seven of nine U-boat losses were to unknown causes. Shipyard repairs took too long. About 30 per cent of the new magnetic torpedo detonators were duds. The illogical realities of Hitler's 'Führer state' meant solutions could be far off.

The harsh winter of 1940, already mentioned in regard to the Winter War and *Weserübung*, hamstrung U-boat operations, too. In January and February, they managed to sink 85 ships, totalling 290,000 tons. The totals dropped drastically during the Norwegian campaign: From March to May, only 43 ships (140,000 tons) fell to the U-boats' torpedoes (by comparison, the Luftwaffe and mines sank 101 ships in May alone). At the same time, largely thanks to the defective torpedo problem, there was no corresponding peak in Royal Navy warships sunk; for example, U-boats attacked HMS *Warspite* on four occasions without causing any damage.

Dönitz ordered a nearly month-long break to carry out maintenance on his boats and shift them to the new bases in France. After seven to eight months, he seemed to have solved the torpedo detonator problem. That June, he experimented with two wolf packs with 13 submarines, but the rendezvous of hunter and prey failed to materialize. For the next five months, the U-boats enjoyed their *glückliche Zeit* (lucky, or happy times) when each patrol averaged eight victims. Subsequent wolf packs succeeded and 'Ace' U-boat captains were feted like their Luftwaffe peers. Convoy escorts seemed unable to protect their charges. But Dönitz's force was exhausted and had to return to base. As 1940 turned to 1941, *U-52* was his only boat at sea. The year ended successfully, with 2,186,180 tons sent to the bottom over the previous 12 months.

Meanwhile, the British technological edge added new arrows to their quiver, in particular airborne radar sets that could locate surfaced U-boats. Dönitz met this with increased construction and, by early 1941, new arrivals outnumbered the number of submarines sunk. The Royal Navy responded with more effective escorts, and soon half of all U-boat victims consisted of 'stragglers' that had fallen out of convoys and thus had no protection. In March, *U-47*, of *Royal Oak* fame, succumbed to depth charges launched by the World War I destroyer HMS *Wolverine*. That month marked the end of attacks by individual boats. Phase I of the U-boat was over.

---

38 These were 750-ton types VIIA and VIIB (with a radius of 6,500 miles and armed with 12 torpedoes) and the 1,100-ton type IXA (radius 8,100 miles, 22 torpedoes).

39 Peter Padfield, Dönitz: *The Last Führer*, Victor Gollancz: London, 1984, p. 206.

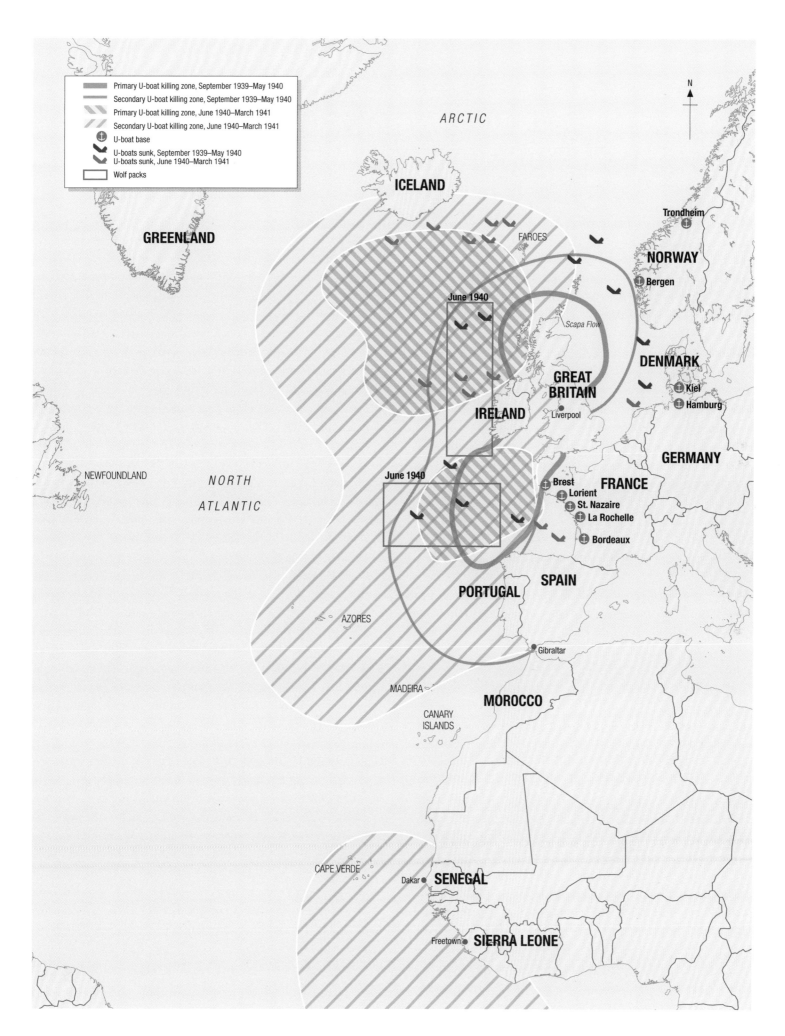

MAP 83: U-BOAT OPERATIONS (II), APRIL–DECEMBER 1941

In early 1941, the constant pendulum of war – action, reaction, counter-reaction – had swung against the U-boats. Growing British experience managing convoys, end-to-end surface escorts and radar-equipped aerial escorts (to name but a few Allied advances) had gained the upper hand. That March, the Royal Navy had defeated Germany's top three Ace submariners (Günther Prien, Otto Kretschmer and Joachim Schepke). Not only was the individual U-boat tactic more dangerous for the boats, but suitable targets in fixed hunting areas were becoming ever fewer. Dönitz and his men came up with a solution: Wolf pack surface attacks at night. Here, one submarine tracked the convoy during the day while the rest of the wolf pack trailed. Once night arrived, the U-boats surfaced. In the darkness their small conning towers were almost invisible, and their elevated position provided a better ability to search the horizon (compared to by periscope). Finally, surface speeds were much greater. The radio communications necessary to make the wolf pack work, both to and from Dönitz's headquarters and between boats of the group, remained the system's Achilles heel. British direction-finding and code-breaking exploited these transmissions. For the next 18 months or so, however, a rough balance existed between the two foes.

Dönitz pushed his men west and north. In mid-April, a wolf pack located convoy SC 26 and sank 14 ships in one night. That spring, according to British data, U-boats sank 142 ships, totalling 818,000 tons, with 58 ships (325,500 tons) sunk in May alone. Half of this last number fell to a six-boat group operating astride the poorly protected Freetown convoy routes. A major failure of the submarine force that May came during the sortie by *Bismarck*; the 'West Group' boats, only a couple of hundred miles from the battleship, failed to make contact, while *U-556* shadowed the Royal Navy's battlefleet, but earlier had run out of torpedoes.

June 1941 represented a mixed blessing for the U-boat war. Construction of new units boomed, with 15 boats per month coming off the ways. However, Operation *Barbarossa* was a step backwards so far as Dönitz was concerned. With so much of the Luftwaffe deployed east, even the normally problematic cooperation between submarines and reconnaissance/bomber aircraft declined. Initially, some U-boats deployed to the Baltic, but after two months, these withdrew because of the inactivity of the Soviet fleet. Perhaps worse, Hitler demanded a further dilution of effort towards Arctic waters to intercept ships heading for Archangel and Murmansk. Accordingly, Raeder ordered 10–12 boats north. Dönitz argued that he could not spare a single submarine from the Atlantic. Besides, where did higher headquarters think merchantmen destined for Soviet ports began? The answer was, in

the Atlantic. Hitler, always irrationally afraid of a British move against occupied Norway, did not relent. In mid-August, the first tentative Allied convoys departed Iceland for the USSR.

Therefore, that summer, with the number of operational boats greater than ever (63, with a further 93 in training), sinkings declined to 22 ships – only 94,200 tons. British code-breaking improved (on 8 May, they captured an intact Enigma machine when depth-charge attacks forced *U-110* to the surface, and escorts captured the submarine), while Roosevelt empowered the US Navy to aggressively escort convoys farther and farther east. Not wanting to provoke the Americans, Hitler authorized fighting back only in cases of self-defence[40].

Problems assaulted Dönitz from all sides. Maintenance still moved at a glacial pace: The average U-boat spent 35 per cent of its existence at sea and 65 per cent under repair (the admiral wanted the ready-rate closer to 50–50). Then, in August, Hitler offered to send Mussolini 29 boats to help in the Mediterranean, and Raeder agreed. The Führer ordered six more there in September and a further four in November and December. The U-boat damage to the carrier *Ark Royal* and sinking of the old battleship HMS *Barham* that autumn seemed to confirm the decision. Almost in vain, Dönitz fought for his Atlantic plan; he barely had more submarines in this critical theatre now than he did in 1939.

The U-boats had a good month in September, sending 53 ships totalling 202,000 tons to the bottom[41]. Near the coast of Greenland, a wolf pack attacked the heavily escorted convoy SC 42, destroying 16 ships (68,000 tons) out of 65. One Sierra Leone convoy lost nine vessels sunk and two more damaged. As part of that action, *U-107* set a record for tonnage sunk on a single patrol: 90,000 tons. With 80 boats now operational, U-boats sank 156,500 tons of shipping in October. A month later, that number slipped to 13 vessels totalling only 62,000 tons, the submariners' lowest total for the year. Encounters with the US Navy escalated in a potentially dangerous fashion, merely engaging destroyers USS *Greer* on 4 September, damaging USS *Kearney* on 16–17 October and sinking USS *Reuben James* on the 31st. When Hitler declared war on the United States on 11 December 1941, he removed all restrictions on attacking American ships.

40 Hitler's caution in September is hard to reconcile with his recklessness three months later, when he illogically, unnecessarily and counter-productively declared war on the USA. In a long list of terrible decisions – Dunkirk, *Barbarossa*, etc. – this is among his worst.

41 In any given period discussed here, on average U-boats accounted for between roughly 55 and 70 per cent of Allied losses. For example, losses in September to 'all causes' (i.e. including Luftwaffe, surface ships, mines, etc.) was 84 vessels totalling 285,000 tons.

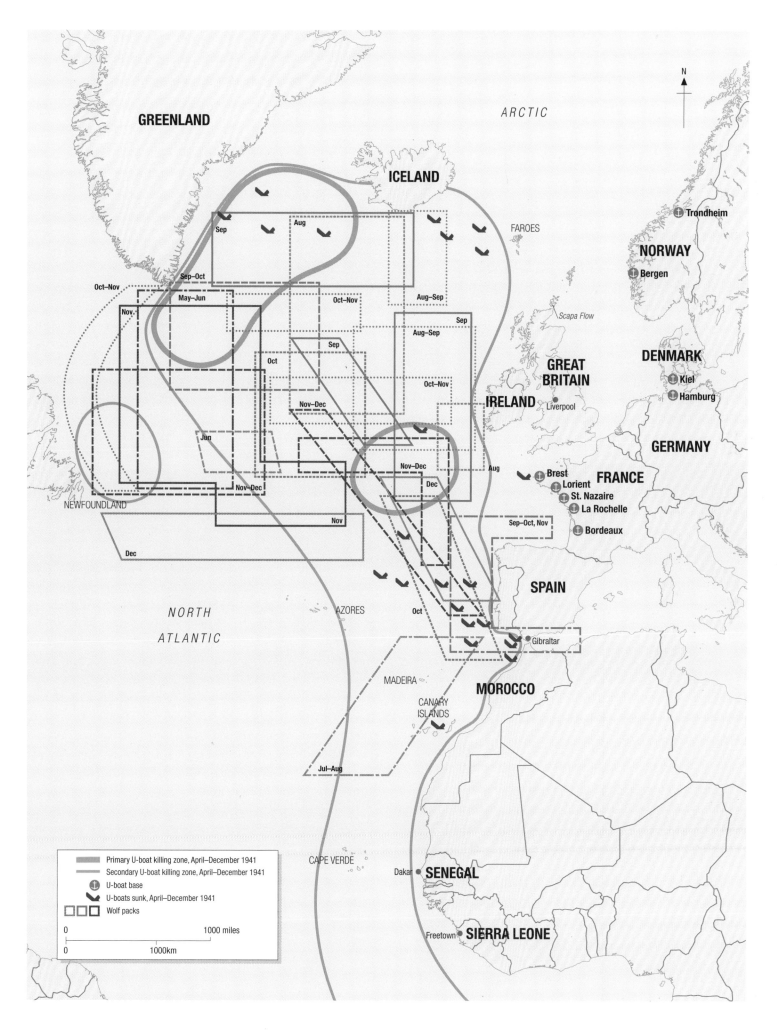

GREENLAND

ARCTIC

ICELAND

FAROES

NORWAY

Trondheim

Bergen

DENMARK

Scapa Flow

Kiel

Hamburg

GREAT
BRITAIN

IRELAND

Liverpool

GERMANY

Sep

Aug

Sep–Oct

Oct–Nov

May–Jun

Nov

Oct–Nov

Aug–Sep

Sep

Aug–Sep

Sep

Oct

Oct–Nov

Nov–Dec

Jun

Nov–Dec

Dec

Aug

Brest

Lorient

St. Nazaire

La Rochelle

FRANCE

NEWFOUNDLAND

Nov–Dec

Nov

Dec

Sep–Oct, Nov

Bordeaux

SPAIN

NORTH

AZORES

Oct

Gibraltar

ATLANTIC

MADEIRA

MOROCCO

CANARY
ISLANDS

Jul–Aug

Primary U-boat killing zone, April–December 1941
Secondary U-boat killing zone, April–December 1941
U-boat base
U-boats sunk, April–December 1941
Wolf packs

CAPE VERDE

Dakar ● SENEGAL

0   1000 miles
0   1000km

Freetown ● SIERRA LEONE

181

MAP 84: GERMAN CRUISER WARFARE (I)

Guerre de course is recognized as a poor man's naval war. While it cannot be considered decisive, it can certainly contribute to a navy's war effort. The Kaiser's fleet had tried this technique early in the Great War, until the Royal Navy cleared the seas of German ships in a series of well-known actions. During the 1920s, still restricted by Versailles, Germany could only build lighter ships, the type suitable for cruiser warfare. After Hitler became chancellor, he half-seriously delegated Kriegsmarine commander Raeder the freedom to build whatever navy he wanted. Raeder only had one sort of navy in mind and besides, the Third Reich did not have the resources to build a world-conquering navy, even if Hitler had allowed him to.

Hitler inherited much of his wartime navy: The panzer ships and light cruisers had already been built, while the battlecruisers and heavy cruisers were designed a year after he took office and were begun a year later. The diesel-powered panzer ships were perfect for their missions, but the light cruisers proved unsuited to year-round operations in the brutal Atlantic. The battlecruisers and heavy cruisers were beautiful, symmetrical vessels, although they would be plagued by problems with mechanical reliability. Small fuel bunkers equated to reduced endurance: For long cruises, they required supply ships and tankers staged around the ocean. German destroyers, while good ships, could not keep station with heavier units, especially in rough seas, meaning larger warships were usually unescorted. The largest guns of any of these vessels were 11in., although all also carried numerous torpedoes, according to the German preference begun by Tirpitz. Later, the massive *Bismarck* joined the fleet, armed with 15in. guns and enough fuel oil to sail the North Atlantic. In part due to losing political turf battles against the Luftwaffe, German ships lacked dedicated air cover, since the Kriegsmarine never operated an aircraft carrier.

Raeder issued his war plans in May 1939. He wanted a continuous series of commerce raids, which would simultaneously stretch the Royal Navy. The surface fleet, augmented by merchant raiders and the U-boat arm, would cut Britain's maritime lifeline. When World War II began, only the panzer ships *Admiral Graf Spee* and *Deutschland* were combat ready; *Admiral Scheer* was undergoing an overhaul, *Scharnhorst* and *Gneisenau* were experiencing teething troubles, *Admiral Hipper* was in training following its modernization, while *Blücher, Prinz Eugen* and *Bismarck* were still in various stages of construction. In accordance with orders published on 4 August, *Admiral Graf Spee* departed Wilhelmshaven on the 21st, followed by *Deutschland* three days later. Supply ships *Altmark* (leaving from Texas) and *Westerwald* were to join

them. All managed to slip into the North Atlantic unnoticed by the British. On the last day of peace, the Royal Navy learned that the two panzer ships were no longer in port; that same day, *Admiral Graf Spee* sailed past the Azores.

After breaking into the Atlantic, *Admiral Graf Spee* was to wait off the Cape Verde Islands for the war to begin, and further orders. After pausing two weeks in a 'waiting area' midway between Rio de Janeiro and Cape Town, she began to hunt. *Admiral Graf Spee's* operational area was the central and southern Atlantic and south-west Indian Ocean, and her targets were the 2,500 ships (21 million tons) flying the red ensign worldwide on any given day. Her first sinking on 30 September was also the first indication the British had of a raider at sea. The Admiralty assembled hunting groups all over the Atlantic and western Indian Ocean. Making good use of her spotting plane, *Admiral Graf Spee* captured two ships and sank two others before heading to the Indian Ocean. There, she sank one ship before returning to the South Atlantic, where she bagged three more.

Thanks to the *Admiral Graf Spee's* many ruses, and sightings in two oceans, by late October the Royal Navy was not sure which ship they were pursuing or where she was. Hunting groups crisscrossed the South Atlantic throughout November and early December, until the 6in. gun-armed cruisers HMS *Ajax* and *Achilles* plus the larger HMS *Exeter* found *Admiral Graf Spee* early on the 13th. In a running gun battle, *Admiral Graf Spee* punished *Exeter* and, to a lesser degree *Ajax*, but *Achilles* poured shells into the panzer ship. After receiving 25–30 hits, *Admiral Graf Spee* limped into Montevideo just before midnight. With many British and French ships approaching the South American coast and, after much diplomatic wrangling between Britain, Germany and Uruguay, on 17 December, *Admiral Graf Spee* was scuttled in the River Plate estuary.

The cruise of *Deutschland* was much less exciting. She sank two ships and captured one before returning to Gotenhafen on 17 November. Between 21 and 27 November, *Scharnhorst* and *Gneisenau* made a brief sortie into the North Sea and sank the merchant cruiser HMS *Rawalpindi*, before returning to Wilhelmshaven.

Admiral Scheer conducted probably the Kriegsmarine's most epic raiding cruise, from 23 October 1940 until 1 April 1941. She roughly followed the combat track of *Admiral Graf Spee*, including an Indian Ocean detour. *Admiral Scheer* logged 46,000 miles, sank the merchant cruiser HMS *Jervis Bay* and 17 merchantmen, and captured four prizes, all totalling between 150,000 and 160,000 tons, before safely returning home.

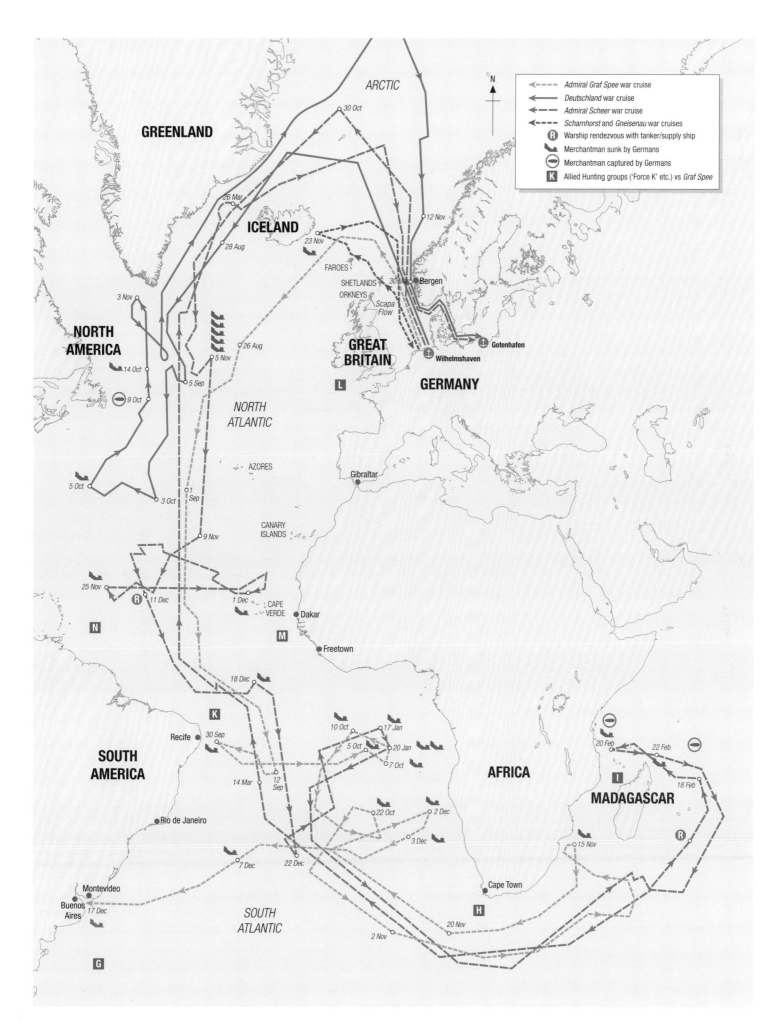

MAP 85: GERMAN CRUISER WARFARE (II)

The 1939 war cruises of *Admiral Graf Spee* and *Deutschland* cast a shadow on the Germans' cruiser warfare philosophy. In five months combined at sea, they only managed to sink 11 ships (57,000 tons), despite achieving complete surprise when Allied navies were most disorganized. Worse from a tactical standpoint, in a battle lasting only a few hours, *Admiral Graf Spee* had been bested by three inferior ships. Strategically, the fact that Germany had no bases for essential repairs demonstrated the fallacy of fighting a global maritime war from its little corner of Europe. The November raid by *Scharnhorst* and *Gneisenau,* which was intended to draw the Royal Navy away from *Admiral Graf Spee,* had to be curtailed when they attracted too much British attention. The Kriegsmarine had misjudged the nature of the upcoming war and the strength of the Royal Navy: Their principal enemy *could* handle multiple threats at the same time.

The Kriegsmarine would have to fight the war with the fleet it had. Ship captains were admonished to be more aggressive and not let a feeble opponent like *Rawalpindi* hold back two battlecruisers. German propulsion systems remained a worry. Combined operations by surface units and U-boats never came together, often because of too few submarines. The Kriegsmarine could not cooperate well with the Luftwaffe; neither could its two main branches cooperate with each other. In early March 1940, as the two battlecruisers prepared to sail,[42] Hitler ordered Operation *Weserübung.* Since the Kriegsmarine did not have the strength for both regular combat operations and cruiser warfare, the latter would have to wait first for the Scandinavian and Western campaigns, and then for preparations for *Seelöwe.*

ADMIRAL HIPPER: OPERATION *NORDSEETOUR*
Leaving Germany on 27 November, *Admiral Hipper* braved terrible winter weather in the Denmark Strait. Besides trading shots with the escorts of troop convoy WS 5A on Christmas Day, she sank two ships before putting into Brest on 27 December. A year after the panzer ship fiasco, it turned out that German heavy cruisers had many problems as well. Their short endurance meant that fuel worries preoccupied the captain as much as enemy ships. While tied up in France, *Admiral*

Hipper added some Flak guns and, more importantly, a B-Dienst radio intercept team.

Admiral Hipper slipped out of Brest on 1 February 1941 after a month of repairs, but then spent the 5th to the 7th refuelling at sea. Late on the 11th, she sank a straggler from convoy HG 53, and then hours later, came upon 19 ships of the unescorted convoy SLS 64. *Admiral Hipper* opened fire with her guns and torpedoes and the convoy scattered. Consuming two-thirds of her 8in. ammunition and 12 of her 14 torpedoes, she sank seven ships, totalling 33,000 tons. Two days later, she returned to Brest with only 59 tons of fuel oil remaining. *Admiral Hipper* required major repairs that could not take place in France, and besides, Brest was too dangerous: on 24 February, 15 RAF bombs landed within 220 yards of her. She left for Germany on 15 March, arriving on the 28th.

SCHARNHORST AND *GNEISENAU*: OPERATION *BERLIN*
Under Admiral Günther Lütjens, both ships departed Kiel on 22 January 1941, and reached the Atlantic on 3 February. Nineteen days later, they came across an empty convoy and bagged four ships. The duo spent early March avoiding British battleship-escorted convoys, but did guide two U-boats against SL 67, sending 29,000 tons of shipping to the bottom. Over a five-day period, they sank two and captured three. Then, on 16 March, they caught up with a cluster of stragglers, and sank 13 ships totalling 62,000 tons. They arrived at Brest on 22 March. However, after the successful cruise, they became frequent targets for RAF bombers, until 11 months later, when they escaped back to Germany in the famous Channel Dash.

BISMARCK AND *PRINZ EUGEN*: OPERATION *RHEINÜBUNG*
The Kriegsmarine's most famous commerce raid quickly turned into a combat cruise and the loss of the pride of the fleet. *Bismarck* would be the answer to convoys escorted by World War I battlewagons, such as HMS *Ramilles* and *Malaya,* that had stymied the battlecruisers. Raeder wanted her to sail before *Barbarossa,* after which he knew Hitler would have little interest in his navy, so had Lütjens go right back to sea on 18 May. The usual sprinkling of support ships had enough supplies to take care of the pair for three months. In Norway, they topped off with fuel and painted out their air-recognition stripes, and then put to sea on the 21st. Lütjens believed he had made a clean break, but the Home Fleet was onto him. The two ships entered the Denmark Strait on 23 May, and sank HMS *Hood* the next day. The commerce raid by heavy surface units was done.

---

42 Not shown on this map. For 48 hours, from 18–20 February, *Scharnhorst,*
    Gneisenau and *Admiral Hipper* conducted the truncated Operation *Nordmark*
    between the Shetland Islands and Norway. Almost as soon as the operation began,
    the raiders realized they had missed their intended convoy and so returned home.
    From 27 July to 11 August, *Admiral Hipper* sailed the Norwegian Sea as far north
    as Spitzbergen, before returning to Germany. Only a few ships were sunk or
    captured.

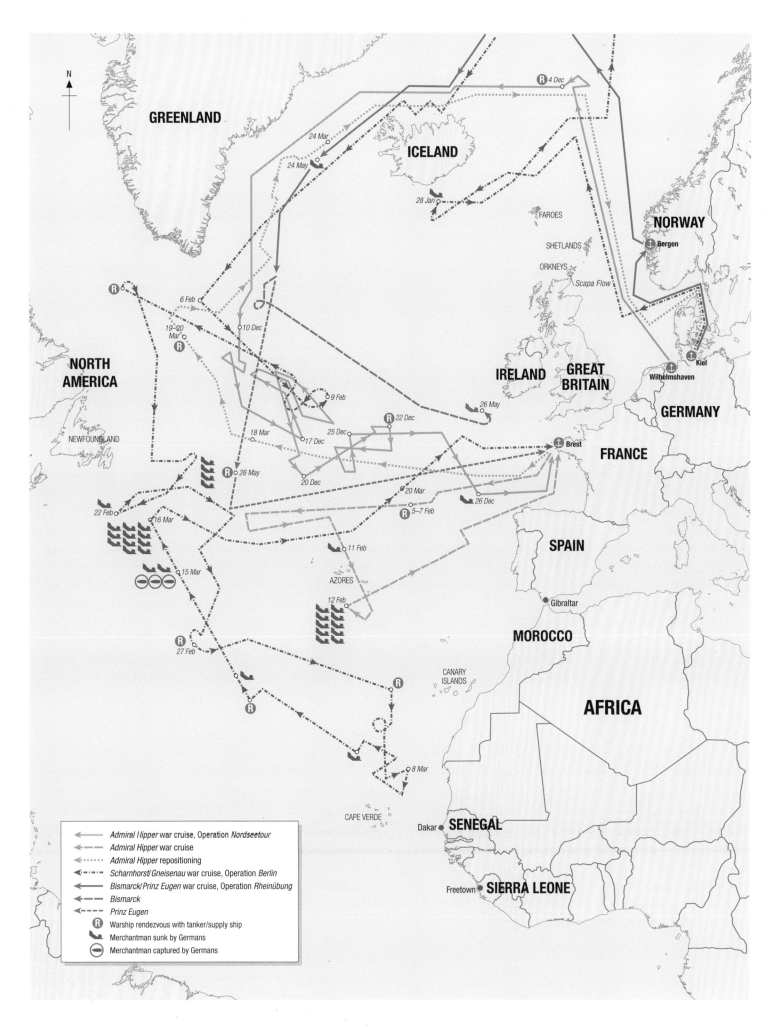

N

GREENLAND

ICELAND

NORWAY

FAROES

SHETLANDS
ORKNEYS
Scapa Flow

Bergen

NORTH
AMERICA

NEWFOUNDLAND

IRELAND

GREAT
BRITAIN

GERMANY

Kiel

Wilhelmshaven

Brest

FRANCE

SPAIN

Gibraltar

MOROCCO

AZORES

CANARY
ISLANDS

AFRICA

CAPE VERDE

Dakar

SENEGAL

Freetown

SIERRA LEONE

4 Dec

24 Mar
24 May

28 Jan

6 Feb

19–20
Mar

10 Dec

9 Feb

18 Mar

17 Dec

22 Dec

25 Dec

20 Dec

26 May

26 May

20 Mar

5–7 Feb

26 Dec

22 Feb

16 Mar

15 Mar

11 Feb

12 Feb

27 Feb

8 Mar

Admiral Hipper war cruise, Operation *Nordseetour*

Admiral Hipper war cruise

Admiral Hipper repositioning

Scharnhorst/*Gneisenau* war cruise, Operation *Berlin*

Bismarck/*Prinz Eugen* war cruise, Operation *Rheinübung*

Bismarck

Prinz Eugen

Warship rendezvous with tanker/supply ship

Merchantman sunk by Germans

Merchantman captured by Germans

MAP 86: GERMAN COMMERCE RAIDERS (I), 1940

The most common criticism of the Kriegsmarine is that Hitler went to war five years too early.[43] As we have just seen, however, its problems went way beyond simple numbers of surface ships and U-boats. Its strategy became suspect within the first months of World War II, as did its isolated diplomatic and geographic position. Its admirals and captains made numerous questionable decisions, and actual combat missions revealed problems with the design and construction of its ships.

Early in World War II, geography, limited numbers of both warships and submarines, combat damage and mechanical breakdowns, plus the short range of Luftwaffe bombers, all negatively impacted the German commerce war. An expedient weapon appeared on the scene: armed merchant ship commerce raiders. Another example of the Kriegsmarine fighting a 'poor mans' war', these converted freighters served a useful purpose. There was nothing new to them, a legacy of earlier privateers, which the Kaiser's navy had also used in World War I.

These plain, drab merchantmen were armed with hidden guns (5.9-inch was the largest) and torpedo tubes. They usually carried float planes for scouting wide open oceans, plus a large supply of mines to drop where the Allies might least expect them, for example, Auckland and New Zealand. Two of the raiders actually carried small torpedo boats capable of 40 knots. They also carried oversized crews, usually between 300 and 400 men, mainly so some sailors could serve as prize crews to sail captured ships back to German-occupied Europe. These merchant cruisers needed range finders, fire-control facilities and other combat systems of a standard warship. In addition, they carried

carpentry materials, wood and canvas, plus paint in order to constantly disguise themselves as other vessels. They had oversized maintenance crews to make repairs in far-away places. Raiders operating in the Pacific occasionally used Japanese bases for supplies and repairs. Further, they participated in deception operations directed by the naval staff, such as making false reports about sighting German warships to draw away Royal Navy pursuers.

Atlantis left Germany on 31 March, followed by five other raiders that summer and another in December. Each had an assigned operational area. *Komet* arrived in the Pacific; thanks to friendly relations with Stalin, she sailed across the north of the USSR assisted by a Soviet icebreaker. Hunting was good since merchant captains were still new to the concept of the raiders. Raeder's staff also assisted by cleverly shifting the ships' operational areas. Even if the raiders went through dry spells when they did not sink or capture many ships, they disrupted commercial routes and schedules, and tied down Royal Navy assets. Captured ships often held a wealth of valuable intelligence, from codebooks to the whereabouts of British hunting groups. In conjunction with U-boats, weather ships or blockade runners the raiders created a scouting line across shipping lanes. Some had old propulsion plants and other fragile systems that could not be fixed by expedient means while underway, so returned to Europe.

The peak of German commerce raider success came in the summer and autumn of 1940. By that time, however, they had lost the element of surprise since merchantmen captains avoided suspicious ships' masts at first sight. The German gunners' initial targets were radio rooms and antennae, to prevent emergency calls going out. Gun battles (the 5.9-inch guns were the raiders' preferred weapons) often caused so much damage to the victim that hoped-for prize ships had to be sunk instead.

43   Whether Raeder's battleship-heavy 'Plan Z' would have succeeded in World War II maritime warfare dominated by aircraft carriers is doubtful.

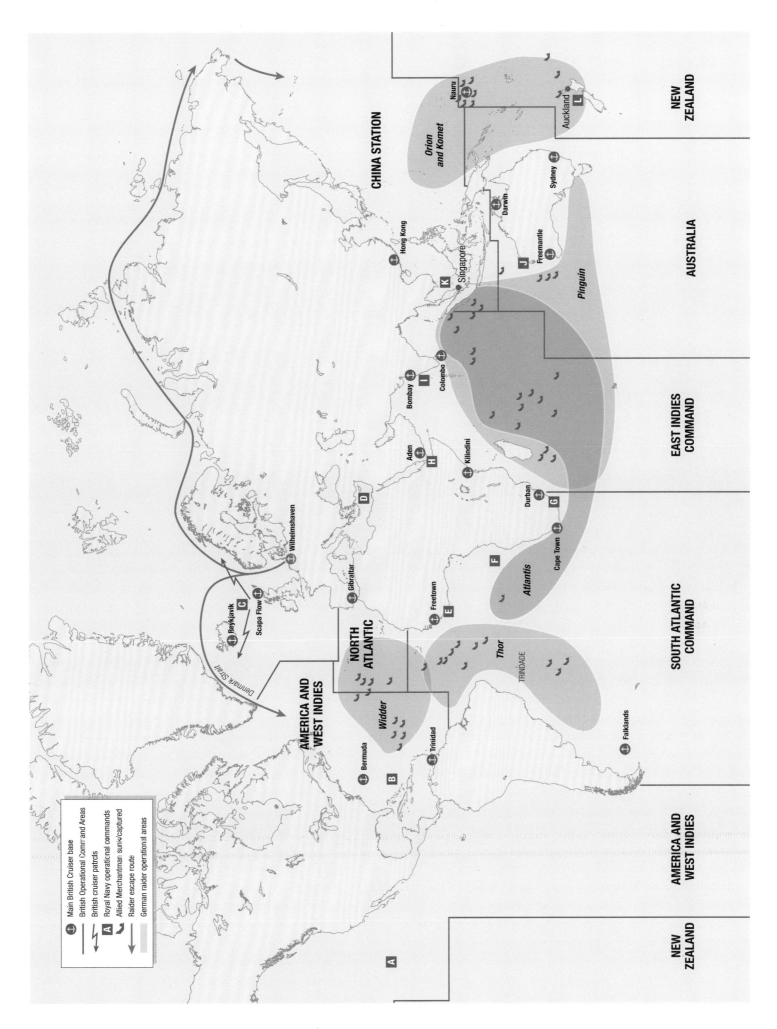

NEW ZEALAND

AMERICA AND
WEST INDIES

SOUTH ATLANTIC
COMMAND

EAST INDIES
COMMAND

AUSTRALIA

NEW
ZEALAND

CHINA STATION

Main British Cruiser base
British Operational Comm'and Areas
British cruiser patrols
Royal Navy operational commands
Allied Merchantman sunk/captured
Raider escape route
German raider operational areas

Reykjavik
Scapa Flow
Wilhelmshaven
Denmark Strait
Gibraltar
Bermuda
Trinidad
Falklands
Freetown
Cape Town
Durban
Kilindini
Aden
Bombay
Colombo
Singapore
Hong Kong
Darwin
Freemantle
Sydney
Auckland
Nauru

NORTH
ATLANTIC

AMERICA AND
WEST INDIES

Widder
Thor
TRINDADE
Atlantis
Pinguin
Orion
and Komet

A
B
C
D
E
F
G
H
I
J
K
L

187

MAP 87: GERMAN COMMERCE RAIDERS (II), 1941

Cunning and aggressive captains and crews were essential for successful merchant raider operations. So was good intelligence from Raeder's HQs, concerning ship and convoy locations, and escort size. These raiders worked in conjunction with warships, U-boats, blockade runners, and the supply-ship network. With its limited resources, the Kriegsmarine had to coordinate all weapons at its disposal in intricate and constantly changing operations across all the world's oceans. Raider captains had to adjust as merchant ships got wise to them by avoiding suspicious vessels, too readily radioing 'QQQ' (questionable raider, hence the nickname 'Q ship') or 'RRR' (raider), sure to attract enemy warships. Intended victims often tried to turn and run rather than submit, while many actually fought back, knowing that a lucky hit from a single old gun might disable the raider's fire controls, navigation, communications, etc. In many cases, capturing a victim was preferable to sinking it. This was especially true of tankers and whale-factory ships full of oil much needed by the Reich. In fact, the captain of *Thor* received a reprimand for sinking a captured whaling ship carrying 17,662 tons of oil.

Disrupting shipping lanes and distracting the Royal Navy ranked equally important with capturing or sinking merchant ships. Raiders provided other valuable services such as bombarding enemy shore installations. For example, *Komet* shot up the phosphate pier, oil tanks and other machinery on Nauru Island north of the Solomons. Raiders often carried their own *B-Dienst* radio intercept and jamming detachments, which could provide real-time intelligence to the raider's

captain, other German ships at sea, or Kriegsmarine HQs.

Many raiders either remained at sea or returned to various hunting grounds in 1941 (therefore the same ship on the same cruise is shown here and on Map 86). In the constant learning competition of war, both sides went through the normal cycle of measure and countermeasure. Raider captains had to resort to new tactics, such as hanging grappling hooks from spotter planes, flying between a victim's masts and ripping its radio aerials with the hook. Encounters and combat with Royal Navy warships and armed merchant cruisers increased in 1941. In the Indian Ocean, *Pinguin* fell to HMS *Cornwall* on 8 May. She had sunk 32 ships of 154,619 tons. *Kormoran* got into a violent gunfight with the light cruiser HMAS *Sydney* on 19 November. Both ships sank: 315 of 400 Germans were saved, but none of the 644 Allied sailors were. Another successful raider, *Atlantis,* credited with 22 ships totalling 145,697 tons, was sunk two days after her last attack by HMS *Devonshire.* She had been fuelling U-126 when the heavy cruiser spotted her; the submarine dived but could not sink the British warship. *Atlantis* had spent 622 days at sea and had sailed 102,000 miles.

By mid-November 1941 all the raiders had been sunk or returned to port. Over the next few months a couple sailed again, and one or two could still be found at sea in 1943. Together the raiders sank 136 merchant ships totalling 890,000 tons at a fraction of the cost of the panzer ships and heavy cruisers. This made them second only to U-boats when it came to damaging Allied shipping.

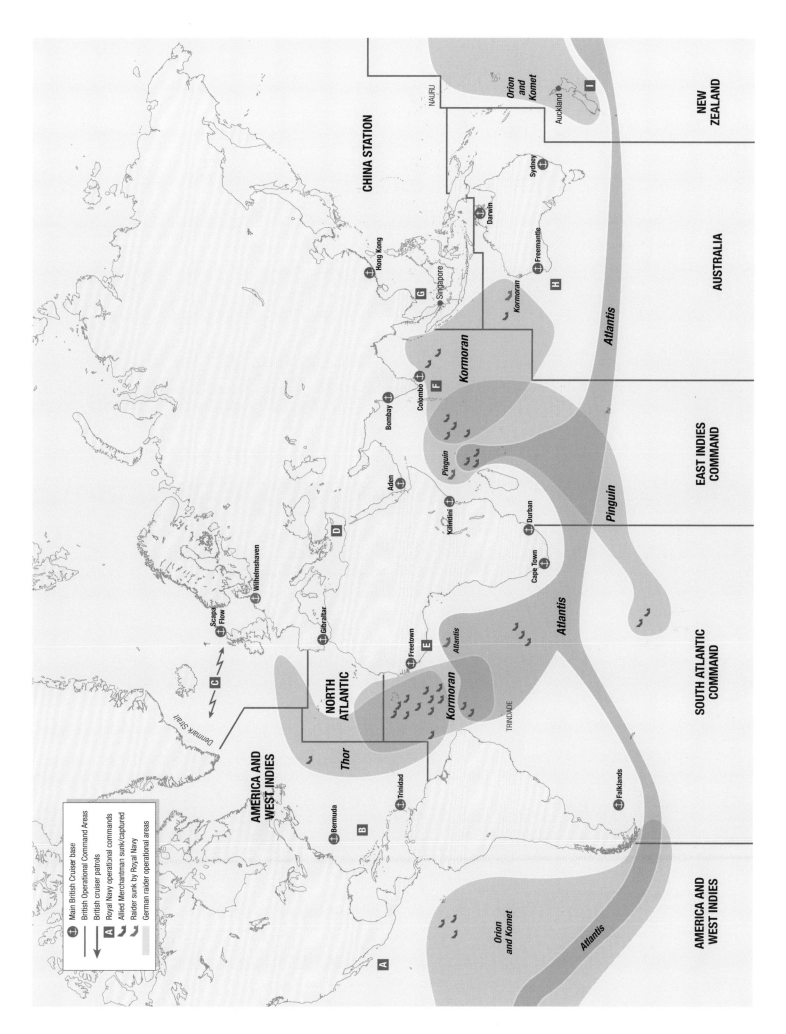

Main British Cruiser base
British Operational Command Areas
British cruiser patrols
A Royal Navy operational commands
Allied Merchantman sunk/captured
Raider sunk by Royal Navy
German raider operational areas

NEW ZEALAND

AUSTRALIA

Orion and Komet

NAURU

Auckland

I

CHINA STATION

Sydney

Darwin

Freemantle

Hong Kong

Singapore

G

H

Kormoran

Kormoran

Colombo

Bombay

F

Pinguin

EAST INDIES COMMAND

Aden

Kilindini

Durban

Cape Town

Pinguin

Atlantis

Scapa Flow

Wilhelmshaven

Gibraltar

Freetown

D

E

Atlantis

Atlantis

Denmark Strait

C

NORTH ATLANTIC

Thor

Kormoran

SOUTH ATLANTIC COMMAND

TRINIDADE

Falklands

AMERICA AND WEST INDIES

Bermuda

Trinidad

B

A

Orion and Komet

Atlantis

AMERICA AND WEST INDIES

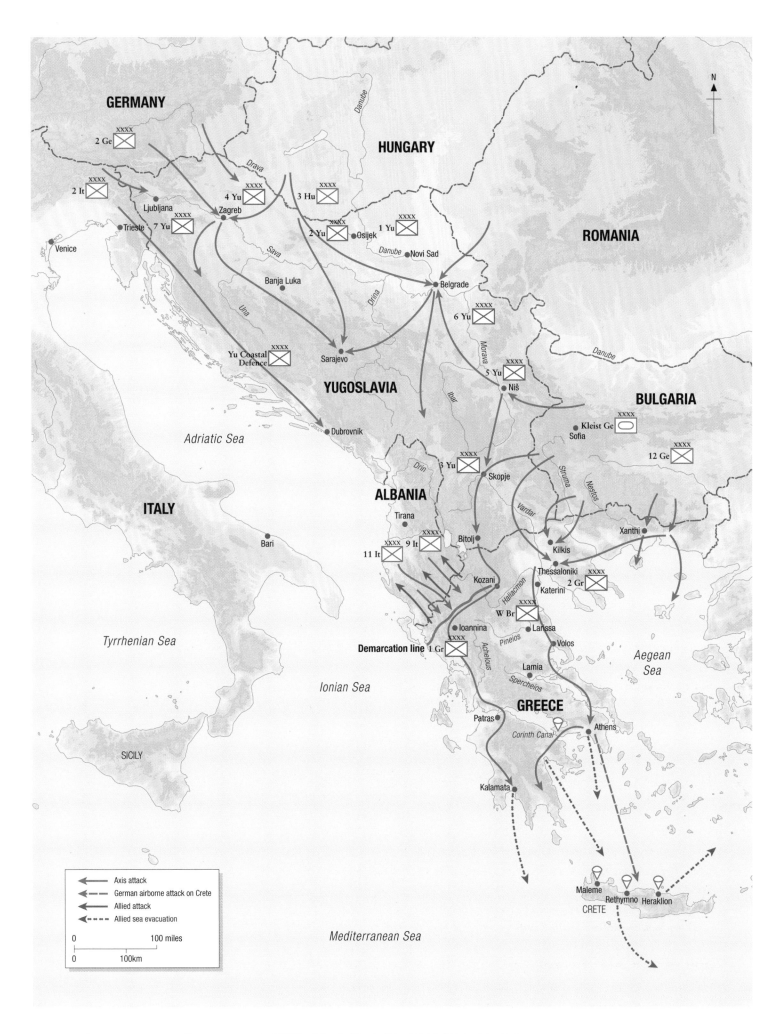

GERMANY

2 Ge XXXX

2 It XXXX

HUNGARY

Drava

4 Yu XXXX
Ljubljana
Zagreb
7 Yu XXXX
Trieste
Venice

3 Hu XXXX

2 Yu XXXX
Osijek

Sava

1 Yu XXXX

ROMANIA

Danube
Novi Sad

Banja Luka

Una

Belgrade

6 Yu XXXX

Morava

Yu Coastal
Defence XXXX

YUGOSLAVIA

Adriatic Sea

Dubrovnik

Sarajevo

Drina

5 Yu XXXX
Niš

BULGARIA

Ibar

Kleist Ge XXXX
Sofia

Drin

3 Yu XXXX
Skopje

12 Ge XXXX

ITALY

ALBANIA

Tirana

Bari

11 It 9 It XXXX
Bitolj

Kozani

Struma

Vardar
Nestos

Kilkis

Xanthi

Thessaloniki
Katerini

2 Gr XXXX

Tyrrhenian Sea

Haliacmon

W Br XXXX

Ioannina

Demarcation line 1 Gr XXXX

Pinelos
Larissa
Volos

Achelous

Lamia

Aegean
Sea

Ionian Sea

Spercheios

GREECE

Patras

Corinth Canal

Athens

SICILY

Kalamata

Maleme
Rethymno Heraklion
CRETE

Axis attack
German airborne attack on Crete
Allied attack
Allied sea evacuation

0   100 miles
0   100km

Mediterranean Sea

CHAPTER 8:
THE BALKAN CAMPAIGN

Hitler would have preferred that the Balkan Peninsula remained a compliant resource area for Germany and a strategic backwater in the larger war – hopefully ignored by both sides. The Führer's naive wishful thinking had little basis in reality: The entire region was a product of the post-World War I treaties, so subject to all the tensions associated with those documents. Firstly, at least two of the countries, Romania and Yugoslavia, were integral parts of France's Little Entente defensive arrangements against Germany; secondly, since the early 1900s, Italy considered much of the area its sphere of influence. And thirdly, Great Britain's interest in the eastern Mediterranean, including the Aegean Islands, was considerable in view of its proximity to the Suez Canal – to name but three reasons. Furthermore, with the recent example of the World War I beachhead at Thessaloniki (Salonika) as a demonstration of Allied maritime capabilities (which had only grown during the interwar period), there is some truth to Churchill's 'soft underbelly of Europe' assessment. For this reason alone, Hitler should have anticipated trouble in south-east Europe.

The trend towards fascist, or at least conservative authoritarian, regimes throughout the Balkans, and general anti-communism which lessened traditional Russian (and then Soviet) influence there, may have given some comfort to the Führer. Heavy-handed German–Italian reactions to some issues, such as the two Vienna Awards (which granted disputed territory to Hungary), gave the impression of decisive 'Führer state' solutions. In reality, the two dictators merely hung a fig leaf over lingering, systemic problems. Finally, the Western campaign had three main effects in the Balkans: It completely ended French influence, damaged British prestige and greatly enhanced Hitler's standing and German power. The numerous military successes the Third Reich enjoyed during the first year of World War II threatened Mussolini's fragile ego and prompted him into Balkan adventurism; this also wrecked Hitler's hopes for the area. In response to Czechoslovakia, the Duce invaded Albania in April 1939 and made it part of the Italian Empire. The two countries had a long common history, so this did not upset Hitler. However, 18 months later, Mussolini invaded Greece from his Albanian base.

This attack immediately failed and, worst of all from Hitler's viewpoint, brought Britain actively to the aid of Greece. Italian incompetence and unpreparedness, rough terrain and terrible weather condemned the invasion. The Greeks promptly shifted forces to the threatened area and launched effective counterattacks. The Italians had barely penetrated 20 miles into Greece along the south-western half of the front, but soon the

Greeks shoved them 40 miles back into Albania along the entire front. The fighting then stalemated until Operation *Marita* in April 1941.

Britain gave guarantees to Greece in April 1939 and landed troops at Piraeus and on Crete six months later. Within days of the 1940 Italian offensive, the Royal Navy sent a mission to Athens and RAF squadrons began to arrive on 4 November. A week later, aircraft from HMS *Illustrious* attacked the Italian naval base at Taranto, demonstrating British power and Italian impotence to all, especially Hitler. Germany had already sent a military training mission to Romania in October and in November he 'asked' Bulgaria for permission to station air defences there to protect the Romanian oilfields. Weeks later, Hungary signed the Tripartite Pact. That winter, German influence and military strength grew in the region (in both ground and air forces). All the while, Hitler had an uneasy feeling about Stalin's possible reactions, especially after the occupation of Bessarabia indicated potential Soviet mischief in the Balkans (see Map 33). Turkey's stance was also a major question mark. After waiting for the death of Greek dictator General Ioannis Metaxas, sufficient success against the Italians in North Africa and tortured negotiations, a new BEF (called the Imperial Expeditionary Force or IEF) began to arrive in Greece on 7 March 1941. These 53,000 ANZAC troops were all the impetus Hitler needed.

Planning for the invasion of Greece, Operation *Marita,* had been underway since the RAF arrived in November. A week later, Hitler issued Directive No. 18, which spelled out objectives for the Mediterranean in general and on 13 December he added Directive No. 20 for *Marita.* The 12. Armee under Generalfeldmarschall Wilhelm List, assembling 24 divisions in Romania and (after 28 February) Bulgaria, drew up the operational and tactical plans for Panzergruppe 1 and three subordinate corps. Preparations went according to plan throughout March, with an attack date planned for early April.

Except for its approximately 100-mile border with Greece, Yugoslavia became encircled when Bulgaria joined the Tripartite Pact. Practically surrounded by revisionist neighbours, the new situation motivated the country to see things Hitler's way. Having Yugoslavia as an Axis partner would greatly ease logistics for *Marita.* Meetings between Hitler and top Yugoslav officials on 28 November 1940 and 14 February 1941 went nowhere, but on 4 March, Prince Regent Paul acted more agreeably. Hitler explained he did not want to transit combat troops, just supplies. On 18 March, the Yugoslavs abruptly decided to join the Axis and the prime minister and foreign minister signed an agreement on the 25th in Vienna (protests prevented them from doing so in their own capital). The uncomplicated preparations for *Marita* seemed assured, but that all changed fewer than 48 hours later. A military coup tossed out Prince Regent Paul and the existing government, enthroned King Peter II, formed a new government and, on the 29th, began mobilization.

The new regime claimed it wanted to get along with Germany, although anti-German protests swept most of Yugoslavia (except for Croatia). Hitler minimized the first and accentuated the second, so mere hours after the coup, he said that with 'merciless harshness' he

wanted to 'destroy Yugoslavia as a military power and sovereign state'.[44] That same day, he issued Directive No. 25, which gave the operation against Yugoslavia its name and wrote to Mussolini about the change of plans. With speed of the utmost importance, on the 29th, the OKH held a conference to coordinate Operations *25* and *Marita.* The underdeveloped infrastructure and rough terrain in both Greece and Yugoslavia complicated everything. As before, logistics was the Germans' main concern, in particular the Belgrade–Niš–Thessaloniki road and rail line, plus free navigation on the Danube. The new plan added 2. Armee attacking out of Austrian Germany, with its *Schwerpunkt* coming between the Drava and Sava Rivers. Near Belgrade, it would meet Kleist coming north from Bulgaria and Romania.

The two operations began on 6 April. Yugoslavia, a two-decade-old artificial creation of the Versailles system, gave only the illusion of national unity. Its one-week mobilization clearly did not allow enough time. Greece, already decisively engaged against the Italians, had limited forces with which to resist the Germans. The 12. Armee attacked in two directions: The panzers north and westwards into Yugoslavia and infantry southwards into Greece. It took Kleist less than a week to reach Belgrade and to cover the 100 miles to Albania, cutting off Yugoslavia from Greece. Despite the rough terrain, it took even less time to conquer the rest of the country. Yugoslavia would not be subdued, however, and the brutal four-year guerrilla war began immediately.

Greece had a series of defensive lines across Macedonia and Thessaly, but had only half a dozen divisions left to hold them. The Australians and New Zealanders sent to bolster the Greeks barely made a difference and within a week the Germans had broken through or gone around most of the defenses. By the 25th, they had created two pockets in Epirus, trapping the Greek troops that had previously fought the Italians. They also approached Athens, which fell two days later. By the end of April, 12. Armee had defeated the last Allied forces in the Peloponnese.

Hitler issued his Directive No. 28 governing Operation *Merkur* on 25 April, which was set to begin on 20 May. In the meantime, Richthofen's Flieger-Korps VIII redeployed to bases around Athens and in the eastern Peloponnese and began asserting its power over the area. The Royal Navy had just conducted yet another evacuation and was reinforcing and resupplying Crete. According to plan, starting on the 20th, parachutists and glider troops of Flieger-Korps XI would land at three key locales in western and central Crete: Maleme, Rethimno and Heraklion. The attacks generally confused the defending troops from Britain and the dominions, and the native Greeks; they held in some places, withdrew in others and occasionally launched ineffectual counterattacks. Despite the loss of some senior leaders, all three German landing zones managed to survive the critical first day.

At this point, an air–sea battle developed in the Aegean, as both sides tried to impact the battle for Crete. A ragtag German flotilla of impressed Greek vessels set sail for Crete on the 19th with mountain troops from the 5. Gebirgs-Division. On 21 May, Royal Navy cruisers

---

44 Helmut Greiner et al., *The German Campaign in the Balkans* (Spring 1941),US Army: Washington, 1953, p. 22.

and destroyers crushed one convoy and caused heavy losses and on the next day they forced another convoy to turn back. Luftwaffe bombers hunted down the ships throughout the 22nd, sinking many, while damaging others. The seesaw battles on Crete continued unabated: Allied forces again had trouble coordinating defence and counterattack, while Ju 52s flew in Gebirgsjäger reinforcements at a rate of 20 transports per hour. The Germans suffered many casualties, but had gained the upper hand by the 24th and 25th. On the 28th, the Royal Navy began to evacuate British soldiers once again.

Crete represented the death knell of German airborne operations. In hindsight, their efforts would have been better employed against Malta, a much more painful thorn in Hitler's side. Crete never dominated the eastern Mediterranean as the Wehrmacht had hoped. Similar to Norway at the other extreme of Nazi-occupied Europe, it was a cul-de-sac. It sat at the end of an extended, tenuous and primitive logistical trail, so the Germans could never fully exploit its potential. But similar to Norway, we must ask what would have been the consequences if Hitler had allowed the British to keep Crete? Their maritime capabilities could have turned the island into a base from which to threaten the Führer's Balkan flank.

MAP 89: ITALY AGAINST GREECE, 28 OCTOBER 1940–13 APRIL 1941

Mussolini attacked Albania. Italy already dominated it politically and economically, prompting King Victor Emmanuel III to ask the dictator why he bothered to invade 'a handful of rocks?'

During the summer of 1940, Italy built up its troops in Albania to 125,000 (a fact noticed by German agents there). It also made air and naval attacks on the Greek coast and shipping, hoping to provoke a warlike reaction. On 22 August, Mussolini ordered plans to invade Greece. On 18 September, he gave the German foreign minister Ribbentrop his ludicrous justification: 'when our land forces have advanced into Egypt, the English fleet will not be able to remain in Alexandria and will seek refuge in Greek ports.'[45] A nation of 43 million invading another with nine million should be easy. On 15 October, the Duce held a war council in Rome, where senior generals blatantly lied about their troops' eagerness and enthusiasm. At 0300 hours on 28 October, Italy's ambassador to Athens delivered an ultimatum. Two and a half hours later, Mussolini attacked with 200,000 men supported by up to 200 aircraft.

Italian generals were so confident of victory they had prepared only superficial orders and made flimsy arrangements. They correctly assessed that, with its spread-out population and rough geography, Greek mobilization would be difficult and slow. In fact, only three to four Greek divisions were ready when the invasion came. Regardless, the Italians made slow progress along confined mountain roads, which even small detachments of Greek soldiers could effectively block. Only the Eleventh Army in the south could advance, covering 6 miles in two days. Greek defenders completely frustrated the Ninth Army in the north.

The Greeks laboured under many handicaps besides slow mobilization: They had few field fortifications, since they assumed an invasion would come from Bulgaria, not Albania; their weapons were World War I French and German models; transport, anti-aircraft and anti-tank weapons were in short supply; and their 150 aircraft were obsolete French and Polish types. However, against the Greeks, even 'elite' Italian Alpine troops on the main axes towards Konitsa and Mestovo crawled forward. Armoured and motorized forces closer to the coast likewise proved incapable of any sort of Italian blitzkrieg. By the first week of November, defensive reinforcements arrived in the form of more Greek troops and RAF squadrons. Metaxas launched small counterattacks against Mussolini's road-bound columns, with deadly effects. The weather went from bad to worse. By the second week

of November, Greek counterattacks surrounded and destroyed Italian divisions that had managed to advance 20–25 miles. Mussolini replaced the incompetent General Sebastiano Visconti Prasca with General Ubaldo Soddu, who, with the centre collapsing, withdrew the army.

On 14–15 November, the Greeks launched their general counteroffensive into Albania. These soon created breaches in the Italian front and cut off advanced Italian units. Again, the main action occurred in the centre. Greek advances here threatened the Italians on the coast with encirclement against the Adriatic, though such an ambitious manoeuvre by marching infantry in the mountainous country was beyond Greek capabilities. The Italians nevertheless streamed back north, with the invigorated enemy in close pursuit. The Greeks proved much more adept at attacking in the Viosa and Drino river valleys than the Italians had. The entire turn of events infuriated Hitler, who, on the 18th, met the Italian foreign minister Galeazzo Ciano in Berchtesgaden and told him as much and sent a strongly worded letter to Mussolini.[46] The following day, the last Italian soldier retreated out of Greece. Through the latter part of November, the Greeks pushed on and captured Italian soldiers, weaponry and supply bases. In early December, they took Pogradec on Lake Ohrid, again threatening the entire Italian front, this time from the north-east. Mussolini replaced Soddu with General Ugo Cavallero. The Greeks continued to advance down the Viosa, taking Përmet and continuing northwards. By the end of 1940, they had taken the southern quarter of Albania.

By early January 1941, the hard-marching Greek Army had reached its limit. Final attacks towards Berat and Vlorë failed due to the harsh winter more than to Italian defences or counterattacks. On the 29th, the 70-year-old Metaxas died and the new Greek prime minister, Alexandros Koryzis, worried about the threat of a German intervention if Mussolini lost Albania. The front stabilized until early March, when the Italians sent numerous new divisions across the Adriatic.

On 9 March, under Mussolini's watchful eye, seven of his 28 divisions attacked near the coast, only to have the Greek defences halt them five days later. Ten days after Mussolini's offensive began, the front stabilized again. In four and a half months, the Italians suffered 20,000 killed, 40,000 wounded, 26,000 captured and 18,000 crippled by frostbite. Strategically, Mussolini had lost Hitler's trust and had revealed Fascist Italy's political and military bankruptcy to the world.

---

45 Edwin Packer, 'Italian Fiasco: The Attack on Greece', in *History of the Second World War*, Marshall Cavendish: New York, 1973, part 10, p. 259.

46 Mussolini later said of Hitler's letter, 'He really smacked my fingers'; Packer 1973, p. 268.

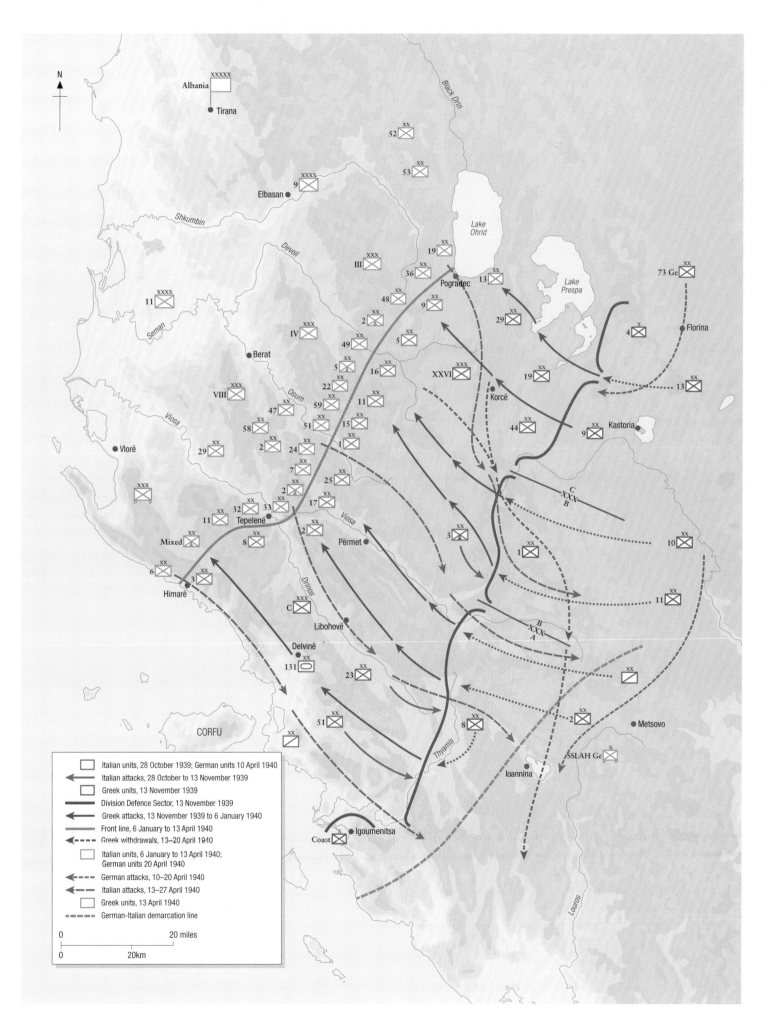

N

Albania XXXXX

● Tirana

52 XX

53 XX

Black Drin

9 XXXX
Elbasan ●

Shkumbin

Devoll

Lake
Ohrid

19 XX

III XXX

36 XX

Pogradec ●

48 XX

9 XX

13 XX

Lake
Prespa

29 XX

73 Ge XX

11 XXXX

Seman

IV XXX

2 XX

5 XX

XXVI XXX

19 XX

4 X

● Florina

49 XX

Korçë ●

13 XX

● Berat

5 XX

16 XX

Osum

11 XX

44 XX

9 XX Kastoria ●

VIII XXX

22 XX

59 XX

47 XX

51 XX

15 XX

1 XX

Viosa

58 XX

2 XX

24 XX

● Vlorë

29 XX

7 XX

25 XX

3 XX

C
XXX
B

2 XX

17 XX

Viosa

1 XX

10 XX

32 XX 33 XX

11 XX Tepelenë ●

Mixed XX

8 XX

2 XX

● Përmet

6 XX

3 XX

Himarë ●

Drinos

11 XX

B
XXX
A

C XX

Libohovë ●

● Delvinë

131 XX

23 XX

XX

51 XX

8 XX

XX

● Metsovo

CORFU

XX

2 XX

Thyamis

SSLAH Ge X

● Ioannina

	Italian units, 28 October 1939; German units 10 April 1940
	Italian attacks, 28 October to 13 November 1939
	Greek units, 13 November 1939
	Division Defence Sector, 13 November 1939
	Greek attacks, 13 November 1939 to 6 January 1940
	Front line, 6 January to 13 April 1940
	Greek withdrawals, 13–20 April 1940
	Italian units, 6 January to 13 April 1940; German units 20 April 1940
	German attacks, 10–20 April 1940
	Italian attacks, 13–27 April 1940
	Greek units, 13 April 1940
	German-Italian demarcation line

Coast X ● Igoumenitsa

Louros

0   20 miles

0   20km

195

MAP 90: OPERATION 25 (I), 6–12 APRIL 1941

Mussolini's reckless attack on Greece impacted the entire Balkan Peninsula. Initially, when most experts agreed with Italian generals that the war would be a quick and easy victory, the Yugoslavs worried about the fate of Thessaloniki, its main commercial outlet. First, it quickly became clear that Italy was in for a long and ultimately unsuccessful war. Then, months later, when Hitler tried to woo Yugoslavia, Mussolini's meddling in the area represented the biggest obstacle to any sort of accommodation. In addition, the invasion made real the one thing the Führer wanted to avoid most: RAF bases in Greece (on Crete and Lemnos) that could threaten oilfields in Romania. Finally, it complicated *Marita* and, more critically, *Barbarossa*.

Hitler hoped that he would not have to invade Yugoslavia; he preferred creating a client state, like Hungary and Romania. Throughout December 1940 and January 1941, he believed that the Yugoslav government was flirting with him, while the military and other segments of society opposed him. On 19 March, Hitler gave Yugoslavia five days to join him, simultaneously giving an anti-government conspiracy new life. Yugoslavia signed the agreement at the last minute and the coup took control of the capital Belgrade two days later.

The Führer demanded the conquest of Yugoslavia, including terror bombing of the capital. The OKH got to work with no time to lose. Heer chief of staff Halder telephoned Mussolini and Hungarian regent Horthy to enlist their help; both indicated eagerness to join. On 30 March, Hitler approved the plan, which saw List's 12. Armee as the *Schwerpunkt* coming from the east and Generaloberst Maximilian von Weichs' 2. Armee coming from the north[47]. Axis-aligned forces – the Italian Second Army and the Hungarian Third Army – would join in, while Bulgaria protested that it did not have time to prepare. Forces allocated for Operations *25* and *Marita* were clearly overkill, but reflected the hasty planning, poor intelligence and exaggerated estimation of both Yugoslav powers of resistance and the geographical difficulties.

The Yugoslav Army had 28 infantry and three cavalry divisions. All were based and recruited regionally and therefore of suspect ethnic composition. Some, especially Croatian and Slovenian units, were of doubtful reliability. The Yugoslav defensive plan called for contesting the entire border, so its forces were thinly spread. After the war, one

general said that only seven divisions, one-quarter of the military, actually fought against the Germans. Critics later claimed that a frontier screen, with the mass of the army withdrawing to fight in the mountainous interior of the country, would have worked better.

The invasion began on 6 April, taking Yugoslavia by surprise; Hitler specifically prohibited the usual ultimatum. The Führer had demanded the destruction of Belgrade and Göring gave Operation *Strafgericht* (*Retribution*) to 4. Luftflotte, despite the fact that the capital had been declared an open city. Bombs fell for two days, killing 17,000 inhabitants, while the obsolete Yugoslav Air Force (600 ageing machines) looked on ineffectually. The government immediately withdrew to Užice. Meeting the next day, it concluded that the situation was not desperate. A day later, with one intermittent phone line to the army high command, it realised the situation was indeed desperate.

The XL Panzer-Korps opened the attack in the south and made directly for Skopje. The Yugoslav Third Army offered minimal resistance and began to withdraw through Kosovo towards Albania. On the principle route to Niš and Belgrade, 4. Gebirgsjäger-Division opened the way for XIV Panzer-Korps, set to attack on the 8th. The 5. and 11. Panzer Divisionen attacked on schedule, split the two divisions attempting to bar the way and raced down the Nišava and Morava Rivers to Niš; they captured Yugoslavia's second city the next day. With remnants of the Yugoslav Fourth Army behind him, only scattered units without anti-tank weapons, or reservists assembling at their depots, blocked Kleist. At that point, 5. Panzer-Division veered west to cut off Yugoslav units retreating southwards, while 11. Panzer-Division made directly for Belgrade. By nighttime on 12 April, it had advanced 125 miles and stood 40 miles from the capital.

The 2. Armee began its attack on 10 April. Its XLVI Panzer-Korps split in two directions, 8. Panzer-Division racing up the Drava River valley towards Belgrade and 14. Panzer-Division attacking towards Zagreb with LI Armee-Korps and XLIX Gebirgs-Korps. *Volksdeutsche* (the German minority that had lived in the region for centuries) rose up and also gave the Wehrmacht any assistance they could. Croats, which made up the mass of the Fourth Army defending there, had little loyalty to the Serb-dominated Belgrade regime. They often melted into the woods without much of a fight. The Italians (eight infantry, three cavalry, two motorized and one armoured division) and Hungarians (six brigades) also moved out in order to stake their claim at the peace table. The Yugoslav defenders, already demoralized at this early stage, struggled against the Axis troops and snowstorms.

---

47   List already had 650,000 men in Romania and Bulgaria to defend Ploesti and execute *Marita* and *Barbarossa*. Weichs' army originally represented the OKH reserve for *Barbarossa*.

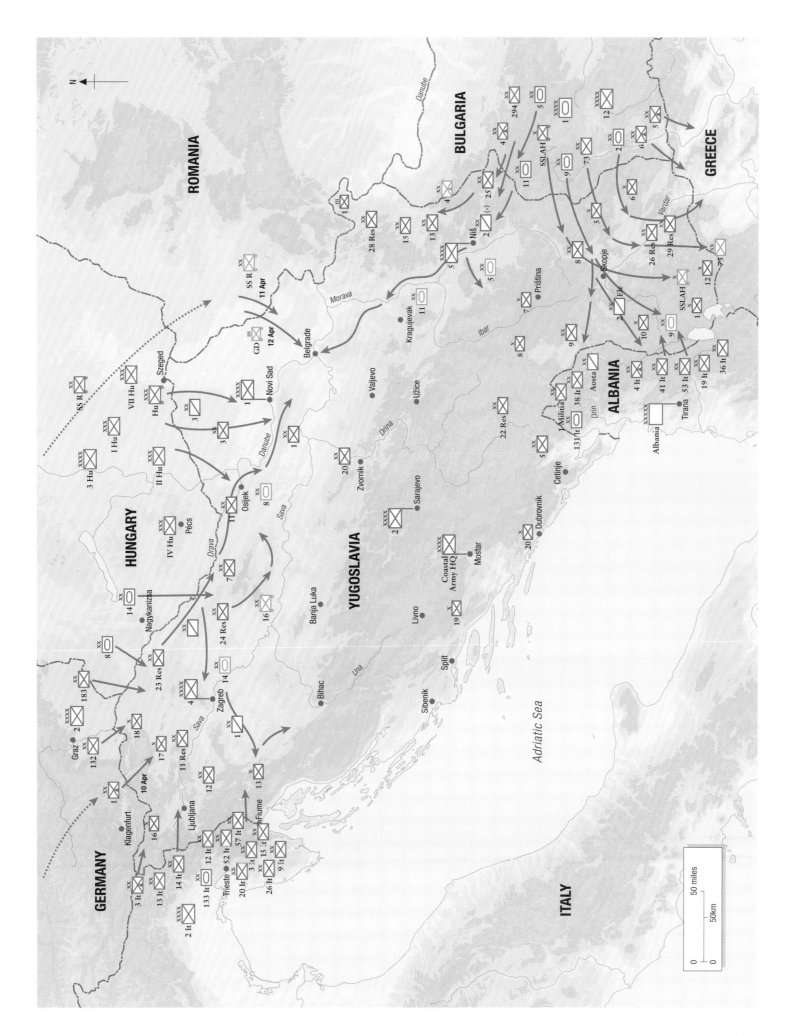

MAP 91: OPERATION *25* (II), 13–18 APRIL 1941

Friendless, overmatched and basically surrounded by Germany and its Axis confederates, Yugoslavia had little chance in this war. Ethnic tensions exacerbated these problems; in Slovenia, an entire brigade gave themselves up to a German motorcycle infantry company. Between the border and Zagreb, the Wehrmacht received the surrender of 15,000 Yugoslav troops (300 were officers, including 22 generals, among whom were the First Army Group and Seventh Army commanders). The Germans reached Belgrade on the night of 12 April and quickly entered the capital.

In the north, 2. Armee displaced its command post to Zagreb and continued towards Sarajevo. Aided by four divisions attacking north from Albania, the Italian Second Army fought its way down the Dalmatian coast. Entire Yugoslav divisions surrendered to them and they took Dubrovnik on 17 April. Likewise, against no resistance the Hungarians quickly overran the Banat, supposedly to protect the Hungarian minority there.

On 13 April, Easter Sunday, the German military officially took control of Belgrade, as the new, young King Peter and his government tried to run the country and its war effort from outside Sarajevo. The next day, Peter flew to Cairo where he established a government in exile, before ultimately going to London. As he departed Yugoslavia, he gave his generals the authority to conclude an armistice with the Germans.

The Yugoslavs had decided to withdraw to the mountains around Sarajevo and fight it out from there, but it was too late. The Germans laboured under two time constraints: Firstly, in order not to give the Yugoslavs a break in which they could establish defences in the difficult terrain of Bosnia, Herzegovina and Montenegro; and secondly, to allow themselves to redeploy against the USSR as quickly as possible. Weichs (now commanding the Germans north of the line Prizren (Yugoslavia)–Sofia (Bulgaria) ordered a robust pursuit by two groups: Four infantry divisions of XLIX and LI Armee-Korps, plus 14. Panzer-Division from the west and six divisions from Panzergruppe Kleist led by 8. Panzer-Division from the east. The 4. Luftflotte provided air support. By 14 April, Yugoslav resistance had disintegrated, as Serbs and Croats battled each other throughout Dalmatia. Elsewhere that day, Kleist's men took 40,000 POWs at Užice and another 30,000 at Zvornik. On the 14th, the 8. and 14. Panzer Divisionen entered Sarajevo from east

and west, capturing the Second Army headquarters, ending fighting in the centre of the country.

In the south, List pursued the Yugoslav Third Army westwards; its Serbian troops fought back, but others, such as its Macedonians, gave up in large numbers. Aided by Flieger-Korps VIII, units of the XL Panzer-Korps reached Albania on the 12th and, by the 13th, had contacted the Italians there. This diversion, ordered by Hitler against the wishes of General Halder, brought a sense of relief to Mussolini and the Italians. With Macedonia now secure, 9. Panzer-Division and the Leibstandarte SS Adolf Hitler regiment drove south towards the Greek frontier, soon joined by 5. Panzer-Division.

By 17 April, the Axis powers had crushed the defenders. That day, General Weichs negotiated with the Italians and Yugoslavs to end the fighting, which became effective the next day. Germany suffered light casualties: 151 killed, 15 missing and fewer than 400 wounded; XLI Panzer-Korps, attacking Belgrade from the south, reported one man dead. A quarter of a million Yugoslav soldiers went into captivity (large numbers of German, Hungarian, Bulgarian and Croat nationals who had been conscripted into the Yugoslav Army were released). Approximately 15,000 Yugoslav soldiers escaped to fight another day with the Allies. However, many also escaped captivity and fled into the mountains in one of two groups: Monarchist Chetniks and communists under Josip Broz, later famous as guerrilla leader Tito.

Being so close to the Third Reich, German dominance over the Balkans was assumed. The delay caused to Operation *Barbarossa* of more than a month is often considered the greatest effect of Operation *25* (and to a lesser degree, *Marita*). Without a doubt, the Balkan operations cost Heeresgruppe Süd in terms of time, losses and wear and tear on high value units, specifically XIV, XL and XLI Panzer-Korps, plus Flieger-Korps VIII. Some of these formations promptly redeployed towards the USSR in mid-April, while others fought in Greece for an additional five weeks (in particular to Richthofen's close air support experts, heavily involved against Crete). However, there were many other reasons for postponing *Barbarossa* that had nothing to do with the Balkan campaign. Mainly, these include shipping units east from the Reich and occupied France, plus completing logistical arrangements for the invasion of the Soviet Union. Therefore, while Hitler's attack on the Balkans contributed to delaying *Barbarossa*, it did not cause it.

199

MAP 92: OPERATION *MARITA*, 6–30 APRIL 1941

Hitler had been planning Operation *Marita* since November 1940, when Mussolini's invasion of Greece turned into a debacle and the RAF deployed Blenheim bombers there. Throughout the following winter, the Wehrmacht built up substantial forces for its own offensive into the country, as well as to attack the USSR as part of *Barbarossa*. The 27 March 1941 Yugoslav coup added Operation *25* to the equation and added urgency to any attack on Greece.

Great Britain had been in a quandary over what to do about Greece. It did not have the assets in the Mediterranean Theatre, especially ground troops, to both defend the Suez Canal and help Greece. Discussions through late February spoke of between 50,000 and 100,000 Commonwealth troops coming to Greece's aid. Buttressed by the stout Metaxas Line along the border with Bulgaria and the mountainous geography of northern Greece, the Allies thought this could be the place to finally halt the blitzkrieg. A stronger line, along the Aliakmon River near Mount Olympus, had the added advantage of distance from airfields in Bulgaria. The whole arrangement had one main weakness, however: If the Germans came through Yugoslavia, like the Maginot Line these fortifications could be outflanked.

Greece had six divisions not fighting the Italians: Three manning the Metaxas Line, two on the Aliakmon Line and one in western Thrace. By the first week of February, the British had conquered Cyrenaica in North Africa, so felt comfortable sending Commonwealth troops to Greece (Operation *Lustre*). General Henry Wilson would command this ground organization, known as the IEF – often called 'W Force' after Wilson – but not the three RAF squadrons, comprising one each of Blenheims, Hurricanes and Gladiators. Throughout March, they shipped over 58,000 men of the I Australian Corps (6th Australian and 2nd New Zealand Divisions) and 1st Armoured Brigade Group. W Force took up positions behind the Aliakmon in a somewhat piecemeal fashion.

The Yugoslav coup surprised the Allies as much as Hitler. The German attack ten days later surprised them as well. The XXX Armee-Korps and XVIII Gebirgs-Korps made a frontal assault on the Metaxas Line, with the mountain troops having the main mission of opening the Rupel Pass across the 7,000ft-high peaks. The 2. Panzer-Division did exactly what the Allies feared such a formation would: It came out of south-west Bulgaria and made a left hook around the exposed end of the Metaxas Line. This manoeuvre by List cut Allied forces into three parts: Greeks facing the Italians in Albania, Greeks in eastern Macedonia and Thrace and W Force plus a few Greek units on the Aliakmon River. The 12. Armee would defeat each part in detail, especially after the XL Panzer-Korps came south through Skopje into the Monastir Gap and into central Greece. The Germans made short work of the Evros and Nestos brigades in eastern Thrace and penetrated the Metaxas Line in numerous places.

The 2. Panzer-Division battled the Greek 19th Motorized Division in Axios. On 8 April, it approached Thessaloniki, a major port, and in the process turned the Metaxas Line, which still resisted in places. The city fell and the Eastern Macedonian Army capitulated the next day. Meanwhile, XL Panzer-Korps advanced from Yugoslavia into central Greece, where W Force screening units conducted a fighting withdrawal. Wilson's main forces waited on the Aliakmon and a second line close behind it. The two enemies first made contact on the 9th. The Germans launched attacks over the next two days. ANZAC troops accounted for themselves well, effectively fighting from camouflaged positions and marching at night to avoid the Luftwaffe. By 12 April, Australian battalions began to give way; one British tank battalion had lost 42 of 52 tanks. A day later, the centre caved in, initiating a general withdrawal. Also on the 13th, the Western Macedonian Army in Albania began to disengage from the Italians. Unfortunately for it, List's 73. Infanterie-Division came in from behind and cut off its escape routes. Divided into a number of small pockets, it surrendered to the Germans on 21 April.

Between 14 and 17 April, the Allies briefly held up the Germans on either side of Mount Olympus. When the Germans had this obstacle behind them, the Allies knew they had little chance of holding on. To save Greece from unnecessary devastation, Allied commanders agreed on the 19th that the IEF would leave immediately. It turns out that 'immediately' meant a few days, since Stukas had made Athens' main port of Piraeus unusable. Most Commonwealth troops would have to withdraw under German pressure to the southern Peloponnese and ship-out from there. While the Greeks fought rearguard actions at Thermopylae and elsewhere, around 50,000 imperials made good their escape (11,000–12,000 became POWs, while they left behind 100 tanks, 400 guns and 8,000 vehicles). German casualties were about 1,100 killed and 4,000 wounded.

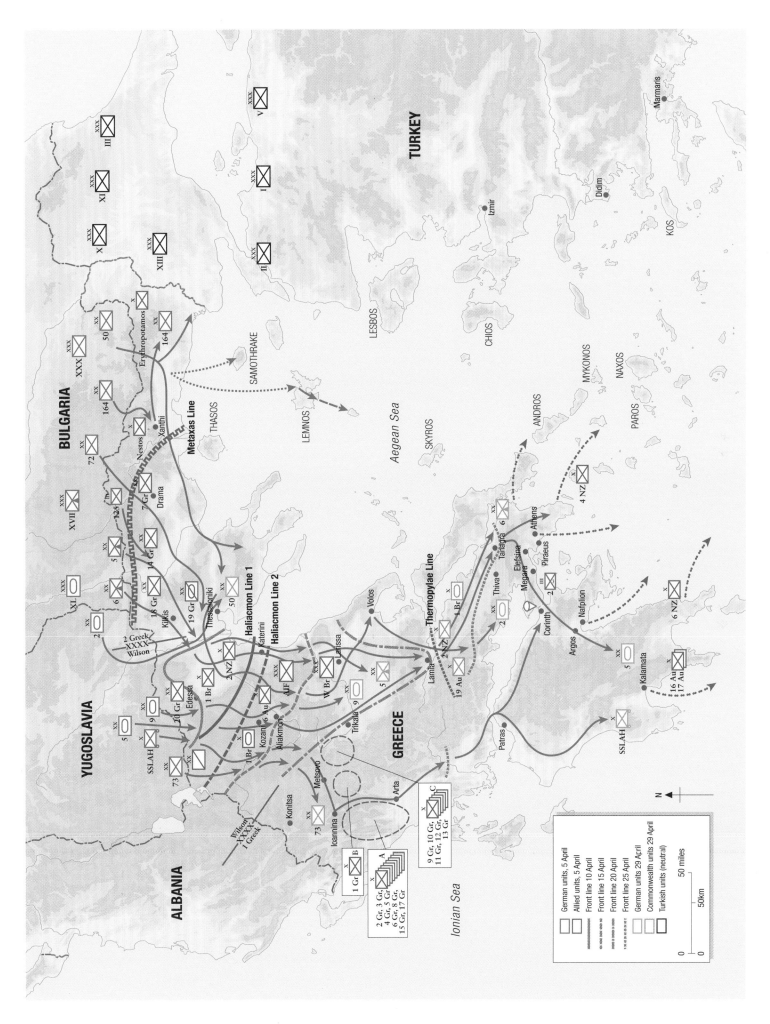

BULGARIA

TURKEY

YUGOSLAVIA

ALBANIA

GREECE

Marmaris

Didim

Izmir

KOS

LESBOS

CHIOS

MYKONOS

NAXOS

PAROS

ANDROS

SKYROS

SAMOTHRAKE

THASOS

LEMNOS

Aegean Sea

Ionian Sea

Eryhropotamos

Xanthi

Nestos

Drama

Metaxas Line

Thessaloniki

Katerini

Kilkis

Edessa

Konitsa

Ioannina

Metsovo

Arta

Trikala

Kozani

Aliakmon

Larissa

Volos

Lamia

Thermopylae Line

Haliacmon Line 1

Haliacmon Line 2

Thiva

Tatragra

Elefsina

Megara

Athens

Piraeus

Corinth

Argos

Nafplion

Patras

Kalamata

SSLAH

2 Greek XXXX Wilson

Wilson XXXX 1 Greek

1 Gr

2 Gr, 3 Gr,
4 Gr, 5 Gr,
6 Gr, 8 Gr,
15 Gr, 17 Gr

9 Gr, 10 Gr,
11 Gr, 12 Gr,
13 Gr

N

50 miles

50km

German units, 5 April

Allied units, 5 April

Front line 10 April

Front line 15 April

Front line 20 April

Front line 25 April

German units 29 April

Commonwealth units 29 April

Turkish units (neutral)

201

MAP 93: AIR AND SEA ACTION AROUND CRETE, 20 MAY–2 JUNE 1941

Crete held strategic importance in the eastern Mediterranean and Balkan region throughout recorded history. At 160 miles long and up to 40 miles wide, it was the largest island in the Aegean. It had good, large harbours on the north coast and a number of airfields. After the destruction of Piraeus,[48] the island became home to the Royal Navy forces involved in Greece.

Vice Admiral Henry Pridham-Wippell had his headquarters at Souda Bay, initially with four cruisers, three anti-aircraft cruisers, around 20 destroyers and numerous smaller craft under command[49]. Operation *Demon,* the evacuation of the Greek mainland at the end of April, took place under near-constant Luftwaffe attack which sank or damaged eight ships. British aircover was practically non-existent, limited to nine planes at the Maleme airfield that had escaped destruction on Crete and a few planes aboard the carrier HMS *Formidable* (heavily damaged during the Operation *Tiger* convoy to Malta and available to Crete only after 25 May). The British believed an amphibious attack on Crete would come on 15 May, so Pridham-Wippell sent his ships on a futile sweep of the waters north of the island. But Richthofen's mixed bomber force made the Aegean too dangerous to stay long. The Luftwaffe had been bombing Crete since 1 May and had markedly stepped up their attacks on the 14th. At the beginning of the battles for Crete, Flieger-Korps VIII consisted of the following: KG 2 – three *Gruppen* of Do 17s, at Tatoi; LG1 – two *Gruppen* of Ju 88s and KG 26, one *Gruppe* of He 111s at Eleusis; StG 2 – three *Gruppen* of Ju 87s, one each at Myene, Molai and on the island of Scarpathos; ZG 26 – two *Gruppen* of Bf 110s at Argos; JG 77 – three *Gruppen* of Bf 109s and LG 2, one *Gruppe* of Bf 109s at Molai.

The Operation *Merkur* plan called for the attack on 20 May. Due to the small size of the Ju 52s carrying 7. Flieger-Division paratroopers, ship convoys would have to bring over heavy equipment, as well as reinforcing mountain troops from 5. Gebirgs-Division. A motley collection of 63 Greek caïques and fishing boats escorted by Italian destroyers would carry 4,000 men, plus bulky weapons and equipment, to Maleme and Heraklion. The Maleme convoy staged through the island of Milos and departed there once it became dark on the 20th. Alerted by Ultra intelligence, Force D (three cruisers and four destroyers) intercepted it 20 miles north of Crete and, despite the heroics of the Italian destroyer *Lupo,* sank most vessels, causing about 1,500 German deaths. Around dawn on the 22nd, Force C (four cruisers and three destroyers) came across the Heraklion convoy 25 miles south of Milos. Escorting Luftwaffe planes attacked the British ships while the convoy turned back. Throughout the day, the bombers (and Bf 109s carrying bombs) sank two cruisers and a destroyer.

On 22 May, the 5th Destroyer Flotilla from Malta, under Captain Lord Louis Mountbatten, took part in the convoy battles. The following day saw similar action, until 24 Stukas discovered the destroyers. They sank two, including Mountbatten's flagship, HMS *Kelly.* A long-distance test of wills ensued between the Admiralty and Mediterranean Fleet's commander, Admiral Andrew Cunningham. He argued that the Luftwaffe made the Aegean too dangerous for his ships, but London insisted he do everything possible to help save Crete. The RAF needed to do its part, too. It had withdrawn what was left of its nine planes at Maleme the day before the Germans arrived. After four days with no air cover, six Hurricanes and a few Blenheims arrived from North Africa on 24 May. They tried to operate out of Heraklion, but abandoned the effort the next day due to the unfavourable situation; Bf 109s were now operating out of the Maleme airstrip.

After five days, the battle on Crete had finally turned in the Germans' favour. On 25 and 26 May, Cunningham attempted to relieve the pressure by attacking Richthofen's airbase on Karpathos (Scarpanto). But *Formidable* only had a dozen fighters aboard, while her World War I-era escorts HMS *Barham* and *Queen Elizabeth* could not match the bombers; the carrier and one battleship were damaged. On the 27th, London gave its permission to commanders on the scene to plan the evacuation of Crete. Mostly using the small fishing ports on the south of the island, the next day, Cunningham began removing the beleaguered defenders. The evacuation of around 15,000 men took until 2 June; the Luftwaffe harassed the endeavour, sinking a cruiser and two destroyers, while damaging many other ships. The British also took 4,000 troops from Heraklion.

---

48 As part of a resupply convoy, the 12,000-ton ship SS *Clan Fraser* arrived on the night of 6 April. The next day, German bombers hit her when she still had 250 tons of explosives aboard, blowing the ship sky high. The explosion destroyed much of the harbour's facilities and sank 11 nearby ships totalling 41,589 tons.

49 This also included the use of the guns of the heavy cruiser HMS *York*, beached since 27 March in the harbour after being severely damaged by Italian torpedo boats. Later, more ships, including battleships, joined his flotilla.

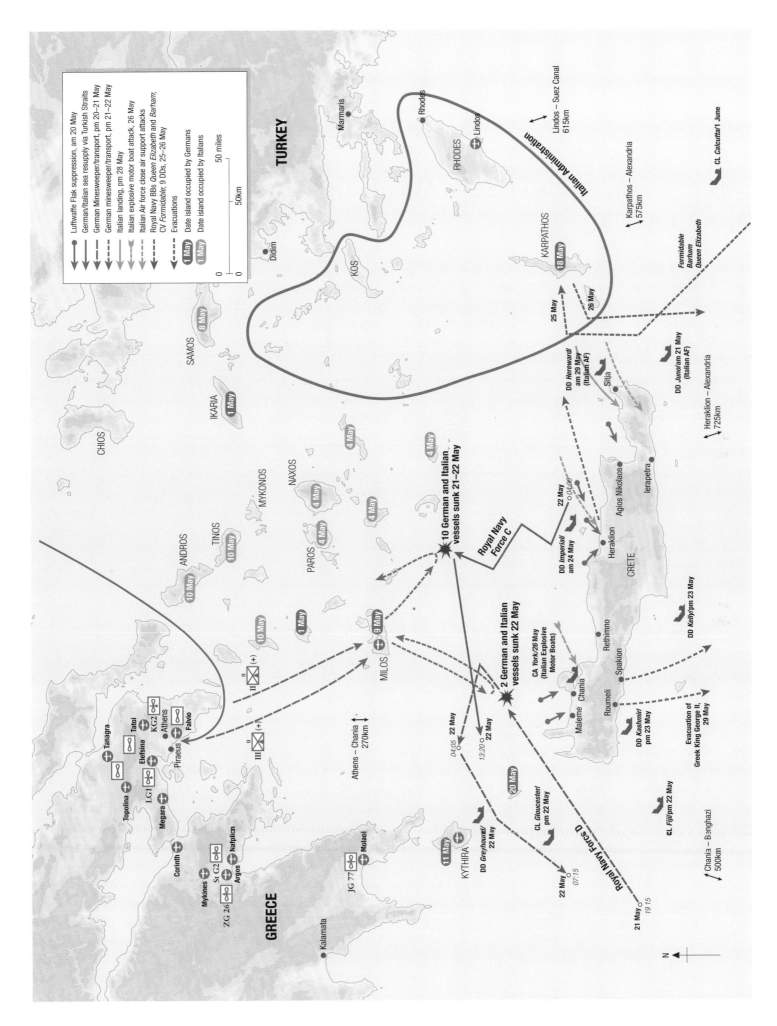

Legend:

- Luftwaffe Flak suppression, am 20 May
- German/Italian sea resupply via Turkish Straits
- German Minesweeper/transport, pm 20–21 May
- German minesweeper/transport, pm 21–22 May
- Italian landing, pm 28 May
- Italian explosive motor boat attack, 26 May
- Italian Air force close air support attacks
- Royal Navy BBs *Queen Elizabeth* and *Barham*; CV *Formidable*, 9 DDs, 25–26 May
- Evacuations
- 1 May Date island occupied by Germans
- 1 May Date island occupied by Italians

0   50km
0   50 miles

TURKEY

Marmaris
Didim

Rhodes
Lindos

RHODES

KOS

SAMOS   8 May

Lindos – Suez Canal
615km

Karpathos – Alexandria
575km

Italian Administration

KARPATHOS   18 May

CHIOS

IKARIA   1 May

25 May   26 May

Heraklion – Alexandria
725km

Formidable
Barham
Queen Elizabeth

DD *Hereward*/
am 29 May (Italian AF)

DD *Juno*/am 21 May
(Italian AF)

Sitia

MYKONOS

NAXOS   4 May

4 May   4 May

22 May ○ 04:00

Agios Nikolaos

Ierapetra

ANDROS   10 May

TINOS   10 May

PAROS   4 May

10 German and Italian
vessels sunk 21–22 May

Royal Navy Force C

DD *Imperial*/
am 24 May

Heraklion

CRETE

GREECE

II ⊠ (+) II
10 May

1 May

DD *Kelly*/pm 23 May

Tatoi
Tanagra
Elefsina
KG2
LG1
Topolino
Athens
Megara
Piraeus
Falvio

Corinth
Mykines
St G2
ZG 26
Argos   Natplion

JG 77   Molaoi

KYTHIRA   11 May

DD *Greyhound*/
22 May

CL *Gloucester*/
pm 22 May

20 May

Royal Navy Force D

21 May   19:15

22 May ○ 07:15

MILOS   9 May

2 German and Italian
vessels sunk 22 May

04:05 ○
22 May

13:20 ○
22 May

CA *York*/26 May
(Italian Explosive
Motor Boats)

Rethimno

Roumeli   Spakion

Maleme   Chania

CL *Fiji*/pm 22 May

Evacuation of
Greek King George II,
29 May

DD *Kashmir*/
pm 23 May

Athens – Chania
270km

Chania – Banghazi
500km

CL *Calcutta*/1 June

N

203

MAP 94: OPERATION *MERKUR*, 20 MAY–2 JUNE 1941

On 15 April 1941, nine days into the Balkan operations, Göring met 4. Luftflotte commander Löhr, who had been advocating a Luftwaffe seizure of Crete. On the next day, the Reichsmarschall went to Hitler with the idea. The Führer asked, 'You know that this operation in the Balkans has delayed our time schedule for *Barbarossa*, yet with this knowledge, you ask me to delay even more and get involved with an attack on Crete?' Göring, doubtless repeating Löhr, replied that if Germany left Crete in Allied hands, it would be '*Pfuhl im Fleish*' ('A thorn in our side') and would interfere with Axis designs for the eastern Mediterranean and Suez Canal. Hitler met his airborne commander, Generalleutnant Kurt Student, five days later and issued his Directive No. 28 four days after that.

Student would take Crete with paratroopers, 13,000 from 7. Flieger-Division, plus the Luftlande Sturmregiment (including glider troops), reinforced later by 4,000 men from the 5. Gebirgs-Division. Richthofen's Flieger-Korps VIII would support them with 280 level bombers, 150 Stukas, 180 fighters and 40–50 reconnaissance aircraft. About 490 Ju 52s would do the heavy lifting (and would lose 200 planes). Their first objectives consisted of the airfield at Maleme and the island's administrative centre of Chania; the second wave landed around the airfields at Rethimno and Heraklion.

About 25,000 evacuees from the mainland defended Crete, mainly from the 6th Australian and 2nd New Zealand Divisions, who had arrived with their individual weapons but little else. Three British battalions were already on the island and two more arrived before the Germans, totalling 8,700 fresh, well-armed troops. Added to these were about 11,000 Greek soldiers. The British also had to care for 15,000 Italian POWs, captured in Africa, but incarcerated on Crete. The New Zealander Major-General Bernard Freyberg commanded the garrison, named Creforce. The defenders had little heavy equipment or weapons (they did have 22 tanks), a poor radio network, no air power and they laboured with a primitive transportation infrastructure, to name but a few of their challenges. Guided by Ultra, Freyberg's three defensive sectors generally corresponded to Student's main objectives, i.e. the airfields.

Following two hours of Luftwaffe bombardment, the Germans started landing near Maleme at 0700 hours on 20 May: 5,000 paratroopers and 53 gliders. The landings did not go well and the attackers suffered numerous senior leader casualties (including the division commander killed). Some units landed on top of alerted defenders and others spread out over the drop zones. The New Zealanders fought back, began aggressive patrolling and launched counterattacks. That afternoon, the Ju 52s came back to the eastern drop zones (only seven transports had been shot down in the morning), where landings generally went better than around Maleme.

On the morning of 21 May, despite enemy artillery fire, Ju 52s managed to land at Maleme, with reinforcements and supplies and to remove wounded. Throughout the day, other transports came and went. They dropped more parachutists and brought in the Gebirgsjäger-Regiment 100. The Germans consolidated their dispersed groups, but did not advance far. The defenders held in some places and counterattacked in others, but their failure to hold the airfield, or at least make it unusable, represented a major problem. The seesaw battle continued at Rethimno, while reinforcements dropped into Heraklion. Richthofen's flyers made sure the defenders could safely move only during darkness.

Pre-dawn Allied counterattacks near Maleme on the 22nd came up short and, after sunrise, the Luftwaffe returned. Regardless, the defenders attacked during the day, with indecisive results. The two sides had rough equilibrium at Rethimno, with neither able to gain the upper hand. The same was basically true at Heraklion and was likely to remain so; on the 24th, the Argyle and Sutherland Highlanders began to arrive from the south, but another battalion of paratroopers also dropped in. On the 23rd, the Germans began to assert themselves, attacking from Maleme towards Chania, with paratroopers on the coast and Gebirgsjägers inland. The 5th Brigade pulled back. The 5. Gebirgs-Division's Regiment 85 had arrived and made its presence felt south of Chania.

German reinforcements and attacks began to have a decisive effect on 25 May. They squeezed around Chania and Gebirgsjäger-Regiment 85 cut the coast road to the south-east. That day General Student arrived and King George II of Greece left. By the 26th, the Germans had 17,000 troops on Crete and the British began to consider another evacuation. Arrangements for the withdrawal began the next day, as all over the island the Germans pressed their clear advantage.

On 28 May, the Royal Navy started pulling Freyberg's soldiers off Crete, mainly from the southern fishing ports, but also all along the coast wherever isolated groups of men had been fighting. Rearguards held back the Germans, who did not pursue all that aggressively. Fighting and evacuations, the latter usually at night to avoid the Luftwaffe, continued for the next four days.

The fate of Commonwealth troops can be divided into three categories: 3,967 became casualties (plus 2,200 sailors), 11,370 ended up as POWs and 15,000 were saved. The Germans lost about 7,000 troops, nearly half of them parachutists and 320 aircrew. Student's crack Flieger-Korps XI had been decimated. Although Hitler would continue to create parachute units, he never again ordered an airborne operation of any size.

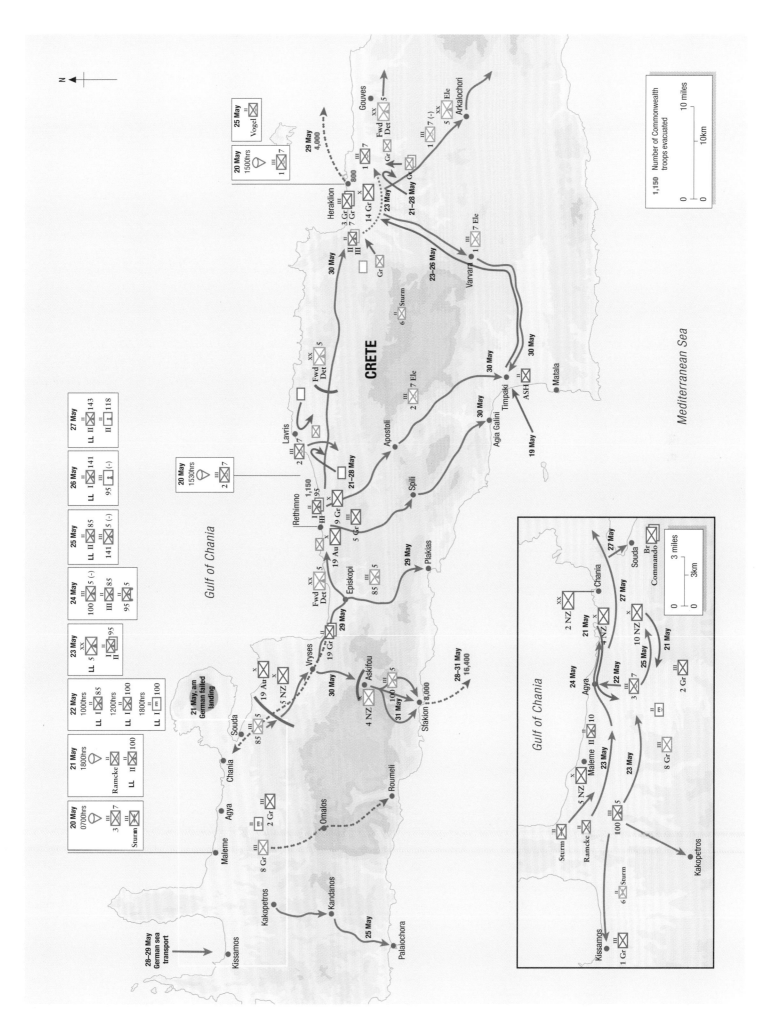

CONCLUSIONS

Depending on how one computes the time, the blitzkrieg dominated European warfare for the first 26–38 months of World War II in Europe, from the summer of 1939 until the autumn of 1941 or even 1942. After reaching an equilibrium around the first half of 1943, the Soviets' version of the blitzkrieg ruled the battlefield until May 1945. The blitzkrieg's interwar competition for a war-winning technique, heavy 'strategic' bombing, did not deliver promised results until employment of the war's ultimate weapons system, the Americans' marriage of the B-29 with an atomic bomb.

As mentioned at the outset of this atlas, war is a learning competition. It took the rest of the world's militaries two or three years to learn how to defeat the blitzkrieg. Ironically, in 1918 the Allies, in particular the French with their groundbreaking Renault FT tanks, had the clear starting advantage. But after the end of the Great War, they unanimously turned away from their successful technique, considering tanks a *sui generis* solution to the *sui generis* problem of trench warfare, not to be repeated. During the interwar period, the doctrinal and technological path to blitzkrieg was open to all nations; therefore it is improper to talk of delayed development or arrested modernization on the part of the Allies. Following a generation of choices made after 1918, their advantage had evaporated. Even if these choices were not 'wrong', such as the 1920s decision to build the Maginot Line, by 1939 neither could they simply be reversed or undone. Further, exporting these same decisions had negative ripple effects, such as French techniques adopted by its Little Entente clients in Poland, Belgium and Yugoslavia.

World War II, especially the first two years or so, was a come-as-you-are affair. In the joyless realities of the learning competition, there can be a time lag between observation and experience of a problem and developing and fielding workable solutions The six months between the end of the Polish and the start of the Western campaigns was not enough time for the Allies to adjust. An entire additional year of uneasy peace prior to *Barbarossa* did not give the Red Army enough time, either. It took them a year of crushing and humiliating defeats to discover their own counter to the blitzkrieg.

Strategically, Hitler's blitzkriegs were aided immeasurably by the fact the Allies did not have a Tsar to the Reich's east: quite the opposite; in Stalin the Führer actually had a willing enabler. Germany also used a healthy dose of enemy mistakes to ensure the blitzkrieg's early successes.[50]

Although Operation *Weserübung* proved that panzers were not essential for a successful blitzkrieg campaign, they certainly helped. After years of military parades and Nürnberg Nazi Party rallies, the Wehrmacht's panzers were no secret to the world's other armies. Likewise, after the battles of the summer and autumn of 1918, the effects of concentrated tanks should have surprised no one, least of all the French and British.

We also know that during the 1940 Western campaign, the Allies had more and, often better, armour. Perhaps knowing the small proportion of the Heer represented by its panzers, the Allies can be excused for underestimating their coming impact. But the blitzkrieg is not so much a matter of 'what you've got, but how you use it.' Interestingly, notably in a war that put a premium on flexible and quick thinking, on average French generals were 8–10 years older than their German counterparts. Further, perhaps since in the Polish campaign panzers did not fulfil a truly novel, operational role, we can be sympathetic to the fact that the Allies did not anticipate the Ardennes manoeuvre by Kleist's massed Panzergruppe.

By June 1940, General Wilhelm Keitel, Chief of the OKW and unofficial leader of Hitler's sycophant corps, dubbed the Führer the Grösster Feldherr Aller Zeiten (the Greatest Field Commander of All Time).[51] On 19 July, immediately after giving his 'Last Appeal to Reason'

speech to the Reichstag, Hitler handed out promotions and field marshal batons to a grateful Generalität (including Keitel). However, the good mood was about to get a splash of cold water; the Battle of Britain was only a couple of weeks old and would soon prove to be more than Germany or the Wehrmacht could handle.

Hitler's relatively easy victories ended with the Balkan campaign and for another year thereafter things became more difficult. Despite *Barbarossa's* blitzkrieg beginnings, the Nazi–Soviet War turned into a war of attrition that Germany could not possibly win, so long as Stalin remained in power. Months of 'decisive battles' in the east, equivalent to the Ardennes manoeuvre of 1940, could not win *Barbarossa*. In the new generation of young, battle-hardened Red Army generals, the blitzkrieg had a worthy adversary in the learning competition.

For the better part of two years, Hitler's blitzkrieg dominated Europe. Small nations like Poland, Denmark, Norway, the Netherlands, Belgium, Yugoslavia and Greece, plus larger ones such as France, fell one by one. Great Britain, from the relative safety of its island home, could not be invaded and defeated. Successfully fighting the British Empire required a strategy and doctrine, a navy and air force and cooperative and worthwhile allies that the Third Reich simply did not have.

This unfortunate reality was magnified when relatively small and resource-poor Germany took on the USSR and USA. The vast Soviet Union dissipated the blitzkrieg's blows and diluted its synergy. The technique may have been the perfect weapon to win limited continental wars against nearby neighbours, such as those fought by Frederick and Bismarck, but not massive worldwide wars such as those started by Kaiser Wilhelm II and Adolf Hitler.

---

50 Nothing new here as the victors of Cannae, Austerlitz, Chancellorsville, Midway, Stalingrad, Dien Bien Phu, 1967 Six Day War and numerous other battles could attest.

51 Gordon Craig, *Germany, 1866–1945*, Oxford, 1978, p. 714. When the tide turned against the Wehrmacht, German love of acronyms and black humour combined to create the nickname Gröfaz, ibid.

APPENDIX
MAP 95: THE OCCUPATION OF POLAND

No one in their right mind would want to live in the space between Hitler and Stalin around the time of World War II, yet that is exactly where Poland found itself. By mid-October 1939, this poor country had been divided into four categories of occupation: Annexed by Germany, annexed by the USSR, annexed by Lithuania and administered by Germany (the General Government). After the start of *Barbarossa*, the German military took over the Soviet and Lithuanian zones, which the Nazis turned into their *Reichskommissariats*[52]. The brutality and murder began part way into the 1939 campaign as an SS Sicherheits Dienst (SD) Einsatzgruppe accompanied each field army. Further, the Germans had captured 587,000 POWs, way more than expected, and these were abused from the start. New Nazi rules stated: 'Poles who have failed to understand that they are conquered and we are conquerors and who act against the above regulations, expose themselves to the most severe punishment.'[53] By the end of October, the Polish resistance movement had begun; it would eventually number half a million souls. The unfortunate Poles suffered occupation by one tyrannical regime or other for more than five years.

On 8 October, Hitler annexed 35,000 square miles in the east that included approximately 9 million Poles, an extended version of the 1914 *Kaiserreich*, plus areas around Łodz and the Suwalki 'beak' between East Prussia and Lithuania. Four days later, he took 37,000 square miles in central Poland, home to 12 million Poles, known after the 26th as the General Government and headed by Hans Frank[54]. Lithuania took a strip of Polish territory to its south-east, generally around Vilnius (Wilno). The Soviet Union took Vilnius (minus the city), Nowogród, Bialystok and Polesie, (which together they rechristened Western Belorussia) and Wołyń and Galicia (now Western Ukraine).

In those areas absorbed outright into the Reich, the Nazis sought to remove all vestiges of the centuries of Polish culture and habitation. They forbade use of the Polish language, prevented the emergence of any sort of Polish political leadership and shut down schools, libraries, museums, etc. Hitler delegated to Heinrich Himmler and the SS the tasks of evicting about 1 million Poles from these regions and 'Germanizing' them (on the 17th, Hitler exempted SS units from military jurisdiction). This expulsion took place during the terrible winter of 1939/40, while *Volksdeutsche* (ethnic Germans from the Baltic States, eastern Poland and Romania) often replaced the Poles. In the

annexed areas, they confiscated property worth 6.6 billion zloty and in the General Government property valued at 1.9 billion zloty. This represented 80 per cent of Poland's pre-war GDP overall. In both German-occupied areas, they resettled 2.5 million Poles

In the General Government, the Germans began harsh and repressive measures in late October, starting with police round-ups. Soon, there followed the usual university and school closures, the destruction of Polish monuments and looting of cultural artefacts. Frank intended on turning his fiefdom into one huge forced-labour camp. In January 1940, the Germans severely restricted movement of Jews and then began to herd them into ghettos in most large cities. Jews found outside of the ghettos after October 1941 could be shot, as could any Poles helping them. By early 1941, the Germans had reduced the food intake of Poles to 669 calories per day and Jews to 184 (Germans received 2,613 calories). Later that year, Hitler decreed the Germanization of the General Government and began to expel Poles to make the area 80 per cent German. Later in 1941, the SS began the first concentration camps in the east at Stutthof near Danzig and Gross-Rosen near Breslau. Between 1939 and 1941, the Germans executed about 120,000 Poles for a variety of flimsy reasons.

The Soviets managed their occupation zone in a much less organized fashion. At first, they merely stood by as Belorussian and Ukrainian peasant groups meted out vigilante ('revolutionary') justice to Poles, especially civil officials and military officers. They instituted forced land redistribution, mandatory state-sponsored atheism, the Sovietization/Russification of schools, the confiscation of state, church and private property and instituted arbitrary taxes on businesses, among other things. They confiscated Polish property worth 2.1 billion zloty and resettled 1.25 million Poles to the USSR. In the much poorer and sparsely populated east, this represented about 20 per cent of the pre-war GDP, but about the same proportion of the population was evicted as in the German sectors. Killings in the Soviet-occupied areas were much higher by comparison, however; in June and July 1941 alone, they murdered 100,000 Poles. By previous agreement with Hitler and without warning, they uprooted those of German ancestry in their zone (including the Baltic States) and deported them to western Poland.

Jews, of course, received especially harsh treatment in all occupied areas. At the Bug River during the autumn and winter of 1939, groups of Jews fleeing one regime were surprised to encounter Jews from the other regime fleeing in the opposite direction; each group assumed that they would get better treatment in the other region. The Germans created a 'Jewish reservation' east of Lublin into which they deported Jews from all over occupied Europe.

---

52 For these, see Robert Kirchubel, *Atlas of the Eastern Front, 1941–45*, Osprey Publishing: Oxford, 2016, Appendix 3, Map 125.

53 Martin Gilbert, *The Second World War: A Complete History*, Henry Holt & Co.: New York, 1989, p. 24.

54 The corresponding military jurisdiction was called Oberost after its World War I ancestor.

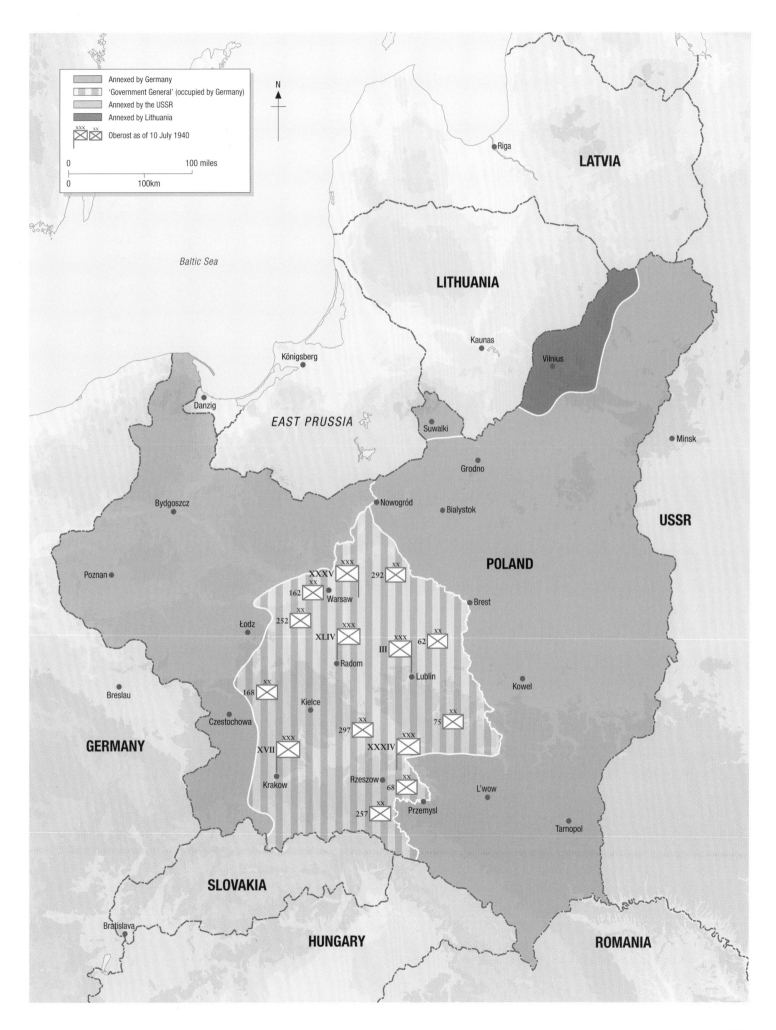

MAP 96: THE OCCUPATION OF SCANDINAVIA

The Germans expected an easy occupation in the 'Aryan' Nordic countries and they were right. As mentioned above, Denmark submitted before noon on the day Germany invaded, while after the fall of Norway, Quisling established a puppet government that the Nazis barely tolerated. The latter, because it had the temerity to resist conquest, could expect a much rougher occupation.

According to international law, Denmark had never technically been at war with Germany. It would also be the only nation conquered by the Nazis that did not have to pay for its occupation. In this small country, the realities of occupation became evident starting on the day following the German conquest. The new masters initiated the usual police state measures, such as press censorship, prohibition of contrary political activities, outlawing the Communist Party, among other things. The Danes formed a new coalition government on 8 July 1940, with the main premise of cooperating with the occupiers. Otherwise, it feared the Germans would only tighten the screws. However, up until 29 August 1943, when the Germans declared martial law, Denmark remained an independent nation. Around 100,000 Danish workers went to Germany and after the summer of 1941, a Danish Free Corps fought alongside the Wehrmacht against the USSR.

The German *Reichskommissariat* would supervise the economic exploitation of Norway and guide its civil administration. Quisling's administration did not last long, and that summer leading government officials and other civil leaders decided to reach an accommodation with the Germans. Similar to the Danes, they chiefly wanted to just get along and avoid trouble with the occupying power. A number of factors complicated the relationship: The existence and competing claims of legitimacy of exiled King Haakon VII, plus elements of the Norwegian military (notably the navy) still fighting the Germans. On 25 September 1940, Reichskommissar Josef Terboven appointed Nazi ministers over government offices. He later tried to have the rump parliament legitimize his appointments, but nothing came of it. At the lower levels of government, Norwegians either remained at their posts out of patriotism, or resigned in large numbers, in which case collaborators appointed by the Germans ran day-to-day operations.

The pre-war Norwegian economy depended heavily on imports, especially foodstuffs, carried by the nation's huge merchant fleet. This dried up completely due to the Royal Navy's blockade of Nazi-occupied Europe. The Norwegian people responded by growing their own versions of 'victory gardens'.

An unarmed resistance sprang up as soon as the government fled Norway. Within a year, the British Special Operations Executive (SOE) contacted Norwegian representatives through intermediaries in Sweden. By October 1940, the militarized Home Forces came into being. But the Norwegians and British did not agree on raids and sabotage, with the former leery of acting for fear of German reprisals. The two would not cooperate until 1943. On 9 April 1941, first anniversary of *Weserübung*, Norwegians conducted silent demonstrations in schools, streets and workplaces. However, with a dozen divisions garrisoning the country and a compliant populace, Norway remained quiet.

When the Germans arrived, Denmark and Norway had 6,000 and 1,400 Jews respectively. Many were refugees from the Reich. Within six months, the Nazis closed academic and professional positions to them, but otherwise they suffered little of the abuse Jews did elsewhere under Nazi domination. Not all Scandinavians were sympathetic, however. With anti-communism as a prime motivation, more than 500 Danes and Norwegians joined SS-Standarte 'Nordland', one of three regiments of the new SS-Division 'Wiking' that took part in *Barbarossa*.

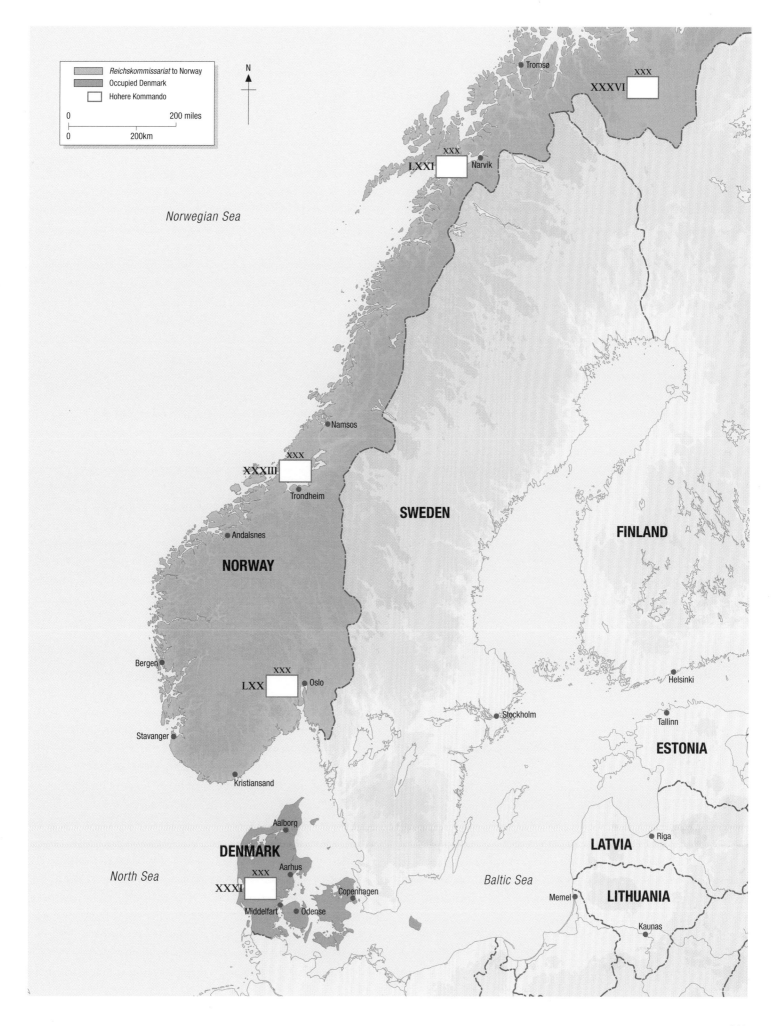

MAP 97: THE OCCUPATION OF THE NETHERLANDS, BELGIUM AND FRANCE

The Germans had a lot invested in their occupation of Western Europe. They wanted to regain territories lost at Versailles. They wanted to exploit the region's manpower reserves, natural resources and industry. They needed its air and naval bases and had to fortify its coast against the outside world.

The Germans divided their new holdings into numerous categories and jurisdictions. The two broadest categories were occupied (most of the area) and unoccupied (the French State or 'Vichy'). They brought Alsace-Lorraine 'back to the Reich', as well as three Belgian towns and environs. They created a resettlement zone in north-eastern France, where French people would eventually be removed and German colonizers brought in. On the Atlantic, Bay of Biscay and Channel coasts, they instituted a narrow military zone. Supposedly, this would be cleared of French people, but in practice that would have been impossible. Two civilian *Reichskommissariat* and *Militärbefehlshaber* shared power in the Netherlands and Belgium/northern France (Artois and Flanders), while a *Militärbefehlshaber* oversaw occupied France. The boundary between occupied and unoccupied France was treated as an international border. In the south, Italy annexed a few small French areas along their common border and occupied a larger stretch of land.

Like other countries in occupied western Europe, through 1941 inhabitants here accepted the new austerity and took a 'wait and see' attitude about the course of the war. The defeated nations experienced a combination of police state conditions (heavy-handed rules, arbitrary arrest, censorship and propaganda) and military occupation (troops billeted everywhere). All three had their share of collaborators, an extreme example being the many thousands of volunteers to the SS-Standarte 'Westland' (another regiment in SS-Division 'Wiking').

With Queen Wilhelmina in exile and the Dutch fighting the Axis in the Pacific, the Netherlands divided along the lines of Norway, explained in the previous map. Austrian Nazi Arthur Seyss-Inquart supervised the economic exploitation of the country His mission consisted of squeezing out all possible manpower, agricultural produce and manufactured goods.

Belgium had a unique experience in that King Leopold III remained in the country, so it had no government in exile, unlike many of Hitler's victims. It lost Eupen, Malmedy and St. Vith (absorbed in 1919) to German annexation. Despite the presence of a *Reichskommissar*, in Belgium the relatively efficient military administration dominated. In accordance with Hitler's wishes, they manipulated differences between the pro-German Flemish and French-leaning Walloons, favouring the former. As in other occupied nations, a dynamic tension existed between German occupiers and Belgian bureaucrats and civil servants, who tried to make life for their fellow countrymen as painless as possible. Belgium had a long history of industrial productivity (exploited by the Kaiserreich from 1914 to 1918), which was badly needed by the Nazi war effort.

German and Belgian administrators maintained an uneasy truce to balance the demands of the Reich with the needs of the Belgian people. Both also hoped to avoid the attention of the SS and its extremely wide reach. As elsewhere, Belgium had a number of collaborationist groups, as usual led by pre-war fascists. Belgian Rexist leader Leon Degrelle created the Walloon Legion (Légion Wallonie), which fought against the USSR.

Nazi symbols, police state regulations, German road signs, ubiquitous *Feldgrau* uniforms, constant shortages and forced labour dominated life in occupied France. The military administration managed to keep the SS and Gestapo at arm's length, at least through the time period shown here.

The new French State walked a fine line between the initially popular head of state, Marshal Philippe Pétain and the increasingly unpopular regime in Vichy. This government, a French creation (i.e. not mandated by the Germans) administered both parts of France, although its influence in the unoccupied south was clearly greater. As elsewhere in Nazi Europe, dutiful French civil servants wanted to avoid overly antagonizing the Germans, while at the same time maintaining French traditions and helping the Nazi war effort as little as possible. As part of the harsh armistice terms, over half of the government's revenues went to reimburse German occupation costs. French commercial enterprises had to serve their only two remaining trading partners, Germany and Italy, while also taking care of the French populace. Industrial and mineral production plummeted, in part since France's wealthiest areas now fell under the Germans' Belgian *Reichskommissariat*. Approximately 1.6 million POWs still in captivity exacerbated labour problems. With so much output going to Germany, the civil authorities had to ration food and other essential goods at an early point. The daily food intake was supposedly 1,200 calories, a goal rarely achieved. Among other challenges, between 8 and 10 million refugees created in May and June 1940 had to return home.

In the unoccupied French State, little remained of the old republic. The Vichy regime had clear authoritarian and conservative tendencies. It advocated a return to a rural patriarchy of non-Paris in bygone France and a prominent place for the Catholic Church. Any sense of unity, centred on veneration for Pétain, had largely evaporated by 1941. Collaboration, a word first used by Pétain in a meeting with Hitler in October 1940, remains a sore subject in France even today, but occurred at the highest reaches of the Vichy government. French resistance to their Nazi overlords is also well known, with de Gaulle's 18 June 1940 radio address from London often receiving credit as its proximate cause. Throughout the occupation, it offered active and passive, violent and non-violent opposition, carried out by a diverse range of French citizens.

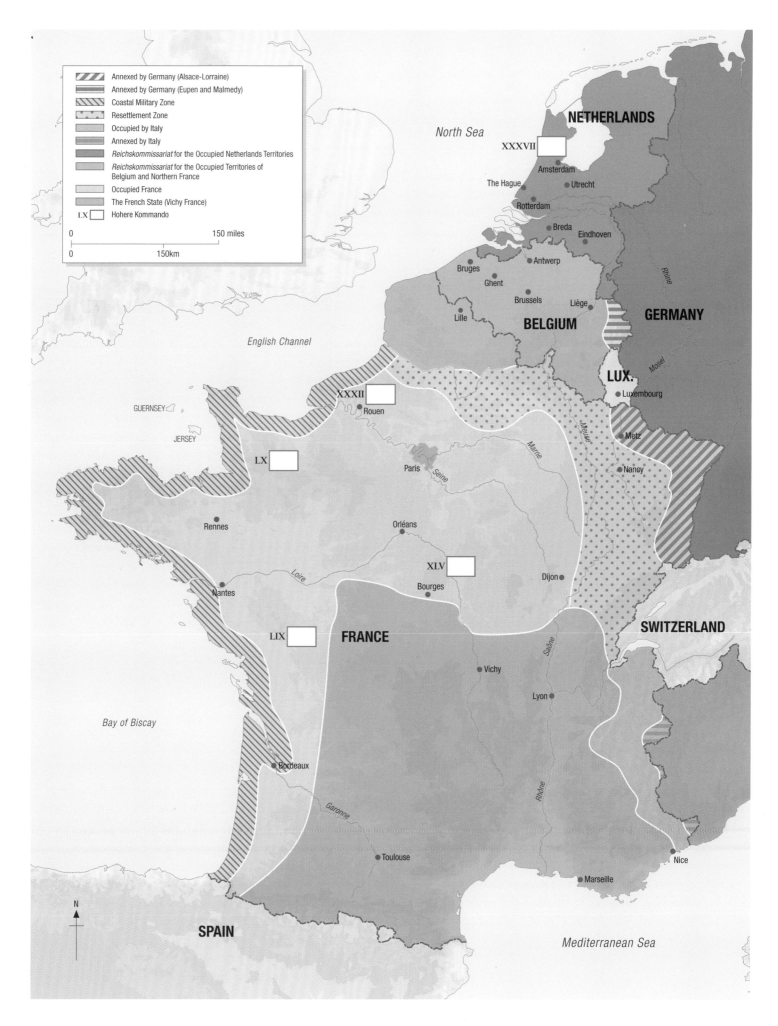

	Annexed by Germany (Alsace-Lorraine)
	Annexed by Germany (Eupen and Malmedy)
	Coastal Military Zone
	Resettlement Zone
	Occupied by Italy
	Annexed by Italy
	Reichskommissariat for the Occupied Netherlands Territories
	Reichskommissariat for the Occupied Territories of Belgium and Northern France
	Occupied France
	The French State (Vichy France)
LX	Hohere Kommando

0   150 miles

0   150km

North Sea

NETHERLANDS

Amsterdam

The Hague

Utrecht

Rotterdam

Breda

Eindhoven

XXXVII

Bruges

Ghent

Antwerp

Brussels

Liège

BELGIUM

GERMANY

Lille

Rhine

English Channel

LUX.

Luxembourg

Mosel

GUERNSEY

XXXII

Rouen

Metz

Meuse

JERSEY

LX

Paris

Marne

Nancy

Seine

Rennes

Orléans

Loire

XLV

Bourges

Dijon

SWITZERLAND

Nantes

LIX

FRANCE

Saône

Bay of Biscay

Vichy

Lyon

Bordeaux

Rhône

Garonne

Toulouse

Nice

SPAIN

Marseille

N

Mediterranean Sea

MAP 98: THE OCCUPATION OF YUGOSLAVIA AND GREECE

The Axis occupations of the Balkans was even more complicated than that of Western Europe, if only because of all the additional players. To Germany and Italy, we can add Hungary, Bulgaria and Albania, alternately turning the calendar back to 1914 or conducting a shameless landgrab regardless of history or tradition. Furthermore, Hitler established the puppet state of Croatia from the wreckage of Yugoslavia.

The Germans annexed much of Slovenia directly to the Reich. In Serbia, it set up a civilian administration around Belgrade and a military administration, primarily to provide a German buffer between antagonists Hungary and Romania. In Greece, it also occupied the region surrounding Thessaloniki, the border with Turkey (another buffer) and selected Aegean islands. Harkening back to the glory days of the Venetian Republic, Italy annexed significant portions of the Dalmatian coast. It occupied the majority of Greece, including most Aegean islands, and administered Montenegro. Albania, Bulgaria and Hungary all annexed, or occupied and administered, portions of Yugoslavia and Greece. Hitler's uncharacteristic generosity to his four compatriots came mainly from his twin desires to conserve German manpower and share the headaches that were sure to come. Yugoslavia and Greece had both de jure governments in exile (which in all cases included the support of the major Allied powers) and de facto governments at home that had the unenviable position of accommodating the occupying victors and providing essential services for their people.

As part of his racial war, Hitler wanted to eliminate Slavic Serbia as a nation[55]. More practically speaking, Yugoslavia had many natural resources prized by Germany and had been part of the latter's informal economic sphere for many decades. The new country also had extensive, rich farmland and sat astride many miles of the Danube. Hitler made sure that its best mines fell inside the German areas, or that he had first claim to their output. The other four Axis powers chiefly used their areas of occupation for aggrandizement, resettlement and colonialization, or occasionally, ethnic cleansing. The new Independent State of Croatia indulged in massive resettlement and ethnic-cleansing actions as well. In particular, they persecuted the 2 million Serbs now found within its

borders, killing 250,000 in the first three months alone. By October and November the reprisals began across occupied Yugoslavia, with entire villages burned down, all their men murdered and so on.

Among Hitler's so-called allies, competition and resentment between many of them – Italy versus Croatia – and brutality – by Germans, Bulgarians, Croats and even Italians – made for a messy occupation. This directly gave rise to perhaps the most fearsome resistance movement in the Führer's new Europe. German garrisons in small towns lived in constant fear of attack, as did convoys and outposts. The Italians in Montenegro suffered from a spectacular raid. Because of Operation *25* and the Croats' excessive behaviour, Serbs led the two main guerrilla armies: Monarchist Chetniks and communist Partisans. Later, the two groups turned on each other, a situation aggravated by their respective sponsorship by Churchill and Stalin. This 'Yugoslav Civil War' literally decimated the nation's population and its effects continued to be felt until the late 1990s and perhaps beyond.

As distinct from Yugoslavia, the Axis' main attraction in Greece was not natural resources but its strategic position in the eastern Mediterranean. Also in contrast, the Greek communist resistance, which sprang up early in the summer of 1941, had little competition from other groups. With *Barbarossa*, it took an unambiguous pro-Soviet stance and helped form a National People's Liberation Army six months later. Thanks to contacts made in Greece during the previous spring, the British sent SOE operatives there almost as soon as *Marita* had ended. They helped establish both communist and non-communist insurgent cells. Otherwise, the Germans generally respected the Greeks, easing the pain of occupation a bit.

Of course, Jews fared very badly, especially in Yugoslavia. Early on, the Croats launched a pogrom that would make the Nazis proud. Beginning late in 1941, nearly 3,000 Croatian Jews escaped into the Italian's new Dalmatian area.

The two Balkan countries represented both a disappointment and a liability to the Axis occupiers. Work stoppages and sabotage meant Germany could never properly exploit Yugoslavia's natural wealth. Poor infrastructure throughout the Balkans, the weak condition of Mussolini's navy and air force, plus Axis strategic overstretch after *Barbarossa* meant that Crete would never dominate the Mediterranean Sea. Active and effective resistance movements required ever more Axis might to combat and even then, they could not pacify the Balkans.

---

55 In part, his virulent anti-Serbian attitude was a holdover from his days a subject of the Austro-Hungarian Empire.

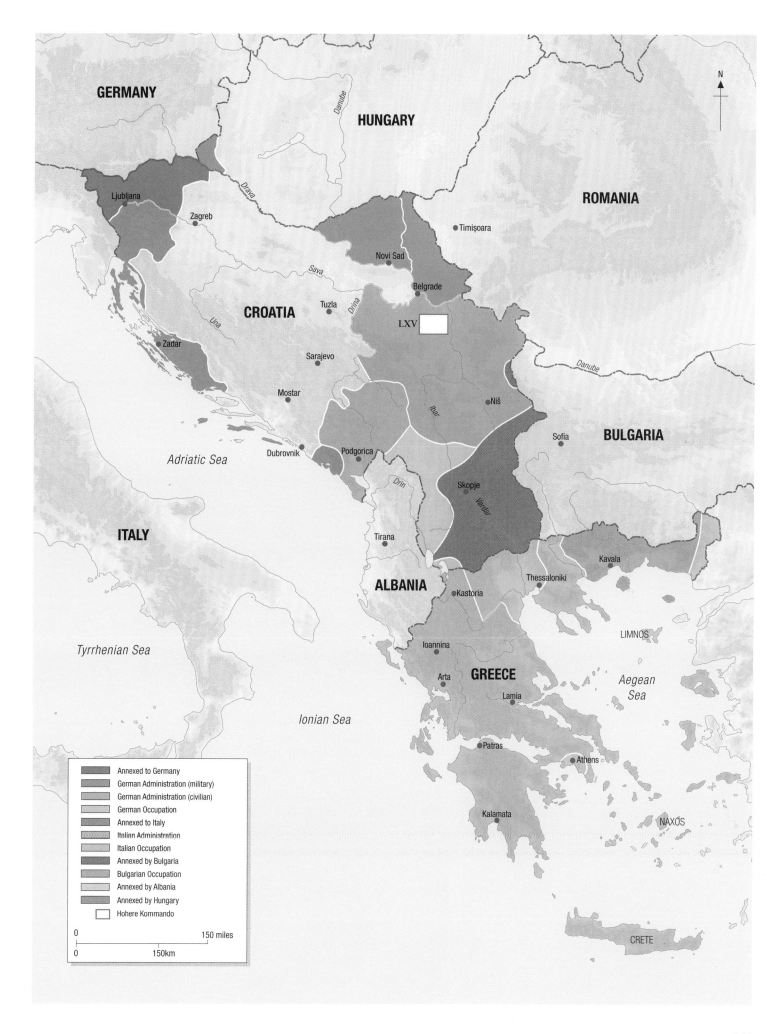

GERMANY

HUNGARY

ROMANIA

Danube

Ljubljana

Zagreb

Drava

Timișoara

Sava

Novi Sad

CROATIA

Tuzla

Drina

Belgrade

LXV

Una

Zadar

Sarajevo

Mostar

Ibar

Niš

Danube

Sofia

BULGARIA

Adriatic Sea

Dubrovnik

Podgorica

Drin

Skopje

Vardar

ITALY

Tirana

ALBANIA

Kastoria

Thessaloniki

Kavala

LIMNOS

Tyrrhenian Sea

Ioannina

Aegean Sea

Arta

GREECE

Lamia

Ionian Sea

Patras

Athens

NAXOS

Kalamata

CRETE

	Annexed to Germany
	German Administration (military)
	German Administration (civilian)
	German Occupation
	Annexed to Italy
	Italian Administration
	Italian Occupation
	Annexed by Bulgaria
	Bulgarian Occupation
	Annexed by Albania
	Annexed by Hungary
	Hohere Kommando

0   150 miles

0   150km

N

BIBLIOGRAPHY

Antil, Peter, *Crete 1941: Germany's Lightning Airborne Assault,* Osprey Publishing: Oxford, 2005

Baldwin, Hanson, *Battles Lost and Won,* Avon Books: New York, *1968*

Barnett, Correlli, *Hitler's Generals,* Grove Weidenfeld: New York, 1989

Barry, R. H., 'Military Balance', in *History of the Second World War,* Marshall Cavendish: London, 1973

Bekker, Cajus, *Hitler's Naval War,* Ballantine Books: New York, 1964

——, *The Luftwaffe War Diaries,* Ballantine Books: New York, 1969

Bergstrom, Christer, *Battle of Britain: An Epic Conflict Revisited,* Casemate, Oxford, 2015

Bishop, Chris, *German Panzers in WWII: Order of Battle,* Zenith Press: Minneapolis, 2008

Bishop, Patrick, *Battle of Britain: A Day-by-Day Chronicle,* Quercus: London, 2009

Bond, Brian, *France–Belgium, 1939–1940,* Davis-Pointer: London, 1975

——, *Britain's Two World Wars against Germany: Myth, Memory and the Distortion of Hindsight,* Cambridge University Press: Cambridge, 2014

Boog, Horst (ed.), *The Conduct of the Air War in the Second World War: An International Comparison,* Oxford University Press: Oxford, 1988

Bullock, Alan, *Hitler and Stalin: Parallel Lives,* Alfred A. Knopf: New York, 1992

Busch, Harald, *U-boats at War,* Ballantine Books: New York, 1962

Calder, Agnos, *The People's War,* Ace Books: New York, 1972

Cervi, Mario, *The Hollow Legions: Mussolini's Blunder in Greece, 1940–1941,* Doubleday: New York, 1971

Charles, Jean-Leon, 'Invasion of Holland and Belgium', in *History of the Second World War,* Marshall Cavendish: London, 1973

Churchill, Winston, *The World Crisis,* Free Press: New York, 2001

Collier, Basil, *The Defence of the United Kingdom,* Her Majesty's Stationery Office: London, 1957

Collier, Richard, *Duce!,* Fontana/Collins: London, 1972

Coox, Alvin, *Nomonhan: Japan versus Russia, 1939,* Stanford University Press: Redwood City, 1985

Crowhurst, Patrick, *Hitler and Czechoslovakia in World War II,* I. B. Tauris: London, 2013

Dean, Maurice, *The Royal Air Force and Two World Wars,* Cassell: London, 1979

Dear, L. C. B. and Foot, M. R. D., *Oxford Companion to World War II,* Oxford University Press: Oxford, 1995

Deighton, Len, *Blitzkrieg,* Triad/Granada: London, 1980

——, *Blood, Tears and Folly,* Castle Books: Edison, 1999

DeJonge, Alex, *Stalin and the Shaping of the Soviet Union,* Fontana/Collins: London, 1987

Dildy, Douglas, *Denmark and Norway 1940: Hitler's Boldest Operation,* Osprey Publishing: Oxford, 2007

——, *Dunkirk 1940, Operation Dynamo,* Osprey Publishing: Oxford, 2010

——, *Fall Gelb 1940 (1): Panzer Breakthrough in the West,* Osprey Publishing: Oxford, 2014

——, *Fall Gelb1940, (2): Airborne Assault on the Low Countries,* Osprey Publishing: Oxford, 2015

Doughty, Robert, *The Seeds of Destruction: The Development of French Army Doctrine, 1919–1939,* Archon Books: Hamden, 1985

Drea, Edward, *Nomonhan: Japanese–Soviet Tactical Combat, 1939,* Combat Studies Institute: Fort Leavenworth, 1981

Edwards, Roger, *Panzer: A Revolution in Warfare, 1939–1945,* Arms and Armour: London, 1989

Emerson, James, *The Rhineland Crisis,* Iowa State University Press: Iowa City, 1977

French, David, *Raising Churchill's Army: The British Army and the War against Germany, 1919–1945,* Oxford University Press: Oxford, 2000

Frieser, Karl-Heinz, *The Blitzkrieg Legend: The 1940 Campaign in the West,* Naval Institute Press: Annapolis, 2005

Fuller, J. F. C., *The Second World War,* Duell, Sloan and Pearce: New York, 1962

Garzke, William and Dulin, Robert, *Battleships: Axis and Neutral Battleships in World War II,* Naval Institute Press: Annapolis, 1985

Gilbert, Martin, *The Second World War: A Complete History,* Henry Holt: New York, 1989

Glantz, David, *Red Army Operations, August 1939–March 1940,* (n.p.), 2006

Goralski, Robert, *World War II Almanac, 1939–1945,* Perigee Books: New York, 1981

Grayling, A. C., *Among the Dead Cities: The History and Moral Legacy of the WWII Bombing of Civilians in Germany and Japan,* Walker & Co.: New York, 2006

Greiner, Helmut et al., *The German Campaign in the Balkans (Spring 1941),* Department of the Army: Washington DC, 1953

Gross, Gerhard, *The Myth and Reality of German Warfare: Operational Thinking from Moltke the Elder to Heusinger,* University Press of Kentucky: Lexington, 2016

Gross, Jan, *Revolution from Abroad: The Soviet Conquest of Poland's Western Ukraine and Western Belorussia,* Princeton University Press: Princeton, 2002

Guderian, Heinz, *Panzer Leader,* Ballantine Books: New York, 1961

Hellenic Army General Staff, *An Abridged History of the Greek–Italian and Greek–German War, 1940–1941,* Army History Directorate: Athens, 1997

Horne, Alistair, *France 1940: To Lose a Battle,* Macmillan: London, 1969

Jackson, Robert, *Dunkirk,* Playboy Press: New York, 1980

Kaufmann, J. E. and Kaufmann, H. W., *Hitler's Blitzkrieg Campaigns,* Combined Books: Conshohocken, 1993

Keegan, John (ed.), *Churchill's Generals,* Grove Weidenfeld: New York, 1991

Kemp, Peter, 'Struggle for the Sealanes', in *History of the Second World War,* Marshall Cavendish: London, 1973

Kennedy, Ludovic, *Pursuit: The Sinking of the Bismarck,* Fontana/Collins: London, 1974

Kesselring, Albert, *The Memoirs of Field Marshal Kesselring,* Presidio Press: Novato, 1989

Killen, John, *A History of the Luftwaffe, 1915–1945,* Berkley Medallion Books: New York, 1969

Kroener, Bernhard et al., *Germany and the Second World War, Vol. V, Organization and Mobilization of the German Sphere of Power, Part 1, Wartime Administration, Economic and Manpower Resources,* Clarendon, 2015

Lucas, James, *Hitler's Mountain Troops,* Arms and Armour Press: London, 1992

McNab, Chris, *The Fall of Eben Emael: Belgium 1940,* Osprey Publishing: Oxford, 2013

Maier, Klaus et al., *Germany and the Second World War, Vol. II, Germany's Initial Conquests in Europe,* Clarendon Press: Oxford, 2015

Manstein, Erich von, *Lost Victories,* Presidio Press: Novato, 1982

Marres, Juliete, 'Nazi Overlords', in *History of the Second World War,* Marshall Cavendish: London, 1973

Mel'tiukhov, M. I., *Upushchennii shans Stalina: Sovetskii Soiuz i bor'ba za Evropu: 1939–1941,* Veche: Moscow, 2000

Michaelis, Klaus, *1938: Der Krieg gegen die Tschechoslowakei,* Michaelis-Verlag: Berlin, 2004

Moulton, J. L., 'Conquest of Norway', in *History of the Second World War,* Marshall Cavendish: London, 1973

Müller, Rolf-Dieter, *Enemy in the East: Hitler's Secret Plans to Invade the Soviet Union,* I. B. Tauris: London, 2015

Murray, Williamson, *Strategy for Defeat: Luftwaffe, 1933–1945,* Chartwell: Secaucus, 1986

Nissen, Hendrick, *Scandinavia During the Second World War:* University of Minnesota Press: Minneapolis, 1983

O'Neill, H. C. (ed.), *Odhams History of the Second World War,* Odhams Press: London, 1951

Overy, Richard, *The Road to War,* Stoddart: Toronto, 1989

Packer, Edwin, 'Italian Fiasco: The Attack on Greece', in *History of the Second World War,* Marshall Cavendish: London, 1973

Padfield, Peter, *Dönitz: The Last Führer,* Victor Gollancz: London, 1984

Pettibone, Charles, *Organization and Order of Battle of Militaries in World War II, Vol. VI, Italy and France,* Trafford Publishing: Bloomington, 2010

——, *Organization and Order of Battle of Militaries in World War II, Vol. IX, The Overrun and Neutral Nations of Europe,* Trafford Publishing: Bloomington, 2014

Papaderos, Emmanouil, *Axis Against Greece: The Greco–Italian and Greco–German Conflict of 1940—1941,* (n.p.), 2013

Pointing, Clive, *1940: Myth and Reality,* Ivan R. Dee: Lanham, 1993

Porten, Edward von der, *The German Navy in World War Two,* Ballantine Books: New York, 1969

Rochat, Giorgio, *Le guerre italiane, 1935–1943,* Einaudi: Turin, 2005

Romanych, Marc and Rupp, Martin, *Maginot Line 1940: Battles on the French Frontier,* Osprey Publishing: Oxford, 2010

Salmaggi, Cesare and Pallavisini, Alfredo, *2194 Days of War,* Gallery Books: New York, 1988

Schmidl, Erich, *Der 'Anschluss' Österreichs,* Bernard und Graefe: Bonn, 1994

Schreiber, Gerhard et al., *Germany and the Second World War, Vol. III, The Mediterranean, South-East Europe, and North Africa, 1939–1941,* Clarendon Press: Oxford, 1995

Sawczynski, Adam and Nehring, Walther, 'Two Sides of the Polish Campaign', in *History of the Second World War,* Marshall Cavendish: London, 1973

Seaton, Albert, *The German Army,* Sphere Books: London, 1983

—— and Seaton, Jean, *The Soviet Army, 1918 to the present,* New American Library: New York, 1986

Shepherd, Ben H., *Hitler's Soldiers: The German Army in the Third Reich,* Yale: New Haven, 2016

Shirer, William, *The Collapse of the Third Republic,* Simon and Schuster of Canada: Toronto, 1971

Shukman, Harold, *Stalin's Generals,* Grove Press: New York, 1993

Snyder, Louis, *The War: A Concise History, 1939–1945,* Dell Publishing: New York, 1964

Thies, Klaus-Jurgen, *Der Zweite Weltkrieg im Kartenbild, Der Polenfeldzug,* Biblio-Verlag: Osnabruck, 1989

——, *Der Zweite Weltkrieg im Kartenbild, Weserübung. Die Besetzung Dänemarks und die Eroberung Norwegens 9.4.–10.6.1940,* Biblio-Verlag: Osnabruck, 1991

——, *Der Zweite Weltkrieg im Kartenbild, Der Westfeldzug, 10 Mai–25 Juni bis 1940,* Biblio-Verlag: Osnabruck, 1994

Thomas, David, *Nazi Victory: Crete 1941,* Stein & Day: New York, 1972

Trotter, William, *A Frozen Hell: The Russo–Finnish War of 1939–1940,* Chapel Hill Press: Chapel Hill, 1991

Weinberg, Gerhard, *Germany, Hitler and World War II,* Cambridge University Press: Cambridge, 1995

Whitley, M. J., *German Cruisers of World War Two,* Arms and Armour Press: London, 1985

Williams, John, *France: Summer 1940,* Ballantine Books, New York, 1969

Willmott, H. P., *The Great Crusade* (revised edition), Potomac Books: Nebraska, 2008

Zaloga, Steven and Madej, Victor, *The Polish Campaign 1939,* Hippocrene Books: New York, 1985

Zaloga, Steven, *Poland 1939: The Birth of the Blitzkrieg,* Osprey Publishing: Oxford, 2002

Ziemke, Earl, *German Northern Theater of Operations,* US Government Printing Office, 1960.

ABOUT THE AUTHOR

Robert Kirchubel, PhD, is a retired US Army Armor branch lieutenant colonel and currently a post-doctoral military history researcher at Purdue University. This *Atlas of the Blitzkrieg* is the product of his life-long study of World War II.